THE
SECONDARY
SCHOOL
TODAY

THE
SECONDARY
SCHOOL
TODAY

PETER F. OLIVA

University of Florida

 THE WORLD PUBLISHING COMPANY
Cleveland and New York

Published by the World Publishing Company
2231 West 110th Street, Cleveland, Ohio 44102

Published simultaneously in Canada by
Nelson, Foster & Scott Ltd.

First Printing

Library of Congress Catalog Card Number: 67–12078

Printed in the United States of America

TO RUTH, EVE, AND MARC

PREFACE

The material of this book is planned to meet the requirements of comprehensive courses in secondary school principles and methods. Seven units are presented in the text. Each unit is divided into four parts, the first of which states the objectives of the unit in terms of competencies that the unit seeks to develop. The second part, the commentary, is the author's text material, and consists of numbered chapters. The third part suggests class and evaluation activities, which the class may use during and at the end of its study of the unit. The fourth part consists of selected annotated bibliographical references and references to instructional aids and sources. This format parallels instructional patterns proposed for the secondary school in Unit III of this book.

The units to be found in this text are as follows:

Unit I: *The Emergence of the Modern Secondary School.* We begin the book with a brief survey of the history and status of secondary education. We discuss some of the administrative aspects of secondary education and the status of the secondary school teacher.

Unit II: *The Secondary School Curriculum Today.* In this unit we consider some of the sociological forces affecting the curriculum, examine curricular developments in the major subject fields, and describe current curricular practices and plans, including innovations.

Unit III: *Planning for Instruction.* Here we discuss types of planning with which secondary school teachers are involved. The unit gives illustrations of different types of plans.

Unit IV: *The Instructional Process.* This unit describes selected techniques of instruction and discusses learning theory in some detail.

Unit V: *Guidance for the Classroom Teacher.* Material in this unit is aimed at developing understanding of the guidance role of the teacher. Here the reader will find discussion of selected guidance techniques, elementary statistics, and standardized testing.

Unit VI: *Discipline and Control.* The unit analyzes discipline in its democratic setting. It describes causes of behavior problems, suggests remedial and corrective measures to be employed, and stresses the development of self-discipline.

Unit VII: *Evaluation.* We consider in this unit principles of evaluation, test construction, and means of evaluation other than tests.

It was the intent of the author to include many illustrations, examples, anecdotes, actual cases, comparisons, and activities. The book is designed to be read and easily understood. For this reason every effort has been made to make the style of writing readable. Further, the book is designed to be used as well as read. For this reason the author has suggested class and evaluation activities that have proved helpful during study of each unit and at the conclusion of the unit. Individual instructors who use this book may wish to reserve some of the suggested activities and questions as items on written tests in their course.

The selected bibliography for each unit provides references to some of the better reading on the topics of the unit. When films or other teaching aids are available and will prove helpful in the study of a unit, these are mentioned in the final section of each unit. It is to be hoped that generous use of the bibliographical references and the instructional aids and sources will give depth to the study of the units.

Each unit is, in a sense, self-contained. Each unit deals with understandings, appreciations, attitudes, skills, and facts that the secondary school teacher should seek to develop. Careful cross-referencing is made in the units when relationships between topics are encountered.

The author is indebted to the National Association of Secondary School Principals for permission to use in this book the material from his own article, "High School Discipline in American Society," published in *The Bulletin of the National Association of Secondary School Principals,* XL (January 1956), pp. 1–103.

PETER F. OLIVA

Gainesville, Florida
February 15, 1967

CONTENTS

THE EMERGENCE OF THE MODERN SECONDARY SCHOOL

OBJECTIVES OF UNIT I

At the conclusion of his reading and correlated study-discussion activities the reader should

A. understand that
   1. the American secondary school began with European antecedents;
   2. the American secondary school today is a unique secondary institution;
   3. the American secondary school has experienced both achievements and shortcomings;
   4. the American secondary school attempts to provide for all educable adolescents;
   5. the junior high school and the junior college are developments of the twentieth century;
   6. early secondary schools were sectarian in nature;
   7. there are great variations in financial support of schools among the states;
   8. the federal government has aided education since the eighteenth century;
   9. the dropout problem continues to be a serious one in secondary education;
   10. secondary education in actual practice is still not universal nor free;
   11. the schools have always had their critics;
   12. criticism can be either constructive or destructive in its effect on the schools;
   13. a European system of education is not necessarily appropriate for American society;
   14. shortages of teachers of secondary school subjects vary from state to state and from subject to subject;
   15. the tangible rewards for teachers have improved in recent years;
   16. standards for admission to the teaching profession are rising;
   17. there are many opportunities for advancement in the profession.

B. show appreciation for
   1. the uniqueness of the American secondary school,
   2. the accomplishments of the American secondary school,
   3. the efforts of universities, public schools, state departments of education, and professional organizations to raise professional standards,

    4. the efforts of secondary schools to meet the needs of a diversified student body,

    5. the historic struggles to develop the American secondary school.

C. adopt attitudes of

    1. commitment to the goal of universal education,

    2. understanding of and confidence in the unique qualities of the American secondary school,

    3. support for higher standards of professional preparation and certification,

    4. willingness to support professional organizations,

    5. acceptance of the code of ethics of the profession,

    6. willingness to assume responsibility for student teachers and interns when employed as a full-time teacher,

    7. willingness to make teaching a real profession.

D. be able to demonstrate skill in

    1. analyzing some of the current problems in secondary education,

    2. planning for himself a program which will meet the realities of personal interests and ability as well as job opportunities,

    3. finding out the purposes and nature of various professional organizations,

    4. finding out certification requirements in the various states,

    5. applying for a job.

E. be familiar with

    1. the dame school,

    2. the Latin Grammar School,

    3. the academy,

    4. the "Old Deluder" Law,

    5. the role of Benjamin Franklin in the development of secondary education,

    6. the English High School,

    7. the Kalamazoo Case,

    8. federal acts in support of education,

    9. certification procedures,

    10. placement procedures,

    11. National Council for Accreditation of Teacher Education.

CHAPTER 1

THE DEVELOPMENT OF THE SECONDARY SCHOOL

Robert Watson, age sixteen, turns his used car into the school parking lot. The time is eight-twenty, ten minutes before the first bell. He hops out of his car, waves to two buddies on the football field across from the parking lot. He hurries toward the front entrance of the imposing brick structure, a sprawling, single-story building which with its covered walks and outside lockers stretches into the distance. This modern edifice, the area's new central high school, is set in the middle of some thirty acres of grounds, providing ample space for adolescents to stretch and run about. Tennis courts, a baseball diamond, and even an Olympic-size pool are provided for Robert and his fellow students. The parking lot for students is rapidly filling as Robert heads toward his homeroom.

Robert enters his cheerful, bright homeroom. The walls glow with friendly colors. He plops down in a movable chair, equipped with large tablet arm. Most of the students have arrived and are sitting in their own chairs, which have been constructed in different sizes, some even equipped for left-handed students. The bell rings, and over the electronic public address system the principal reads announcements to all his twenty-five hundred students in grades ten through twelve.

As we follow Robert through the day we find him exposed to the latest in equipment and material. We find his teachers using a variety of audio-visual techniques. We see him in a large, well-stocked library which has not only a generous supply of books but also magazines, pictorials, filmstrips, and other materials. For Robert is fortunate. He is a student in one of the finest, newest, and most modern high schools in the country. The community has spared no expense to give him and all his schoolmates the finest education possible. The essential features of Robert's school have been repeated in many communities throughout the country. These bustling up-to-date, well-equipped establishments are a far cry from the earliest schools of our country. Robert's ancestors in the United States were not quite so fortunate.

The modern secondary school has evolved from European antecedents into a unique American educational institution. The colonists brought to the New World not only types of educational institutions but also a burning desire for education. Religiously oriented, the colonist wanted to make sure that every man could read the Scriptures for himself. For purposes of tracing some of the major developments in the history of secondary education in the United States, we will break our discussion into four periods: (1) 1607–1635, (2) 1635–1751, (3) 1751–1821, and (4) 1821 to the present. We remind the reader that in any period of history, there is rarely a clear-cut dividing line where one movement ends and another begins. This is equally true in the history of education. Some of the educational institutions that began in the times of the early colonists still exist today.

THE PERIOD 1607–1635

Youth in the earliest days of our country were educated without the benefit of well-developed educational institutions. Boys and girls were taught in the home the skills needed for survival in the New World—the earliest form of "life-adjustment education." Boys learned the arts of agriculture, hunting, trapping, building construction, and defense from Indians and the elements. Girls learned from their mothers the art of homemaking and, with male approval, incidentally, the attitude that the woman's place was in the home.

The church served as a principal educational agency to the young of early colonial days. The young were taught the codes of behavior of their church, be it Episcopalian in Virginia or Congregational in New England or Catholic in Maryland. Much of the instruction was by rote, the young people repeating the words of the minister until they could recite them verbatim. The catechism of the particular church provided the meat of the instruction. By the minister's sermons the parishioners were taught and guided in daily living.

The wealthier families frequently imported tutors from England or France to teach their young people the social graces and to give them a liberal education. This system of education was especially popular among the landed gentry of the South. Needless to say, the struggling, dirt-poor laborer had little time, money, or inclination for private tutoring.

The ancient guild system made its way across the ocean and provided a means of vocational training in America. Apprenticeship in the crafts gave young men the opportunity to work for an expert craftsman over a period of years and to master the skills of his trade. This type of education, dating from the Middle Ages, is still an effective means of training, utilized by our present-day labor unions.

The first "school" of the colonial United States was the "dame school" or "kitchen school." As these names imply, a woman of the community who possessed a rudimentary education herself gathered together in her kitchen a few of the youngsters who wished to learn and taught them the three R's. For this civic-mindedness the dame received a few pennies from each of her charges. She was able to give her pupils only the most elementary education. Her efforts, however, helped to combat illiteracy and prepared some of the pupils for further education as other schools were established.

The earliest colonists relied on the home, church, tutors, apprenticeship, and the dame school for educating the young. But it was soon apparent to the colonists as they gained a foothold in the New World that a more formal type of school was needed.

THE PERIOD 1635–1751

THE LATIN GRAMMAR SCHOOL

From the middle of the seventeenth century to the middle of the eighteenth century the Latin Grammar School dominated the educational scene in America. While previous forms of instruction were still in existence, the Latin Grammar School came into its own as a European transplant on American soil. Boston Latin School, the first Latin Grammar School in the United States, opened its doors in 1635 and has been in continuous operation ever since. The curriculum of Boston Latin School, like the curriculum of all Latin Grammar Schools to follow, was largely classical in nature.

The purposes of the Latin Grammar Schools were simple: instruction of selected boys for admission to college—i.e., Harvard, later William and Mary, Yale, and Princeton—where they studied to become ministers and teachers. Many of the ministers who were graduated from these colleges came back to the Latin Grammar Schools to train a new generation for admission to the colonial colleges. It is worthy of passing note that the National University of Mexico and the University of San Marcos in Lima, Peru had already been in existence eighty-five years before Harvard was founded.

The Latin Grammar School was open only to boys. Not until the middle of the eighteenth century would it become common for girls to attend secondary schools. The clientele was limited to the upper classes, the sons of men who could pay a fee for the boys' education in the grammar school and university.

The Latin Grammar School should be thought of not as a truly secondary school but as a combined elementary-secondary school. Boys were admitted at the age of seven or eight, a time when today's pupils enter the first or second grades. They continued their studies in the Latin Grammar School for seven to eight years, entering the university at a tender age of fourteen or fifteen. The sons of the wealthier colonists finished college at an age when today's adolescents are finishing high school. The curriculum at both the grammar school level and the college level was decidedly different and much narrower than the curriculum of today's high school and college.

As the name "Latin Grammar School" implies, the curriculum was oriented toward classical studies. The boys enrolled studied Latin, Greek, Hebrew, history, the Bible, and mathematics. Systematic study of neither English nor science was considered worthy in this era. The curriculum of the Latin Grammar School was dominated by the requirements of the college. Bossing cites the entrance requirements of Harvard University in 1643:

> When any Schollar is able to understand Tully, or such like classicall Latine Author extempore, and make and speake true Latine in Verse and Prose, suo ut aiunt Marte [independently, as they say]; and decline perfectly the Paradigm's of Nounes and Verbes in the Greek tongue: Let him then and not before be capable of admission into the Colledge.[1]

We may note in this quotation not only the influence of the college on the secondary school but also the evolution of our language in spelling, use of the possessive, and punctuation. As we see today's youth striving to enter the "closing college door," we are well aware that the impact of the college on the curriculum of today's secondary school is still strong.

CHURCH AND STATE

While today only twenty to thirty per cent of our school teachers are males, instruction in the Latin Grammar School of colonial times was a man's job. Religious instruction permeated the entire curriculum. Reading materials, the *Hornbook*, the *Psalter*, the *New England Primer*, and the catechism, served the dual role of inculcating religious doctrine and at the same time teaching language skills. In the current dialogue over the meaning of the First Amendment to the Constitution of the United States and the interpretations of the issue of separation of church and state we must realize that in our early schools church and state were inseparable. With church elders dominating local governmental bodies, many of the colonial communities could properly be called theocracies. The schoolmasters of

---

[1] Nelson L. Bossing, *Principles of Secondary Education*, 2nd ed., (Englewood Cliffs, N. J.: Prentice-Hall, 1955), p. 27. As quoted from "New England's First Fruits," *Massachusetts Historical Collections, 1792*, I, p. 242. By permission of Prentice-Hall, Inc.

colonial days served in a community with the approval of the minister of the local dominant church.

The issue of separation of church and state has been debated for centuries and continues today to occupy a prominent place in the list of unresolved educational problems. We should recognize that the establishment of secular schools open to all pupils of all faiths has not evolved without conflict. Nor is the modern high school yet completely secular. Many issues in this area remain unsettled in spite of recent court decisions. Among these issues are prayer reading, school devotionals, Christmas and Easter celebrations in the schools, aid to parochial schools, released time for religious instruction, and the employment of clergy as teachers in the public schools. In some of the small rural communities of the nation the stamp of approval of the local clergy on teachers and administrators to be hired is still a potent factor.

The schoolmaster of the Latin Grammar School was not, however, perplexed by such problems of a pluralistic society. He knew his duties and he performed them. He relied heavily on the technique of rote-memorization. When he conducted a recitation, he expected his pupils to do exactly what the word "recitation" implies. He spoke or dictated passages that his students repeated until they had committed them to memory. Ready corporal punishment served to jog the wayward, the mischievous, the uninterested, the slow, and the negligent. The grammar school was a stern institution, affected by Calvinist views of mankind. The schoolmaster subscribed to the belief that man was innately evil. The best way for him to overcome his sinfulness was to suffer physical and mental rigor, thereby disciplining himself. Corporal punishment and rote-memorization, therefore, were good for the pupils, since these techniques would curb their tendencies toward sinfulness.

The Latin Grammar School had few of the niceties of the modern high school. The school plant itself was unimpressive. The schoolmasters were not concerned about the "whole child" or with appealing to individual differences. There were no bands nor football teams to make life more interesting for the Latin Grammar School student. The schoolmaster cared nothing about motivating the learner. The findings of experimental and perceptual psychology were long in the future. With his hickory stick in one hand and his *Primer* in the other he schooled several generations of colonial leaders. To him we must give his due.

THE "OLD DELUDER" LAW

The Commonwealth of Massachusetts led the way toward public support for schools. The "Old Deluder" Law of 1647 is a landmark in the history of public education. By this law the colony of Massachusetts required communities of fifty families to provide instruction in reading and writing, and towns of one hundred families to establish a grammar school and hire a teacher for it. Small penalties were provided for failure to follow its provisions. The law derives its nickname, "Old Deluder," from the intent of the colonists to require instruction so that citizens could read the Scriptures and not be deluded by Satan.

The "Old Deluder" Law set a precedent for our present public school system in recognizing the state's responsibility for education of the young. Although the penalties for noncompliance were trivial and not enforced, the law established the principle of state sanctions against communities that did not provide an educational system.

For more than a hundred years the Latin Grammar School fulfilled the needs of a small segment of the colonial population. It educated an elite group for college entrance and ignored the needs of the general populace. The Latin Grammar School, although aided by colonial legislation, was not truly a public institution: it was neither free nor open to all; its curriculum was classical and sectarian in nature. As the times and needs of society changed, the secondary school was also forced to change. A new institution rose to meet the challenges of the times.

THE PERIOD 1751–1821

The rapidly growing American population was pushing the frontiers of the country westward. A continuing stream of colonizers and later immigrants brought with them their own educational needs. The early nineteenth century saw the dawn of the Industrial Revolution in the United States, bringing with it demands for skilled workers and for a more functional education than that provided in the Latin Grammar School. The academy was created to satisfy these demands.

THE ACADEMY

From the middle of the eighteenth century until the Civil War period the academy was the principal instrument of secondary education in the United States. Benjamin Franklin is credited with the establishment of the first academy, The Philadelphia Academy and Charitable School, which formed the basis for the establishment, years later, of the University of Pennsylvania. It was Franklin's intention that his academy provide an education which would equip young people for success in life and the business world. He believed the academy should teach subjects that would be useful in the New World, with emphasis on the study of English. Reluctantly, to gain financial support, he agreed to the incorporation of Latin in the curriculum. Somewhat offsetting the classical influence, modern languages were added to the curriculum. Science became an acceptable discipline for study by secondary school students.

Opened in 1751, Franklin's academy started with three departments, English, Latin, and mathematics, and shortly afterward added a fourth division, the philosophical. Some of the proposals Franklin made for the academy reveal insights into school curriculum and methodology that are as timely today as they were two hundred years ago. He recommended:

That a house be provided for the academy, if not in town, not many miles from it; the situation high and dry, and if it may be, not far from a river, having a garden, orchard, meadow, and a field or two.

That the house be furnished with a library (if in the country, if in the town, the town library may serve) with maps of all countries, globes, some mathematical instruments, an apparatus for experiments in Natural Philosophy, and for Mechanics; prints of all kinds, prospects, buildings, machines, etc.

All should be taught to write a fair hand. . . . To form their style, they [students] should be put on writing letters to each other, making abstracts of what they read; or writing the same things in their own words; telling or writing stories lately read, in their own expressions.

While they are reading Natural History, might not a little Gardening, Planting, Grafting, Inoculating, etc. be taught and practiced, and now and then excursions made to the neighboring plantations of the best farmers, their methods observed and reasoned upon for the information of youth?[2]

In his proposals Franklin advocates such modern notions as large attractive sites with ample room for varied activities, instructional materials centers, the teaching of the language arts through a functional approach, and field trips for educational purposes.

The academy achieved its greatest popularity in New England and the Middle Atlantic States. As the years passed girls were admitted to this institution. Some academies which have become well known were established in the late eighteenth century. Phillips Academy at Andover, Massachusetts, dates from 1778 and Phillips Academy at Exeter, New Hampshire, from 1781. Though we now think of these academies as "prep schools," Phillips Academies were founded "for the purpose of instructing youth, not only in English and Latin grammar, writing, arithmetic, and those sciences wherein they are commonly taught, but more especially to learn them the great end and real business of living."[3]

Today's institutions that bear the name "academy" are largely private schools, college-preparatory secondary institutions, or military schools. For

[2] Ibid., pp. 38–39. As quoted from T. H. Montgomery, A History of the University of Pennsylvania, 1749–1770 (Philadelphia: George W. Jacobs and Co. 1900) pp. 497–500. By permission of Prentice-Hall, Inc.

[3] Emma Reinhardt, American Education: An Introduction, rev. ed. (New York: Harper & Row, 1960), p. 305.

sentimental reasons, a few high schools also have continued to call themselves academies. The academy served as a transitional institution between the selective Latin Grammar School and the public high school. It obtained its support from endowments, tuition, and, in some cases, the state. The academy as an institution was neither wholly public nor wholly private. Methods of instruction in the academy were not totally different from those employed by teachers in the Latin Grammar School. Memorization continued to be a principal technique of pedagogy. Although Franklin's academy offered a six-year sequence of studies beginning at age eleven, students entered most academies around the age of thirteen and commonly pursued a four-year sequence.

For a time the academy was recognized as a popular institution for the mass of students while the children of the well-to-do continued to attend the Latin Grammar School, but as more and more young people entered the academies the Latin Grammar School declined in importance. The colleges began to turn to the academies for their students. Once again the heavy hand of the college could be felt on the secondary school. The schoolmasters of the academy began to feel that their primary mission was the preparation of young people for institutions of higher learning. The Latin and philosophical curricula grew to dominate the academy much as the college-preparatory curriculum dominates many high schools today. The next step in the evolution of the American school was to be a free, publicly supported institution with an expanded curriculum and doors open to all youth.

THE PERIOD 1821 TO THE PRESENT

From 1790 to 1820, a short span of thirty years, the population of the United States grew from just under four million persons to just under ten million. These thirty years brought an increase in the number of states in the Union from seventeen to twenty-six plus the District of Columbia. A secondary school favoring the needs of the college-bound, whether it be called a Latin Grammar School or an academy, could not adequately serve a rapidly growing nation. An institution free of European traditions and origin was essential.

MASSACHUSETTS, A LEADER IN EDUCATION

Massachusetts has since the early colonial period offered the nation leadership in education. It was Massachusetts that established the first grammar school, and the first university in the United States. Massachusetts passed the first laws requiring local communities to establish schools. Horace Mann, as secretary of the Massachusetts State Board of Education from 1837 to 1848, succeeded in obtaining strong support for a system of public schools. Massachusetts recognized the state's responsibility in the preparation of teachers when, under Mann's leadership, it established in 1839 the first state normal school in the United States.

The first high school in the United States was the English Classical School, founded in Boston in 1821. Three years after its opening the name of the school was changed to the English High School. The term "high school" is believed to have been borrowed from the name of a secondary school in Edinburgh, Scotland. Boys of age twelve who had mastered the three R's were admitted to the English High School. (High schools for girls and coeducational instruction were several years yet in the offing.) The three-year sequence stressed English, mathematics, history, and science. Foreign languages were conspicuous by their absence from the curriculum. A secondary school for all the people was the aim of the English High School.

The extension of secondary education in the United States was aided by a series of laws and court cases in various states. Most significant of these were two laws in Massachusetts and a precedent-setting court case in Michigan. In 1827 the Commonwealth of Massachusetts decreed that towns with five hundred or more families must maintain a high school with a ten-month program. The state went so far as to specify that during those ten months Americian history, geography, surveying, algebra, and bookkeeping must be taught. Towns with four thousand or more residents were required to include also in the curriculum Latin, Greek, rhetoric, logic, and general history. Twenty-five years later the state of Massachusetts passed the first compulsory attendance law. Today most states compel children to attend school until they reach the age of sixteen.

THE KALAMAZOO CASE

For another quarter-century the battle was waged throughout the United States to provide public education by means of taxes. The high school continued to exist along with the academy. As communities sensed their obligations to establish popular institutions where the children of all people could be educated, enrollments in the high schools increased. The state of Michigan gave the public high school a powerful push with the decision in the famous Kalamazoo case.

The board of education of Kalamazoo, Michigan, decided to establish a high school with public funds and hire a superintendent of schools. A taxpayer of the community brought suit against the board of education, contending that the board had exceeded its authority. It was the taxpayer's position that the board had no right to use public funds for secondary education. He maintained that secondary education should be paid for by the parents of children who want that instruction. The Supreme Court of Michigan took the case under advisement and in 1874 decided that a school district was not limited to the support of elementary education but could establish whatever levels of schools it wished as long as the voters of the school district were willing to pay the taxes. The court, in essence, ruled that secondary education is a legitimate part of the program of public schools. By this historic decision school districts have been able to justify extension of public education both upward into the college level and downward to kindergarten and nursery school.

Secondary education today has grown in a variety of ways. Until recent times the eight-four pattern—eight years of elementary school (or elementary and junior high school) and four years of high school—has been popular in many parts of the country. Moderate-size communities tend toward the six-six pattern—six years of elementary school and six years of junior-senior high school. Large communities frequently use the six-three-three pattern—six years of elementary school, three years of junior high school, and three years of senior high school.

JUNIOR HIGH SCHOOLS

The junior high school and the junior college are both developments of the twentieth century. In the early stages of our educational history grades seven and eight were considered a part of the elementary school. The pupils in these grades were taught in a self-contained classroom in much the same way as those in the lower six grades. The abrupt transition at ninth grade from elementary to secondary school was difficult for many youngsters to make. It became apparent that the needs of preadolescents were not adequately served by either the elementary scihool or the senior high school. For this reason a school was created for the specific purpose of educating children in the twelve-to-fourteen age bracket. The junior high school could give to these students a program especially suited to them, and teachers specially trained for handling this level of education could be employed. A departmentalized program, as opposed to the self-contained classroom, could get the pupils ready for the highly departmentalized program of the senior high school. With their own program junior high school pupils would not be swallowed up in the senior high schools.

The first junior high schools were founded in Columbus, Ohio, and Berkeley, California, in 1910, by separating grades seven, eight, and nine from the elementary and senior high program. Since that date the junior high school has spread throughout the country. It is generally recognized by educators that, when enrollments permit, it is most desirable that the junior high school be provided with buildings, materials, staff, and administration separate from those of the other levels. One of the real concerns of educators today is the pressure exerted by the senior high and college on the junior high school. A steady downward shift of subject matter from the college to the senior high school, from the senior high school to the junior high school, and even from the junior high school to the elementary school may destroy the original intent in the establishment of junior high schools.

There is a growing belief that the junior high school is no longer serving its original purposes and is more and more taking on the characteristics of the senior high school. American children today are reaching adolescence much earlier than children of many years ago. Some educators believe that a new organizational plan is necessary. On the horizon are several new plans, one of which is the four-four-four—four years of elementary school, four years of middle school, and four years of high school. Advocates of the middle school, which combines the former grades five, six, seven, and eight, believe that this pattern of organization will more nearly meet the needs of present-day preadolescents.[4] Some communities are now experimenting with the middle school.

JUNIOR COLLEGE

The first public junior college was built in Joliet, Illinois, in 1902. The junior college is one of the most rapidly growing developments in education. The junior or community college, as it is often known, comprises grades thirteen and fourteen and serves a triple function. It offers a terminal education in commercial and vocational subjects for those students who will go no further in their formal education. It provides a transfer program consisting of the freshman and sophomore years of college, after which students go on to four-year colleges and universities. It serves the community with an adult education program in a wide variety of fields. The existence of a junior college within commuting distance of students makes possible post-high school education for many young people who would otherwise not be able to afford a college education. The ultimate goal of junior college education is the establishment of enough of these institutions within commuting range of all those young people who wish to obtain advanced education. It is possible that in years to come the community college may take on all the vocational education now offered at the high school level. California, Mississippi, New York, and Florida have made great strides in providing junior college education for the students in their states.

Since the junior college provides both advanced secondary education and beginning college education, there has been some disagreement on the administration of these schools. In Florida the junior college operates under the administration of the superintendent of the county public school dis-

---

[4] See William M. Alexander, "What Educational Plan for the In-Between-Ager?" *NEA Journal*, 55 (March 1966), 30–32; and W. M. Alexander and Emmett L. Williams, "Schools for the Middle School Years," *Educational Leadership*, 23 (December 1965), 217–23.

trict. In California the majority of junior college presidents are directly responsible to the school boards of their junior college districts. A continuing problem is maintaining the junior college for the specific purposes for which it is intended. There is a pronounced tendency for the junior college to aspire to become a four-year college and ultimately a university. The college emphasis has on some occasions caused the terminal and adult education programs to be neglected or abandoned.

GROWTH OF SECONDARY EDUCATION

From modest beginnings secondary education in the United States has grown to enormous proportions. From the classical studies of the Latin Grammar School the secondary school curriculum has developed into a multicurricular program. Whereas the Latin Grammar School served only an elite, the modern high school strives for universal education of adolescents. The comprehensive high school of today offers a broad program of general and specialized education in a variety of curricular patterns. Some cities have erected specialized vocational high schools. Teachers utilize many techniques and aids in their attempts to implement the latest findings in the fields of psychology, learning, and instruction.

The statistics of secondary education today are impressive. Over sixteen million adolescents enter the doors of our secondary schools daily. More than eleven million of these are enrolled in grades nine through twelve. It takes close to 30,000 public and private high schools to house these sixteen million students. Out of a total of some 1,800,000 teachers, approximately 735,000 instruct secondary school pupils.[5] In 1967–68 we can expect the number of secondary school teachers to surpass 800,000. The demand for teachers has in recent years exceeded the supply of trained teachers.[6]

With centralization and consolidation of school districts the number of small high schools in the country is declining. In 1930, 82 per cent of the high schools enrolled 300 or fewer pupils. In 1958–59, 57 per cent of all high schools, a total of approximately 11,000 schools, enrolled fewer than 300 pupils. The average enrollment of the small high school is 145 pupils. Although the majority of high schools may be classified as small, only some 13 per cent of the high school student population, about 2,000,000 pupils, are in attendance at these small schools.

Educators regard the trend to centralization and consolidation as beneficial. The small high school cannot provide a modern, diversified curriculum. It cannot offer a wide choice of electives. It cannot, as a rule, attract and hold capable teachers. Most small high schools exist in rural areas

---

[5] National Education Association, *Estimates of School Statistics, 1965–66* (Washington: Research Division, N.E.A., 1965), pp. 9, 13.

[6] National Education Association, *Teacher Supply and Demand in Public Schools, 1966* (Washington: Research Division, N.E.A., 1966).

where support of education is at a low financial level. In some regions small high schools continue to exist within several miles of each other, which means that facilities must be duplicated at each school. Local community pride in maintaining the small school has taken precedence over the educational needs of young people. Some small schools are able to fill their needs for staff only because of the presence of local teachers who have made their homes in the area and are content to reside there. On a nation-wide basis only one in four of the high schools classified as small is accredited by the regional associations. James B. Conant, former President of Harvard University, had the limitations of the small high school in mind when he recommended in 1959 that the total number of high schools in the United States be reduced to 9,000 and that each high school have at least 100 pupils in the graduating class.[7]

SOME PROBLEMS OF TODAY'S SCHOOLS

DISPARITIES IN FINANCIAL SUPPORT

It is obvious that the quality of education is related to the amount of money put into it. The states vary greatly in their abilities to support education. In 1964–65, while the national average expenditure per pupil in average daily attendance stood at $483, New York State spent $790 and Mississippi spent $273.[8]

Financing of schools, both elementary and secondary, becomes a more difficult problem as the years go by. Ways must be found to increase the percentage of tax revenues that go to education. The United States is in an unparalleled period of affluence. In 1964, when the gross national product, the value of all goods and services produced, was about $629 billion, expenditures for education totaled approximately twenty-one billion dollars. In the same year citizens of the United States spent about twenty-four billion dollars for recreation. The financial plight of the schools becomes more severe as schools must be built and faculty employed for the growing population. Costs of construction, labor, textbooks, and instructional materials have risen sharply. More young people are remaining in school for a longer period of time. Today two out of three young people continue until graduation from high school.

It is the belief of many educators, as well as of the professional education organizations, that the federal government must provide a larger share of the financing of education. Typically, 56 per cent of school rev-

[7] James B. Conant, *The American High School Today* (New York: McGraw-Hill, 1959), pp. 77–85. By permission of A Study of American Education, Princeton, N.J., which holds the rights to all of Conant's studies of American education.
[8] National Education Association, *Rankings of the States, 1965* (Washington: Research Division, N.E.A., 1965), p. 49.

enues come from the localities where the schools are located. Most of this money is raised through taxation of property. Some communities, though by no means all, have reached a limit in assessing property taxes. Forty per cent of the school revenues come from the state through a variety of taxes, some earmarked for education and some from general revenues. Four per cent of the schools' finances come from the federal government. (Nebraska and Delaware depart from these patterns of support in that 95 per cent of the school revenues of Nebraska come from local sources and 83 per cent of Delaware's from state sources.)

FEDERAL PARTICIPATION IN EDUCATION

The mobility of the population and the inability of the poorer states to finance adequately a system of education make increased participation of the federal government imperative. The federal government has the most efficient system for tax collection. State and local debts have been increasing faster than the federal debt. Participation in financing of education is not a new role for the federal government. Past federal legislation on education has included the following:

a. The Northwest Ordinance of 1785 provided that "there shall be reserved the lot number 16 of every township for the maintenance of public schools within said township."

b. The Morrill Land-Grant Act of 1862 granted to each state public land for the support of colleges where students could study agriculture and mechanical arts and take military training (R.O.T.C.).

c. The Smith–Hughes Act of 1917 provided grants for vocational education.

d. The George–Reed Act of 1929 increased aid for vocational education in the schools.

e. The George-Dean Act of 1936 extended aid to vocational education and included the distributive occupations.

f. The National School Lunch Act of 1946 gave to public and private schools funds and foods for school lunch programs.

g. The GI Bills of 1944, 1952, and 1966 provided federal funds for the education of veterans of World War II and the Korean War, and for individuals discharged from the Armed Forces after January 31, 1955.

h. Several acts in 1941, 1950, and 1958 provided funds to areas that are "impacted," i.e., adversely affected by federal activities. One example of this is the Cape Kennedy area in Florida, which has had to accommodate a large number of persons engaged in the space projects.

i. Public Law 85-926 in 1958 extended federal grants to train teachers of the mentally retarded.

j. The National Defense Education Act of 1958 has provided millions of dollars to strengthen critical areas in education: science, mathematics, modern foreign languages, guidance, and research in the use of mass media. The 1964 amendments to this act broadened the scope of the act. Through matching federal-state grants schools could obtain funds for instruction in history, civics, geography, English, and reading as well as science, mathematics, and modern foreign languages. Teacher training institutes were authorized in history, geography, reading, English, library science, educational media, and instruction of the culturally disadvantaged.

k. The Manpower Development and Training Act of 1962 provided funds for training or retraining of unemployed adult workers and for counseling and training of youths sixteen years of age or older.

l. The Higher Education Facilities Act of 1963 authorized funds for construction of facilities at institutions of higher education, including public community colleges and public technical institutes.

m. The Vocational Education Act of 1963 greatly expanded opportunities for occupational training and provided funds for construction of vocational education facilities.

n. The Economic Opportunity Act of 1964 established an Office of Economic Opportunity to combat poverty. This legislation authorized the Job Corps, work-training programs for unemployed youth, work-study programs for needy college youth, a community action program (including "Operation Headstart," a program for preschool children of low-income families), adult basic education, special programs for low-income farm families and migratory workers, and recruitment of volunteers to further programs of the act (VISTA—Volunteers in Service to America).

o. The Civil Rights Act of 1964 provided help to school districts involved in the process of desegregation. Institutes and consultant help were provided for school personnel who wished assistance in establishing equal educational opportunities in their districts.

p. The Higher Education Act of 1965 authorized loans and scholarships for students, community service programs, improvement of libraries, and assistance to developing institutions for improvement of instruction. It also transferred the college work-study program from the Office of Economic Opportunity to the Office of Education.

q. The Elementary and Secondary Education Act of 1965 is one of the most significant pieces of federal legislation affecting education. It doubled the amount of federal aid to the public schools and provided general aid as opposed to aid for specific fields. The act was mainly intended to meet the needs of the culturally disadvantaged. It provided payment of one-half the average per-pupil expenditure for children from families with an income of less than $2,000 per year, funds for library resources, textbooks, and audio-visual materials, money to establish supplementary education centers, funds for the establishment of regional educational research and training facilities, and financial aid to strengthen state departments of education.

The administration of President Lyndon B. Johnson, a former school teacher himself, must be credited with the first massive federal support to education.

For more than one hundred years the minimum of a secondary education for all pupils who could profit from it has been the goal of public education in the United States. The high school diploma is almost an essential requirement for employment in today's competitive labor market; the college degree is rapidly becoming a requirement for admission into jobs with a future. The estimated lifetime earnings of men who had less than eight years' schooling amounted in 1963 to $131,000; of those with eight years of elementary education, $178,000; with four years of high school, $246,000; and with four years or more of college, $386,000.[9]

Statistics for the year 1963 show that men with fewer than eight years of education earned an annual mean income of $3,641; with four years of high school, $6,693; and with four years or more of college, $10,062.[10] A high school education today is essential. Yet, the goal of a high school education for all youth who have the ability to pursue it is far from realized.

SCHOOL DROPOUTS

The dropout figures are always dramatic and startling. The National Education Association states that only slightly more than half of all fifth-graders finish high school.[11] The percentage of dropouts varies from community to community and from state to state. Some communities are, of course, wealthier than others. Pupils in well-to-do communities stay in school until they graduate.

The dropout rate, however, has been decreasing through the years. In 1940 two out of three young people failed to complete high school. By 1949 the dropout rate had been reduced to slightly more than fifty per cent. The year 1950 was the first year in the history of the United States that a greater percentage of students graduated from high school than dropped out. The present national dropout rate from high school has been estimated at thirty to thirty-five per cent.

The increased competition for jobs and the growing wealth of the country have combined to keep more adolescents in school longer. A conservative estimate places the number of high school dropouts at 900,000 annually.

[9] U. S. Department of Commerce, *Statistical Abstract of the United States, 1966*, 87th annual ed. (Washington: U. S. Government Printing Office, 1966), p. 116.
[10] *Ibid.*
[11] National Education Association, *Research Bulletin* (February 1960), 11.

During the decade 1960 to 1970 we may expect the total number of dropouts to approach 12,000,000.

The fortune of birth plays a critical role in the dropout problem. If a child is born in a rural family, in a Negro family, in a migrant family, or in a family whose head is an unskilled worker, that child will tend to drop out of school before a child from an urban, white, nonmigrant, professional family. A look at the United States Census figures for 1960 illustrates this point. Of the total number of white persons twenty-five years of age and over (under 90 million), 26 per cent had finished high school and 8 per cent had finished college. Of the total number of nonwhite persons twenty-five years of age and over (under 10 million) 15 per cent had finished high school and less than 4 per cent had finished college. Put another way, in 1960 the median number of school years completed by white persons was calculated to be 10.9, while the median number of school years for nonwhites was 8.2.[12]

The reasons why pupils drop out of school are varied. The National Education Association found the average dropout to be sixteen years of age, one who does not participate in extra-class activities, and one whose parents are uninterested in education.[13] Although many dropouts are of less than average intelligence, approximately two-thirds of them possess at least average intelligence. The typical dropout is lacking in academic aptitude. He finds little in school to interest him and little that meets his needs. He is anxious to get out into the "real" world, earn some money, marry, and raise a family. Frequently he comes from a culturally disadvantaged or broken home.

Some pupils do leave school for financial reasons and to assist their families. Some, however, give as reasons for leaving school socially acceptable excuses, "have to work," "folks need me at home," when actually they mean "not interested in school" and "the program is not suitable for me." The National Education Association's Project on School Dropouts corroborates previous findings to the effect that among the dropouts are many potentially able young people.[14] Some of these young people come from favored home environments. For one reason or another they have elected or been forced to drop out of school before graduating. Recent studies of the creative child show that regimentation and conformity cause creative boys and girls to do poor work in school. Although we are now speaking of students who do not finish high school, we should take cognizance of the fact that of those adolescents who do graduate only about fifty per cent go on to college. Thus, about one high school student out of three goes on to college.

[12] U. S. Department of Commerce, *Statistical Abstract of the United States, 1966,* 84th annual ed. (Washington: U. S. Government Printing Office, 1966), p. 113.

[13] *Research Bulletin* (February 1960), *op. cit.*

[14] Daniel Schreiber, ed., *The School Dropout* (Washington: National Education Association, 1964).

COSTS OF A HIGH SCHOOL EDUCATION

Several factors prevent the goal of universal secondary education from being realized. In spite of the fact that high schools are, in theory, free, in practice they are often expensive, as parents who foot the bills will quickly attest. A high school education involves both apparent costs and concealed expenses. Many high schools assess a number of student fees, the bulk of which go to provide materials for courses.

Although it is general practice for public schools to furnish textbooks at public expense, some schools require their pupils to buy all or some of their own textbooks. Whenever expenses must be paid by the student or his parents, the poor student who cannot pay the fees is confronted with a serious problem. Many students from lower-socioeconomic-level homes have left school because the fees and other expenses were so great that they could not afford to remain.

Hidden costs force many adolescents to drop out of school. These are costs, which some people refer to as "hidden tuition," that are not required by the school but that are nevertheless very real to students and their parents. These are the expenses for various activities that adolescents feel they must take part in to maintain their status and to belong to their peer group. We could compile a long list of these expenses, from the car that junior drives to school, to the evening gown daughter must have for the freshman hop, to class rings. Some expenses which should be optional have crossed the line to become, in fact, required. The student activity fee that is assessed each pupil in some schools is a prime example. Hidden tuition may run from $100 to $200 a year per child, not including such items as motor scooters and automobiles. This is an enormous expense for some families, especially large families from lower socioeconomic brackets. The middle-class bias in our schools is readily detected in the extent to which the school permits hidden tuition to be a factor. The school must help to keep expenses to a minimum. It is more than probable that with leadership from the school staff, parents would welcome attempts to keep hidden tuition down.

DESEGREGATION

The courts have aided children of minority groups by outlawing segregation and the Congress has furthered the work of the courts in its 1964 Civil Rights Act and 1965 Voting Rights Act. The pace of desegregation will be swifter than has been true in the past. In the "separate-but-equal" days, up until the United States Supreme Court decision on segregation in 1954, support to Negro education was minimal, particularly in some of the Southern states which were attempting against overwhelming financial odds to maintain two separate systems of education. Some progress toward desegregation had been made even before the Civil Rights and Voting Rights Acts. *The*

Southern School News, which gathers factual information on the racial prob-lem in the schools, reported in 1963 that 1,129 school districts of a seventeen-state southern region had integrated to some extent. Since 1954, 962 of these districts acted voluntarily, while 167 were ordered by the courts to desegregate. In the year 1963–64, 130 school districts desegregated volun-tarily, 20 by federal court order.[15]

For a more accurate picture of the situation it should be pointed out that there are 6,197 school districts in this seventeen-state southern region. About half of these, 3,053 districts, are districts in which both whites and Negroes reside. Most of the remaining are districts which have in them only whites. By June 1963 about one-third (1,129) of the school districts where both whites and Negroes live had desegregated. In many cases, however, de-segregation has been nominal or token. Of some three and one-half million Negroes enrolled in schools in 1965 in the seventeen-state region, 568,000 or about 16 per cent of the Negro enrollment, were attending school with whites.[16]

The problem of segregation is not confined to the South. Trouble has broken out in New York City, Chicago, Los Angeles, and other cities of the nation. Discrimination against Mexican and Indian minority groups is a continuing problem in the West and Southwest, as well as discrimination against the Puerto Rican in cities of the East.

SOLUTIONS TO THE DROPOUT PROBLEM

School systems are attempting a variety of programs to reach more pupils and to keep them in school. In rural areas the trend toward larger, modern, centralized high schools with efficient systems of school-bus transportation brings more adolescents to school. Agriculture is included in the curriculum, where needed. Some "rural" schools miss an essential point, however. Where they had been truly rural in past years, they are now semirural or even urban. The economy has shifted in many small towns from a basically rural one to a basically industrial one. In many cases the nature of farming itself has changed from small farms where all the work is done by hand to large, mechanized farms. Schools in some areas have failed to change their cur-ricula with changes in the community.

Schools are seeking out migrant children—though by no means to the extent they should—and encouraging them to come to school. In some cases, as in Florida, bilingual teachers work with these students. New York City has under way a project to raise the cultural sights and academic achievement of both culturally disadvantaged youngsters and other pupils generally.[17]

[15] Southern Education Reporting Service, *Southern School News* (Nashville, Tenn., September 1963), p. 1.

[16] U. S. Department of Commerce, *Statistical Abstract of the United States, 1966,* 87th annual ed. (Washington: U. S. Government Printing Office, 1966), p. 123.

[17] See reference to the Higher Horizons Project in Unit IV, pp. 250–51.

Some schools are instituting a nongraded program so pupils may proceed through high school at their own speeds.[18] Detroit's program, called Job Upgrading, has set aside in ten high schools classrooms for dropouts, where they receive special instruction, work experience while learning, and assistance in finding permanent jobs after they have completed their period of training. Some of the dropouts return to regular high school studies while others go to work. Students in the program receive pay for their work while in training and a generous amount of counseling.

Detroit's Eastern High School, opened in 1965, has broken its program into occupational categories such as retailing in place of traditional subjects. Communities are operating night schools for those students who have dropped out and then have realized that they needed a high school education. Night school gives them a second chance. Also enrolled in night schools are many girls who had become pregnant during their high school days. The number of unmarried teen-age girls who become pregnant each year is an alarming problem for society. Hobart reports that pregnancies among unmarried girls, ages 15 to 19, have almost doubled since 1940. While there were 6.58 such pregnancies per 1,000 girls in 1940, in 1957 there were 13.11 per 1,000.[19]

The junior college is filling a need for aiding dropouts by offering adult, noncredit educational programs in vocational subjects. The newly authorized vocational boarding schools may also succeed in alleviating this serious problem in education.

PRAISE AND BLAME FOR THE SECONDARY SCHOOL

Periodically the schools are subjected to sharp criticism. In our decentralized system citizens feel that their schools are a personal concern. Our educational system has nurtured the school-community concept, has promoted Parent-Teacher Associations, has invited laymen to sit on advisory committees, has emphasized the importance of cooperating with the home, and has put on shows and athletic contests for the community. The schools serve as rallying-points in some communities. Frequently, they also serve as scapegoats for other ills in our society. Since almost all persons have attended school for at least a few years, each person feels himself to be an expert on education; indeed, the American public is as quick to make judgments about education as about politics and baseball. It is far easier to criticize the schools than to criticize the home, the church, or society in general.

THE CYCLES OF CRITICISM

Criticism of the schools seems to come in cycles. During World War I our schools were blamed for teaching German, the language of the enemy.

[18] See reference to the nongraded high school in Unit II, pp. 121–22.
[19] Charles W. Hobart, "The Pregnant High School Girl: An Analysis and a Proposal," *The Personnel and Guidance Journal* (May 1962), 786–90.

They also suffered criticism because the health of our young men was discovered in military examinations to be deficient. Somehow, it was implied, the schools were responsible for the malnutrition, mental illness, physical handicaps, and dental decay found in the boys examined by draft boards.

In the 1930's a reaction to some of the experimentalist philosophy and practice burst forth with condemnations of "lollipops in education." The public felt some schools were sugar-coating all learning, that schools were too permissive, and that pupils were not learning anything. The few schools that might have been guilty of such practices were multiplied in the public image until all schools became guilty of excesses.

Two bitter waves of criticism have hit the schools—one in the early and middle 1950's, the second since the launching of the first sputnik, in 1957. The character of these two waves differed considerably. Although both were unpleasant in nature, sometimes exasperating, often exaggerated, and frequently unjustified, the wave of criticism in the fifties was essentially negative, whereas criticism since 1957 and on into the sixties has been essentially positive.

The criticisms of the 1950's focused on the "excessive" costs of education, "communist influence" in the schools, and the "permissiveness" of education. Thus, we heard that communities were building "costly palaces" as high schools. We heard "what was good enough for grandpa is good enough for my son." The schools were accused of wasting tax moneys. Pamphlets were circulated about "The Little Red School House"—"Red" referring to "communist" or "socialist" influence. Teachers were labeled subversive if they mentioned the United Nations or the Tennessee Valley Authority. "Pink" and "red" textbooks were censored, although many had not been read by the censoring vigilantes. The schools were accused of being irreligious, usurping functions of the home, and striving for "one-worldism." While the schools were performing all these horrible functions, they were "coddling" pupils. They were offering too many fads, frills, and snap courses, it was claimed. Pupils were "frittering away" their time in extra-class activities.

We must remember that while some critics believed in the validity of their criticisms, some used one point of attack to further their own ends. It has been fairly common practice for disgruntled taxpayers to seize upon any straw that might result in lower taxes. Thus, the charges that the schools were "irreligious," "communistic," or "anti-intellectual" were often masks for a desire to cut financial support to the schools.

The criticism of the post-sputnik era has been centered upon the issue of excellence and scholarship. We no longer hear frequent complaints about the high costs of education. The public is almost reconciled to the fact that education of a high quality costs money. Educators have responded to previous criticism by finding ways to reduce construction costs and to economize wherever possible. When we look at the paucity of instructional materials and library books, the shortage of teachers, and the lack of classrooms, we cannot say that schools are extravagant. Further, with the increased need for quality in education and the presence of additional dollars in the pocketbook, the criticism that education is too costly has receded.

The scare of "red" influence in the school has diminished since the 1950's. Very few people actually believe that teachers, principals, or textbooks are subversive. Occasionally super-patriots and right-wing groups attack some statements of teachers or some library books. Study of the United Nations and its organizations raises a few hackles now and then. The storm center today, however, is the issue of scholarship. To be sure, Arthur Bestor, Albert Lynd, and Mortimer Smith, critics of public education, were writing before sputnik about "anti-intellectualism" in the schools.[20] Sputnik crystallized critical opinion. In fact, it put the American public in a panic. The Russians had beaten us into space. Who was to blame? Casting around frantically for a culprit, the public found the old scapegoat—the schools.

ACHIEVEMENTS OF OUR SCHOOLS

The wonder of American education is not that our schools are so bad, but that they are so good. It is true that our schools have not always been as good as we would have liked them to be. With nearly 30,000 high schools in the country, for example, we can find some that are abysmally poor in quality. We can also find secondary schools unequaled by any in the world.

Within the short span of our nation's life our schools have unified one of the most diverse populations in the world. It is to the credit of our schools that democratic institutions have been preserved and that our nation has achieved leadership in the free world. Our schools have made significant contributions to our position in world affairs.

Our public school system has taught generations to apply knowledge and use the resources at our command. We have been able to use our natural and human resources in such a way as to ensure one of the highest standards of living in the world. An uneducated population could not have achieved such successes in technology, industry, and farming as has the citizenry of the United States.

Most of our engineers and scientists have come through our public school system. The United States is recognized today as a leader in the fields of science, technology, and medicine. For this reason thousands of students from other lands by-pass the ancient centers of learning in France, Germany, and England to come to the United States for advanced study.

[20] See Arthur Bestor, *Educational Wastelands: the Retreat from Learning in Our Public Schools* (Urbana, Ill.: University of Illinois Press, 1953), and *The Restoration of Learning: a program for redeeming the unfulfilled promise of American education* (New York: Knopf, 1955); Albert Lynd, *Quackery in the Public Schools* (Boston: Little, Brown & Co., 1953); Mortimer Smith, *And Madly Teach* (Chicago: Henry Regnery, 1949), *The Diminished Mind* (Chicago: Henry Regnery, 1954), and *The Public Schools in Crisis* (Chicago: Henry Regnery, 1956).

More students continue in high school and go on to college in the United States than anywhere else in the world. Some critics object to this quantitative argument, but it is an accomplishment that should not be minimized.

EUROPEAN EDUCATION

We are advised by some critics of American education to emulate the European systems of education. If we may generalize on systems with their unique differences, in Europe young persons are separated early in their educational life by means of tests to determine their future education and careers. These critics praise, for example, the French baccalaureate exam, a stringent written and oral examination that is the basis for admission of French secondary school pupils to the universities.

The needs of the scholastically able and highly motivated students in Europe are served admirably. An intellectual elite is developed, from which come the leaders of European nations. It is currently popular to show adulation for the schools of Switzerland, England, and the Netherlands. Several years back the German gymnasium and the French lycée were the ideals. When sputnik was launched, the Russian system of education immediately took on superior characteristics. But as we probe beneath the surface, we find that other nations have their own educational problems.

Strangely enough, while we are advised to adopt European patterns once again, as we did in the days of the Latin Grammar School, more countries of the world are attempting to emulate American patterns of life and education. England and France have made attempts in this direction in education. There is considerable unrest in England over the "eleven-plus" examinations that their young people must undergo. The secondary "modern" schools of England, which are not held in high esteem by graduates of elite "public" schools like Eton and Harrow, may play an increasingly greater role in English life. In France protests are being heard more often against the baccalaureate. It is conceivable that in years to come this hurdle will play a decreasing role in French education. It would be ironic, indeed, if, in our zeal to reform American education, we adopted European patterns while they, in turn, found value in American models.

Chapter 2

THE SECONDARY SCHOOL TEACHER

A COMPOSITE PICTURE

The National Education Association drew a picture of the public school teacher in a monograph published in 1961.[1] The median age for all secondary school teachers was 35.9 years. Secondary school teachers tend to be somewhat younger than their elementary counterparts. The median age for secondary male teachers was 33.7 years and for secondary women teachers, 42.6 years. Seventy per cent of all secondary school teachers were married. Of the total teaching force, elementary through secondary, over 31 per cent were men, over 68 per cent women.

SALARIES AND HOURS

In 1960–61 the mean salary for men teachers in the secondary schools was $5,664 and for women, $5,251. Apparently a cultural bias continues to operate in favor of men, who are more frequently heads of households. Salaries have been edging up, for in 1965–66 the estimated average salary of secondary school teachers was $6,768.[2] Secondary school teachers fare better than elementary school teachers, whose estimated average salary in 1965–66 was $6,293. This difference in salary between elementary and secondary school teachers appears to perpetuate a differential of long standing.

Salaries are considerably higher in large school districts. Those districts that employ 2,500 or more teachers paid in 1960–61 a median salary of

[1] *The American Public School Teacher, 1960–61*, Research Monograph 1963—M2 (Washington: Research Division, National Education Association, 1963). See also *Teacher Supply and Demand in Public Schools, 1964*, Research Report 1964—R9 (Washington: Research Division, N.E.A., 1964); *Economic Status of Teachers in 1963–64*, Research Report 1964—R7 (Washington: Research Division, N.E.A., 1964).

[2] National Education Association. *Rankings of the States* (Washington: Research Division, N.E.A., 1966), p. 24.

$6,359, while districts with 1 to 49 teachers paid a median salary of $4,591. Needless to say, those with more years of teaching experience earned higher salaries than beginners.

Salaries vary a great deal from state to state. During the 1965–66 school year California led the nation with an estimated average salary for secondary school teachers of $8,600. New York and Illinois followed California. Secondary school teachers in South Carolina and Mississippi were paid estimated average salaries of $4,850 and $4,349, respectively.

The typical secondary school teacher instructs 155.8 pupils per day. Average class size in the secondary school is 26.6, which may come as a surprise to teachers in schools with crowded classrooms. The secondary school teacher puts in an average workweek of 45.9 hours, which includes class instruction, out-of-class instructional duties, and miscellaneous duties. The average number of pupil periods per week, i.e., number of pupils in each class times the number of periods per week, totals for all classes 684 pupil periods. A fortunate 57.6 per cent of secondary school teachers have at least one conference period per day. The mean length of class period is 54.5 minutes.

TEACHER TRAINING

Most secondary school teachers are well prepared, at least as far as number of years of college is concerned. Male secondary teachers showed a median of 5.5 years of college completed; female secondary teachers, 4.9. Although 2.3 per cent of secondary school teachers lacked a bachelor's degree, 36.1 per cent had earned a master's degree or higher. It is safe to conclude that secondary school teachers generally have a higher level of educational attainment than elementary school teachers. In 1960–61 the median number of years of college for elementary teachers was 4.5, and 23.8 per cent of elementary school teachers were without a bachelor's degree.

More men than women teach social studies, science, mathematics, physical education, industrial arts, agriculture, music, and driver education. More women teach English, business education, home economics, foreign languages, art, and core courses.

ATTITUDES AND BACKGROUNDS

Most of the teachers felt a sense of identity with their communities. Overall, 64.4 per cent of secondary school teachers reported they lived in the community where they taught. The percentage of teachers living in the community decreased as the size of the school district increased.

The report showed that 55.9 per cent of secondary school teachers are active members of teachers' associations. Significantly, the percentage of teachers who are active members of a teachers' association increases as the size of school district decreases. More than 51 per cent are active members of a church or synagogue. Only 7.5 per cent are active members of a political party, and 69.2 per cent of all teachers are not political-party members.

Of particular interest are the attitudes teachers hold about teaching. Of the male secondary school teachers, 59.2 per cent felt that their teaching loads were light or reasonable; 64.1 per cent believed that the strain of teaching was little or moderate; and 61.3 per cent certainly or probably would teach again if they had to make the decision another time. Of the female secondary teachers, 60.2 per cent felt that their teaching loads were light or reasonable; 64.2 per cent said the strain was little or moderate; and 78 per cent certainly or probably would teach again if the choice had to be made over. In the minority were those men and women who felt their loads were heavy and unreasonable, who believed the strain was considerable, and who would certainly not or probably not choose teaching a second time.

Eleven per cent of our secondary school teachers are employed in school districts with 2,500 or more teachers, 55.3 per cent teach in school districts with 199 or fewer teachers, and 21 per cent in school districts with 1 to 49 teachers. The National Education Association study confirms the fact that teachers are drawn from the middle, upper-middle, and lower-middle classes. The fathers of 70.2 per cent of the secondary school teaching force were farmers, skilled or semiskilled workers, managerial workers, or self-employed; the fathers of 16.1 per cent were in professional or semiprofessional work; and only 13.7 per cent of the teachers' fathers did clerical or sales work or unskilled labor. These figures reinforce the fact that our schools are largely middle-class institutions where pupils are taught by middle-class teachers who promote middle-class values.

Before the prospective teacher is able to move into the classroom on his own he has to take three steps. First, he must complete his teacher preparation and obtain his degree. Second, he has to obtain certification. Third, he has to secure a contract for a job. These three steps, preparation, certification, and placement, bear our consideration.

PREPARATION OF SECONDARY SCHOOL TEACHERS

TRENDS IN TEACHER PREPARATION

The typical program of preparation of secondary school teachers consists of (1) general education, (2) a major in a teaching field, and (3) professional education courses. The program of teacher preparation at teacher education institutions in the various states is organized in such a way that at graduation the prospective teacher qualifies for both a degree and a state certificate to teach. These institutions work closely with the state certification authorities within the state department of education to assure certification for their graduates.

In the preparation of secondary school teachers we see a number of trends, among which are the following:

1. *The preparation of teachers at the college level has become the concern of both professional educators and specialists in various fields.* There has been a rapprochement between these two groups. In institution after institution educators and scholars in the field have sat down together and designed programs of teacher preparation that meet the approval of both groups. Professional education in the large universities is becoming an intercollege task, rather than the sole responsibility of the college of education.

2. *In recent years the number of credits required in the major field has been increased.* It has been recognized as the responsibility of the college to turn out graduates who have depth in their field of specialization. Accompanying this intercollege approach to teacher education is the decline of the teachers' college. Many of the teachers' colleges have become state colleges offering a variety of programs to both students who are planning to teach and students who are going into other fields. Some of them have taken on the characteristics of liberal arts colleges with a department of education for the preparation of teachers. The teachers' colleges per se are expected to continue this transformation into general state colleges serving the needs of more young people of the state. Some have moved from the position of teachers' college to state college to state university as the population of the area served has grown.

3. *The character of professional education has been changing.* The number of credits in education courses has either held constant or declined in total. With a general increase in the total number of hours required in the major fields and for graduation, the percentage of credits in professional education courses has decreased slightly. This has meant that the colleges have had to study carefully their offerings in professional education. They have had to limit these offerings to only the essential courses. It is generally agreed in professional circles that some knowledge of educational psychology or human growth and development, some understanding of the place of the school in society, some concept of the secondary school curriculum, some work in techniques of teaching, and a field experience such as student teaching are necessary areas of professional preparation.

4. *Colleges of education, like the public schools, are making use of newer techniques, such as instructional television and team teaching.* Some institutions are using closed-circuit television in their courses and in observation of teachers in the classroom. Educational technology may be expected to play a greater part in the preparation of teachers. It is possible that a portion of the field experiences will be replaced by simulation of classroom experiences on the campus by means of films, slides, and tape recorders. Student

teachers will be able to react to controlled situations, receiving immediate reinforcement of their reactions. If they make mistakes in this part of their training, they do not suffer the consequences that ensue when they make the same mistakes in actual classrooms. Through simulation the period of field experiences may be shortened. Experimentation with the use of simulation in the preparation of teachers is under way in a number of universities.

5. *There is a trend toward a longer period of preparation for teachers.* It is conceded that it is not possible to provide depth in a field, broad general preparation, and professional education in the usual four-year college program. Five-year programs for teachers are already in operation in some states. We may expect to see more of these coming into the picture as our general and professional knowledge continue to expand. Some of the five-year programs culminate in a master's degree, others do not.

6. *Student teaching or internship, which most prospective teachers feel to be the most significant part of their teacher preparation, is experiencing change too.* The older program of practice teaching, in which students were placed for a period or two a day in schools near the college, has all but been replaced by a period of full-time experience. Colleges vary in the length of their· student teaching programs. Generally, student teachers are assigned to directing or cooperating teachers in the schools for a period of eight weeks to a full semester. During that time they are on duty the full day and are expected to assume the role of a staff member under the guidance of the directing teacher to whom they are assigned.

Colleges are moving toward paid internship programs. These usually operate in the fifth year of preparation. Interns are placed in schools for one semester or for a full year and are paid by the school district at the rank of a beginning teacher. During this period of internship they are supervised by a specially designated teacher supervisor and by a member of the college faculty. The University of Hawaii, for example, has a fifth-year internship program in which it assigns three interns per semester to a teacher whose sole responsibility is working with these interns. The teacher is paid jointly by the university and the state. The intern is paid by the state.

To supervise the student teachers more "clinical professors," as recommended by Conant, will be trained and assigned.[3] It is Conant's contention, which most professional educators will accept, that the supervision of interns requires a high degree of skill and is a task essential in the preparation of teachers.

Today's secondary school teacher is better prepared in all areas—general education, teaching field, and professional education—than the teacher of

[3] James B. Conant, *The Education of American Teachers* (New York: McGraw-Hill, 1963), pp. 62, 140–45.

a number of years ago. The emphasis on scholarship and excellence has reached the colleges as well as the public schools. Educators and scholars have joined forces to assure a better-prepared product. Applicants for admission to teacher education programs are more carefully screened than has been true in the past. The raising of scholarship standards of the profession has had a salutary effect. Teachers can command higher salaries and greater respect when they are well prepared. More able students are attracted into teaching when they realize that teaching is a respected profession.

CERTIFICATION OF SECONDARY SCHOOL TEACHERS

From early colonial days through the first quarter of the nineteenth century each locality hired its own teachers. Standards of employment varied from community to community. Standards within the states were so varied and so lax that some centralized system of licensing teachers became imperative.

THE STATE AS CERTIFYING AUTHORITY

In the early nineteenth century county officials began to assume the task of certifying teachers in their communities. With the appointment of chief state school officers in the various states the responsibility for certifying teachers shifted to the state level. Today the state licenses teachers as it licenses members of other professions. The state derives this authority from the Tenth Amendment to the United States Constitution, which reserved to the states powers not delegated to the United States nor prohibited to the states. The state legislature has delegated the power of certification, in most cases, to the state department of education. Certification is administered customarily through the division of teacher certification within the state department of education. A few large cities (New York City, for example) conduct their own examinations and certification.

The division of certification of the state department of education has the responsibility of analyzing the preparation of an applicant for a teaching certificate and issuing him a certificate. It is generally true that requirements for certification by the states have been lower than the requirements for a degree in the teacher-preparation institutions. For example, a state may require twenty-four hours of French to be certified while a college major requires thirty hours. Throughout the United States, however, certification requirements are on the rise, particularly requirements in the teaching field. We may expect the state requirements to approach the college requirements soon.

DIVERSITY IN CERTIFICATION REQUIREMENTS

The number of credits required in various fields has differed considerably from state to state. Many states have required for certification special courses not required by other states. Such diversity in certification requirements has prevented the mobility of teachers from state to state. In fact, states which needed teachers to alleviate a shortage were discouraging teachers from moving into their communities. In 1954–55 this author did a study of restrictions on mobility of teachers, examining certification requirements of the states.[4] At that time Texas required teachers to complete a course in the Texas Constitution; California stipulated a course in audiovisual education; teachers in the state of Washington had to take a course in Washington school problems; Utah wanted a course in health education; a five-dollar nonrefundable fee had to accompany applications for Florida certificates; a course in conservation of natural resources was required of teachers in Arkansas; and New York gave oral examinations for foreign-language teachers. The list of specific requirements could go on interminably. To be sure, many of these requirements are still in existence. The states also permit teachers to come in and make up the requirements after taking residence in the state. Many teachers, however, are reluctant to take additional courses, especially if they have been through a bona fide teacher preparation program.

To solve this problem some of the states have joined together in a reciprocity compact. The notable illustration of this is the eight-state compact in effect since 1949 among the New England States, New York, and New Jersey. Teachers can move within these states with a degree of ease and can obtain certification with a minimum of restriction.

THE NATIONAL COUNCIL FOR ACCREDITATION OF TEACHER EDUCATION

The most significant development in the field of certification is the influence of the National Council for Accreditation of Teacher Education. This council, which was organized in 1952, is composed of representatives of the National Council of Chief State School Officers, the National Association of State Directors of Teacher Education and Certification, the American Association of Colleges for Teacher Education, the National Education Association on recommendation of the National Commission on Teacher Education and Professional Standards, and the National School Boards Association. A major task of the National Council for Accreditation of Teacher Education (NCATE) is the accreditation of teacher education programs of member institutions.

Although there has been some dissension over the role of NCATE, the general principle of an accrediting association is sound.[5] It has been charged

---

[4] Peter F. Oliva, "Mobility of Teacher Supply Restricted by Certification Laws," *The Nation's Schools* (December 1954), 44–46; and "Four Steps Toward Greater Mobility of Teaching Personnel," *The Nation's Schools* (January 1955), 71–72.

[5] See "Will Wisconsin Accredit NCATE?", *Phi Delta Kappan* (January 1963), 154–59; Lindley J. Stiles, "Reorganizing Accreditation for Teacher Education," *Phi Delta Kappan* (October 1963), 31–37; and Chester C. Travelstead, "NCATE Yesterday, Today, and Tomorrow," *Phi Delta Kappan* (October 1963), 38–42.

that NCATE interferes with institutional programs, forces conformity, and is often arbitrary. On the positive side of the picture, an accreditation body can help raise standards nationally. Certainly, the quality of teacher education programs in some colleges of the country has left much to be desired. The effect of NCATE on certification has been significant. In 1966 twenty-seven states granted reciprocity privileges in the certification of teachers to graduates of their teacher education institutions which had been accredited by NCATE. This meant, for example, that a graduate of an NCATE accredited teacher education program in Vermont could obtain a certificate in Arizona or North Dakota or Colorado. NCATE has increased the mobility of teachers on a nation-wide basis.[6]

Two other trends in certification may be noted. The states have moved away from the granting of lifetime certificates to teachers. In days gone by a teacher obtained a certificate that permitted him to teach as long as he lived without ever doing any further study. Today teachers must earn periodically a certain number of credits to maintain their certificates. With the rapid increase in knowledge and newer techniques of instruction it makes sense that teachers should bring themselves up to date periodically. States vary in their requirements for up-dating certificates. Some require a specific number of college credits, e.g., six credits every five or ten years. These credits may be taken in almost any subject. Other states permit professional and educational travel to count for part of the credit to be earned. This travel ordinarily must be approved in advance by the superintendent. Some states permit teachers to earn credit toward this requirement by supervising student teachers.

GREATER FREEDOM FOR THE TEACHER EDUCATION INSTITUTION

More freedom is being granted by the state to the teacher education institutions. The states' divisions of teacher certification have been in the past somewhat inflexible in interpreting courses taken by applicants for certificates. Colleges have had to tailor their programs to make sure their graduates had the exact courses set forth in the certification requirements. Conant has advocated that the higher institutions be permitted greater flexibility in preparing teachers.[7]

It is possible within the existing framework for the state to permit greater freedom to the colleges while still retaining the authority for certification. When the college can show a program to be sound, the state division of teacher certification should accept this program even if it departs somewhat

[6] Included in the states that grant reciprocity of certification to graduates of teacher education institutions accredited by NCATE are Alabama, Arizona, Colorado, Delaware, Florida, Georgia, Illinois, Indiana, Iowa, Kentucky, Maine, Maryland, Mississippi, Missouri, Nebraska, North Carolina, North Dakota, Oregon, Pennsylvania, Rhode Island, South Dakota, Tennessee, Texas, Utah, Vermont, Washington, and West Virginia.

[7] Conant, *op. cit.*, p. 63.

from usual patterns of preparation. Such a working relationship between the colleges and the state department of education will encourage experimentation in teacher education and the attempt to develop new and more effective programs of preparation. The state departments of education must resist the tendency to read transcripts and accept courses by number and title alone. They must be willing to accept a statement of the content of the course from the university. If the course meets the intent of the certification requirements, it should be accepted toward certification whether or not it bears the "right" number or title.

It is to be hoped that organizations such as NCATE will help standardize some of the terminology of certification. The states refer to "certificates," "credentials," "provisional certificates," "temporary certificates," "graduate certificates," and so on. The meanings and requirements have differed from state to state. It would be helpful to the teacher if the same terms could be used in each of the states.

As he continues in the profession the teacher will undoubtedly wish to obtain additional certificates. He may wish to add a second or third teaching field or to enter guidance or administration fields. He may seek a higher level certificate by taking graduate study and obtaining a master's degree. School districts recognize higher levels of certification, which are based on advanced study, by differentials in salary.

Students interested in the current certification requirements of a particular state should write to the Division of Teacher Certification of the State Department of Education in that state for latest information. They may also consult a manual on certification requirements in the United States.[8]

PLACEMENT OF SECONDARY SCHOOL TEACHERS

PATHS TO EMPLOYMENT

After the prospective teacher has completed his period of preparation and has obtained his certificate, he is ready to accept placement in a teaching job. It is surprising how many teacher candidates come through a teacher preparation program without some knowledge of procedures for finding jobs. The ethical paths to employment are three: First, the applicant may apply directly to the superintendent of schools of the school district. In large counties personnel officers are often designated to recruit and hire teaching personnel, in which case application is made to these officials. He may also apply to the secondary school principal, who, should he wish to hire the

---

[8] See W. Earl Armstrong and T. M. Stinnett, *A Manual on Certification Requirements for School Personnel in the United States* (Washington: National Commission on Teacher Education and Professional Standards, 1964 ed., 1964), published biennially. Also, Elizabeth H. Woellner and M. Aurilla Wood, *Requirements for Certification* (Chicago: University of Chicago Press, 30th ed., 1965), published annually.

applicant, refers him to the superintendent for approval. Personal interviews are required, as a rule. Recommendations are made by the superintendent to the local school board, which has the power to employ teachers.

Ethical conduct would preclude exerting pressure on school board officials through ties of family and friends. It would also preclude indiscriminate application to many school districts when the applicant is fairly certain he would not care to teach in certain districts. It is a further breach of ethics to apply for a teaching job which the applicant knows to be filled. Strong enough emphasis cannot be placed on the necessity for submitting neat, accurate applications. Since the written applications represent the first contact a school system has with the applicant, it is essential that he present the best picture of himself. Many applicants for teaching jobs are rejected because their applications are incomplete and sloppy.

A second route to employment is through the college placement bureaus that most teacher preparation institutions maintain for their graduates. School officials get in touch with the college bureaus, which, in turn, recommend their graduates for placement. A final path to employment may be found in the commercial teachers' agencies, which place applicants for a fee. The customary fee for placement by a commercial agency is four to five per cent of the first year's salary.

FACTORS IN EMPLOYMENT

Whether or not an applicant is employed depends upon a number of factors. The turnover in positions is an important factor in teacher employment. Jobs in smaller communities and in lower paying school districts tend to open faster as teachers move to larger communities and better paying school districts. The teacher's field of specialization is a salient factor. At this time employment opportunities are bright for teachers in the fields of library science, Latin, home economics, and women's physical education. Opportunities in mathematics, science, and modern foreign languages are good, though the supply of teachers in these fields is rapidly reaching a point where it will meet demands. The fields of social studies and English are overcrowded in many areas of the country. The most crowded field and one posing greatest problems of employment is men's physical education. The shortage of teachers is not nearly so critical at the secondary school level as at the elementary level. Shortages are greatest in the critical fields mentioned above and in certain states which are experiencing rapid growth. Few teachers, however, fail to find employment if they have the requisite training, personal traits, and references. Many teachers must make adjustments in their preferences. Those who wish to teach at the senior high level may have to accept employment at the junior high level, or vice versa. They may also have to make an alternate choice of community or school district if their first choice is already saturated. Sometimes they will find it necessary to pull up stakes and move to another state in order to find the type of employment they would like.

Opportunities for advancement in the profession are many. Teachers may aspire to the position of department head, master teacher in a teaching team, supervisor, personnel worker, or administrator. Each step upward requires additional training which brings with it additional salary.

When he signs his contract, the teacher joins the ranks of the profession. He is expected to honor the provisions of his contract. Once he has signed he ceases looking for positions. The ethical teacher does not at the last moment, when a school is expecting him, turn down his contract for a higher-paying position. Teaching is recognized as a profession because it (1) requires a period of professional preparation, (2) requires persons with specialized competencies, (3) maintains certain admissions standards, and (4) maintains a professional code of ethics.

PROFESSIONAL ORGANIZATIONS

Standards for the profession are upheld through the professional organizations, of which the teacher should be a member. The beginning teacher whose pay dwindles in a hurry often finds it difficult to justify the $25 to $50 he pays annually to various professional organizations. His dues, however, bring with them tangible benefits. The professional organizations speak in a unified voice for the teaching profession. The increased benefits that teachers receive today, from salary raises to sick leave to tenure, have been achieved through the action of professional organizations. The dues should be considered a small investment in advancing the profession. Most of the professional organizations sponsor conferences and publish periodicals that help the teacher to keep up to date in his field. It would not be unrealistic for the teacher to maintain active membership in (1) a general national professional organization, (2) a state-wide professional organization, (3) the national organization in his field of specialization, (4) the state organization in his field of specialization, and (5) a local school district professional organization. Membership further permits contacts among teachers so they may exchange views and learn from each other.

In his relationships with students, other teachers, the public, and administrators, the truly professional teacher maintains the highest standards of ethical conduct. He should not only be familiar with but should also subscribe wholeheartedly to the code of ethics of his state and national professional organizations. The Code of Ethics of the National Education Association is a comprehensive, clear statement which, if followed by teachers and administrators, would contribute a great deal toward making teaching a real profession.[9]

[9] The N. E. A.'s Code of Ethics appears in the *National Education Association Handbook* (Washington: National Education Association), published annually.

SUMMARY

The American high school has developed from European antecedents into a unique institution serving a diversity of students. The American high school has a record of which we can be justifiably proud. With increased enrollments have come problems in financing, staffing, and instruction.

Standards for the preparation and certification of teachers of the secondary schools have been on the rise. Higher standards and ethical conduct serve to make teaching an honored profession.

CLASS AND EVALUATION ACTIVITIES

1. Use the following check list to clarify your own thinking about criticisms of education.

Check List on Criticisms

For each of the following criticisms made against education check whether you believe that criticism is True, Partially True, or False.

True   Partially True   False

1. The schools are not teaching the fundamentals.
2. Modern educators believe that schools ignore the wishes of parents.
3. The schools cost too much.
4. The schools are anti-intellectual.
5. There is no discipline in the modern school.
6. Modern marking, reporting, and promotion practices are bad.
7. There is not enough homework.
8. The schools are irreligious.
9. The schools, teachers, and textbooks are "red" or "pink."
10. The schools are controlled by professional educators.

True   Partially True   False

11. The schools are coddling too many uncooperative, unwilling students.
12. The schools have usurped the functions
of the home.
13. The schools are neglecting basic areas
of education.
14. There are too many snap courses in our
schools.
15. The curriculum is too broad.
16. There are too many extracurricular activities in the curriculum.
17. Teachers are overtrained in methods of
teaching.
18. Teachers are required to take their advanced credits in education rather than
in their subject field.
19. The schools are promoting international
government.
20. The schools have no business teaching
about sex.

2. Follow up the check list by group discussion of each criticism. Find
evidence in articles, books, or interviews with informed persons to support
your beliefs about each criticism.

3. Find out the dropout rate of secondary schools in the immediate
community or your home town. Find out the reasons for the dropouts. Consult the superintendent, principal, or guidance personnel for this information.

4. Find out the numbers and percentages of increase in enrollments
in the junior and senior high schools of the immediate community or your
home town. Try to obtain projections of enrollments in these schools for
the next five years; the next ten years.

5. In any selected secondary school find out

a. Expenditures per pupil in average daily attendance.

b. Mean and median salaries for secondary school teachers in the
school. Obtain separate figures for classroom teachers as a group and classroom teachers plus other school personnel, including administrative persons
and specialists on the staff.

c. Percentage of teachers who possess regular teaching certificates.

d. Median number of years of experience of the teaching faculty.

e. Number of teachers who are teaching out of their field.

f. Average rate of turnover of teaching staff.

g. Percentage of teachers who are members of professional organizations.

h. Percentage of men on the faculty.

6. Compare data obtained in the selected secondary school with data for the state and nation. See publications of the research division of the state department of education and publications such as *Rankings of the States* and *Research Bulletins* from the National Education Association's Research Division.

7. Study literature of the National Education Association and the American Federation of Teachers. Study the purposes and nature of each of these organizations. If possible, have a member of each of the two organizations speak to the class on the topic, "Why I Am a Member of the N.E.A." or "Why I Am a Member of the A.F.T."

8. Determine employment opportunities in the various teaching fields in your state. Consult the state department of education and college placement officials.

9. Prepare a letter of application such as you would send to a superintendent when it comes time for you to seek employment.

10. Role-play the situation: a graduate of a teacher preparation program appears for interview with the secondary school principal. Repeat in several teaching fields. Take turns playing the roles of the principal and applicant. Conduct a critique after each instance of role-playing.

11. Prepare as a group a simple code of ethics for teachers.

12. Compare certification requirements for teachers in your field in your state with requirements in four or five other states in which you may be interested.

13. Evaluate your own period of teacher preparation as to:

   a. adequacy of general education.

   b. adequacy of professional education.

   c. adequacy of preparation in your teaching field.

   Suggest ways by which your preparation could have been improved.

14. Debate the topic: Courses in professional education are necessary for the preparation of teachers in the secondary schools.

15. Evaluate certification requirements in your state with respect to (1) adequacy and (2) procedures.

16. Defend the present certification system in your state or present an alternative to the present system.

17. Debate the topic: The National Council for Accreditation of Teacher Education is a positive influence on teacher education.

18. Debate the topic: Teachers should be paid on a merit basis, i.e., better teachers would receive higher salaries.

19. Discuss the advantages and disadvantages of

   a. a single salary schedule.

   b. across-the-board salary raises.

   c. tenure.

20. Prepare a summary of both tangible and intangible benefits of teaching.

21. Discuss the merits and demerits of teachers' strikes.

22. *a.* Identify the following professional organizations and name their major periodicals:

    A.F.T.

    A.A.S.A.

    A.S.C.D.

    Kappa Delta Pi

    N.A.S.S.P.

    N.E.A.

    Phi Delta Kappa

    Pi Lambda Theta

    Your state education association

    b. Name a national professional organization in your teaching field and its periodical.

    c. Name a state professional organization in your teaching field and its periodical, if any.

    d. Name two periodicals exclusively for secondary school teachers.

23. Trace the evolution of the American secondary schools. Look into an imaginary crystal ball and describe a secondary school one hundred years hence.

SELECTED BIBLIOGRAPHICAL REFERENCES

1. Alexander, William M., and Saylor, J. Galen. *Modern Secondary Education: Basic Principles and Practices.* New York: Holt, Rinehart, and Winston, 1959. 765 pp.

    Pertinent chapters in: Part One, "Teachers and Pupils in Secondary dary School"; Part Two, "The Secondary School in American Life"; Part Three, "Secondary Education in Four Other Nations of the Western World"; and Part Six, "The Administrative Structure of Secondary Schools."

2. Conant, James B. *The Education of American Teachers.* New York: McGraw-Hill, 1963. 275 pp.

    Presents Conant's recommendations for teacher education. Stresses importance of practice teaching. Calls for clinical professors to supervise student teachers and greater flexibility for university teacher education programs. De-emphasizes foundations of education and methods courses and the role of the National Council for Accreditation of Teacher Education.

3. Kinney, Lucien B. *Certification in Education.* Englewood Cliffs, N. J.: Prentice-Hall, Inc., 1964. 178 pp.

Paperback analyzing the history, purpose, and procedures of teacher certification.

4. Koerner, James D. *The Miseducation of American Teachers.* Boston: Houghton Mifflin, 1963. 360 pp.

Presents Council on Basic Education's views on teacher education.

5. Metcalf, Lawrence E., DeBoer, John J., and Kaulfers, Walter V., eds. *Secondary Education: A Textbook of Readings.* Boston: Allyn and Bacon, 1966. 530 pp.

This textbook on readings is divided into six parts: The Commitment to Universal Secondary Education in the United States, The High School Population, The Goals and Curriculum of the Free Public High Schools, Explorations in the Subject Fields, Recent Developments in Secondary Schools, and Problems, Trends, and Issues.

6. Schreiber, Daniel, ed. *The School Dropout.* Washington: National Education Association, 1964. 214 pp.

Series of papers presented to symposium called by National Education Association's Project on School Dropouts. Papers discuss societal factors of the dropout problem and implications for school programs.

7. Stiles, Lindley, McCleary, Lloyd E., and Turnbaugh, Roy C. *Secondary Education in the United States.* New York: Harcourt, Brace and World, 1962. 528 pp.

Comprehensive text on purposes of secondary education, organization of secondary schools and curriculum, and current concerns in secondary education.

8. Stinnett, T. M., and Huggett, Albert J. *Professional Problems of Teachers.* 2nd ed. New York: Macmillan, 1963. 516 pp.

Extensive treatment of professional personnel policies and working conditions, responsibilities and rights of teachers, professional organizations, preparation of teachers, certification of teachers, and accreditation of teacher education.

INSTRUCTIONAL AIDS AND SOURCES

FILMS

Education in America: The Seventeenth and Eighteenth Centuries. 16 min. Sound. Color or black and white (Coronet).

Historical developments in education in New England, the South, and the Middle Colonies. Includes the dame school, Latin Grammar School, pauper school, and academy.

Education in America: The Nineteenth Century. 16 min. Sound. Color or black and white (Coronet).

Describes significant historical developments in education in the nineteenth century, including the establishment of the first high school, work of Horace Mann, and compulsory education laws.

Education in America: The Twentieth Century. 16 min. Sound. Color or black and white (Coronet).

Historical developments in American education in the twentieth century. Relates developments to social, economic, and cultural aspects of United States life. Discusses educational theories and major trends and problems.

Passion for Life. 83 min. Sound. Black and white. Feature length film. French dialogue, English subtitles (Brandon Films).

Superb French film which portrays a schoolmaster's struggles to introduce modern principles of education in the school of a small village.

UNIT II

THE SECONDARY SCHOOL
CURRICULUM TODAY

OBJECTIVES OF UNIT II

At the conclusion of his reading and correlated study-discussion activities, the reader should

A. understand that

1. the secondary school curriculum is undergoing constant change;
2. sociological forces effect educational change;
3. the purposes of education in the United States are different from the purposes of education in other societies;
4. various individuals and groups have formulated thoughtful statements of the purposes of education;
5. curricular needs differ in different communities;
6. the comprehensive high school is uniquely American;
7. the fixed-track system in the secondary school curriculum is disappearing;
8. balance in the curriculum is essential;
9. there is a general increase of stress on scholarship and excellence throughout the curriculum;
10. every subject in the curriculum is experiencing change; some subjects are undergoing drastic changes;
11. there remain many unresolved issues in respect to the secondary school curriculum.

B. show appreciation for

1. the unique qualities of the American high school,
2. the great effort of our schools to try to meet the needs of all learners,
3. schools that are daring to be different and that are trying out new ideas.

C. adopt attitudes of

1. recognition of the inevitability of change,
2. willingness to try out new ideas,
3. interest in changes taking place in the various subjects of the curriculum,
4. open-mindedness and willingness to suspend judgment about innovations in the curriculum.

D. be able to demonstrate skill in

1. formulating his own concepts of the purposes of secondary education,

2. investigating changes that are taking place in the secondary school,

3. interpreting to the uninformed changes that are taking place in his own field of specialization.

E. know the following:

1. the meaning of the term "curriculum,"

2. principal forces that are causing change in the curriculum,

3. the names and recommendations of prominent individuals and groups concerned with secondary education,

4. some of the major changes in content and implementation of the secondary school curriculum.

CHAPTER 3

SOCIOLOGICAL FORCES AFFECTING THE CURRICULUM

The ancient Latin word "curriculum" had a variety of meanings. It was used to signify "chariot." It referred to the track that the chariot followed. It came to mean the race that the charioteers ran. Finally, it was used to mean course or career. The term has been used in educational terminology to mean the course of studies that the learner pursues. As we see some of the frenzied pace of the modern secondary school, we might wonder if we are reverting to the definition of curriculum as a "race." To many observers of the secondary school scene education appears to be taking on the characteristics of a race. Students are racing with one another for merit awards, scholarships, top groupings, scholastic honors, early graduation, and college admission. Our society through its schools is racing to keep up with and surpass the Russians, the Europeans, and the as-yet-unverified residents of distant planets. Our scholars are racing to keep up with the mass of knowledge pouring forth daily like an educational horn of plenty. Our teachers are racing through the textbooks and sundry other duties. Like the Roman chariot, education on wheels is tearing along toward distant, undefined goals.

A DEFINITION OF CURRICULUM

In common educational usage the curriculum of the school consists of all the experiences that a young person encounters under the direction of the school. This definition of curriculum is broader than that used in earlier periods of our educational history. It was formerly equated with the program of studies or a particular sequence of courses or track, e.g., college-preparatory curriculum. Although we still use the word popularly to denote these meanings, we have expanded its meaning to encompass a range of experiences. Included within the modern concept of curriculum are (1) the program of studies, (2) the methods of instruction employed in each course, (3) the guidance program of the school, and (4) the extra-class activities program. We shall use the word in this broad sense.

The secondary school curriculum has changed rapidly in the last decade. Readers of this textbook who have been graduated from high school only three or four years ago may find it difficult to conceive of a time when closed-circuit television was not in use, when classrooms were all pretty much the same standard size, when teaching teams were unheard of, when the study of communism was considered a waste of time, when fifty per cent of the entering student body failed to complete high school, when language laboratories were nonexistent, when the new mathematics had not made its appearance, and when standardized tests made infrequent intrusions in the school's program.

We may continue to expect change in the curriculum. Ten years from now, most of our high school students may be studying cybernetics, computer programming, Chinese, space science, hydroponics, and nucleonics. The school may be a windowless structure with air conditioning and artificial lighting. The ways we utilize staff and the organization of the courses may be quite different. The interior design of the school building will reflect new advances in pedagogy as well as in school architecture. The gadgetry we use as aids to teaching will be refined, more sophisticated than those currently in use.

Change and the ability to adapt to change have always been a constant challenge in human society. A static society cannot long survive. A healthy educational system must, like other human institutions, adapt to change and help its students to prepare for living in a society where change is the way of life.

CHANGES IN SOCIETY

It is not change alone, however, that has brought on many of the problems we encounter in education today. It is the astounding rapidity of changes in our twentieth-century society. What are some of the sociological changes which have created a new setting for our schools? Let us consider a few of them.

POPULATION INCREASE

Commonly referred to as the population explosion, the great increase in numbers of people has brought with it a multitude of problems. The increased demand for more teachers, more classrooms, more schools, more equipment, more books and supplies has taxed the resources of most communities. The explosion of population continues as one of the great unresolved issues of our times. Critics of Malthus, the eighteenth-century economist who predicted that population would in time outstrip our food supplies, have labeled him a prophet of doom. They may well ponder some of the impressive and hair-raising statistics pertinent to the population increase:

Every 7.5 seconds an infant is born in the United States.

The population of the United States shows a net gain of 1 person every 12 seconds, or 3,000,000 per year.

By 2000 A.D. there will be 350 million persons in the United States.

The world population is growing at the rate of 5,400 per hour, or 47,000,000 per year.

By 1980 A.D. we can expect a world population of 4 billion; by 2000 A.D., 6 billion.

The secondary school curriculum and its patterns of organization must change considerably to accommodate the masses of students demanding to be educated. Unique ways of meeting the problem of increased enroll-ments must be tried out. Original solutions must be forthcoming. It will not prove an effective answer to continue adding pupils to already over-loaded classes. Some of the newer practices which we shall explore later in this unit are attempts to provide a partial answer to the school popu-lation problem.

INCREASED MOBILITY OF THE POPULATION

If we could stand off in space and watch the American continent, we would see thousands of our citizens with bags packed driving off to new destinations. We would see hundreds of trucks and moving vans loaded to capacity carrying the paraphernalia of thousands of mobile families. We are a highly mobile, restless population. Mobility has accompanied our population growth, our increase in affluence, our technological develop-ment, and our improved means of transportation. Thousands of American citizens have moved into California, Arizona, Nevada, and Florida in search of the "good life." While states favored by climate and job opportunities continue to grow at fantastic rates, some of the lesser favored states have lost population. Uneducated citizens of both the white and Negro race have moved from some of the Deep South communities to urban areas of the north.

The United States Census Bureau reported that in March 1965 about one-fifth of the American population lived at an address different from that of the preceding year. Suburban residents are much more mobile than rural residents. As the income of the wage earner increases, there is the tendency for the family to change its place of residence for better dwelling. National figures show that only a little over a quarter of the population continue to live in the same house for a period of ten years or more.

The constant shifting of population creates many burdens for school sys-tems, particularly in the states that are drawing large numbers of permanent residents. The task of providing enough schools, teachers, and materials is in itself enormous.

INCREASE IN KNOWLEDGE

Whether we are speaking of an expansion in knowledge in the field of mathematics or science or technology or, for that matter, in any of the disciplines of the school program, we are struck by the rapidity with which man is adding to his fund of knowledge. We can, for example, fly from New York to Chicago in a jet in about as long as it took George Washington to ride in a carriage over the rough path from Mount Vernon to Washington, D.C. The supersonic transport will hurtle passengers across the Atlantic in two and one-half hours by 1970. The first manned flight to the moon is scheduled for 1970 and our scientists have begun to speak of flights to Mars by 1982. Our explorers are probing the depths of the skies and the ocean. Whole new fields of mathematics have been created within the last twenty-five years.

The implications of the explosion of knowledge for teachers are staggering. We cannot continue to add content without end to the same period of three or four years of the high school program. Choices must be made as to what content will be included in the curriculum. Content must be continuously revised. In fact, the content we teach today may become obsolete by tomorrow. Some of the truths which we hold today may be outmoded by tomorrow. We are, for example, already revising our views on how human beings learn. We are confronted with new theories on the formation of the universe. We have created for the first time a man-made protein. On the other hand, we have barely begun to unlock the secrets of life, space, and atomic energy. Though our medical pioneers have conquered polio, smallpox, tuberculosis, malaria, trachoma, and typhus, the mysteries of the common cold, cancer, heart disease, and multiple sclerosis are still to be solved. The educator has to decide what content and what ways of approaching that content will be most beneficial in preparing citizens in a changing society.

INDUSTRIALIZATION

We may trace the beginning of the Industrial Revolution in the United States to the establishment of the textile industry in New England in the late 1700's. The Industrial Revolution, although it has produced in the United States a civilization with one of the highest standards of living in the world, has also brought with it the ills of an industrial society. We have learned to utilize our natural resources, but at such a rate that we are now in danger of depleting our rich storehouse of natural wealth. Our timber, particularly our redwood, is in danger. We have tapped our oil and mineral wealth at a dizzying rate. We have polluted our water and air. Although we have had natural wealth in plenty during the past, we must now turn our attention in our educational institutions to the development of attitudes and techniques of conservation of resources.

Industrialization has encouraged the growth of cities and the urban complexes and has caused a steady trek from farm to factory, from the country to the city. With modern mechanization of agriculture fewer farmers are needed to supply the needs of city dwellers. In fact, our farming methods have been so efficient that we have piled up surpluses of grain and non-perishable edibles.

Modern industrialization has brought with it greatly improved means of transportation and communication. Our millions of deluxe automobiles speed across the super-highways of the country. Super-highways have not only helped the farmer to get his crops to market and the child to travel to a spanking new central school, but have also welded the nation together. We can drive from New York to Chicago on super-highways without a single red light. We will soon reach the goal of uninterrupted travel on super-highways from New York to California. We may also see finished one day the Pan American Highway, which will take us from the United States to Buenos Aires. In the realm of communication modern cables link us with both Europe and Asia. For approximately ten dollars we can talk for three minutes with friends and relatives in countries across the oceans. Telstar and its kindred satellites now permit us to relay through space events as they are transpiring on distant continents. A "hot line" links the President of the United States and the Premier of the U.S.S.R.

DIVISION OF LABOR

Industrialization has resulted in a sharp division of labor. Job holders perform highly specialized skills for which special training is needed. The trend in society is toward an ever-increasing degree of specialization. This has been caused in part by the growth in knowledge that makes it virtually impossible for an individual to have expertise in a number of fields. The general practitioner, for example, the friendly old country doctor whom we knew and admired, has all but been replaced by physicians who are specialists in internal medicine or geriatrics or pediatrics or eye-ear-nose-throat or urology or gynecology. The local garages advertise specialization in transmission repair or brake relining or tire servicing or electrical repairs. The labor unions have refined the division of labor into a virtual science with even the most minute jobs performed by persons who are specialists in one function or skill.

The teaching profession is no exception to the movement toward specialization. We find a host of educational specialists: classroom teachers, guidance counselors, deans of students, curriculum specialists, principals, and others. Classroom teachers within a given subject area have specialized training in aspects of the subject, e.g., the biological sciences and the physical sciences.

Education for an age of specialization must differ from education for an age of generalists. The choices of vocational training to be taught in the high school are as plentiful and as complex to make as the choices of academic content. Surely, no school can teach young people all the skills they will need for specialized jobs. A vital curriculum will provide a basic education which will equip students to learn their specialties after high school. It will equip them with general work skills, habits of study, and attitudes toward work upon which they can build.

Since more goods can be mass-produced in less time than in the days of handmade products, more time is available to the average citizen for leisure. The workweek has steadily declined over the years. The days of the sixty-hour workweek or the fifty-hour week or the forty-five-hour week have all but disappeared. Even the forty-hour week is giving way. The electrical unions in the early sixties were the first to obtain a thirty-five hour week as their basic workweek. In the next decade it will be common for employees to work at gainful jobs thirty-five hours per week. The reduced workweek results in more leisure time which can be put to use profitably or squandered. The development of lifelong interests and hobbies can be initiated in the elementary and secondary school. These interests can carry through the age of retirement. With improved health the life span has increased. Today's American citizen can look forward to an average life span of seventy years.

UNEMPLOYMENT

Progress is not without its displacements and anxieties. Automation hangs like a sword of Damocles over the heads of American workers. The worker displaced by automation must find means of retraining, and must, even at an adult age, develop new skills by which he can earn a living. Nothing can be so detrimental to our society and so deadening to the individual as unemployment. In spite of our high standard of living, in spite of all-time employment records and unparalleled national production, unemployment is still a problem. We find "pockets of poverty" in some of our mountain areas, in cities where industries have moved on, and in slum areas. The continuing problem of poverty and unemployment in a land of plenty is one with which Americans must contend. The school cannot by itself solve complex social problems such as unemployment, but it can help students to develop skills and knowledge that will keep them off the bread lines. It can help students develop the abilities to cope with social problems and it can inculcate positive attitudes to the effect that complex problems are possible of solution. In Unit VI on discipline and control, we shall return to the subject of industrialization as it impinges upon the behavior of the individual.

INTERDEPENDENCE OF PEOPLE

We live today in close physical proximity not only nationally but internationally as well. Our cities serve as large melting pots for all types of citizens—skilled and unskilled, law-abiding and criminal, adjusted and maladjusted, rich and poor, black and white. For all our progress in the technological sphere, we have made feeble progress in understanding among peoples. Prejudice against races and creeds and class consciousness die hard, but education can serve a liberating function by making people feel a sense of responsibility to their fellow man and by dispelling misunderstandings and ignorance.

Modern transportation and communication and mass media link us closely with peoples of other lands. The myriad of globe-trotters between the United States and other countries increase communication through tourism and business. As individuals get to know each other through personal contact, prejudices begin to disappear. As we study the cultures of other peoples at home and abroad we become more tolerant, more understanding, more human.

We use the foregoing to illustrate the prevalence of change in our society. Change will continue. The increase in population may be checked slightly through birth-control measures, but population projections will continue to show a rise. As more diseases are conquered the death rate will continue to decline in all countries. We will continue to add to our fund of knowledge at ever-increasing rates of speed. Although this is a desirable feature of change, it is not without its educational irony. To cope with change we need a constantly higher standard of education. With the advanced standard of education we have the intellectual equipment to continue to add to knowledge, to make new discoveries, indeed, to create knowledge. Change in the direction of improved education sparks new knowledge which in turn necessitates continual improvements in education.

With the continuing mobility of our population, what is being taught in one state will become increasingly important to the citizens of all other states.

SOCIAL MOBILITY

Along with geographical mobility has come a vertical or social mobility. In the United States we cling to the notion that citizens of a democracy may by their own efforts move upward to positions of increased responsibility, status, and earning power. As our citizens get to know each other better, acceptance among individuals becomes possible. The direction of social mobility at the present time is by no means clear. We can see evidence of greater acceptance and social mobility, with a great deal of fluidity on social lines. Persons from lower socioeconomic status, equipped with ability and training, may rise in the social scale to positions of wealth and influence.

On the other hand, we can see a tightening of social lines and an almost desperate effort to raise social barriers between socioeconomic classes and castes in the United States. The country-club set maintains its untainted exclusiveness. Only the "right" people are admitted to membership in some of the elite social, business, and professional clubs. Although law may have extended the civil rights of minorities, it does not and cannot compel social acceptance. True social mobility can be accomplished only when men are willing to acknowledge the worth of all individuals. It may be inevitable that there will always be some kinds of social gradations, be they gradations of wealth or ability or tradition. It is the mission of an open society, however, to maximize opportunities for social and personal advancement. No doors should be arbitrarily closed to able individuals. The American dream must be maintained as a vital force in our society.

The public schools can make a powerful impact in the area of social mobility. For many of the formative years the children of persons of all walks of life are in the schools, and it is in the public school that children learn to understand and accept one another. They learn to exchange views, form attitudes, and understand the nature of democracy.

Change, then, in social conditions dictates change in the curriculum.

DECIDING ON THE AIMS OF EDUCATION

Our educational institutions are parts of our changing society. Continuous change for the better is essential. Change in the curriculum should be sought and valued. Leadership is to be encouraged. Changes should be steady and gradual. Parties affected should share in the process of making changes. Any change should offer hope for improvement and should be done with specific purposes in mind.

Change is inevitable, both in man's biological development and in his sociological institutions. Those who resist change—any change— and those who wish to return to the mythical "good old days" are unhappy individuals indeed. We have in our school systems teachers who refuse to make changes in their programs and techniques even when they are forced to admit these programs and techniques no longer apply. Education is such an all-pervading institution, striking the lives and fortunes of young and old alike, that it must be subjected to constant scrutiny. As our times change an unending flow of decisions about education must be made by the lay public and professional persons. Decisions must be made in respect to (1) the purposes of education, (2) the content of education, and (3) the implementation of education. We shall consider each of these three areas of decision-making.

EDUCATIONAL AIMS IN HISTORICAL PERSPECTIVE

Every society must define the aims of education in that society. In a static society the purposes of education would remain unchanged. Ostensibly, the major purpose of education in any society and at any period of history is the education of that society's young. On this goal all societies, even the most static and most primitive, can agree. But when we look beneath this generality further definition of the aims of education in a particular society becomes necessary. The questions, Education for whom? and Education for what? enter the picture. For centuries formal education, i.e., schooling, was restricted to males. We have still not eradicated the ancient idea that the woman's place is in the home, and that girls need not receive as much schooling as boys. Only in recent years in the United States have women been encouraged to enter the professions of law, medicine, and engineering. For centuries also formal education has been treated as a privilege of the upper classes, the well-to-do, or the especially intelligent.

The ancient Greeks, who contributed so much to Western civilization, stressed education of boys for a life of leisure and for positions of social leadership. With the Greeks education was not a matter of bread-and-butter, vocational training to equip young people to go out and earn a living, but a leisurely course in the liberal arts. In their purest form the liberal arts were those that liberate man and were pursued by men who had the time to pursue them. The liberal arts were those studies that gave men the background for philosophizing. The philosopher-king was the superb product of ancient Greece.

Unfortunately, an education limited to an elite, be it in Greece or Rome or medieval Europe or seventeenth-century America, ignores the needs of seething masses. It stifles the productivity of a nation. It perpetuates serfdom and slavery. We may marvel at the engineering wonders of the Pyramids or the Colosseum or Persepolis, astounding feats of human intelligence and endurance. Yet, our wonderment is beclouded by the knowledge that many of the enduring wonders of the world were built by brute force and by the sweat, pain, and death of those who were denied the fruits of education and citizenship. It has been the history of totalitarianism in all ages to deny education to large segments of the population.

Modern societies, be they democratic or totalitarian, seek to use education to further their own purposes. Though the general function of school-

EDUCATION IN UNDERDEVELOPED COUNTRIES

ing is the education of the young, the specific purposes of education differ from culture to culture. Since purposes differ, the content of education and the way it is implemented differ as well.

Each generation within a culture must redefine the aims of education to befit the times and current needs of the culture. The aims of education in a culture as old as Iran, for example, are considerably different today from what they were five centuries before Christ when Persia ruled the East. In former days Iran was a center of trade, science, and the arts. Its physicians, mathematicians, and poets were world renowned. Today, exhausted by centuries of wars, spoiled by countless conquering armies, Iran, like many of the "underdeveloped" or "newly developing" countries, is struggling for a comeback on the world stage. Once a mighty power it now fights poverty, disease, archaic agricultural methods, and lack of industry to become once again a productive power. Its educational needs and therefore its educational purposes today are completely different from those in the times when it was under Darius or Alexander the Great or Genghis Khan or Shah Abbas the Great or the Arabs. Social and political conditions combined to change the course of history for this country. The illustration of this one Middle Eastern country can be repeated many times with countries of the Near and Far East, South America, and to some extent the countries of southern Europe and the Balkans. The illustrations would point up the fact that an educational system must be in harmony with the needs of the people in its time. They would demonstrate the fact that the purposes of education cannot remain eternal and unchanging but must change with the demands of the times.

CHAPTER 4

THE PURPOSES OF
SECONDARY EDUCATION

Influential individuals and groups in the United States have spoken on the purposes of education. As we have noted, the Puritans of New England espoused education as a means of combating the works of the devil by equipping the colonists to read and comprehend the scriptures. The versatile Benjamin Franklin offered his ideas for an academy in order to prepare young men for life in mid-eighteenth-century America. Thomas Jefferson recognized the importance of education in a democratic society in many of his speeches and writings.[1]

The purposes of secondary education in the United States have undergone revision as the times changed. College preparation was the foremost objective of the classical education of the Latin Grammar School. Preparation for a useful life was the goal of instruction in the academy. Welding a heterogeneous population together with common civic ties has been a goal of the high school. Periodically, professional groups have been called upon to express their views on the purposes of education. Some of the groups have been highly persuasive and have had a pronounced effect upon the structure of education. The most significant statements of this nature have come from the National Education Association. From the 1890's on groups and commissions of the National Education Association have attempted to define the purposes of education. Their statements have always been colored by the demands of the times. Although we could chronicle these statements at length, we have arbitrarily selected for our discussion here the *Report of the Committee of Ten on Secondary School Studies*, the report of the Commission on the Reorganization of Secondary Education, and the Education Policies Commission's statement on *The Central Purpose of American Education* to illustrate the changing conceptions of educational aims.

[1] See Saul K. Padover, ed., *Thomas Jefferson on Democracy* (New York: Penguin Books, 1939).

NATIONAL EDUCATION ASSOCIATION STATEMENTS

THE REPORT OF THE COMMITTEE OF TEN

The Report of the Committee of Ten, issued in 1894, is a remarkable document.[2] It demonstrates very clearly how individual biases can distort recommendations for the curriculum. The Committee, headed by President Eliot of Harvard University, proceeded on the assumption that the purpose of secondary education was not exclusively preparation of young people for college. From this premise, however, the Committee outlined a college-preparatory program which they felt would suit the needs of both the college-bound and the noncollege-bound. It seems but natural that a Committee of Ten, only one of whom was a public school person, a high school principal, would conclude that the needs of both college-preparatory and noncollege-preparatory students would be met by a college entrance curriculum.

The curriculum of the secondary school has been torn between the two sets of goals, college-preparatory and noncollege-preparatory, almost as if they were antitheses of each other. We have seen periods in our history when the college-preparatory aims were in the ascendance: the 1600's, early 1700's, late 1800's, and again in the middle 1900's. We have seen the nonacademic and vocational aspects of the curriculum stressed in the late 1700's, the early 1800's, the early and middle 1900's. The college-preparatory and noncollege-preparatory aspects of the curriculum are not mutually exclusive. One does not have to be sacrificed for the other. Both can live in harmony, reinforcing each other and strengthening each other.

THE COMMISSION ON THE REORGANIZATION OF SECONDARY EDUCATION

The Commission on the Reorganization of Secondary Education grasped this concept when it reported in 1918 on the needs of young people. The Commission's report set forth the famous Seven Cardinal Principles of Secondary Education.[3] These principles, which are statements of purposes of secondary education, were issued in a time when the United States was involved in a great World War, when young men who were examined for military service showed up with serious physical and educational deficiencies, when the last tides of immigration were diminishing, when men were just taking to the air, when the age of the automobile was just beginning, when industry was gearing for war, when mass production was demanding specialized skills, and when American families were feel-

[2] National Education Association, *Report of the Committee of Ten on Secondary School Studies* (New York: American Book Co., 1894).

[3] Commission on the Reorganization of Secondary Education, *Cardinal Principles of Secondary Education* (Washington: U. S. Office of Education, Bulletin No. 35, 1918).

ing in earnest the tensions of industrialization. The Commission listed the following seven purposes of secondary education:

1. Health
2. Command of fundamental processes, i.e., the fundamentals or basic skills
3. Worthy home-membership
4. Vocation, i.e., the development of vocational skills
5. Citizenship
6. Worthy use of leisure
7. Ethical character

This succinct statement of purposes issued a half-century ago has been modified by ensuing study commissions. It has scarcely been improved, however. The goals enumerated by the Commission on the Reorganization of Secondary Education have not been fully achieved even today. Statements such as the report of the Commission on the Reorganization of Secondary Education help to keep before us worthy goals. They serve as guidelines and keep us conscious of the directions we should take.

We have had what amounts to a cacophony of voices demanding to be heard. Thorndike, Watson, and other behaviorists describe the purpose of education as the shaping of the mind by eliciting the right responses by means of the right stimuli. The philosopher John Dewey and his fellow experimentalists viewed education as life.[4] Professor Arthur Bestor, who has been a sharp critic of education, believes that the goals of modern education are anti-intellectual.[5] Admiral Hyman Rickover advises us to emulate Swiss schools.[6] The Council on Basic Education, an organization critical of many practices in our schools, warns us that our schools are falling down on their job of education for scholastic achievement.[7] James B. Conant encourages sound secondary programs for all with particular emphasis on the academically talented.[8]

THE EDUCATIONAL POLICIES COMMISSION

Among the most influential and persuasive statements of purposes of education are those that have come from the National Education Association's Educational Policies Commission. Over the years a series of im-

---

[4] See Unit IV of this text.

[5] *The Restoration of Learning: a program for redeeming the unfulfilled promise of American education* (New York: Knopf, 1956). Also, *Educational Wastelands; the Retreat from Learning in Our Public Schools* (Urbana, Ill.: University of Illinois Press, 1953).

[6] *Swiss Schools and Ours; Why Theirs Are Better* (Boston: Little, Brown, 1962).

[7] James D. Koerner, ed., *The Case for Basic Education; a Program of Aims for Public Schools* (Boston: Little, Brown, 1959).

[8] *The American High School Today* (New York: McGraw-Hill, 1959). By permission of A Study of American Education, Princeton, N. J.

pressive reports on American education has been issued by this group, composed of noted educators and lay persons in the United States. The Educational Policies Commission appears to have become progressively less wordy, and simultaneously less specific, as it recorded its views periodically in the last thirty years. Its 1938 statement spelled out in minute detail the purposes of American education as the commission saw them. It defined the objectives of self-realization, human relationship, economic efficiency, and civic responsibility. It described the competencies an educated person would display in each of these areas.[9] Its next significant statement has been popularized as the Ten Imperative Needs of Youth. The commission attempted in its 1944 report, *Education for All American Youth*, to look at our society and decide what educational needs would be common to all American boys and girls. This statement has a close resemblance to the Seven Cardinal Principles.[10] Its most succinct statement was issued in 1961 as *The Central Purpose of American Education.*[11] The commission took note of the changes in the world of today when it said:

> Many profound changes are occurring in the world today, but there is a fundamental force contributing to all of them. That force is the expanding role accorded in modern life to the rational powers of man. By using these powers to increase his knowledge, man is attempting to solve the riddles of life,. space, and time which have long intrigued him. By using these powers to develop sources of new energy and means of communication, he is moving into interplanetary space. By using these powers to make a smaller world and larger weapons, he is creating new needs for international organization and understanding. By using these powers to alleviate disease and poverty, he is lowering death rates and expanding populations. By using these powers to create and use a new technology, he is achieving undreamed affluence, so that in some societies distribution has become a greater problem than production.[12]

Consequently, the commission concluded:

> The rational powers of the human mind . . . are central to individual dignity, human progress, and national survival. . . . The purpose which runs through and strengthens all other educational purposes—the common thread of education—is the development of the ability to think.[13]

[9] Educational Policies Commission, *The Purposes of Education in American Democracy* (Washington: National Education Association, 1938).

[10] See Unit V of this text, pp. 281–82, and Educational Policies Commission, *Education for All American Youth* (Washington: National Education Association, 1944), pp. 225–26.

[11] Educational Policies Commission, *The Central Purpose of American Education* (Washington: National Education Association, 1961).

[12] *Ibid.*, p. 9. By permission of N.E.A.

[13] *Ibid.*, pp. 11–12.

As we have traced the thinking of prominent lay and professional groups about the purposes of education, we find them wrestling with perennially unresolved issues. We experience the necessity for making decisions as to purposes which fulfill at a particular time in history both the needs of the learners and the needs of society. We must resolve the following questions about the aims of education in the United States before we can hope to specify content and means for implementing content. Focusing on secondary education, we may ask:

1. *Should secondary education be for all youth in America or should it be for a select few?* Should students be permitted and encouraged to continue as long as possible in school or should those who are unwilling or unable to meet arbitrarily set standards be rigorously weeded out? Would America be stronger if young people were screened for secondary education? Would the causes of democracy be served if secondary education were limited to those of high scholastic aptitude? Perhaps it would simplify teaching somewhat. Perhaps it might save taxes if we could restrict education to the chosen few: the gifted, the geniuses, the academically talented, the bright, the quick, and the motivated. But such restrictions would run counter to the long struggle in the United States for free public schools open universally to all. The demands for education today are so great that a minimal level of secondary education for all, with a small percentage of subnormal individuals excepted, is an essential goal.

2. *Should secondary schools stress college preparation or should they seek to prepare both college-bound and noncollege-bound students?* Though on a national scale about one-third of our high school graduates go on to college, many secondary schools consider their primary, indeed, their only responsibility the preparation of students for college. Since the days of the Latin Grammar School the needs of the college-bound have been served before the needs of others. The academically oriented program does not serve the needs of a large segment of our secondary school population. The American secondary school must seek to achieve competencies which will aid in the development of citizens in all walks of life. The ability to think may be the central purpose of education but instruction can be varied to accomplish this goal.

3. *Should the secondary school serve as the transmitter of existing culture or should the secondary school serve as an instrument of change?* Persons who espouse the transmission of the cultural heritage point of view see the school in a passive role of handing down truth, or at least truth as it is known today. To them the school is oriented largely to the past

and present. It is their belief that if students know well the truths of the past and present, they should be able to cope with the problems of the future. If the school aims only to pass down to the young the lore of the ages, its job is somewhat simplified. What is known can be packaged in text materials that students may study. Answers are readily apparent. The school need not concern itself with unresolved issues that may be controversial in nature. It need not teach ways of solving problems. Life for the teachers, administrators, and parents is a little more comfortable. The status quo is good enough. No one is rocking the boat with disturbing ideas. Besides, there is a vast amount of content to be learned and students' energies are best spent learning the wisdom of the ages.

Transmission of the cultural heritage is, of course, a major role of the secondary school, but it is far from enough for young minds of this century. We cannot be satisfied with transmission of knowledge alone. We should seek means of teaching young people to tackle unsolved problems. We should find ways of stimulating discovery rather than constantly permitting passive learning. The modern school can sacrifice neither transmission of the heritage from the past nor an orientation to the future. The best secondary school curriculum is the curriculum that effectively utilizes the wisdom of the race, applies it to the problems of the present, and on the basis of our limited knowledge seeks to anticipate problems and solutions to these problems which we may encounter in the future.

DECIDING ON THE CONTENT OF EDUCATION

The administrator and teacher in today's schools continuously faces the responsibility for making decisions about the content of education. Typical questions demanding decision are: What will the scope of the curriculum be? What subjects, units, or topics will be included? Should we offer both general mathematics and algebra? Should the vocational offerings be expanded? Is vocational agriculture necessary? Should we have a junior high school band? Should physical education be required of all students in every year of high school? Should we institute a modern mathematics program? Which version of the new biological sciences programs will we follow? Questions of this nature are not easily answered. Decisions that educators make about content are influenced by the following factors.

1. *The educator's beliefs about the purposes of education.* Until some direction is given to a program it is impossible to specify content. The content of a curriculum would be an aimless hodge podge without some clear statements of purposes. If we believe, for example, that the secondary school serves multiple functions, we provide varying kinds of programs. If we believe it is mainly a college-preparatory institution, we study the college catalogues to see what our graduates will need and plan our cur-

riculum accordingly. If we decide that secretaries are in demand in the community, we offer a secretarial training program. If we believe it is our function to help students with personal problems, we provide counseling services. If we aim to cultivate good reading habits, we put money into our libraries. If we believe the school should help peoples of the world understand each other, we incorporate study of other nations. If we decide that young people need to learn to buy intelligently, we offer instruction in the purchase of homes, clothing, and insurance. No decision in respect to content can be made intelligently until the purposes of the content are first identified.

2. *The educator's understanding of past history, contemporary society, and changing social conditions.* The modern educator possesses a broad background of education and experience. He knows that the content of the curriculum of a school in a highly industrialized urban society must be decidedly different from the content of the curriculum of a school in an agrarian society. He realizes that technology and expansion of knowledge have rendered obsolete much of the content that we have traditionally studied. The contemporary social setting affects choices of content.

3. *The clientele served by the school.* Although there is strong similarity in the curricula of schools throughout the country, there are also striking differences. The science-oriented schools of Brevard County (Cape Kennedy), Florida, are much different from those in rural areas of the nation. The high schools in the vicinity of Scarsdale, New York, where most high school graduates go on to college, provide programs that differ from those of schools in communities where a minority of pupils go on to college. The socioeconomic level from which a school draws its pupils affects decisions about content. The needs of children of the slums and children of the suburbs are as different as ranch houses and tenements.[14] Decisions about content bear close relationship to the needs of the student population of the school.

4. *The activity of scholarly groups.* Specialists are at work in many of the subject fields of the high school curriculum modifying, revising, and up-dating the content of each field. They are preparing new materials and proposing new methods of instruction. The subject-matter specialist on the high school staff has a responsibility for keeping up to date on the work of study groups in his field. He should examine their proposals and materials. He should make recommendations to the principal and faculty for changes in content which have been proposed by study groups in which he has confidence.

5. *State and local requirements.* Decisions about content have already

14 See James B. Conant, *Slums and Suburbs* (New York: McGraw-Hill, 1961).

been made for administrators and teachers in some areas of the curriculum. The public, acting through its legislatures and state departments of education, has set certain limits on choice of content. Most states require a minimal number of credits for graduation from the states' high schools. Many localities by action of the school board go beyond minimal state specifications and require additional units. Some state legislatures have mandated portions of the curriculum. Almost all schools are required to offer work in the history of the state. Some legislatures have prescribed units on elections, alcohol, tobacco, and Americanism. Decisions about content cannot ignore mandates of state law and local policy.

DECIDING ON THE IMPLEMENTATION OF EDUCATION

After the purposes have been defined and after content has been selected, the ways of implementing and organizing that content must be decided. On the secondary school level some far-reaching decisions must be made. Among the pertinent questions to be answered are the following.

COMPREHENSIVE OR SPECIALIZED SCHOOLS?

Should the secondary school be organized as a comprehensive high school or should specialized secondary schools be established? The comprehensive high school is one that offers a variety of programs under the same administration. Conant, who gives the comprehensive high school favorable consideration, lists the main objectives of this type of school:

> First, to provide a general education for all the future citizens; second, to provide good elective programs for those who wish to use their acquired skills immediately on graduation; third, to provide satisfactory programs for those whose vocations will depend on their subsequent education in a college or university.[15]

The comprehensive high school attempts to provide for the needs of all kinds of learners. The alternative to the comprehensive high school is the separation of curricula in specialized high schools. In many of our large cities we find high schools established for specialized purposes. New York City is a prime example of this with its Bronx High School of Science, its Food and Maritime Trades Vocational High School, its High School of Art and Design, its High School of Commerce, and so on.

In the comprehensive high school all programs are under a central administration. The principal and his assistants are charged with the operation and administration of all the curricula of the school. The programs can be administered with greater ease, efficiency, and economy. The most

---

[15] James B. Conant, *The American High School Today* (New York: McGraw-Hill, 1959), p. 17. By permission of A Study of American Education, Princeton, N. J.

important advantage of the comprehensive high school is the unifying force it creates among students of all backgrounds and interests. In the comprehensive high school students from varying socioeconomic levels meet together in many of the classes. Another drawback to separate schools is the inevitable tendency to place the poorer students and the disciplinary problems in the vocational or technical high schools, reserving the academic schools for the brighter students and the college-bound.

In recent years educators have inclined toward the comprehensive high school. On this point the Association for Supervision and Curriculum Development (ASCD) says:

> The secondary school should be a comprehensive school. If a major task of the public school system in America is to develop the basic values of a free society, and mutual respect for the range of persons and groups within our diverse culture, students must have an opportunity to live and work together. The comprehensive secondary school is an essential element in the development of a common viewpoint sufficiently strong to hold our nation together. If specialized high schools which divide the population along social and economic lines were substituted for comprehensive high schools, it would further the division that exists among groups and decrease the possibility of maintaining and developing the qualities that unite us as a free people.[16]

The ASCD further points out that more flexibility in choice of courses can be allowed in the comprehensive high school, since there is a wide range of choices open to the student. The ASCD states:

> For example, even though he may be preparing for college, he may elect typing or bookkeeping as one of his electives because he wishes to have one of these skills for his personal use. If high schools were highly specialized, the two courses mentioned above would be in the commercial school and not available for the student in the college preparatory school. Neither would it be possible for the student who is preparing to work in business or industry to elect courses in the humanities of the kind offered in a college preparatory high school.[17]

The comprehensive high school is a uniquely American institution. It has no parallel in other countries of the world. Specialized high schools continue to be the norm in other nations. Decisions whether to build only comprehensive high schools or specialized high schools will have to be made community by community. Size of school enrollments, funds available, and the specialized skills needed in the community are major factors to weigh in this decision. Wherever the comprehensive high school

[16] Kimball Wiles, and Franklin Patterson, *The High School We Need* (Washington: Association for Supervision and Curriculum Development, N.E.A., 1959). By permission of the ASCD.

[17] *Ibid.*, p. 6.

can adequately serve the needs of the community, a decision in favor of this type of organization is to be desired. In large cities where many diversified skills are needed specialized high schools may prove a more satisfactory solution. Speaking of large cities, Conant advises:

> As to the education of vocational students in separate schools, one can only say that from the point of view of economy this arrangement seems to be the only practical scheme in many of these cities. The school boards are unwilling, as a rule, to allocate sufficient money to each of the high schools in a large city to purchase equipment necessary for a full vocational program.[18]

As a training ground for citizenship the comprehensive high school excels the specialized high school. The comprehensive high school is well on the way of becoming the norm for secondary schools in the United States.

THE TRACK SYSTEM OR FREE CHOICE?

Should the curriculum be organized in separate tracks or should the total range of courses be available to all students on an individual choice basis? A standard method of organizing content has been the differentiation of the curriculum into multiple tracks, such as the college-preparatory sequence, the vocational sequence, and the commercial sequence. A specified pattern of courses is suggested or required in each of the sequences or tracks.

It has not been uncommon for students to be restricted to the courses prescribed by the track they are following, but today more and more high schools are leaning in the direction of free choice of courses from any of the offerings without regard to specific tracks. The school may outline a particular sequence which will seem to fulfill the needs of the majority of students in a certain grouping, but it will, however, through normal counseling, permit students to choose appropriate elective courses. Choices of courses are permitted on the basis of the student's interest and motivation rather than on a fixed plan set for the student.

Many schools restrict offerings to specific grade levels, but courses without prerequisites and courses with prerequisites which a student has satisfied should be open to all students on an individual basis. More effective implementation of this principle is achieved when students are permitted to select courses without designation as to specific grade level. An eleventh-grader who wishes and needs to take first-year Latin should be permitted to do so even though the first year is commonly taught to eighth, ninth, or tenth graders. A student of unusual ability in science, who is in ninth grade, should be able to select chemistry or physics though these

[18] Conant, *op. cit.*, p. 87.

courses are normally junior or senior level courses. By making the total range of offerings available to students programs can be tailor-made for each individual.

ORGANIZATION OF GENERAL EDUCATION PROGRAM

The use of the term "general education" has created some confusion, for it can be interpreted in a variety of ways. When some speak of "general education" they have in mind a group of separate subjects that are required of all students in the school. This is the interpretation of general education given by the Harvard Committee on the Objectives of a General Education in a Free Society in its 1945 report.[19] A prescribed set of subjects, or constants, has been the time-honored means of providing general education. Normally included within this concept of general education are English, social studies, mathematics, and science.

THE CORE CURRICULUM

An alternative to general education in the form of required constants is the core curriculum. The core curriculum is known by a variety of names: general education, block-time, common learnings, basic living, and basic education. Unfortunately, our professional language lacks precision, as is well illustrated in the use of the term "basic education." This term has at least three widely different meanings. It is used by some to refer to the core curriculum. To others it signifies the three R's and the arts and sciences. This is the meaning in which it is used by the Council on Basic Education. It is also used to describe a program offered to below-average students. In recent years the term "core curriculum" as well as the concept itself, has lost some popularity. Schools tend now to use the other terms, such as "general education" or "block-time program" when referring to the core curriculum.

A core program combines or unifies under one instructor two or more subjects which are taught in a block of time. Two or three consecutive periods are scheduled together for the core program. The most frequent combination of subjects for core programs is English and social studies. In a true core program no effort is made to distinguish between English and social studies in the experiences provided in the program. Nor, for that matter, do core teachers attempt to exclude the use of other disciplines as needed. Topics are chosen that cut across subject lines. The basic technique of instruction is the development of a unit for each topic studied. A prime objective in the core program is the teaching of problem-solving techniques. The core organization permits students to begin with problems and apply to the solution of these problems any and all materials

[19] Harvard Committee, *General Education in a Free Society* (Cambridge, Mass.: Harvard University Press, 1945).

available. A multiplicity of learning experiences is planned with the cooperation of the learners. The core curriculum, when offered by a school, is
required of all students.

Core programs may be structured, that is, planned with specific topics
in mind at each grade level. Or, they may be unstructured, that is, left
to the decision of the teacher and pupils as they plan together. Some
of the current unpopularity of core curriculum stems from the lack of
structuring in some schools. This creates a kind of what-do-you-want-to-
study approach to learning. It also permits duplication of topics at succeeding grade levels, a notoriously wasteful procedure. Core programs that
extend through the high school years usually have some over-arching theme.
A core program may be organized around periods of man's history and
development: at each grade level a certain period of history may be the
theme for the year. Or it may be organized around problems of society
such as employment, mental health, and the United Nations. A core curriculum may be organized to consider institutions of man, such as religion,
transportation, government, and education, or to understand the needs of
adolescents.

If the structure of the core has been carefully thought out and if qualified core teachers can be found, the core curriculum can be a vital way
of organizing the required portion of the curriculum. The most significant
piece of evidence we have in this regard is the report of the Eight-Year
Study.[20]

THE EIGHT-YEAR STUDY

The results of the Eight-Year Study have been widely disseminated and
have influenced curriculum building. During the period 1933–1941 the
Progressive Education Association, sponsors of the study, followed students of thirty experimental high schools from high school through college. Each graduate of the experimental schools was matched with a coun-
terpart in a conventional high school. The colleges and universities that
the graduates of the experimental schools chose permitted them to enter
without the usual college entrance requirements. The thirty experimental
high schools were encouraged to try out new ways of organizing the curricula and new methods of instruction. The graduates of the experimental
schools did as well as or better than their counterparts in college in all
subjects except foreign languages. The graduates of the experimental schools
excelled their counterparts in scholastic honors, leadership positions, study
habits, intellectual curiosity, and extra-class activities. The Eight-Year Study
showed rather conclusively that a single pattern of required courses is
not essential for success in college.

[20] Wilford M. Aiken, *The Story of the Eight-Year Study* (New York: Harper &
Row, 1942).

The core curriculum has had a checkered history from the thirties. It has been castigated as being unproductive and a waste of time. Critics of the core curriculum believe that students do not learn enough subject matter when the subject lines are erased. But in spite of the criticism the core curriculum has held on. Core programs have been most popular at the junior high school level. It has not gained nor does it seem likely to gain a strong foothold at the senior high level. Block-time classes have been especially strong in Maryland, Washington, California, Illinois, and Wisconsin.

We find, however, conflicting advice concerning core programs. Conant recommends that the block-of-time arrangement be established in grade seven only so that a smoother transition between elementary and secondary school is possible. He recommends departmentalization from grade eight on.[21] The Association of Supervision and Curriculum Development recommends block-of-time instruction each year for the three years of junior high school, grades 7-8-9.[22] There are strong arguments on both sides of this issue. Given an outstanding teacher and adequate materials and facilities, a core program has considerable merit, especially during the junior high school years.

PROBLEMS OF THE JUNIOR HIGH SCHOOL

To what extent should the junior high school assume responsibilities and functions of the senior high school? The junior high school offers to young people who are at a critical stage of growth courses especially for them. The basic courses are taught with the preadolescent in mind. Junior high school pupils can pursue exploratory courses to help them decide what fields they would like to study in depth in senior high school. Extraclass activities that fit their stage of development are a part of the program. A major emphasis in the junior high school is on guidance, since preadolescents have a multitude of problems with which they need help.

Students in seventh and eighth grades have not had to concern themselves with the ubiquitous Carnegie unit by which we count credits for graduation. The junior high school has had flexibility in scheduling of courses. It has not been tied down to the definition of the Carnegie unit; i.e., one credit is allotted for each course taught a full academic year one period a day five days a week. Six-week, quarter-term, and half-year courses have been common at the junior high school level, particularly in the exploratory courses such as art, homemaking, industrial arts, and music.

[21] James B. Conant, *Recommendations for Education in the Junior High School Years* (Princeton: Educational Testing Service, 1960), p. 22.

[22] Jean D. Grambs, Clarence G. Noyce, Franklin Patterson, and John Robertson, *The Junior High School We Need* (Washington: National Education Association, 1961), p. 15.

The status of the junior high school as a unique institution with a curriculum planned especially for preadolescents is threatened today. As a partial answer to the quest for scholarship and the explosion of knowledge the junior high school is taking on the characteristics and function of a senior-high preparatory school. Subject matter, which admittedly has expanded with each passing day, is gradually being pushed downward from the senior high school into the junior high school. Pupils are encouraged to begin their sequences of courses sooner and continue them longer. Students are now beginning to earn credit toward graduation for work completed in the eighth grade. It is relatively common now to find courses in algebra and foreign languages offered for credit in the eighth grade. At present these courses are generally offered to the academically talented students. The practice of pushing subject matter lower in grade level can be defended for the more able students. The danger, however, is that the exception may become the rule. If more and more students, regardless of their interests, are encouraged to begin academic sequences at an earlier level than senior high, a great deal of the vitality of the junior high school program will be lost. We must apply the criterion of balance here to maintain offerings of an exploratory nature as well as initial courses in an academic sequence.

The pressures from the senior high school and college have caused junior high school youngsters to start worrying about college admission. For many students the college preparatory sequence now starts in grade eight. Prematurely at ages twelve and thirteen the pupils begin to shop around for colleges and to decide on occupational goals, in spite of the fact that the interests of preadolescents fluctuate as they mature. The junior high school has in the past allowed students to grow in maturity and find themselves before making decisions about careers and college which may turn out to be hastily and prematurely made.

Intelligent faculties can channel the downward movement of subject matter and make it serve the needs of students. Downward placement of content will cause teachers to re-examine their subject matter and be more selective in what they teach. The needs of abler students can be served by offering courses earlier in their academic careers. Further, we must admit that many times we have underestimated the abilities of young people. We have had preconceptions as to when pupils could begin to read, to handle fractions, and to understand concepts of science or history. The downward shift of subject matter has caused us to test our preconceptions. If teachers are not steam-rollered by pressures from the senior high "to cover the text," "to get the student ready for second year," "to prepare the student for the teacher at the next higher level," downward placement of subject matter may be made to benefit learners.

Teachers at both the junior high school level and the senior high school level must be prudent and cooperative in dealing with placement of subject matter. One of the scandals of our profession is the lack of cooperation or articulation between levels of the academic ladder. In school system after school system there is no cooperative planning between the elementary school faculty and junior high schools which receive the elementary school students. There is similarly no cooperative planning between senior high school faculties and the faculties of the feeder junior high schools. The curriculum taught to students from elementary school on through senior high school should follow a well-articulated plan worked out cooperatively by all faculties concerned.

Chapter 5

THE CHANGING CONTENT OF THE SECONDARY SCHOOL CURRICULUM

The subject matter of the basic disciplines, as well as their organization and methods of instruction, has been undergoing dramatic change. The subjects that today's adolescents take bear little resemblance to those their parents and grandparents took in school. Sometimes it seems to the confused parent, indeed to the bewildered teacher, that only the names of the subjects have remained the same—and in some cases even the names themselves have changed. Today's teacher often has the feeling that he is on a gigantic roller-coaster traveling at a speed that is hair-raising, frightening, but at the same time exciting.

In this section of our discussion it will be our purpose to sketch an overview of some of the salient developments in content in the basic subjects and extra-class activities found in the modern secondary school curriculum. We shall give a brief account of some of the objectives, emphases, and directions in the major fields—language arts, social studies, mathematics, science, foreign languages, fine arts, industrial arts, vocational education, business education, physical education, health and safety education, and homemaking—and in extra-class activities. Our discussion will serve as an introduction to the content of the modern secondary school curriculum and provide the reader with a basis for further study in depth.

THE LANGUAGE ARTS CURRICULUM

Some English teachers feel that the English curriculum is evolving. Others believe that it is eroding. The English curriculum of the high school is changing, perhaps, more slowly than some of the other subjects but no less dramatically. The remedies proposed by English teachers range from more of the same to totally new approaches to English instruction. Nothing less than a totally new approach will yield solutions to some of the problems English teachers face.

New approaches are appearing in schools throughout the country with the impetus given them by the National Council of Teachers of English and by some of the grants now being provided for research, experimentation, and teacher training institutes in English instruction. Changes have been slower in the English curriculum than in some of the other disciplines for a number of reasons. Only belatedly have the foundations and federal government provided funds for research in English and for institutes for the retraining of English teachers. Literature has held a stranglehold on the English curriculum from the secondary school through college, creating a situation which has minimized the importance of language and composition. English teachers and English classes are more numerous than those of any other discipline, with the exception of physical education. But in spite of the obstacles to improvement in the content of the English curriculum changes are being made, among them the following:

1. *Not entirely new, but recent enough in relative terms, is the amalgamation of English language and literature into the broad field of the language arts.* The language arts encompass all phases of English instruction: speaking, reading, spelling, writing, listening, grammar, and literature. Many teachers resist the use of the term "language arts" because they feel that this combining of the English language arts destroys some of the purity of each of the subdisciplines. Yet, the language arts orientation provides a broad framework for uniting the various phases of language instruction. Reading, speaking, and writing are not entities unto themselves; every English teacher deals with the entire range of language experience. Though we may use the popular term "English" for the sake of brevity, a modern English program should be more rightfully designated "language arts."

2. *The infant science of linguistics has been demanding the attention of English teachers.* The implications of this developing science have stirred considerable controversy and unrest in English circles. Some of the findings and recommendations of the linguists have aroused the hackles of the traditionalists among English teachers. The implications of linguistics cannot, however, be swept under the rug nor shunted off any longer.

Linguistics is the study and analysis of language. It comes in a variety of forms: historical, comparative, descriptive, structural, and applied. The linguists are more concerned with the way humans speak and the language they use than with the reasons why humans speak as they do. They make no claim to teaching other humans what they *should* say or write. Equipped with tape recorders and an esoteric, but in effect rather simple, phonetic alphabet, they record a language as it is spoken and used today. They recognize, as some English teachers do not, that the English language is changing. A few moments of reflection would make any teacher realize that we do not speak English today as it was spoken in Chaucer's time or even in great-grandad's time. Although those who wish to maintain the status quo or to be arbiters of the correctness or incorrectness of English usage decry the findings of the linguists, applied linguistics has made itself felt in the classroom in a variety of ways.

Because speech is recognized as a skill important to successful daily living, a significantly greater portion of the curriculum is being devoted to the use of the spoken language. The linguists point out that language is spoken on varying educational and socioeconomic levels. Stress is placed in the modern English curriculum on language as it is currently used by educated middle-class persons. Thus, "It's me" and "Who did you see?" are acceptable usage in spite of the fact that an outmoded English grammar book may dictate "It's I" and "Whom did you see?" The linguists urge language teachers to refrain from insisting on archaic language usage. The language as used orally by educated persons rather than the printed word of the textbook is becoming the standard of correct speech.

Formal grammar is giving way, reluctantly, to functional grammar. In the formal approach a rule of grammar cited by an authority is presented. Students learn the rule first, then work exercises applying the rule. Usually, they work too few exercises to make the grammatical principle habitual with them. Thus, we see the anomaly of a student's writing in a workbook correctly, "He doesn't," and then turning around and saying to his classmate, "He don't." The bitterest controversy in English language instruction centers around the teaching of grammar. The solution recommended by the traditionalists to the "he doesn't—he don't" problem is increase in drilling on the rules and exercises. The linguistically oriented teacher approaches the teaching of grammar through patterns, a repetition of the models of structure of the language. These patterns are repeated often enough to make the pattern habitual. A pattern for teaching the use of singular verbs with singular subjects would look like the following:

> Model: He doesn't.
> She ....
> It ....
> John ....
> Mary ....
> The boy ....
> The man ....
> The girl ....
> The mother ....

The patterns are worked and reworked into conversation and writing drills. The linguistically oriented teacher is little concerned for rules of grammar. He supplies rules only when needed and then only the most common rules. He points out that when we learn our own language as babies our mothers and fathers do not teach us first a rule and then the application. They go directly to the application and we infer the rule.

It is often said that modern English instruction neglects the teaching of grammar. Nothing is further from the truth. The modern English teacher teaches grammar, but he teaches it differently in a functional, nontextbook fashion. To teach English in the modern way, however, necessitates a complete change in the techniques and materials of instruction.

3. *Increased attention is being given to writing.* Studies of students at all levels have revealed their inability to write coherently, to express thoughts clearly, and to organize their ideas. Errors in spelling and punctuation abound in themes of students, and lamentably, of teachers. The blame for this situation may be attributed to a number of reasons. First, English teachers are overworked. Since all students must take English at all levels, class enrollments are unreasonably large. If a teacher is to teach writing effectively, he must have time to correct the papers. This would be a superhuman task for overloaded English teachers. This is why James B. Conant and the National Council of Teachers of English, among others, propose a teacher-pupil ratio of 1 to 100 in English programs. Secondly, we have moved too far in the direction of objective testing, which requires a single answer or a tiny mark on a paper. Only essay questions, themes, compositions, and papers can check on a pupil's ability to write. Thirdly, the traditional approach to English burdens the student with a batch of rules that he must first recall before he writes. The reliance on rules impedes the development of writing skills. In cliché form we hear modern English teachers state that "You learn writing by writing."

With the new emphasis on the nurture of creativity throughout the curriculum English teachers are encouraging creative writing, permitting students to turn loose their thoughts and imaginations. Further, English teachers are giving their students, particularly the college-bound students, opportunities for writing disciplined research papers calling for the use of libraries and outside sources of information. Some teachers recommend that encyclopedias be removed from the school libraries so that students will not be able to copy their reports out of already digested articles. Students would then have to dig through many sources of information.

4. *The secondary school English curriculum is accepting the responsibility of assisting adolescents to improve their reading skills.* English teachers realize that not all students will develop reading skills at the same rate. The modern English curriculum offers both remedial reading, using modern gadgetry such as Reading Accelerators and the Tachistoscope, and developmental reading programs to help all students improve in this essential skill. With proper training even bright students and good readers can become faster and better readers.

5. *The literary content of the English curriculum has been expanded.* Traditionally, we have made American students familiar mainly with works of American and British literature. Today we find world literature being introduced. We find greater choice of reading matter allowed students. We no longer find all students reading all of the same books. Students may choose with the teacher's guidance works of literature of special interest to them and are encouraged to select from the hundreds of excellent paperback books now available at low cost.

The teaching of literature itself has undergone change. The English teacher is less concerned with dissecting literature and examining students on their recall of specifics of place, persons, and time. Instead he emphasizes with students the underlying ideas of the works and seeks to develop students' understandings of people and of themselves. The teacher hopes that reading good works of literature will give the student pleasure rather than agony. He hopes that the choice and reading of good writing will carry over and be a source of enjoyment to the individual throughout his lifetime. It is impossible to estimate how many students have had their interest in literature killed by tortured dissection of the plots of literary works.

6. *The high school is offering a selection of elective courses in the language arts.* Speech, dramatics, and journalism are among choices students may make in this field. These courses permit students to go deeper into these studies than they are able to in the limits of the regular, required language arts sequence.

7. *A concern for the exceptional child has led to the instituting of speech therapy or speech correction, as it is often called.* The speech therapist helps students with speech and hearing disorders to overcome their handicaps and to lead a fuller life.

A number of fundamental changes are under way in the language arts curriculum. They will affect the content, organization, and methods of instruction in this field.

THE SOCIAL STUDIES CURRICULUM

The social studies program is concerned with developing an understanding of man—his history, his institutions, and his problems. Only physical education and English exceed the social studies in total enrollments. Every high school student takes at least two years of social studies, while most take three and many take four. Included in the social studies are history, geography, political science, civics, economics, and sociology. With the possible exception of English the social studies curriculum deals more intimately with man's life and his place on this small planet than any other secondary field. Through the social studies man gets to know not only himself but his neighbors and the world around him. The social studies curriculum is evolving as rapidly as other subject fields. Among some of the changes in the content of the social studies are the following:

1. *In many schools the broad field, social studies, has supplanted the discrete courses, history, geography, etc., in much the same way as the language arts have taken the place of English, speech, etc.* The shift to the broad field has encountered the same resistance as the change to language arts. Recently some schools have shown signs of moving back to separate labeling of each of the subdisciplines within the social studies. Actually, "the social studies" is a more accurate description of the content of this program. It is next to impossible to divorce history from geography, economics from history, sociology from government or political science. We may maintain separate labels for our courses at each level of the high school, but we find elements of the many social studies included in each of the courses. When we plan in terms of the social studies as opposed to the separate disciplines, we can set a general framework for the entire sequence. We have somewhat more flexibility in planning. We can, for example, set up a program centered around periods in man's history or man's institutions or the needs of society. These themes cut across the social studies fields. We can give the entire program a greater unity when we think in terms of the broad field, social studies, instead of a sequence of separate courses.

2. *No subjects change more rapidly than do the social studies.* Every day, every hour, and every minute the march of history continues. The problem of selection of content is, perhaps, more acute in the social studies than in any other subject of the high school curriculum. There are practical limits to demands that can be made for students' time. Each teacher must, then, choose carefully those topics that are most important. He must eliminate some of the content. He cannot even expect to complete the study of all basic textbooks, since they increase in size year by year. Unfortunately, some content has to be sacrificed, particularly if the teacher wishes to move into newer and hitherto untried areas. With so much to be taught in so short a time the social studies teachers of a school system must analyze their curriculum carefully, eliminating unnecessary material and cutting out needless repetition. Constant expansion and judicious pruning of the social studies content are going on simultaneously.

3. *The social studies curriculum aims to equip citizens for living in our democratic society.* Today's citizen needs to know something of his origins. He needs an understanding of the world around him. He further needs to develop skills of getting along with other people and working together to

solve social problems. To accomplish this the social studies stress the democratic process throughout the curriculum. Not only do students learn the forms of the democratic process but they are also encouraged to apply the techniques of the democratic process in their classes through committee work and group action. They demonstrate that complex social problems cannot be solved in our society by one-man action. They attempt to teach young people the duties of citizenship as well as the rights that Americans enjoy. By contrasting American democracy with totalitarian societies teachers help students to gain an appreciation for the benefits which are cherished in our form of government.

4. *The controversial issues of our day take a prominent place in the social studies curriculum of many schools.* It is unfortunate that some schools are so fearful of permitting free discussion of controversial issues that they ban study of some of the most pressing, unsolved problems of our time. Community pressures have succeeded in prohibiting unfettered discussion of some of the more inflammatory issues in the community. As a result, principals have sometimes advised their teachers to omit study of specific controversial issues. Occasionally we find a principal who orders his teachers to omit discussion of any controversial issue.

Prohibition of the study of unsolved issues teaches young people concomitantly that free speech and free inquiry are meaningless phrases. We should be teaching our youth in all courses that the human mind can be trusted and should be set free. The continuous search for answers to controversial social problems by democratic measures must occupy a primary position in the social studies curriculum.

5. *The social studies provide the basis for the core curriculum.* We have mentioned the fact that most core programs consist of a combination of English and social studies. Social studies themes usually supply the framework for the experiences planned in the core program.

6. *The social studies curriculum is expanding along several lines.* A typical secondary school sequence in social studies would look as follows:

7th grade:	State history; geography
8th grade:	American history
9th grade:	Civics
10th grade:	World history
11th grade:	American history
12th grade:	Problems of American democracy

There is pressure in social studies circles to expand the coverage of world history. The one-year sophomore-level course covers too great a scope and overwhelms the student with a mass of facts and understandings. Schools can economize on time by moving civics into the seventh and eighth grades and reducing the American history course, which will be repeated at the eleventh grade. They may also combine American history and problems of American democracy into one unified course. Obviously, something has to give. Americans have historically been ill-informed about the history and life of other peoples of the world. With the United States as leader of the free world, America can no longer afford the luxury of ignorance of the rest of the world.

New emphasis is being given in social studies programs to the East and Latin America. Both areas have been neglected in our social studies curriculum. In our social studies programs we have often given students the idea that any contribution of importance has originated in the Western world. We have failed to teach our young people that the East was civilized when the West was barbarous. Current social studies programs are giving attention to the lands south of our borders, our neglected Latin neighbors, whose economies directly affect life in our hemisphere. In a brief period of time Latin America will become one of the most populous areas of the globe. Our American citizens have had only the most elementary knowledge of the needs, problems, and aspirations of peoples of the Latin countries of our Western hemisphere. The social studies are attempting to close the gaps in our knowledge of the East and Latin America.

7. *There is renewed interest in the teaching of geography.* Prior to World War II the study of geography had hit an all-time low. As America catapulted into a position of leadership in the world the need for education in the field of geography became apparent. The casual study of geography in conjunction with history or other social studies was not enough to overcome the abysmal lack of knowledge of the world around us. Modern programs of social studies have now instituted, or in many cases reinstituted, the study of geography in the junior high school. They also stress geography throughout the social studies sequence.

8. *New elective courses are to be found in some high schools.* Among these courses are sociology, anthropology, and psychology. It is doubtful that these courses will make great headway since the social studies curriculum is already more crowded than is desirable.

Belatedly the federal government has taken an interest in the social studies by supporting research, establishing curriculum study centers for the development of methods and materials, and providing institutes for training teachers of the social studies.

Newer materials, stress on the world around us, and emphasis on broad understandings have combined to make the study of the social studies an enjoyable experience for young people. Nothing can be more stimulating than the study of man himself, which is the essence of the social studies.

On the other hand, nothing can be more deadening than a pedantic approach to history in which students and teacher concentrate on the minutiae of dates, names, and places to the exclusion of great thoughts, concepts, and movements.

THE MATHEMATICS CURRICULUM

The mathematicians tell us that the twentieth century is the "golden age" of mathematics. In the last fifty years more mathematics has been developed than in all previous years. Mathematics has responded to the needs of an age of science and technology with the development of a host of new subjects such as linear programming, functional analysis, topology, abstract algebra, and quality control. These subjects have just made their entry into the college curriculum. At college, secondary, and elementary school levels the mathematics curriculum is experiencing a continuing revolution. Any parent who has struggled to help his child do his math homework recently will verify that profound changes have taken place in mathematics teaching. The parent who has not been trained in the new or modern mathematics will find the task an impossibility. With the possible exception of science no field has undergone such extensive change as the mathematics curriculum. Among the principal changes are the following:

1. *The new programs in high school mathematics stress underlying assumptions and reasons why operations are done.* "Structural" or conceptual aspects of mathematics are emphasized. The "new" mathematics taught in the high school is actually "old" mathematics dressed up in modern garb. Practically all the mathematics in the secondary school program has been known for at least two hundred years; the new programs, however, provide more effective ways of presenting the subject matter. In the traditional approach to the teaching of mathematics the student memorizes rules without understanding the rules, and then he mechanically applies these rules.

Understanding why takes some of the mystery out of mathematics. The modern mathematics curriculum rejects the purely mechanical approach to instruction.

2. *The modern mathematics curriculum is striving to encourage students to develop their own proofs rather than apply a predigested set of proofs.* Mathematics teachers have told students over the generations that this subject makes a person think. They have then proceeded to teach the course par excellence, geometry, as an ordeal in memorization. How many students have gone through high school geometry, even obtaining good grades, by sheer memorization of the theorems and their proofs is hard to estimate. New methods of instruction in mathematics put stress on discovery. The

modern mathematics teacher is never happier than when a student comes up with an original, yet correct, solution to a problem.

3. *The modern mathematics curriculum has been reorganized in terms of unifying themes as opposed to discrete, unrelated topics.* Among these unifying themes are structure, number, operations, measurement, and proof. The new programs have identified themes and basic principles which run through all the mathematics. By stressing underlying themes teachers are able to show students the interrelationships among the various fields of mathematics. The boundary lines between the fields of mathematics are more fluid, less rigid than in past years. An outmoded sequence in mathematics placed algebra in ninth grade, plane geometry in tenth grade, intermediate algebra and solid geometry in eleventh grade, advanced algebra and trigonometry in the twelfth grade. Some schools insisted without any research to support them that plane geometry had to be taken before intermediate algebra. Today we find varying sequences arranged for varying abilities of students. We find plane and solid geometry combined into one course. We find some principles of intermediate or second-year algebra supplementing the first-year algebra course. We find "intermediate mathematics," which includes elements of algebra and trigonometry. When it is realized that there are unifying principles or threads that run through all the mathematics, the patterns of organization of content may possess flexibility.

4. *The modern mathematics uses a whole new symbolism and vocabulary.* For this reason the new programs for high school students place stress on preciseness of vocabulary and definitions. If we were to drop into the modern mathematics teacher's classroom, we might hear him explaining the universal set or the commutative property of addition or the additive inverse or the associative law. To some the new mathematics sounds like a foreign language, which, in a sense, it is. Like foreign languages mathematics should be conceived as a means of communication. If individuals are to communicate mathematically, there must be a clarity of meaning in the "words" or symbols that they use.

5. *The ferment of activity in mathematics education in the last fifteen years has resulted in the preparation of several new, improved programs of mathematics for the schools.* The outpouring of new programs has proved both a boon and a problem to mathematics teachers and school faculties. As a boon the new programs have reorganized the subject matter in the light of modern thinking on mathematics. They present entire sequences written jointly by mathematics scholars and high school teachers. As a problem they confront the schools with the necessity for choosing between programs. They complicate the difficulties of transfer students who move

from a school using one program to a school using another program. Nevertheless, the new mathematics programs are a sign of intellectual activity.

Although there are many projects under way in the mathematics program and many more may be expected in ensuing years, the beginning teacher should be aware of three programs which have become bywords in mathematics education. The chances are better than even that teachers will hear their mathematics colleagues discussing at least one of these programs:

a. The University of Illinois Committee on School Mathematics. Popularly known as UICSM, this project was initiated by the College of Education, College of Arts and Sciences, and College of Engineering at the University of Illinois in 1952 with support from the Carnegie Corporation. It represents the first of the improved programs in school mathematics. Under the direction of Dr. Max Beberman mathematics and mathematics education specialists have written text materials for grades nine through twelve. The committee conceives of this program as a complete four-year sequence rather than as material to supplement existing programs. The present four-year UICSM high school curriculum consists of the following units:

(1) The arithmetic of real numbers
(2) Generalizations and algebraic manipulation
(3) Equations and inequations
(4) Ordered pairs and graphs
(5) Relations and functions
(6) Geometry
(7) Mathematical induction
(8) Sequences
(9) Elementary functions—powers, exponentials, and logarithms
(10) Circular functions and trigonometry
(11) Polynomial functions and complex numbers.

The first year of high school mathematics would consist of units 1 through 4; second year, 5 and 6; third year, 7 and 8; and fourth year, 9 through 11.

There has been a tendency for UICSM programs to be offered to the above-average students in the high school.

b. The School Mathematics Study Group. First quartered at Yale University and now at Stanford, the School Mathematics Study Group has produced a comprehensive set of materials ranging from grades four through twelve. Known as SMSG mathematics, the first materials from this group appeared in the academic year 1959–60. The SMSG project is, perhaps, the most ambitious of the mathematics projects. It has the financial support of the National Science Foundation and the sponsorship of the American Mathematical Society, National Council of Teachers of Mathematics, and the Mathematical Association of America as well as the National Science Foundation. The principal text materials produced by this group have been designed for grades seven through twelve. The materials have been prepared by teams of high school teachers, college professors of mathematics, and specialists in mathematics education. Unlike the UICSM project, the SMSG program shows some concern for the average and below-average student as well as the above-average student. The general plan of the SMSG program is as follows:

> *Grade 7:* Fourteen topics, which include What is mathematics? numeration, nonmetric geometry, measurement, mathematical systems, and statistics and graphs.
>
> *Grade 8:* Thirteen topics, which include equations, scientific notation, real numbers, probability, and volumes and surface areas.
>
> *Grade 9:* Algebra. Seventeen topics, which include sets and the number line, properties of addition, properties of multiplication, factors and exponents, and quadratic polynomials.
>
> *Grade 10:* Geometry. Seventeen topics, which include lines, planes and separation, angles and triangles, geometric inequalities, similarity, and circles and spheres.
>
> *Grade 11:* Intermediate Mathematics. Fifteen topics, which include number systems, quadratic functions and equations, systems of equations with two variables, logarithms and exponents, and permutations, combinations, and the binomial theorem.
>
> *Grade 12:* Elementary Functions. Five topics, which include polynomial functions, exponential and logarithmic functions, and circular functions.
>   Introduction to Matrix Algebra. Five topics, which include matrices and linear systems and transformation of the plane.

The nonmathematician need not understand mathematics to realize that the SMSG program is quite different from traditional programs of secondary school mathematics.

c. University of Maryland Mathematics Project. The University of Maryland Mathematics Project has produced since its start in 1957 mathematics materials expressly for grades seven and eight. It is the only experimental program in modern mathematics that has given special attention to the mathematical needs of students at the junior high school level. Professors in mathematics, education, and related fields at the University of Maryland, assisted by the Carnegie Corporation, have worked with classroom teachers of mathematics to produce the materials. These materials for junior high school consist of two textbooks of thirteen topics each. Arithmetic, algebra, and geometry form the bases for this two-year course. It is of interest to note that the materials include within the two-year sequence the first year of algebra, without using the word "algebra."

Although other experimental projects are under way, the above-named three have received extended publicity throughout the nation. They are indicative and representative of the types of activity going on in the lively field of mathematics.

6. *The mathematics sequence is starting earlier in the school life of the learner.* Programs are frequently found now in eighth-grade algebra, particularly for the academically talented student. Teachers are expressing a concern for teaching mathematics from the earliest days in the school life of the child. It is no exaggeration to say that algebra has even hit the kindergarten and first grade. Today we see young children pondering the problem 6 plus ? equals 10. Perhaps, future generations of Americans will possess more mathematical savoir-faire than does the present generation.

7. *The mathematics curriculum is being extended in the high school years.* Academically talented young people are now encouraged to pursue mathematics for three to four years instead of one or two as in the past. One year, however, remains the general requirement in mathematics for graduation from most high schools.

In the interests of national defense the federal government has pumped millions of dollars into research in mathematics and the improvement of mathematics education. It has provided opportunities for thousands of mathematics teachers to attend institutes in mathematics at colleges and universities so they can be brought up to date on the modern mathematics.

Ability grouping has been an essential accompanying feature of modern mathematics programs. The ability to handle mathematical concepts differs so widely among learners that it is impossible to devise a single satisfactory program that will meet universally the needs of all learners.

Mathematics education has made great strides but it still has a long way to go. The needs of the slow learner have scarcely been met. General mathematics, a simplified, elementary course consisting mainly of arithmetic plus a smattering of algebra and geometry, is often a catch-all course. The modernizing of the general mathematics program as a worthy course for the non-mathematically talented should provide a challenge for mathematics educators.

Working along these lines, the National Council of Teachers of Mathematics has a committee on Mathematics for the Non College Bound. This committee is developing materials and trying out methods for teaching students in elementary and secondary schools who have difficulty in learning mathematics. In 1963 this committee prepared a two-volume experimental text for ninth-grade general mathematics classes. The committee is now in the process of preparing a laboratory type of text materials for use with low achievers in the seventh grade.

Mathematics teachers must undo years of mathematics instruction which conditioned young people to detest mathematics, to fear it, to believe that it was too difficult, and to consider it a special territory for boys only. The "new" math in a little over a decade has begun to combat some of these negative attitudes. The "new" has been helped, of course, by the fact that we are in a technological age where a great premium is placed on mathematics and the sciences.

THE SCIENCE CURRICULUM

Unquestionably the star in today's educational firmament is the science curriculum. The stereotyped wooly-headed scientist has been transformed into a knight in shining armor. It is he who will help us mine the oceans, launch the satellites, conquer disease, and beat the Russians. Millions of dollars pour forth from the coffers of private foundations and the federal treasury to stimulate scientific research and to improve the teaching of science.

Like its sister field, mathematics, the science curriculum is undergoing sweeping transformation. We can observe an almost frenzied activity in science as scholars, science educators, and classroom teachers strive to keep up with the relentless advances being made in this field. As scientists continue to probe the secrets of nature our fund of knowledge will grow. The new science curricula in our schools have been prepared to enable young people to live in a scientific age. The new curricula plummet the learner into the twentieth century and seek to prepare him for life in the twenty-first century. Consequently, there is much of the same vitality, ferment, and confusion in the science curriculum as we find in the mathematics curriculum. Among the changes in the secondary school science curriculum are the following:

1. *The science curriculum has been extended downward into the elementary school and has been expanded on the secondary school level.* More frequently than in the past elementary school teachers are bringing science consultants into their classrooms to assist them with the teaching of science. Students are beginning to study the natural sciences earlier and, particularly the more able students, are continuing their studies longer in the high school. The academically talented are now encouraged to complete at least three years of secondary school science. To do this they may begin their science sequence in the eighth grade. Secondary schools have made improvements in both the quantity and quality of instruction in the sciences.

2. *Admission of students to science courses is more flexible in modern secondary schools.* We have seen high schools in the past, and, to some extent today, which restrict chemistry and physics to eleventh or twelfth graders. By some inner, erroneous logic it has been assumed that only the upper levels of high school students have the maturity to succeed in the advanced sciences. With the recent implementation of grouping practices and

the appearance of the nongraded high school, students are admitted to subjects for which they have the competency regardless of their grade level. Thus, if a student is ready to take chemistry or physics, he may do so whether he is in his ninth, tenth, eleventh, or twelfth year of school.

3. *The sciences aim to develop in the learners an understanding of the basic principles and concepts of sciences.* Perhaps some of the readers of this text will recall their experiences in biology as the sheer exercise in memorization of Latin and Greek nomenclature. Unfortunately, after memorizing the ten animal phyla and the four plant phyla, the learners lacked an understanding of the fundamental truths of the biological sciences. The sciences today are seeking to identify pervading, unifying concepts. They are attempting to show the interrelationships between each of the sciences. The science teacher makes every effort to elicit the generalizations that show the unity of the sciences.

4. *Laboratory work has received a new impetus.* The science laboratory, which is a fundamental part of science education, has been starved for material until recent years. Title III funds of the National Defense Education Act have allowed hitherto impoverished science programs to build up their laboratory equipment and supplies. Science educators stress the value of laboratory experiences to accompany science instruction. Through the laboratory students develop skills of inquiry which they cannot learn in the classroom.

Unfortunately, laboratory instruction can become as stereotyped as any other phase of science education. If all students must work the same laboratory problems in a step-by-step arrangement dictated by laboratory workbooks, the laboratory is not achieving its primary value. Students should be encouraged to make discoveries of their own rather than work through predigested experiments whose conclusions are already known to them. A few schools have enabled students to work through classic experiments in the laboratory without telling them what to look for. Students are encouraged to make their own deductions and to feel the thrill that comes from discovery. Some schools are allowing more and more independent laboratory work. A traditional laboratory places all students on the same laboratory problem at the same time. Modern schools provide facilities and time for students to work individually on laboratory problems in which they have a particular interest.

In order to allow class time for laboratory work some schools have scheduled double periods for science classes. The additional time introduces more flexibility in the program. The laboratory will remain an important feature of science education in the schools for many years to come. At least one dissenting voice, however, is heard to disagree with this view. Kimball Wiles in discussing the high school of the future states:

> Small science laboratories will be kept open for full-time use by the individual researchers from the seminars. In fact, students who are not expected to become scientists or technicians in an area will not use laboratory facilities. Laboratory experience will have been abandoned as a general education procedure by the seventies.[1]

If laboratory instruction remains a step-by-step, by-the-numbers experience which all students follow in identical procedure, the science laboratory should be abandoned. A lecture-demonstration by the teacher can accomplish this purpose faster, more efficiently, and less expensively. If laboratory instruction can enable students to experience the joys of discovery, it can remain a valuable part of science education.

5. *Science fairs have served as a motivating force in the high school science curriculum.* No one who has seen some of the amazingly intricate projects of youth talented in science can help but be impressed with the intelligence and creativity of some of our young people. The complex projects that students of the sciences prepare for competition in the science fairs demonstrate clearly that our educational system has its moments of triumph.

The science fair program has established a series of school-wide, local, regional, state, and national competitions in which students enter an original project which they have planned and carried through. The local science fair has become an occasion of considerable community interest. This program provides a channel for giving recognition to students who are able in the sciences.

Some criticism, however, has been directed at the science fair. What began as a voluntary activity has become in some schools a compulsory assignment. Some science teachers require all students to prepare an outside project for the annual science fair. The compulsion and pressure destroy much of the value of the science fair. Each project is supposed to be an original project, the student's own work, but it is difficult to eliminate outside help. Parents and friends have been known to assist students in their project and even to do some of the work for them. The pressure to win has taken a great deal of the pleasure out of an otherwise worthy program. As a reaction to unjustifiable and educationally unsound pressures some schools have decided that their students will not participate in science fairs. If the science fair program can be carefully supervised and controlled in such a way that students are not subjected to unnecessary pressures, this program can be a valuable adjunct to the science curriculum.

6. *Several new programs are commanding the attention of educators and the public.* The most prominent of the new programs are the following:

---

[1] *The Changing Curriculum of the American High School* (Englewood Cliffs, N. J.: Prentice-Hall, 1963), pp. 304–5. By permission of Prentice-Hall, Inc.

a. The Biological Sciences Curriculum Study. The BSCS program was launched in 1959 by the American Institute of Biological Sciences and has received the support of the National Science Foundation. College biologists and classroom teachers of biology have collaborated to produce for the high school three separate versions of the biological sciences. Each version includes both text materials and laboratory experiments. The blue version, reportedly the most difficult, emphasizes biochemistry and physiology. The yellow version centers on genetics and the development of organisms. The green version focuses on evolution and ecology. In addition to the basic materials the Biological Sciences Curriculum Study has suggested for academically talented students one hundred research problems for which solutions are not readily available.

b. Two new programs in chemistry have made their appearance: *The Chemical Education Materials Study (CHEM Study) and The Chemical Bond Approach Project.* Both projects have the financial support of the National Science Foundation and both have as their goals the preparation of new courses in chemistry for the high school. The Chemical Bond Approach Project, started in 1959, is the more difficult of the two projects. In fact, to teach the Chem Bond approach science teachers must have special training such as that provided in the federally supported science institutes. Chem Bond emphasizes the atomic and molecular structure of chemical substances, the electrical nature of matter, and energy changes. Laboratory experiments accompany the text materials of this project. The CHEM Study Project, initiated in 1960, gives prime importance to laboratory work. Students spend more time in the laboratory than in the classroom. The experimental nature of chemistry is emphasized and students are taught to make their own discoveries, observations, and deductions. Unlike the Chem Bond Approach Project, which requires special training on the part of the teacher, the CHEM Study program can be taught by any chemistry teacher. The CHEM Study program is designed for all students of chemistry in high school, while the Chem Bond Approach is more suitable for the above-average student.

c. The Physical Science Study Committee. PSSC, as it is commonly known, was started in 1956 and has received the backing of the National Science Foundation, Fund for the Advancement of Education, and the Alfred P. Sloan Foundation. The PSSC high school physics course stresses the method of inquiry, uses laboratory work to enable students to work through experiments and make their own observations and conclusions. The course is unified under four topics: (1) the universe, which includes time, space, matter, and motion; (2) optics and waves, which involves a study of optical phenomena; (3) mechanics, which concerns dynamics, momentum, energy, and the laws of conversation; (4) electricity, which includes electricity, magnetism, and the structure of the atom.

It has been standard practice in many high schools to admit only the above-average students into the BSCS, CHEM Study, Chem Bond, and PSSC courses. One of the reasons for doing so, in addition to the relatively greater degree of difficulty in these courses, is the fact that these courses are still experimental. As schools gain experience in the teaching of the new courses in science, they will undoubtedly extend the courses to a wider range of students. It should be remembered that students who elect to take advanced work in science, specifically chemistry and physics, are usually more able students to begin with and can be expected, as a rule, to handle more advanced concepts.

7. *Several entirely new courses have been added to the science sequence in some schools.* Among these courses are earth science, organic chemistry, and rocketry.

Stipends from federal funds have enabled science teachers throughout the country to go back to college for additional training they need. Science has come of age. Desultory science courses so typical of the past have been displaced by exciting new programs.

THE FOREIGN LANGUAGE CURRICULUM

The foreign language curriculum of the high school has experienced a long series of ups and downs. The classical languages formed the core of the curriculum of the Latin Grammar school. Enrollments in foreign languages rose steadily until the period just before World War I. In the first decade of the twentieth century more than four-fifths of the public high school population were enrolled in foreign language study. By the early 1950's, however, the percentage of high school students enrolled in foreign languages had dropped to one-fifth of the high school population, and in the middle fifties more than half of the public high schools offered no modern languages at all.

Enrollments in recent years have crept steadily upward. About a third of our public high school students are enrolled in foreign languages; moreover, many thousands of elementary school students are learning a modern foreign language. There is new life in the foreign language curriculum and a growing realization on the part of both professional persons and the public that foreign language study does have its value. The changes experienced by the foreign language curriculum are as dramatic as those of the other academic disciplines. Among the changes are the following:

1. *The audio-lingual approach to teaching modern foreign languages is displacing the outmoded grammar-translation approach.* Students today are taught first to understand and speak the modern language. Reading and

writing, formerly primary objectives of language instruction, now follow development of the skills of aural comprehension and speaking. In many modern language classrooms students see no printed materials at all for the first weeks of the course. They are trained to distinguish sounds and patterns of speech and to reproduce them, largely in the imitative fashion by which they learned their native tongues. After a thorough grounding in the oral and aural aspects of the modern language students are then introduced to visual materials. For teachers who have been trained with the reading objective in mind the audio-lingual approach necessitates retraining.

2. *The modern foreign language is used as much as possible in the classroom from the earliest level.* It is spoken at a normal rate of speed from the start so that students soon become familiar with the pronunciaticn and intonation patterns.

3. *Modern foreign language teachers follow many of the principles of applied linguistics.* Formal grammar plays a minor part in modern language instruction. Students are taught grammar through patterns or models of structures of the language. Through pattern drills rather than learning grammatical rules language habits are established.

4. *The modern languages make frequent use of electronic equipment in the form of a language laboratory.* The language laboratory permits students to practice language forms, to hear authentic foreign voices, and to develop skills of comprehension. The language laboratory serves as an aid to the teacher. In a modern language laboratory the teacher can monitor the performance of students and help each one individually. The language laboratory can perform for the teacher some of the exhausting repetitive work that is so essential in modern language teaching.

A typical high school language laboratory is equipped with four channels which permit simultaneous transmission of four programs. Three of the channels may be equipped with tape recorders and one with a record player. The laboratory aids the teacher in handling individual differences by permitting students to tune into a channel which is playing a program at his level of ability. When used often enough, the language laboratory can help language learners to develop rapidly skills of comprehension and speech. By judicious selection of tapes and records to be played the teacher can also enhance the students' knowledge of the culture of the people whose language they are studying.

5. *The foreign language program has been expanded both downward and upward.* It is no longer unusual to find elementary school students learning a foreign language. Commonly students begin the study of a modern language in the third or fourth grade. Junior high schools offer first level of foreign language instruction to eighth graders. Three- and four-year sequences of a foreign language have supplanted the old two-year sequences. It is generally

admitted that two years of a foreign language are insufficient to allow any degree of mastery of the language. Academically talented youth are encouraged to take a full four years of a modern foreign language in high school.

6. *While students continue to study Spanish, Latin, French, and German, some of the less frequently taught languages are making their appearance in the high school curriculum.* More than 10,000 high school students are studying Russian. Chinese and Japanese are taught in the schools of Hawaii and the West Coast, and the study of Chinese has made its appearance in scattered places throughout the country. We can find high schools that offer Hebrew, Italian, Swedish, Armenian, and even Arabic. With the greater stress on the East and Africa we may expect to find large high schools in the future offering more of the lesser-known languages.

The position of Latin in the curriculum presents an enigma. In spite of the emphasis on modern languages Latin remains strong, ranking second to Spanish in total enrollments. In some areas of the country Latin is the leading language in number of students enrolled. Its popularity must be attributed to parental desires for their children to study Latin. They feel that there is a cultural value to the study of Latin that cannot be obtained through study of the modern languages. They believe that Latin provides a basis for improvement in English and for future study of other languages, particularly the Romance languages, which derive from Latin. Most professional educators, somewhat short-sightedly, we believe, have taken a negative or indifferent attitude toward the study of Latin. One of the few who take a favorable view toward Latin is Edward A. Krug, who says, ". . . Latin has much to commend it for purposes of cultural transmission."[2]

It is possible that two years of Latin may become the norm for those students who have the interest or need for taking it. It appears that where a choice must be made between study of Latin or of a modern language, the modern language will be recommended by school personnel.

7. *New tests developed for modern foreign languages include speaking and aural comprehension as well as reading, grammar, vocabulary, writing, and cultural items.* The development of standardized tests of abilities to speak and comprehend the spoken language is a milestone in the improvement of modern foreign language instruction.

The federal government has tied in the study of modern foreign languages with national defense. Federal funds have been allotted through the National Defense Education Act to send language teachers to institutes for training in the new methods of teaching modern languages. NDEA further provides fellowships for graduate study in the foreign languages, has stimu-

---

[2] *The Secondary School Curriculum* (New York: Harper & Row, 1960), p. 270.

lated research in the foreign languages, and has allocated monies for the establishment of language and area centers. Federal funds helped to develop new materials of instruction, including the Glastonbury (Conn.) materials. This completely new set of text materials, tapes, records, and manuals for four levels of language instruction is now known as *A-LM*, shorthand for "Audio-Lingual Materials."[3] The new audio-lingual teaching materials bear little resemblance to standard textbooks. Considerable experimentation is under way in language education. Research is being conducted in the teaching of languages through films, television, and programmed materials. All of the research aims to tune modern language instruction to the "new key," which gives primary emphasis to audio-lingual skills.

THE FINE ARTS CURRICULUM

No area of the curriculum has been as neglected as have the fine arts, music, and art. Perhaps this has been part of the historic pattern of life in our country. In early years of the development of the United States our citizens were busy pushing back the frontiers and taming a wilderness. They had little time for leisurely pursuits. Only in recent decades have Americans come into their own, achieving world-wide recognition in music and art. The cultural exchange of artists between countries has done much to disabuse other nations of the erroneous notion that America is a land of money-grabbing barbarians. Just as America has begun to gain stature in the arts, however, the sciences threaten to dominate the curricula from elementary school through college. The fine arts are in danger of being pushed further into the background. As few as fifteen per cent of the senior high school population are enrolled in the arts. Approximately a third of the senior high school students take some work in music. Many high schools today are still without any organized art program whatever.

Art and music have made their strongest stands in the junior high school. General art and general music are commonly required exploratory subjects at the junior high school level. Beyond junior high school, work in art and music is rarely required. At least one high school, however, has broken this precedent by requiring drawing of all its students. This is Nova High School in Fort Lauderdale, Florida, which admitted its first students in 1963.

Art and music are such a fundamental part of the culture of man that they deserve far greater attention than schools have been paying them. Music has attracted students mainly because of the school and community emphasis on the performing arts—band, orchestra, glee club, and chorus. Even in these arts, however, much of the instruction has been relegated

[3] Modern Language Materials Development Center Staff, *A-LM Programs* (New York: Harcourt, Brace & World). Audio-lingual materials in French, Spanish, German, Italian, and Russian published in four levels at various times since 1961.

to extra-class activities, after-school instruction, and out-of-school private tutoring.

Art and music are considered by many educators to be an essential part of general education. Through art and music young people may develop appreciations and skills that will last throughout their lifetime. Some schools recognize the needs of students by offering electives in music theory, history of music, music appreciation, art appreciation, painting, drawing, history of art, design, and crafts.

With students subjected to pressures to increase their concentration on the academics, it will become more difficult for them to fit the fine arts into their programs. If there must be choices between mathematics and painting, the choice will most often be resolved for mathematics. If they must choose between chemistry and music appreciation, students will be counseled to elect chemistry. The only hope for expansion of the fine arts seems to be in flexible scheduling that will permit students to take some courses less frequently than the usual five times per week. Art and music can be taught, as they often are in the junior high school, on a two- or three-times-weekly basis. The institution of the seven-period day to replace the six-period day will permit more students to find places in their crowded schedules for the fine arts.

A considerable amount of controversy has raged over the maintenance of junior and senior high school bands. Gradually some consensus is evolving among educators to the effect that marching bands should be discouraged in junior high school and de-emphasized in senior high school. In some high schools the band occupies a position completely out of proportion to its educational value. Parents are busy earning money to purchase band uniforms and equipment. Band members are so occupied with practice for performance at the half-time during the next football game that they have little time for their other studies. Interscholastic band competitions are a prime concern of many schools. Publicity and recognition are heaped upon the heads of the principal, the band director, and the musicians. It should be recognized that schools are not in the business of providing entertainment for the public but in the business of educating youth. When kept within bounds the band can offer valuable educational experiences for talented musicians. It can serve as a source of pride to the community, and it can help develop school spirit. But when a school becomes known primarily for its marching band instead of for its achievements in the major subjects, it is time to review the school's curriculum.

The music and art teachers frequently provide guidance to other teachers on the faculty so they may incorporate musical and art activities into their programs. The creativity of students who are talented in music and art should be fostered not only in the elective subjects of music and art but throughout the curriculum. Music and art provide means of expression beyond the customary written and oral reports. Music and art teachers have an uphill battle to overcome the mistaken notion that only gifted students can enjoy and participate in musical and art activities.

THE INDUSTRIAL ARTS CURRICULUM

The industrial arts serve as a bridge or part of a continuum, if you will, between the fine arts and vocational education. Industrial arts performs a dual function in the secondary school curriculum. It contributes to the general education of the learner and in addition forms a foundation for vocational education. In its vocational function industrial arts provides a basis for developing generalized skills rather than training for specific trades. Students become familiar with various tools and processes. They clarify their interests and identify occupations that they would like to enter after a period of vocational training. Industrial arts does not attempt to equip students for careers in specific vocations. In fact, industry has frequently asked that school industrial arts programs not attempt to do this. Industry requests that school industrial arts programs give students an introduction to industrial trades, a few basic skills, understandings about the world of work, and training designed to encourage positive attitudes toward work.

In its general-education or nonvocational function industrial arts helps its students to familiarize themselves with tools and machines, particularly those they will encounter in daily life at home and in the community, and to develop skills such as simple home repairs, electrical work, auto mechanics, woodworking, and metal working, which will carry over into adult life. Industrial arts assists young people to develop hobbies which they may wish to continue for many years. It offers students opportunities to release creative energies and to feel a sense of pride and accomplishment in their own handiwork.

Typical offerings in the industrial arts curriculum are general shop, woodworking, metal working, electricity, auto mechanics, mechanical drawing and crafts. The placement of arts and crafts in the high school program varies from school to school. Some schools place arts and crafts, such as ceramics, leather working, jewelry making, and etching, in the art sequence. Others place the arts and crafts in the industrial arts sequence. Placement is often resolved on the basis of which teacher is particularly interested in or trained for the teaching of arts and crafts.

As a general rule, only boys enroll in the industrial arts. Occasionally, schools offer "Shop for Girls" or admit girls into the industrial arts program, but in practice girls are not encouraged nor counseled into the industrial arts. The decision not to place girls in industrial arts is culturally determined. Our culture has the stereotyped notion that the use of tools is not a ladylike pursuit. As general education the industrial arts can be beneficial to both boys and girls. Certainly, it could help future homemakers to learn skills that would enable them to run a household more efficiently and economically. It would also help them to become better consumers of goods produced by the factory and the artisan.

The standard requirement in industrial arts is a single course in general shop for junior high school boys. The course may run a full year or less than a year. Through the brief acquaintance junior high school boys get with industrial arts they may decide to seek further vocational education. Sometimes the required industrial arts program may include a unit on occupations to give students some realization of the many kinds of occupations available, the employment opportunities, and the training needs for specific occupations. At times this unit is placed in a homeroom period or in civics class or even in English class instead of in industrial arts.

Beyond the required junior high school exploratory course, the industrial arts courses are elective. It is one of the misfortunes of the current high school curriculum that more students are not able to schedule industrial art in their high school program. For students who are going into the professions and white-collar jobs the high school industrial arts program might be the only exposure they get to the manual trades. Many college-educated adults have lamented the fact that they have not had any instruction in the useful skills that can be learned in industrial arts courses.

The industrial arts have undergone transformation from the days when they were known as "manual training." Industrial arts teachers shudder at the use of this term as a description of their courses now. We have moved away from the mistaken belief that learners fall into two categories: the book-minded and the hand-skilled. Industrial arts teachers will vouch for the fact that intelligence as well as manual dexterity is required for success in the industrial arts. It can be demonstrated that those students who do well possess above-average intelligence. For this reason industrial arts teachers resist the practice of schools' dumping misfits into their programs. The machine shop, for example, is no place for the misfit. The student must keep his wits about him to avoid maiming himself and others.

Newer scheduling practices will enable more students to elect industrial arts courses. The pressure for academic subjects should not exclude the possibility for an interested student to take courses in the industrial arts.

THE VOCATIONAL CURRICULUM

We include within our definition of the vocational curriculum agriculture and technical education. The courses in the vocational curriculum provide specific training for specialized fields. Courses in those sequences fulfill the needs of many students, particularly boys, who will not go on to college. They equip students with salable skills by which they may earn a living.

Vocational education is provided in one of three ways: (1) as one of the major divisions of a comprehensive high school, (2) in separate vocational schools, and (3) increasingly more commonly, in community colleges. A vocational sequence that requires extended training may be started in the high school and continued for an additional two years in the community college.

Vocational education is normally geared to the needs of the community. Training programs are established to fill needs for certain types of skilled and semiskilled workers in the immediate area. The schools cooperate with industry in identifying the skills needed in the locality and in working out satisfactory training programs. As the needs of a community change the vocational programs of the schools change. We see, for example, when a community shifts from agricultural to industrial status, a shift from training in agriculture to technical training. There is often, however, a lag between the needs of the community and change in the school's curriculum to reflect new needs in the community.

The federal government since the end of World War I has given financial aid to vocational education. For many years the vocational instructor in many schools has enjoyed the kind of status and recognition accorded to the superintendent, principal, and football coach.

The content of programs in agriculture has changed as the needs of the small independent farmer have become more complex. Agricultural training programs today must concern themselves with the latest in scientific advancements in farming techniques, the use of modern farm machinery, efficient techniques of marketing, and the economics of farming.

High schools and community colleges offer a wide variety of specialized courses, including air conditioning and refrigeration, radio and TV repair, beauty shop operation, commercial art, aviation mechanics, printing, needle trades, and sheet-metal working. High schools have been successful with Diversified Cooperative Training (DCT) programs which place students in jobs in the community for part of the school day. Combined work-study programs under school supervision have appealed to many students and have helped to hold potential dropouts in school.

It is likely that more and more of the specialized vocational training will be placed in the community college as these institutions continue to grow. Until a community college is established in a locality the high school must continue to offer a selection of vocational courses.

THE BUSINESS EDUCATION CURRICULUM

Like the industrial arts, the business education curriculum performs a dual function in the high school. It offers courses of a general nature that are beneficial to all kinds of students. It provides in addition specialized or vocational instruction for noncollege-bound students. The business education sequence often has within it some of the most potentially useful courses in the curriculum. All students could profit from typing, general business, business arithmetic, business law, and consumer economics. Each of these courses could play a role in the general education of the student. Customarily, no courses in business education are required either at the junior or senior high school level. Typing, however, has gained recognition as an extremely valuable tool subject for any student whether he plans to go into commercial pursuits or into college upon graduation from high school. Schools are attempting to fill the new demands for typing by offering courses in personal typing as well as vocational typing. They are permitting junior high school students to enroll in typing, an unheard of practice not many years ago.

Specialized training in business education has centered around two major fields: bookkeeping and stenography. The challenge of technology has hit the business education curriculum with full impact. In some of our schools the business education sequence is completely out of step with the times. Students are being trained for situations which no longer exist, by methods which are archaic. Industry has streamlined its system of record keeping before many high schools have changed the content of their bookkeeping—which for some mysterious reason becomes "accounting" on the college level—courses. Students who labor over double-entry bookkeeping are chagrined when they find out that this system is outmoded in many businesses. In fact, industrial bookkeeping is rapidly becoming a series of specialized functions each of which is performed by a person specially trained. Bookkeeping machine operators may soon be in greater demand than bookkeepers.

Vocational typing is typically taught in a room equipped with twenty-five to forty manual typewriters. Since electric typewriters are in almost universal use in modern business establishments, training secretaries on manual typewriters is akin to instructing students in driver education on the horse and buggy. Many schools are making the shift to electric typewriters as rapidly as funds become available. A few schools, notably Melbourne High School, Florida, which has not feared to try out new ideas, are offering typing to larger classes. Melbourne teaches typing to a class of one hundred and twenty-five students. The teacher is equipped with a microphone hung around her neck. Melbourne believes it to be just as effective to handle one hundred and twenty-five students in typing at one time as to handle twenty-five. Schools which schedule large classes usually reduce the number of class periods assigned to a teacher or provide assistants or both.

The stenographic courses are also experiencing the changes that technology has wrought. More time is being allocated to training in the use of modern office machines, including steno-typing equipment and dictation and transcribing machines, which modern executives like to use. General clerical training provides experiences in the use of new duplicating machines and processes.

The business education curriculum provides a valuable service for students and community alike. Able secretaries are much in demand by our burgeoning industry. A capable secretary can expect to earn a comfortable living. Though the largest majority of students enrolled in business education are girls, a survey of industry will show that there are also many employment opportunities for male secretaries.

Similar to the Diversified Cooperative Training program, the Distributive Education (DE) program of the business education curriculum offers students a combined work-study program. Students in DE are placed in stores in the community so they may gain some experience in sales work. This program recognizes the importance of retail-sales work in the economy of our country.

Advanced training in accounting and secretarial science is an established part of the curriculum for terminal education in the community college. As community college education becomes more accessible to all youth we may see more of the specialized training in business education shifted to this post-high school institution.

THE CURRICULUM OF PHYSICAL EDUCATION, HEALTH, AND SAFETY

PHYSICAL EDUCATION

For many years the objectives of physical education have been set forth by specialists in the field as the development of sound habits of health and safety, the spirit of sportsmanship, leisure-time interests, physical fitness, and endurance. The task for physical educators is not the introduction of new content into the curriculum but the ordering of that content, which is already well known, in such a way as to accomplish these objectives.

We should distinguish between the physical education instructor and the athletic director or coach, though in many small schools he is one and the same person. The physical education instructor is charged with the needs of all boys and girls, while the coach is responsible for a program geared to the needs of a selected group of students. Both the physical education program and the athletic program play important roles in modern schools. Unfortunately, competitive athletics have overshadowed the physical education program. Interscholastic athletics in particular lend high drama to the school's program. They provide excitement to spectators and the community. When the school's teams are winning, school spirit is at a peak. When the teams are losing, heads often roll and the school spirit sinks to a low. High finances are at stake in interscholastic contests. Athletic stars are courted and feted by talent scouts of major universities. The atmosphere can be a heady one for young people.

If a school can maintain both strong competitive teams and a sound physical education program at the same time, there should be little criticism. Interscholastic athletics provide outlets for adolescent energies and opportunities for some students to gain recognition and success that they could not gain otherwise. The competitive sports do develop manly skills on the part of growing boys and do build bodies and endurance. The stress on winning, however, is difficult to keep within bounds. The coach is anxious to maintain his status in the community and must seek to win his games at all costs. Boys are in danger of being exploited. The competitive sports make great demands on their time. It is not unknown in the history of sports for coaches to use an injured star player regardless of the harm the boy may do himself. Pressures from athletics can be felt throughout the curriculum. Teachers often feel pressed to make sure the athletes meet eligibility requirements so they can play in the next game. Criticism of interscholastic athletics is being voiced more and more. A considerable body of opinion opposes the introduction of interscholastic athletics in the junior high school. Those who hold this opinion feel that junior high school pupils are not ready physically or emotionally for the bruising activities of competitive sports, particularly football. Many coaches object to this position, since the junior high school provides them with a training ground in which to spot and develop senior high school athletes.

Many educators have voiced objections to interscholastic sports for girls. They believe that interscholastic athletics are not physically nor emotionally suitable for girls. The criticism of interscholastic sports has had the salutary effect of improving physical education programs in general. Modern physical education programs offer something for all. We find renewed emphasis on intramural sports, which give students of varying degrees of physical ability the opportunity to participate in team games. Rhythms and dancing help students develop socially. The old activities of physical fitness have been dusted off, polished up, and given a new lease on life. Calisthenics, which tumbled in the favor of physical educators, has made a fresh appearance on the scene.

Modern programs of physical education offer aquatics, camping, and a wide range of individual activities. The general education features of carry-over activities, those which will last students a lifetime, are fostered. Golf, bowling, badminton, tennis, and archery are incorporated into the physical education programs of today. The schools are taking cognizance of the needs of handicapped students by providing corrective exercises.

Physical education is universally required in high schools, though there is no uniformity in the country on number of years required. Physical education is normally required for all students in the junior high school. Requirements in senior high school range from one to four years.

The individual never outgrows his need for physical activity. It is possible that schools should look at new ways of scheduling physical education throughout the student's high school program. Perhaps physical education two or three times per week would be adequate. Schools might also consider the desirability of removing credit for physical education or of devising new ways for evaluating the student's work. If any program in the entire curriculum should be evaluated in relation to an individual's own ability, the physical education program is that one. Grades in physical education are often so highly subjective and arbitrary as to be meaningless. They involve grading such elusive traits as "attitude." In an effort to be scientific and precise grades are handed out for "dressing out," "taking a shower," and refraining from asking the school nurse for excuses from physical education. A noncredit course in physical education would take some of the pressures off students and would enable them to feel they were taking physical education for their own improvement rather than for the teacher's sake.

HEALTH EDUCATION

Health education is deserving of more attention than it receives in many schools. Almost all statements of school philosophy give lip service to the health needs of the students. Yet, students are often in dire need of health instruction. Adolescents can use instruction in personal hygiene, nutrition, and sex education. They are in need of knowledge about the physical growth and development of the human body. They are in need of facts which a program of health education can give them.

Health services can be improved in many schools. The school nurse, who provides the most elemental kinds of health service, is a rarity in the schools of many states. There are extremists in communities who view the hiring of school nurses as a step in the direction of socialized medicine. They fail to see the necessity for first aid, the detection of diseases and injury, the referral of students to physicians, the health counseling which a trained nurse can give young people. It has not helped the cause of health education that arguments have arisen between public health authorities and school health personnel as to which agency is better equipped to provide health services to school children.

The physical education instructor, the health instructor, the coach, and the school nurse combine to promote health education and healthful living throughout the school. In health-conscious schools students keep their classrooms, toilets, locker rooms, and drinking fountains clean. The guidance counselors join with health and physical education personnel to help students with health-related problems. Students should find on the staff adults to whom they can go when they have questions that perplex them.

Somewhere in the curriculum, whether in a class in health or in the social studies or other subject, attention should be given to the health needs of the community, state, and nation. Students need instruction in the values of immunization and the purchasing of health and hospitalization insurance. Health education should not be considered the sole responsibility of the physical education or health instructor any more than English is the task of the English teacher alone. Health instruction may find its place in various spots in the curriculum. Healthful living permeates the curriculum.

SAFETY EDUCATION

The National Safety Council points to the dire need for reducing the high rate of accidents in the home, in the community, and on the highways. By providing safety education and driver education schools help reduce the number of accidents. They help promote safer conditions in the home, school, and community by making students conscious of safety hazards.

Physical education, health education, and safety education are oriented to preservation of a strong, healthy body and a healthful, safe environment.

THE HOMEMAKING CURRICULUM

Homemaking is potentially one of the most useful of the subjects in the high school curriculum. The ostensible goals of homemaking education are the development of skills and understandings that will help make girls better housewives and homemakers. Sewing, cooking, baby and child care, marriage and the family, consumer education, and home nursing are topics commonly included in the homemaking curriculum.

Homemaking education has gone through a series of metamorphoses. It has been called "domestic science," "home economics," and "home living" as well as "homemaking." The term "home living" appears to be gaining currency. Homemaking is regularly required of all girls for a brief period of time in the junior high school. In most states it is an elective program at the junior high school level. Like agriculture, homemaking has received federal support.

The homemaking curriculum has been modified slightly in recent years to reflect the new needs of modern homes. The use of labor-saving devices forms a part of the instruction in a modern homemaking sequence. New products and services are considered. New shopping trends are analyzed. Basically, homemaking offers instruction in the time-honored skills and knowledge required by housewives. Occasionally, schools have offered a course in "homemaking for boys." This course has not gained a great deal of popularity, since many feel it sissified for boys to be concerned with household arts. The same kind of cultural attitude that reserves industrial arts for boys is operant.

The homemaking curriculum has met, however, with some criticism. The homemaking course takes the student's valuable time away from other subjects. Students struggling with mathematics or science or other subjects must devote laborious hours to home sewing projects, to preparation of notebooks with pictures of latest fashions, to cooking projects, etc. All this may be valuable training, but the best use of students' time must be a consideration. The world of work and the college place greater stress on students' knowledge of English and the so-called academics than they do on homemaking skills.

Some of the content of the homemaking program sets up conflicts between school training and home training. This situation is particularly noticeable in the case of lower-class students because the homemaking programs of our schools teach middle-class standards and values. The homemaking curriculum would be the subject of less criticism if it made some study of the kinds of homes from which its students come and concentrated on the skills children will need to enrich their lives in their own homes.

A required program of homemaking for junior high school girls can be defended with little difficulty. In this program they learn the fundamental skills that all American housewives and mothers need. Beyond the junior high school homemaking should be an elective course. It would appear that two years of homemaking beyond the junior high school course would be ample time to provide all the instruction in homemaking that any high school girl should need. An elective course in marriage and the family open to both boys and girls would be most beneficial.

A GENERAL STATE OF CHANGE

Having examined the content of the major fields of the curriculum, we find a general state of change. We find that the content of some subject fields bears little resemblance to the content of several years ago. Each of the subject fields is paying greater attention to basic principles and broader understandings. The scholars and classroom teachers have joined forces to examine the basic structures of each of the disciplines and have been engaged in efforts to develop new materials which will make evident the intrinsic structure of each subject.

The period of study of the major subjects has been lengthened through expansion both upward and downward. Greater stress is being placed on the use of problem-solving techniques in all subjects. Students are being encouraged in each subject to make their own discoveries and form their own conclusions.

Although the high school curriculum continues to improve, several needs remain unfilled. We have not yet discovered the most effective ways of meeting individual differences. Far too many students are graduated with inadequacies in the use of the mother tongue and numbers. We are just beginning to put into use in the classroom the fruits of technology. We are searching for better ways of keeping potential dropouts in school. We have just scratched the surface in research into the structure of each discipline. We have made only a slight beginning in providing curriculum materials related to international education. But the challenge of unfulfilled needs should not discourage the teaching staff. A dynamic, changing curriculum can lend a sense of stimulation to the profession.

THE SUPPLEMENTARY CURRICULUM

The supplementary curriculum of the modern high school is a feature uniquely American. By supplementary curriculum we mean all those activities that fall outside the usual scope of the academic program. These activities supplement the school's program, enrich experiences of young people, but are peripheral in nature. The high school could exist and has existed without these activities, but without them the high school would be a drearier, less interesting place than it is. The supplementary curriculum lends an effervescence to the high school's program that is lacking in most other secondary schools throughout the world. Student activities in secondary schools of other nations are, in general, limited. Students from other lands who study in the high schools of the United States are often amazed and agreeably surprised at the range of student activities that form a part of our secondary school curriculum.

Educators have groped for some accurate term by which to designate the student activity program. "Extracurricular" has been used, but this term implies that the activities are something beyond the scope of the curriculum, whereas many of the activities derive from the subjects within the curriculum and cannot rightfully be considered extra or outside. "Co-curricular" seems to give to the activity program a status it should not possess. It implies an equality of importance and does not accurately describe the activities program. "Extra-class" is a more recent term which has grown in popularity. Not all of the activities, however, are outside of class but are often incorporated into the class program. "Extra-subject" meets the same objections, since some of the school activities are subject-related. For this reason we use the term "supplementary" to imply those activities that enrich the academic curriculum but remain subordinate to the subjects themselves. We also use "extra-class" in this text.

A well-rounded supplementary curriculum includes clubs of many kinds, student assemblies, social affairs, athletic groups, class organizations, and a student council.

The supplementary curriculum has grown through the years in response to students' wishes. No phase of the total curriculum is so directly student-centered as the supplementary activities. The chief reasons for permitting a program of this nature in the high school are the following:

1. *It provides worthwhile activities for young people under professional, adult supervision.* The school recognizes the interests of students and furnishes adult leadership and guidance to make participation in the activities beneficial.

2. *It serves as a safety valve, a release of energies that might otherwise be turned into mischievous or even malicious channels.* Students who are busy with projects and programs of interest to them do not have the time to become behavior problems.

3. *It furnishes students with additional opportunities to satisfy psychological needs: the need for recognition, the need for acceptance, the need for approval, and the need for success.* It offers many opportunities for students to accept and display leadership qualities.

4. *It extends the academic curriculum.* Since most of the subject curricula are already overcrowded, many valuable experiences must be left out of the regular classroom work. The supplementary curriculum picks up some of the worthwhile activities that might otherwise be omitted.

5. *It serves as a motivating force for many students, keeping them interested in school.* Many are the boys who have remained in school because they could play football. Many students persist in their studies because of the opportunities to participate in interest groups and social affairs. A program that can encourage students to remain in school is not to be condemned.

6. *It offers students countless opportunities to develop their own creative talents.* The diversified activities give students a chance to select clubs and organizations in which they can bring out and demonstrate their creativity.

7. *It offers students chances to socialize that they do not have in the classroom.* Through clubs and other supplementary organizations students can get to know each other.

8. *It gives the teachers who are activities sponsors many chances to counsel pupils in informal situations.* Outside the classroom the relationship between students and teachers is less structured. Sponsors who have a high rapport with the students in their activities are often called on by the students to assist them with their problems.

9. *It provides opportunities for citizenship training.* Student council, class

organizations, and club offices are training grounds for practicing the democratic process. In committees students learn to take responsibilities, share ideas, and work together to solve problems.

The supplementary curriculum can readily be justified on the foregoing bases. Their value in high schools has been challenged, however. Some of the critics of contemporary American education regard supplementary activities as unnecessary fads and frills. They feel that students should be hitting the books and not "frittering away" time on needless activities. The criticism might be justified if the activities were, indeed, needless. They are certainly not needless from the point of view of the students. Nor are they aimless or inconsequential. Each activity has, or should have if it is to be maintained in the school program, some educational purpose that makes it worthy of inclusion in the curriculum.

It is customary to set limitations on the number of activities to which any one student can belong. Schools frequently set point values for each type of activity and a maximum number of points which a student may carry. The point system in use in schools prevents a student from becoming overloaded with activities. Since holding office in an organization is weighted heavier than membership alone, it is possible to distribute opportunities for positions of leadership.

PROBLEMS OF THE SUPPLEMENTARY CURRICULUM

Even though the supplementary activities program is carefully supervised and controlled it is not without its problems. Each activity must be supervised by a competent sponsor. It is difficult to find trained persons for all activities. In general, teachers are assigned as sponsors to organizations in which they express personal interest and in which they may have participated in high school and college. A good many teachers must train themselves in the skills necessary for sponsoring certain activities. It takes special competencies to sponsor dramatics, debating, golf, and the newspaper, to mention but a few activities. As a general rule, teachers are expected to sponsor an activity without additional pay, although sponsors of some activities—varsity sports, band, and occasionally dramatics—do receive some additional pay for the extra hours they must put in.

Scheduling supplementary activities is a perennial problem for schools. Confronted with the problem of bus transportation, most schools feel the activities must be scheduled during the regular school day. Some schools have resolved this by making the last period of the day either daily or less frequently the activity period. Some high schools schedule all supplementary activities in the evening. Students must find their own transportation, which most of them are able to do. A small rural high school designates alternate Wednesday afternoons for class and club activities. Some schools attempt to hold assemblies, class, and club meetings in the first morning period, designating the particular organizations to meet each morning. It is probable that the scheduling of supplementary activities the seventh or eighth period of the day represents the best compromise.

The supplementary curriculum has a tendency to grow without periodic evaluation. Activities are added and few are dropped. When an activity has outlived its usefulness, it should be permitted to disband. The supplementary curriculum should strive to provide a wide enough variety of activities for all kinds of students. A sense of balance is essential. Priorities on staff, facilities, financing, and student time must be decided. Continuous evaluation of the efficacy of the supplementary curriculum should not be neglected.

The school must be cautious of pressures from outside organizations which seek to involve students in supplementary activities of special interest to these groups. It should be clearly recognized that many of the clubs in the high school are affiliations of civic groups in the community, e.g., Key Club, Keyettes, Wheel Club, etc. Some of the contests in which students are encouraged to take part are promoted by special interest groups, such as the Daughters of the American Revolution, the American Legion, and the American Medical Association, each of which wishes to promote its own point of view. The school must carefully screen activities that originate from outside the school itself.

Organizations under the sponsorship of the school must be open to all students on an equal basis without discrimination as to race, religion, or socioeconomic level. The procedures for selecting students to become members of school organizations must be above reproach. Since one of the major purposes of supplementary activities is training in the democratic processes, no student who is qualified for an organization and wishes to be a member should be rejected by a group of teachers or students merely because they do not like the student. Any activity that permits an undemocratic selection process should be summarily dropped from school sponsorship. For this reason most high schools refuse to have anything to do with fraternities and sororities. These organizations have no place in the secondary school.

The question of awarding academic credit for participation in supplementary activities has received various answers in schools. Where special daily instruction is required, credit is often granted. Some credit is granted in schools for participation in band, orchestra, and chorus. Occasionally a school gives credit toward graduation for performing duties of a service nature, as in the case of library and laboratory assistants. In general, participation in supplementary activities does not and should not provide academic credit.

Student participation in the government of the school presents special problems. It is no easy task to make student participation in government work. Sponsors of the student council, class organizations, and homeroom groups must exercise adequate supervision without stifling student initiative. Principals must set clear limits to the students' responsibilities and authority. Within these limits they should permit students to operate.

CHAPTER 6

CURRENT CURRICULAR PRACTICES AND PLANS

Changes have been made not only in the content of the curriculum but also in implementation of the curriculum. New patterns of organization and new methods of instruction are operating. Some schools have dared to break the bonds of tradition to try out more effective means of achieving the purposes of the curriculum. Some educators are also looking forward and making proposals for schools of the not too distant future.

The dramatic innovations in ways of organizing for instruction have given the high school a bold new look. It is our purpose to examine six of the current practices in curriculum implementation and one challenging proposal for schools of the future.

CURRICULUM INNOVATION 1: TEAM TEACHING

The rapid spread of team teaching in both secondary and elementary schools refutes the general belief that it must always take fifty to one hundred years to translate an educational idea into practice in the schools. Team teaching in its modern form can be dated back to the mid-1950's. Unlike many other educational ideas, some of which have died aborning, team teaching has had powerful backers. The National Association of Secondary School Principals, through its Commission on Staff Utilization and sparked by J. Lloyd Trump, has given team teaching its educational backing and blessing. The Ford Foundation and the Fund for the Advancement of Education have given team teaching financial backing by supporting experimental projects in many school systems in the country.

Team teaching has arisen in response to needs of the schools for better utilization of the limited staff, for better use of limited school facilities, and for providing varied types of educational experiences. The concept of team teaching itself is rather simple. Three or more teachers of the same subject join together to form a team for teaching purposes. They plan together, share teaching responsibilities, and evaluate the program together.

A program organized in a team-teaching framework consists of three distinct features: large-group instruction, small-group instruction or seminars, and independent study. Trump recommends that 40 per cent of the students' time be occupied in large-group instruction, 40 per cent in independent study, and 20 per cent in small-group instruction.[1] Schools vary the pattern considerably.

COMPOSITION OF A TEAM

From a simple team in which three teachers share responsibilities we can go to a more elaborate team with specialists of various types. A full-blown team could consist of master teachers, general teachers, instructional assistants, clerks, staff specialists, general aides, and community consultants. Each specialist has his own function. Salaries are paid according to the job performed. Less highly trained personnel are able to perform some of the more routine duties that teachers heretofore have had to perform. Instructional assistants and teachers' aides, frequently chosen from housewives and former teachers in the community, can render the professional teacher valuable help by correcting tests, reading papers, and keeping records. Each member of a team is assigned that responsibility of which he is most capable. Team teaching in one sense follows the principle of division of labor which is basic to modern industry.

One teacher, often designated the master teacher, serves as team leader. The team meets daily and plans jointly. A school that establishes team-teaching programs must schedule at least one period during which time all of the members of the team may meet for planning. The team must agree on what will be presented, how it will be presented, and what the duties of each member of the team will be in the presentation. In general, the lecture method is used in large groups, which usually consist of 150–250 students. The discussion method is followed in the small groups, which schools attempt to keep down to approximately fifteen. Teachers take responsibilities for the kind of work they do best: the versatile lecturer may deliver the talks to the large groups, teachers who are skilled in conducting group discussion supervise the small groups, and others may work more effectively with students who are engaged in independent research.

Team teaching and planning allow a great deal of flexibility. Teachers can accept responsibility for teaching to large groups the material and topics in which they are well versed. Each teacher may teach the topic he knows best and may take time to become a specialist in his topic. In an ordinary classroom set-up the teacher is expected to know all the topics equally well. He simply does not have the time nor energy to do the kinds of research, study, and preparation necessary to become expert in every

[1] J. Lloyd Trump and Dorsey Baynham, *Guide to Better Schools; Focus on Change* (Chicago: Rand McNally, 1961).

aspect of his subject. Team-teaching programs lead from strength. The teacher in an American history team program who has a special interest in the Civil War period can become an authority in this phase of American history. Students benefit from the increased depth which teachers are able to bring to the topics they teach.

STRENGTHS AND WEAKNESSES OF TEAM TEACHING

The strengths and weaknesses of any educational innovation must be weighed. On the positive side of the scale, team teaching has brought into the high school a stress on excellence from both the teachers' standpoint and the students' standpoint. The teachers involved are attempting to give their best and expect the students to do likewise. In large groups students must accept greater responsibility for their own work. They must learn to listen and to take notes. Since materials and equipment have to be duplicated in each of several sections, better materials and equipment can be purchased and provided for use in the large groups. Many kinds of audio-visual aids are supplied to the teams.

A differential in pay is often granted the master teacher or team leader. This pay recognizes his competency and serves as an incentive to good teachers. We should not overlook the motivating force of increased status and salary which the position of master teacher can bring.

Opportunities are provided students to engage in varied types of learning experiences through the three separate phases of the team-teaching program. The needs of individuals are partially met through independent study; of small groups, through the seminars; and of large groups, through the lectures.

Team teaching has been a creative answer to the improvement of teaching with limited resources and limited personnel. If ever-increasing enrollments are to be cared for, new ways of organizing for instruction must be found.

A successful team-teaching program must be conducted in suitable facilities. Ideally, a school needs special plant facilities, including an auditorium large enough to house the largest instructional group the school would have. Small classrooms would fan out from the auditorium so the large group could be split up rapidly for seminars and follow-up discussions of the lecturing. Places for independent study should be easily accessible. Older schools have had to make do with the facilities they have. As a result, they have assigned groups to the cafeteria, school auditorium, or other large space. They have been forced to use for small groups regular classrooms, which are often distant from the room used for large group instruction. The movement of pupils to and from classrooms causes confusion and wastes time. New schools have been able to overcome this difficulty by planning for team-teaching programs from the very beginning. Special team-teaching facilities are incorporated in the architect's plans.

The success of a team-teaching program is dependent upon the team members' abilities to cooperate, to get along with each other, to respect each other's ideas, to accept and fulfill responsibilities, and to share in the give and take of cooperative planning. We should face the fact that there are teachers who are emotionally and personally unable to work cooperatively with others. It is usually more difficult to form a team of older established teachers who have worked for years on their own than to create a new team. Teachers who have found their own ways of operating over a period of years are often reluctant to abandon their individual ways. It is absolutely essential that teachers join in a team-teaching program voluntarily, rather than by order from the principal. A team-teaching program which does not have the full support of the teachers who make up the team does not have a chance to succeed. Teachers should agree to work in a team only because they believe the educational benefits to be derived by the learners will be superior to what they now receive. An occasional teacher is motivated to participate in a team-teaching program because he gains a planning period which he does not have in the usual schedule. This motivation is little justification for entering into a team project.

Some administrators and faculties have misunderstood the nature of team teaching. They have equated team teaching with large-group instruction and have conveniently omitted the other two essential features of team teaching: small-group and independent study. Large-group instruction can take care of mass enrollments but it places too great a stress on the lecture method. The personal relationships between teacher and pupils cannot be obtained in large groups. Students cannot discuss, ask questions, and clarify their views in large groups. If small groups and independent study are not parts of the program, some of the more important educational experiences are lost. Large-group or mass instruction per se is not team teaching.

"Turn teaching" is also not team teaching. In turn teaching two teachers bring together their two sections of the same subject and alternately teach the large group. One teaches a unit, then the other. While one teacher is teaching, the other teacher may or may not be in attendance at his colleague's presentation. If learners are to achieve maximum values from this type of instruction, both teachers should be constantly at hand during the presentation. Provision for follow-up discussion in smaller classes should be made. A group composed of two average-sized classes is too large for discussion purposes. Since follow-up discussion is essential to clarify lectures, there is little value in bringing the classes together in a large group without subsequent small-group discussion. If two teachers of two sections of a subject wish to participate in turn teaching, each teacher may move from his classroom to the other classroom to present his topic.

Team teaching has been favorably received at the high school level, where there is a pronounced trend toward the use of such teaching techniques. It has been less well received at the elementary school level. Some elementary school educators tend to reject the type of departmentalization that team teaching brings into the school. Team teaching destroys the self-contained classroom which places a group of youngsters under the care and authority of a single teacher. Critics of team teaching at the elementary school level feel that children are not ready to make the abrupt transition from home to departmentalized instruction. They feel further that team teaching accentuates the subject matter rather than the needs of boys and girls. In spite of these objections some elementary schools have utilized team-teaching principles effectively and believe that pupils are not harmed by this newer system of organizing for instruction. Whether at the high school or elementary level any innovation bears constant scrutiny and continuous evaluation.

CURRICULUM INNOVATION 2: EDUCATIONAL TELEVISION

A fairly common sight in high schools today is the ubiquitous electronic box, the television receiver. The introduction of television as an educational aid has come with great rapidity. It was, perhaps, inevitable that this technological instrument with such great potential should be adapted to serve the schools. Like team teaching, educational television has been ecstatically received in some schools and roundly denounced in others.

Educational television has received support from a number of influential sources. The Federal Communications Commission has set aside some 330 channels for the use of educational television. The Ford Foundation has taken an interest in educational television and has furnished funds for experimentation with its use. The Foundation's most notable and extensive experiment is the closed-circuit television system in the schools of Washington County, Maryland.

OPEN- AND CLOSED-CIRCUIT

Aside from the commercial channels, which telecast occasional educational and public service programs that may suit the schools' needs only incidentally, educational television installations are either open-circuit or closed-circuit types. Local open-circuit systems serve surrounding regions, while closed-circuit television serves only its own schools. Houston, Texas, is credited with the installation of the first open-circuit educational television. Open-circuit telecasts are received over the channels that have been reserved for educational television by the FCC. Schools that elect to receive the instructional programs telecast via open-circuit, if they lie outside the sponsoring system, must either enter into cooperative arrangements for teaching, scheduling, and utilizing the telecast courses or, as happens more frequently, they must take what they can get from the source of the programs.

Closed-circuit television links schools by direct cable and offers much more flexibility than does open-circuit television. With a closed-circuit system schools can prepare their own programs, use their own teachers, and shape the programs to the needs of their own students, locality, and time schedule.

A course presented by educational television offers some of the same advantages as the large-group instruction phases of team teaching. A master teacher, in this case a "studio teacher," presents a well-planned, carefully written lecture or lecture-demonstration using the best audio-visual aids available. The lecture may be presented live or recorded on video tape for future showings. Among the high school courses now being presented via instructional television are social studies, sciences, and foreign languages. A typical high school telecast is a half-hour program beamed to a large group and followed by small-group discussion. If the televised course is to be effective, the teachers who are on the receiving end must be included in the planning and evaluating of the course. The teachers must be fully informed of the scope of the course. They should help to develop manuals to accompany the course and should be fully familiar with the content of each telecast. They should seek pupils' reactions and suggestions regarding the televised course.

USE AND ABUSE OF TELEVISION

In spite of glowing reports about the efficacy of televised instruction it is an open secret that many pupils dislike televised courses. This may be attributed in part to poor facilities. Large rooms ill-suited to television are often used. Acoustics may be poor. The television sets themselves may not receive the programs with sufficient clarity. If not enough sets are provided, students in the rear of a large room will have difficulty viewing. A televised program also demands constant attention and allows little opportunity for movement by the viewers. Students cannot, of course, interact with the teacher or the television set. There is an impersonal atmosphere in televised instruction that students tend to dislike.

Educational television can offer superior programs. It can use the services of the best teachers, assuming that these teachers can also adapt themselves to the impersonality and showmanship required of studio teachers. It can impart a considerable body of information to a large group of students in the shortest possible time. It can help overcome the lack of well-prepared teachers. It can assist schools in coping with the problem of increased enrollments. It permits a differentiation in teaching responsibilities between the studio teacher and the classroom teacher.

Educational television can be used as a valuable aid to the teacher. It can also be abused. Administrators have used educational television in much the same way they have seized on team teaching as a device exclusively for taking care of large enrollments. They have crowded large groups into unsuitable rooms and omitted the imperative follow-up feature. Provision must be made for questions and discussion in small groups following each telecast. It is unfortunate if the success of educational television is measured on the basis of achievement tests alone. Achievement tests frequently show that students learn as much or more in televised courses, even without follow-up discussion. But if the imparting of information per se is the goal of instruction, we are taking a very limited view of education. Students should have the opportunity to think through a topic, clarify their views, raise questions, and challenge each other's views. They must learn to express their thoughts orally. They cannot do this in a passive role, soaking up the studio teacher's vision and squeezing it out on achievement tests. In evaluating an innovation all of the goals of instruction must be considered. It must be determined which of the goals the particular innovation satisfies and what measures remain to be taken to meet other goals.

Ed cational television should be considered a worthy supplementary aid to the high school curriculum. Students may receive some of their instruction through television, though certainly not all of their high school courses. Nothing would be more deadening for the student than a schedule consisting of all televised courses. It does not appear desirable that students should be assigned to more than two courses which are taught by television. This further presupposes that only those courses should be committed to television which cannot be taught as effectively under other conditions.

CURRICULUM INNOVATION 3: PROGRAMMED INSTRUCTION

A technological nightmare stalks the teacher in his low moments. He gloomily foresees a fully automated school equipped throughout with devices for self-instruction, pupils busily teaching themselves, while he looks in from the outside shivering in the cold, unemployed. The teaching machine has made its way into the schools and can serve as a help to the teacher. It need pose no threat to the qualified teacher. He can put the teaching machine and programmed materials to effective use as aids to teaching.

When we speak of programmed instruction we refer to teaching that makes use of programs or programmed materials. A teaching machine is an instrument that makes use of a program. Machines come in a variety of forms from very simple to very complex, very cheap ($20) to several thousands of dollars, very naive to very sophisticated. The machine is designed to help the learner use a program.

A program presents the content of a subject in small steps. The learner reacts to each step by answering a question—in open-ended form or multiple choice. If he obtains the correct answer to an item, he moves along to the next step. Ideally, the student can never make a wrong response. If he should do this, a sophisticated teaching machine would refuse to move to the next item, requiring him to remain on the same step until he has mastered it. Complex machines permit a student to branch off and study the item missed before returning to the central program.

Programmed instruction operates on behavioristic principles of learning. Students proceed in tiny steps. They respond to each stimulus presented in the program. Each response is reinforced positively when the student obtains the right answer.

PROGRAMMED TEXTBOOKS

Programs may be presented to the learners without the use of machines. Programmed textbooks are becoming increasingly more common in instruction. In using programmed materials without a machine the learner must exercise self-discipline and not go on to the next item until he has mastered the previous one.

Programmed instruction offers the following advantages:

1. *It can help the teacher to provide for individual differences.* Students can work at their own speed. If they finish a program, they can go on to the next. They can work independently and not be held back by slower learners. Teachers may use programs of differing levels of difficulty for learners of varying abilities within the classes. Programmed instruction can help a good teacher to do his job more effectively.

2. *It can extend the curriculum by offering courses which the school is unable to provide because of limitations on number of staff or lack of qualified instructors.* Programmed instruction can aid the small school to expand its curriculum. The use of programmed materials is undoubtedly superior to instruction by an unprepared, unqualified teacher. Programmed instruction is an aid to students engaged in independent study. Advanced courses not ordinarily taught in the school may be made available by programmed instruction.

3. *Programmed textbooks, as well as some inexpensive machines, may be taken home for independent study.* Since students must obtain the correct responses to items on a program, the teacher does not have to worry about their learning wrong responses, as they frequently do with ordinary homework.

4. *Programmed instruction is especially helpful in remedial work.* Students who enter a course at a low level of achievement may be placed on an individual program at a more elementary level and brought up in achievement as rapidly as possible.

DISADVANTAGES

The teaching machine and its programs have some of the same limitations as educational television and other gadgetry. The learner cannot react with a machine or program in the same way he interacts with his peers and the teacher. The program is highly structured for him. All the steps are predetermined for him. If he were to utilize a program without a teacher, he would be unable to ask questions, express his own thoughts, develop skills of communication, or develop a sense of values.

Exclusive reliance on programmed instruction runs the same risk as mass instruction or ill-used educational television. It makes the false assumption that the imparting of knowledge is all there is to education. It would be devastating and pedagogically unsound to subject learners to entire schedules of courses taught only by means of programmed instruction.

Teachers should be wary of the programs which they purchase for use with students. The idea of self-instruction or automated learning has caught on with the public, who see in this an easy way, they believe, for their children to get a quick and painless education. The quality of programs runs from very poor to superior. Some are turned out in quick fashion to earn a fast dollar while the market is hot. Others have been carefully prepared, tested, and evaluated by competent experts before the materials are sent to the schools. Teaching machines are built, of course, with the profit motive in mind. A machine should be selected, if one is to be used at all, on the basis of the needs of the particular students, teacher, and school. Schools that are pinched for money may well find the teaching machine itself an unnecessary luxury.

Programmed instruction has both its advantages and disadvantages. It can serve as an aid to the teacher but cannot substitute for the teacher.

CURRICULUM INNOVATION 4: ACCELERATION AND ENRICHMENT

The needs of the academically talented and gifted students have received a great deal of emphasis in the present decade. Concern for the waste of prime human resources has led to the search for more effective ways of bringing forth the talents and abilities of students. It is axiomatic in our schools of today that the curriculum must be adapted to the learners rather than vice versa. New arrangements are in operation to care for the needs of the slow, the average, and the fast learners. In previous years we have placed emphasis on suitable programs for the average and slow. Today we find increasing stress on the needs of the above-average. The principle of balance must be applied once again so that we do not find ourselves catering exclusively to the needs of the above-average, the top 3 or 15 or 25 per cent, and ignoring the needs of the mass of our students. A continuing and critical curriculum problem is that of finding ways of organizing an instructional program that serves equitably the needs of students of varying capacities. The public school cannot elect to educate only the top students. The nation cannot afford to ignore any segment of our school population whether that segment is composed of bright students or average students or slow students.

Separate kinds of curricular arrangements are made for students of varying capacities. High schools have instituted a number of accelerated programs for above-average students which allow them to gain in breadth and depth in their studies at a rate not possible under ordinary circumstances. The object of acceleration is to permit faster students to learn as much as they can at as rapid a rate as they are able. Several of the plans in operation are:

1. *Ability grouping.* Students are placed in sections of a course according to their abilities and achievement. We consider the customary practices of ability groupings elsewhere in the text.[2] Phased education or continuous progress plans give grouping a modern twist. We will consider these plans below when we describe the nongraded school, one of the more recent innovations for meeting the educational needs of students of varying academic proficiency.

2. *Independent study.* There is a growing trend, as we have seen in our discussion of team teaching above, to permit brighter students to do more school work individually and independently. Students are encouraged to do independent research, explore special interests, and utilize total school facilities. Independent study can be incorporated into a regular high school program. Teachers may; if they wish, free able students from class periods which the students could well afford to miss. Instead of remaining to recover ground they already know, students can be excused to do independent projects and research. They may work in the library or at independent study centers in the school or even in the back of the classroom. Independent study is an integral feature of team-teaching programs. Programmed materials may be utilized with students who are able to pursue independent study.

3. *Accelerated courses in junior high school.* We have noted already the increasingly common practice of assigning above-average eighth-graders to

2 See Unit V, pp. 293–96.

accelerated courses in various subjects. This practice enables the student to do more advanced work in senior high school in the subjects which he has already begun at the junior high level.

4. *Early school leaving.* The Ford Foundation has for a number of years supported a program by which academically talented young people are identified and enrolled in college at the end of the junior year in high school. Contrary to the misgivings of some critics of this program, those students who have left high school at the end of the junior year have been successful in their college careers.

5. *Voluntary courses outside of school hours.* A few high school instructors have attempted to offer noncredit courses on a voluntary basis in the evenings or on Saturdays for those students who had the interest to take them. In some areas of the country these programs have met with a resounding success. The thirst for knowledge on the part of young people had been totally unexpected. The chance to study something of interest to them without threat of marks motivated many boys and girls to give up their leisure time to take on extra studies.

6. *Cooperation with institutions of higher education in the area.* By cooperative agreement advanced high school students are permitted by colleges in the same community, particularly junior colleges, to take courses at the college. Students also utilize the college's library resources and call on professors for assistance. Educational institutions which are blessed by the factor of geographical proximity and which are concerned with the needs of academically talented boys and girls would do well to imitate and expand a cooperative arrangement of this type.

7. *Special summer programs for able students at colleges and universities.* Some colleges offer summer programs to academically talented students who have completed their junior year of high school. The 1966 directory of *College Programs for High School Students* (Directory Publishers Co., Hillsdale, N. J.) lists over 200 participating colleges.

8. *The Advanced Placement Program.* Initiated in 1954 by a grant from the Fund for the Advancement of Education, the Advanced Placement Program has grown from 18 participating high schools to more than 2,300 in 1964–65. The program has been administered by the College Entrance Examination Board since 1956. Basically, the Advanced Placement Program permits academically talented students to take college-level courses while still in high school. These courses are usually limited to seniors. Students and teachers in advanced placement courses can follow course descriptions in the eleven subjects (American History, Biology, Chemistry, European History, French, German, Latin, Mathematics, Physics, and Spanish) which

are currently tested in this program. At the end of the year an Advanced Placement Examination prepared by the College Entrance Examination Board is administered to students in the program. The results are forwarded to the participating colleges in which the students would like to enroll. On the basis of successful completion of the course and examination the college may grant the student, when he is admitted, either college credit or placement in advanced levels of the subject or both.

Thirty-four thousand pupils participated in the Advanced Placement Program in 1964–65. The 2,300 high schools represent less than 8 per cent of all high schools. At present approximately 900 colleges have agreed to participate in this program. Most of them have been pleased with the results obtained.

The Advanced Placement Program has had an impact on the total program of studies followed by the academically talented pupils. Advanced Placement Examinations are prepared with certain assumptions made about the prerequisite courses students should have completed before entering an Advanced Placement course.

The modern high school is committed to the search for effective ways of differentiating the instruction. Accelerated programs represent means of developing the talents of above-average students.

CURRICULUM INNOVATION 5: THE NONGRADED HIGH SCHOOL

The nongraded high school is essentially a novel form of grouping. Many educators and groups have advocated some types of grouping. James B. Conant and the 1958 Rockefeller Report on *The Pursuit of Excellence*[3] are in general agreement that students should be grouped in sections of a subject determined by their abilities or aptitude in each subject. Typical plans of grouping, as we note elsewhere in this text, weigh such factors as intelligence, teachers' grades, teachers' judgments, and students' intensity of purpose. The nongraded high school, of which Melbourne High School, Florida, is the prototype, dispenses with all criteria except one, achievement scores on standardized achievement tests.

MELBOURNE HIGH SCHOOL

No person in secondary education today can overlook the much-publicized Melbourne High School. In the heart of Cape Kennedy territory, bustling, growing, science-oriented Brevard County Melbourne High School is a center of new ideas and experimentation in secondary school curriculum. In an era when schools have traditionally waited for the other fellow to institute

[3] Rockefeller Brothers Fund, *The Pursuit of Excellence; Education and the Future of America* (Garden City, N. Y.: Doubleday, 1958).

changes and get battered in the process, Melbourne has leaped forward to try out new plans and procedures. Melbourne has taken its greatest strides since 1960. Progress, though, has not come without criticism. Perhaps this is an inevitable cost that the pioneer must pay.

Melbourne is making contributions to education in a number of ways, but its most significant is the nongraded nature of its high school. B. Frank Brown, the effervescent principal, believes that within the next few years every intellectually respectable school will have an element of nongradedness.[4]

Melbourne's plan of nongradedness consists of grouping students in the various subjects in seven phases. These phases are:

> *Phase 1.* Subjects are designed for students who need special assistance, in small classes.
> *Phase 2.* Subjects are designed for students who need more emphasis on the basic skills.
> *Phase 3.* Courses are designed for students who have an average background of achievement.
> *Phase 4.* Subject matter is designed for extremely well prepared students desiring education in depth.
> *Phase 5.* Courses are available to students who are willing to assume responsibility for their own learning and pursue college-level courses while still in high school.
> *Phase Q.* Students whose creative talents are well developed should give consideration to the Quest phase of the curriculum. This is an important dimension of the phased organization designed to give thrust in the direction of individual fulfillment. In this phase a student may do research in an area in which he is deeply and broadly curious, either to develop creative powers or in quest of knowledge.
> *Phase X.* Subjects that do not accommodate student mobility, e.g., typing, physical education, are ungraded but unphased.

Students are assigned to the various phases on the basis of their performance on standardized achievement tests. A student can be moved to a higher phase at any time during the year if it appears he has been assigned to a phase too low for him. Effort is made to prevent placement beyond a student's achievement so that the student has to be reassigned to a lower phase.

On the complex Melbourne schedule subjects appear as "English—Ph 3," "American History—Ph 4," "Spanish IV—Ph 5." The nongraded curriculum is often referred to as "phased instruction" or "continuous progress plan." Nongraded plans permit learners to work comfortably within their levels of competency. In phases 1 and 2 Melbourne omits marks, thereby removing a threat from students of limited ability and those who need work in the basic skills. Students can go through a high school program under this

---

[4] For a complete description of the nongraded high school read B. Frank Brown *The Nongraded High School* (Englewood Cliffs, N. J.: Prentice-Hall, 1963).

plan and obtain a quality of education which best fits their own needs. Melbourne claims that since its nongraded program was started the dropout rate has declined to four per cent. With the national dropout rate standing at 30 to 35 per cent, a reduction of this nature must be recognized as a creditable achievement on the part of school personnel.

As the concept of the nongraded school loses its novelty, we may well expect more schools at the elementary, junior high, and senior high school level embarking upon programs of phased learning.

CURRICULUM INNOVATION 6: FLEXIBLE SCHEDULING

We may consider scheduling as that device by which the curriculum is placed at the disposal of the faculty and learners. Scheduling is essentially an administrative responsibility. A sound educational schedule, however, is adjusted to the curriculum of the school. It is deplorable that in some schools students must adapt to the schedule rather than the schedule to the needs of the students.

Imaginative administrators are creating new patterns of scheduling. They have been aided in this struggle to revise scheduling procedures by the decreasing emphasis placed on the Carnegie unit, which arbitrarily set as the basis for all courses one period per day, five days a week, for one school year. With the stress on scholarship, the shortage of qualified teachers, the newer ways of utilizing staff, and the introduction of technology into the curriculum more satisfactory ways of scheduling had to be found.

Several facts have become obvious to administrators:

1. *Not all courses necessarily need five equal periods of time per week.* Some courses can do with less frequent class meetings. Some courses can use shorter blocks of time and some longer blocks.

2. *A seven- or eight-period day provides more flexibility than a five- or six-period day.*

3. *Scheduling by fixed class size, e.g., 35 pupils, for each period of the day rules out flexible grouping—large and small groups as the occasion may warrant.*

In their efforts to provide less rigid schedules school administrators have designed unique patterns to fit the needs of their schools' programs. Among the approaches in use are the following:

1. *Rotating schedules.* The number of minutes each subject meets is extended and the number of class meetings per week is reduced. One school with a six-period day, for example, has extended its class meeting time to eighty minutes. Each subject meets four times per week instead of five. The fifth

period is placed on a rotating schedule, meeting at a different hour each of four days of the week. The sixth period is an optional period for activities and other courses.

2. *Block scheduling with flexibility within the block of time.* For example, a core class is scheduled for two periods per day. Teachers involved may divide the two hours into any kind of scheduling arrangement they desire.

3. *Combined double and single periods.* A course that formerly met five periods daily per week is rescheduled to meet two days a week in two-hour blocks and one day a week as a single period. Farrington High School, Honolulu, has scheduled courses that meet, for example, two periods on Monday and Thursday or two periods on Tuesday and Friday. On Wednesday every subject meets for one period.

4. *Modular scheduling.* With this arrangement periods are scheduled in modules of time, as 15, 20, 30, 45, or more minutes. The basic or shortest module is determined, for example, as 15 minutes. Those subjects that require a great deal of time are scheduled in multiple modules. Science, for example, may be allotted five or six modules. Art may be given two modules. This kind of schedule recognizes the need for varying time allotments for various courses.

J. Lloyd Trump describes the ultimate goal of a truly flexible schedule and gives an illustration of a school which is striving to reach that goal:

> The goal, then, in a larger school is to develop orderly procedures that permit teachers and students as much latitude as possible in developing various aspects of instruction and learning. The following appear to be necessary ingredients: The class schedule is made daily on the basis of teacher requests. Each student, under competent direction, makes decisions regarding his part in the established schedule. Conflicts for students and teachers are reduced to a minimum. Teacher loads and pupil loads are such that they permit, on the one hand, maximum professionalization of teaching, on the other, they provide maximum potential learning opportunities for students. The school knows what its students are doing and follows reasonably equitable personnel policies for teachers. The whole scheme is financially feasible and logistically operational.

> At least one school is making significant strides in the direction of such a schedule. Gardner Swenson, principal of the Brookhurst Junior High School in Anaheim, California, describes their program somewhat as follows:

> Individual members of teaching teams determine three days in advance what students they want to teach, in what size groups, for what length of time, in what places, and with what technological aids. Teacher job-specification forms containing this information are turned in to their team leaders. The team leaders then assemble to make a master schedule for the day, a procedure that takes approximately twenty minutes each day. The master

schedule is then duplicated and made available to the students and their counselors. In a daily 20-minute meeting, with the advice and consent of their counselor (twenty students to a counselor), each student makes his schedule. A student noting, for example, that the schedule calls for a large-group presentation on a given subject and deciding that he already knows that material, may elect rather to spend his time in independent study in the art room or library or some place else. The counselor either approves or rejects this decision. Then the student makes out his own schedule for the day in quadruplicate. One copy is for himself, one for the the office, one for the counselor, and one for his parents.[5]

In the preceding pages we have examined six innovations in the implementation of the curriculum of modern high schools. Each of the six innovations can be found in operation at the present time. Before we conclude our examination of innovations we should consider a challenging plan for high schools of the future.

THE HIGH SCHOOL OF 1985

Kimball Wiles looks toward 1985 and sees the program of the school divided into four phases: analysis of experience and values, acquisition of fundamental skills, exploration of the cultural heritage, and specialization and creativity. Wiles describes his proposal for analysis groups as follows:

> In the school, each pupil will spend six hours a week in an Analysis Group. With ten other pupils his own age and a skilled teacher-counselor he will discuss any problem of ethics, social concern, out-of-school experience, or implication of knowledge encountered in other classes. No curriculum content will be established in advance for the Analysis Groups. The exploration of questions, ideas or values advanced by group members will constitute the primary type of experience.
>
> The purpose of the Analysis Group will be to help each pupil discover meaning, to develop increased commitment to a set of values, and to offer opportunity to examine the conflicts among the many sets of values and viewpoints held by members of society.
>
> The members of the Analysis Group will be carefully selected to provide a group composed of persons of relatively equal intellectual ability, but varied social and economic values. The group will remain a unit throughout the high school program of its members. . . . Each Analysis Group teacher will meet three groups, or thirty-three students, during the week. His time beyond the eighteen hours in the discussion groups will be for individual counseling with his thirty-three pupils and their parents. The Analysis Group will be considered the basic element of the educational program.[6]

[5] J. Lloyd Trump, "Flexible Scheduling—Fad or Fundamental?," *Phi Delta Kappan* (May 1963), 370.

[6] *The Changing Curriculum of the American High School* (Englewood Cliffs, N. J.: Prentice-Hall, 1963), pp. 301–2. By permission of Prentice-Hall, Inc.

Wiles sees the establishment of a Materials Center in which students may schedule teaching machines for working on their basic skills. He states:

> Machines will teach basic skills as effectively and efficiently as a teacher. . . . Two librarians, one to issue programs and the other to help on request, and a staff of mechanical technicians will supervise the work of two hundred students. Disorder will be at a minimum because each person will work on his own level and with his own goals. Moreover, each student will work in a private sound-proofed cubicle.[7]

Students will spend roughly a third of their high school program exploring their cultural heritage, acquiring knowledge from the humanities, social sciences, and physical and biological sciences.

> Classes in the Cultural Heritage program will be large. Sometimes as many as five hundred or one thousand will be in a single section. Teaching will be by television, films, or a highly skilled lecturer. No provision will be made for discussion, because ideas that produce a response can be discussed in the Analysis Groups. Only one teacher and an assistant will be needed in each subject-matter field in each school. The teacher will lecture or present the material through an appropriate medium. The assistant will prepare quizzes and examinations and record the marks made on the machine-scored tests.[8]

Opportunities to specialize will be provided in a variety of ways—through shops, studios, work laboratories, work-study programs, and seminars in the content fields. These seminars will be limited to fifteen pupils and will meet for two two-hour periods per week. Students will spend the remainder of their time conducting independent research in the library or laboratories. Wiles says:

> Graduation days will have been eliminated. Students will continue to work in the secondary school until they pass their college entrance examinations or move to a job. Most students will enter the secondary school at thirteen, but some will leave at fifteen and others at twenty. A student's decision to leave the program will be conditioned by his completion of the Cultural Heritage experiences, his acquisition of fundamental skills, and his individual goals.[9]

Wiles' proposals for the secondary school of 1985 are challenging and far-reaching. Whether we accept all, part, or none of his proposals we are made to realize that the high school curriculum will continue to change as new ideas are advanced. Today's innovations are tomorrow's outmoded practices. Schools must continue to find newer and better ways of helping learners to learn.

[7] *Ibid.*, pp. 302–3.   [8] *Ibid.*, p. 303.   [9] *Ibid.*, p. 305.

IMPROVING THE CURRICULUM

As we conclude our discussion of the secondary school curriculum today we should stress the necessity for constant curriculum revision and improvement. Every teacher shares responsibilities for keeping the curriculum dynamic, free from stagnation.

The modern secondary school teacher must keep up to date in his field. He will profit from in-service workshops, conferences, professional reading, summer courses, and institutes at colleges and universities. He should be willing to try out some new ideas and support new programs that seem to make sense to him. He should be willing to participate in curriculum studies that have as their purpose improvement of the curriculum. Today's teacher has many opportunities to take part in curriculum planning, development, and evaluation. He may serve on a school's curriculum steering committee. He may work with his department on special committees and projects. He may engage in writing units and curriculum guides. He may participate in an evaluation of a phase of the school's program or the entire curriculum of the school.

The *Evaluative Criteria* of the National Study of Secondary School Evaluation presents a good beginning point for schools wishing to evaluate their curricula.[10] These criteria provide one of the most extensive sets of standards available. Separate criteria for both the junior high school and the senior high school are given. It should be pointed out, however, that these criteria are revised only at ten-year intervals. Schools are now using the 1960 criteria. A school using the criteria will find them very helpful but should not feel bound to reject creative solutions of their own to educational needs in their own schools.

Other faculties tackle curricular revision on a piecemeal basis, studying features which they feel most in need of improvement. Curricular revision often comes as much by example as by planned study. B. Frank Brown refers to the process of "spinning out."[11] By this he means that a few interested teachers try out a new idea or plan. If they are successful, other teachers may follow their example. Schools that wish to try team teaching, for example, would do well to follow this approach. The principal can allow the teachers of one subject to organize themselves into a team and to develop a pattern for teaching their course. It is probably best to avoid wholesale changes by administrative fiat. It still remains sound theory that curriculum change comes only through a change in people.

[10] *Evaluative Criteria* (Washington: National Study of Secondary School Evaluation, 1960).

[11] Brown, *op. cit.*, pp. 209–10.

SUMMARY

We began this discussion with a statement about our changing society and a description of some of the forces that have produced change. We have followed this with a statement of the thesis that the curriculum of the high school must change to reflect changes in society. We have considered briefly some of the principal changes in purposes, content, and implementation of the high school curriculum. We conclude with the proposition that continuous change is inevitable, necessary, and stimulating.

CLASS AND EVALUATION ACTIVITIES

1. Write your definition of "curriculum" and read to the class. Compare and discuss the various definitions. See if you can reach consensus on a definition.

2. Compile on the blackboard a list of changes which have taken place in the United States in the last ten years and draw one implication for education from each change.

3. Break into small groups of five to seven and prepare a group statement on the purposes of secondary education.

4. Prepare a chart showing the rate of population increase in the United States and the world. Draw implications for the high school.

5. Pretest. Identify and/or explain any of the following with which you may be familiar:

   a. Report of the Committee of Ten on Secondary School Studies
   b. The Harvard Report
   c. The Seven Cardinal Principles
   d. The Council on Basic Education
   e. The Educational Policies Commission
   f. James B. Conant
   g. General education
   h. Core curriculum
   i. Team teaching
   j. Programmed instruction

k. Nongraded high school

l. Advanced Placement Program

6. Decide which of the following competencies you believe every high school graduate should possess. Decide whether the high school has any responsibility for developing these competencies. Give reasons for your answers.

a. Know the names and locations of all the fifty state capitals.

b. Prepare a federal income tax return.

c. Recite *The Gettysburg Address.*

d. Play a musical instrument.

e. Swim.

f. Know the plot outlines of at least two of Shakespeare's plays.

g. Demonstrate integrity.

h. Be acceptant of persons of a different race, religion, or color.

j. Be able to dissect a frog.

i. Be able to solve an equation with two unknowns.

k. Spell correctly.

l. Address a group of a hundred people.

m. Enjoy a hobby.

n. Feel a commitment to the United Nations.

o. Speak a foreign language.

p. Appreciate great works of art.

q. Drive a car.

r. Make simple home repairs.

s. Demonstrate proper etiquette.

t. Dress properly.

7. Invite to class specialists in the fields of science, mathematics, and foreign languages to explain to the class new developments in their fields.

8. List a number of the major criticisms you have heard about public secondary education. Find some evidence to support or refute each criticism.

9. Observe in local schools, if possible, ongoing programs of team teaching and educational television. If no such programs are readily available for observation, try to locate experienced teachers who have worked in team teaching and with educational television. Invite them to class to speak about these innovations.

10. Obtain and analyze copies of the schedule of offerings of several high schools—either high schools in the vicinity or the high schools from which class members were graduated. Look for any innovations in scheduling.

11. Assemble samples of programmed materials and teaching machines. Practice using these. If no actual materials or machines are available, find illustrations and descriptions in the literature.

12. Find out what programs (programmed materials) are available in your field. Consult *Programs: A Guide to Programed Instructional Materials,*

U. S. Government Printing Office. This is an annual publication by the Center for Programed Instruction.

13. Show the effects of each of the following sociological forces on the curriculum of the secondary school.

  a. Population explosion
  b. Explosion of knowledge
  c. Industrial and technological explosion
  d. Social and geographical mobility of the population
  e. Increased contacts with peoples of other lands
  f. The struggle for civil and human rights
  g. The threat of communism
  h. The increased percentage of elderly and retired persons in the population
  i. The impact of materialism
  j. The growth of urban and suburban areas
  k. The growing role of the federal government

14. Prepare a statement of the principal changes taking place in your field of specialization. Make your statement clear enough so that a person who is not a specialist in your field would understand it.

15. Explain a number of ways by which the secondary school is serving the needs of the academically talented.

16. Evaluate Kimball Wiles' proposals for the high school of 1985, which are found in Part IV of *The Changing Curriculum of the American High School,* Prentice-Hall, 1963.

17. Develop your own projection of the high school of 1985.

18. Evaluate the following innovations, appraising strengths and weaknesses of each.

  a. Team teaching
  b. Educational television
  c. Programmed instruction

Decide whether these innovations have any relevance for teaching in your subject field.

19. Reply to the following questions:

  a. Do you believe that high schools of the future will be nongraded? Why do you believe this?

  b. Why has the term "supplementary" been used in reference to the student activity program? Would you concur in its use? If not, what term would you use? Why?

  c. What is your reaction to the "core curriculum"?

SELECTED BIBLIOGRAPHICAL REFERENCES

1. Alexander, William M., ed. *The Changing Secondary School Curriculum: Readings.* New York: Holt, Rinehart and Winston, 1967. 479 pp.

   Excellent collection of readings on the secondary school curriculum. This book is divided into four parts: The Bases of Secondary School Curriculum Improvement, Toward a Changing Curriculum, Issues in Secondary School Curriculum Improvement, and The Secondary School Curriculum of the Future. Contains fourteen chapters including readings on the purposes of secondary education, secondary school pupils, changing emphases in secondary school subjects, organization of the curriculum, balance in the curriculum, and means of curriculum change.

2. Association for Supervision and Curriculum Development. *Balance in the Curriculum.* Yearbook 1961. Washington: Association for Supervision and Curriculum Development, N.E.A., 1961. 197 pp.

   Analysis of the principle of balance in the curriculum. Discusses the meaning of balance, the American value system that must be considered when making decisions about the curriculum, the kinds of problems faced by teachers and learners as they struggle to achieve balance in the curriculum, and the roles of various individuals and groups working on the development of school programs.

3. Association for Supervision and Curriculum Development. *New Insights and the Curriculum.* Yearbook 1963. Washington: Association for Supervision and Curriculum Development, N.E.A., 1963. 328 pp.

   Thoughtful book that presents new insights regarding potentiality, knowledge, self-management, relationships across cultures, citizenship, and creativity. In each section a scholar analyzes the facet of his field that he deems most significant. His presentation is paired with the statement of a curriculum specialist who examines the professional implications of the scholar's analysis.

4. Association for Supervision and Curriculum Development. *Using Current Curriculum Developments.* Washington: Association for Supervision and Curriculum Development, N.E.A., 1963. 118 pp.

   Survey of the research and curriculum innovations in the arts, English, foreign languages, health and physical education, mathematics, science, social studies, vocational and technical education, and instructional technology. Two chapters provide guidelines for making judgments about curricular projects.

5. Bair, Medill, and Woodward, Richard. *Team Teching in Action*. Boston: Houghton Mifflin, 1964. 229 pp.

    Good analysis of various aspects of team teaching.

6. Beggs, David W., III, ed. *Team Teaching: Bold New Venture*. Indianapolis: Unified College Press, 1964. 192 pp.

    Twelve authors analyze various aspects of team teaching in this useful volume.

7. Brown, B. Frank. *The Nongraded High School*. Englewood Cliffs, N.J.: Prentice-Hall, 1963. 223 pp.

    Lively presentation of the institution of a nongraded program at Melbourne High School, Florida. Presents advantages of nongradedness over graded programs.

8. Bruner, Jerome. *The Process of Education*. Cambridge, Mass.: Harvard University Press, 1960. 97 pp.

    Jerome Bruner, as director of the Woods Hole Conference, 1959, summarizes views of some thirty-five scientists, scholars, and educators at the conference. This interesting and valuable report discusses the importance of structure, readiness for learning, intuitive and analytic thinking, motives for learning, and aids to teaching.

9. Center for Programed Instruction. *Programs '63. A Guide to Programed Instructional Materials*. Washington: U. S. Government Printing Office, 1963. 814 pp.

    Lists by subject field 352 programs available in 1963. Contains illustrative items from many programs.

10. Conant, James B. *The American High School Today*. New York: McGraw-Hill, 1959. 140 pp.

    Widely read report in which Conant makes twenty-one recommendations concerning the American high school. Contains discussion of the characteristics of American education and the comprehensive high school.

11. ———. *Recommendations for Education in the Junior High School Years*. Princeton, N. J.: Educational Testing Service, 1960. 46 pp.

    Short booklet outlining Conant's fourteen recommendations concerning the junior high school.

12. Costello, Lawrence F., and Gordon, George N. *Teach with Television*. New York: Hastings House, 1961. 192 pp.

    Comprehensive guide to instructional television. Among topics covered are the limits of television, the television studio, the televised lesson, teaching the lesson, using the lesson, and evaluating the results.

13. Cram, David. *Explaining Teaching Machines and Programming*. San Francisco: Fearon Publishers, 1961. 86 pp.

Simplified description of programming with illustrations of both linear programming and branching programs.

14. Department of Classroom Teachers and Department of Audio-Visual Instruction. *And TV, Too*. Washington: National Education Association, 1961. 63 pp.

Helpful booklet on the purposes and uses of educational television.

15. Douglass, Harl R., ed. *The High School Curriculum*, 3rd ed. New York: Ronald Press, 1964. 696 pp.

Extensive sourcebook on the high school curriculum. Among the topics discussed in the chapters by thirty-three contributing authors are the nature of curriculum, current trends, and analyses of each of the subject areas of the junior and senior high school curriculum.

16. Fine, Benjamin. *Teaching Machines*. New York: Sterling Publishing Co., 1962. 176 pp.

Readable, popular treatment of teaching machines and programmed learning. Clever table of contents in form of a program.

17. Foltz, Charles I. *The World of Teaching Machines*. Washington: Electronic Teaching Laboratories, 1961. 116 pp.

Analysis of programmed learning with numerous pictures and descriptions of teaching machines.

18. Fraser, Dorothy M. *Current Curriculum Studies in Academic Subjects*. Washington: National Education Association, 1962. 101 pp.

Provides information about recent developments, projects, and studies in science, mathematics, English language arts, modern foreign languages, and social studies.

19. Goodlad, John I. *School Curriculum Reform in the United States*. New York: Fund for the Advancement of Education, 1964. 96 pp.

Discusses curriculum reform movements in mathematics, the sciences, social sciences, English, and modern foreign languages. The booklet analyzes some problems and issues related to curricular reform and makes recommendations concerning curricular projects.

20. Grambs, Jean D., Noyce, Clarence G., Patterson, Franklin, and Robertson, John. *The Junior High School We Need*. Washington: Association for Supervision and Curriculum Development, N.E.A., 1961. 37 pp.

Short report from the ASCD Commission on Secondary Curriculum. Makes recommendations for the program of the junior high school.

21. Heath, Robert W., ed. *New Curricula*. New York: Harper & Row, 1964. 292 pp.

Fourteen chapters by educational authorities describe goals, history, and status of several key curriculum projects. Discusses educational implications of these projects.

22. Krug, Edward A. *The Secondary School Curriculum*. New York: Harper & Row, 1960. 555 pp.

One of the best comprehensive works on the secondary school curriculum with chapters on the origin of high schools, purposes of high schools, and each of the subject areas of the curriculum.

23. Morse, Arthur D. *Schools of Tomorrow—Today!* Garden City, N. Y.: Doubleday, 1960. 191 pp.

A popularized report on education experimentals including team teaching, nongraded schools, Higher Horizons Project, and educational television.

24. National Education Association. Reports of the NEA Project on the Instructional Program of the Public Schools.

I. Major reports

a. Deciding What to Teach. Washington: National Education Association, 1963. 264 pp.

Discusses bases for selecting curriculum content. Among the topics discussed in the report are the nature of disciplines, individual differences, balance and priorities, controversial issues, and the question, Who should make curriculum decisions?

b. Education in a Changing Society. Washington: National Educational Association, 1963. 166 pp.

Examines forces affecting education in our society, including science and technology, economic growth, large bureaucratic organizations, leisure time, mass media, urbanization, population growth, and international interdependence. Draws implications of these forces for the school program.

c. Planning and Organizing for Teaching. Washington: National Education Association, 1963. 190 pp.

Looks toward improvements in curriculum organization, school organization, classroom organization, personnel, resources, time, and space organization.

d. Schools for the Sixties. New York: McGraw-Hill, 1963. 146 pp.

Makes thirty-three recommendations pertaining to twelve decision areas in education.

II. Auxiliary reports

a. The Principals Look at the Schools: A Status Study of Selected Institutional Practices. Washington: National Education Association, 1962. 76 pp.

Reports of results of a questionnaire sent to elementary and secondary school principals. Questionnaire gathered data on changes in what is taught, changes in organizational patterns, resources used in developing the instructional program, and forces influencing change. Principals were asked to predict status of selected instructional and institutional practices five years hence (from 1961 to 1966).

   b. *The Scholars Look at the Schools: A Report of the Disciplines Seminar.* Washington: National Education Association, 1962. 64 pp.

   Report of 1961 Seminar on Disciplines at the National Education Association Center. Discusses ideas and methods of inquiry in the humanities, the sciences, mathematics, and the social sciences.

25. Rickover, Hyman. *Education and Freedom.* New York: E. P. Dutton, 1959. 256 pp.

   Collection of speeches made by the author on the subject of education. Presents view that drastic upgrading of scholastic standards of the school is essential if freedom is to be maintained. Appendix 1 recommends parents read Albert Lynd, *Quackery in the Public Schools* (Boston: Little, Brown, 1953), bulletins of the Council on Basic Education, and Arthur Bestor's *The Restoration of Learning* (New York: Knopf, 1956). Appendix 2 lauds Dutch secondary schools. Appendix 3 consists of a note on the challenge of Russian education.

26. Rosenbloom, Paul C. *Modern Viewpoints in the Curriculum.* New York: McGraw-Hill, 1964. 312 pp.

   Report of the National Conference on Curriculum Experimentation, September 25–28, 1961, at the University of Minnesota. Sections deal with the stake of society in education, the nature of learning, current problems in various fields, experimentation and evaluation, the role of professional societies, the role of supporting agencies, and the role of government.

27. Shaplin, Judson T., and Olds, Henry F., Jr. *Team Teaching.* New York: Harper & Row, 1964. 430 pp.

   Extensive treatment by several authors covering various aspects of team teaching. Contains in appendix helpful bibliography and list of team-teaching projects.

28. Smith, Mary Howard. *Using Television in the Classroom.* New York: McGraw-Hill, 1961. 118 pp.

   Readable book on instructional television. The three parts of the book deal with the topics: introducing the classroom teacher to television, the role of the classroom teacher, and demonstrations of instructional television in use. Based on the experiences of the Midwest Program on Airborne Television Instruction.

29. Stolurow, Lawrence M. *Teaching by Machine.* Cooperative Research

Monograph No. 6. Washington: U. S. Office of Education, 1961. 173 pp.

Presents much information on teaching machines and concepts and techniques of programming.

30. Trow, William Clark. *Teacher and Technology. New Designs for Learning*. New York: Appleton-Century-Crofts, 1963. 197 pp.

Readable paperback on technological change in the schools, including television, programmed learning, and instructional materials centers. Contains introductory chapters on the educational enterprise and the learner and his environment.

31. Trump, J. Lloyd, and Baynham, Dorsey. *Guide to Better Schools; Focus on Change*. Chicago: Rand McNally, 1961. 147 pp.

Explains clearly the purposes, advantages, and practices of team teaching. Recommends ways to schedule large-group instruction, small-group discussion, and independent study.

32. Wiles, Kimball. *The Changing Curriculum of the American High School*. Englewood Cliffs, N. J.: Prentice-Hall, 1963. 331 pp.

Comprehensive, well-written, readable book on the high school curriculum. Considers bases of curriculum decisions, elements of the curriculum, the process of change, and the high school of the future.

33. Wiles, Kimball, and Patterson, Franklin. *The High School We Need*. Washington: Association for Supervision and Curriculum Development, N.E.A., 1959. 28 pp.

Short report from the ASCD Commission on the Education of Adolescents. Makes recommendations for the program of the high school.

34. Woodring, Paul, and Scanlon, John. *American Education Today*. New York: McGraw-Hill, 1963. 292 pp.

Collection of essays from the education supplement of *Saturday Review*. Sections deal with aims, philosophy, current issues, types of institutions, innovations, and teacher education. Concludes with a perspective on education by Arnold Toynbee.

INSTRUCTIONAL AIDS AND SOURCES

FILMS

And No Bells Ring. Parts I and II. Total of 56 minutes for both parts. Sound. Black and white. Washington: National Association of Secondary School Principals.

Hugh Downs narrates this one-hour program which explains and illustrates team-teaching theory and practice. Shows large-group instruction, small-group instruction, and independent study. J. Lloyd Trump, proponent of team teaching, appears in the film.

And So They Live. 26 min. Sound. Black and white. New York University and University of Kentucky.

Old but excellent film which shows a curriculum completely unsuitable for the children for whom it is intended, young people of poor families in the hills of Kentucky.

FILMSTRIPS

Example of a Teaching Machine. Color. Basic Skill Films, 1355 Inverness Drive, Pasadena, California 91103. Prepared by Dean H. Luxton and Robert E. Corrigan.

Example of a teaching machine program. The example used is a complete program for learning how to read a resistor.

Teaching Machines. Color. Basic Skill Films, 1355 Inverness Drive, Pasadena, California 91103. Prepared by William H. Allen, University of Southern California.

Tells what teaching machines are, what a teaching machine program is like, and what the educational role of teaching machines is. Shows types of teaching machines. A. A. Lumsdaine is technical advisor.

RECORDS

Alberty, Harold. *The Core Program in the High School.* One 33⅓ rpm 12-inch record. 22 minutes each side. Educational Growth Series for Teachers. Educational Recording Service, Los Angeles, California 90045.

Harold Alberty lectures on the nature of the core curriculum, explains different types of core programs, and discusses advantages of the core curriculum.

National Education Association. *Focus on Change.* One 33⅓ rpm 12-inch record and one color filmstrip to accompany record. 23-minute program. Washington: National Education Association, 1962.

Howard K. Smith narrates on the record that accompanies color filmstrip. Describes large-group instruction, small-group discussion, and individual study. Based on the findings and recommendations of the National Association of Secondary School Principals' Commission on Staff Utilization in the Secondary School.

UNIT III

PLANNING FOR INSTRUCTION

OBJECTIVES OF UNIT III

At the conclusion of his reading and correlated study-discussion activities the reader should

A. understand that

1. planning is the process of making instruction manageable and meaningful to the learner;

2. the teacher's success in the classroom depends to a great extent on his planning for instruction;

3. teachers plan for instruction on varying levels: in the classroom, school-wide, school-system-wide, and frequently state-wide, regionally, and nation-wide;

4. teachers work from general, long-range plans to specific, short-range, and daily plans;

5. teachers often share responsibility in planning;

6. the unit method is one effective approach to planning;

7. the unit method of teaching lends itself particularly well to the social studies, core, science, and English classes;

8. careful planning simplifies the problem of classroom control and prevents many disciplinary problems from arising.

B. show appreciation for

1. the skill of the teacher who successfully plans for instruction,

2. carefully conceived long-range and short-range plans,

3. a well-made learning unit,

4. a well-made resource unit,

5. a well-made lesson plan.

C. adopt attitudes of

1. acceptance of the necessity of planning for instruction,

2. willingness to make the effort involved in the construction of plans,

3. willingness to attempt imaginative, creative procedures in planning.

D. be able to demonstrate skill in

1. over-all planning,

2. preparing learning units,

3. constructing resource units,

4. making lesson plans.

E. know the following:

1. the meaning of the terms

    a. long-range planning,
    b. short-range planning,
    c. learning unit,
    d. resource unit,
    e. lesson plan.
2. suggested outlines for preparing a
    a. learning unit,
    b. resource unit,
    c. lesson plan.

Chapter 7

PLANNING A LEARNING UNIT

WHAT IS PLANNING?

If we were to take a whirlwind tour of several classrooms of the nation, we would encounter such common sights as the following:

A twelfth-grade English class in New York State is reciting aloud the dagger soliloquy from *Macbeth*.

A tenth-grade biology class in South Dakota is dissecting a frog.

A ninth-grade mathematics class in Oregon is busy working problems applying the equation, $c^2 = a^2 + b^2$.

An eleventh-grade American History class in North Carolina is discussing the spoils system and the meaning of patronage.

A seventh-grade arithmetic class in Arizona is working with fractions on the blackboard and at their seats.

An eighth-grade physical education class in Indiana is square dancing.

Finally, a sight that makes one stop and ponder for a moment: A twelfth-grade English class in California is reciting aloud the dagger soliloquy from *Macbeth*.

The casual observer moves hastily on, perhaps approving of the diligence of the students or the capability of the teachers. The perceptive observer, however, pauses briefly and asks himself a few searching questions. Why are these students studying the particular subject matter? How did these particular items of content come to be parts of the courses he has observed? What items have been displaced and omitted while the selected items have been incorporated? Who has made the decision to teach the particular items that pupils are studying? How did the teachers know how to proceed in the teaching of the particular content?

It soon becomes apparent that teachers differ widely in their techniques of handling the subject matter of a course. This is especially noticeable when we observe teachers of the same subject in different schools dealing with the same general material. For example, let us extend our imaginary tour to include stops in the classrooms of several teachers of first-year Spanish who are reviewing the verbs *ser* and *estar*. We need not journey to various states to observe differences in techniques of presentation of subject matter. We can find variations among teachers in different schools of the same school system and, indeed, in different classrooms of the same school. In one large school system we can find the following teaching situations:

Teacher A has his group writing out review exercises in a standard commercial workbook.

Teacher B is reviewing aloud the answers to textbook exercises that the students have prepared as homework.

Teacher C is passing out a dittoed set of supplementary exercises which he has prepared and which he wishes the students to undertake.

Teacher D is asking questions orally in Spanish, using the verbs, and is requiring oral answers in Spanish from the students.

Teacher E has his students asking each other original questions in Spanish, using the verbs and responding to each other in Spanish.

Teacher F is using a language laboratory. Students are listening to a tape that employs the verbs and responding aloud to questions on the tape.

Teacher G is using a language laboratory that is more elaborate. Students are listening to a tape, responding aloud to questions on the tape, and recording their responses on tape at their positions.

Teacher H is showing students 20-by-24-inch pictures of situations that evoke oral responses using the verbs under review.

Teacher I is using individual, simple machines with programmed materials that teach the verbs *ser* and *estar*.

Again the perceptive observer asks himself a few pointed questions. Why are the teaching procedures so different in the several classes? Are all the teachers of first-year Spanish after the same objectives? How much effect do the facilities have on techniques of instruction? In what way have the teachers arrived at the techniques in progress? Do students learn as well under one teacher as under another? Seated at home after our tour of selected classrooms of the nation we sift our thoughts and arrive at the following conclusions:

In every classroom visited, teachers and learners were pursuing certain goals. Decisions had been made as to the choice of subject matter, the instructional materials and facilities to be used, and the ways of achieving the goals.

In every classroom some planning had been done by the teacher prior to presentation of the subject matter in the classroom.

In every classroom teachers were using highly individual means of instructing students. Though there were some points of similarity in goals, content and method, there were varying procedures, as demonstrated in the Spanish classrooms, for pursuing the topics under study.

Planning is the means of organizing the instructional program in such a way as to attain the goals of instruction. Planning is the process wherein the content, materials, and activities of the instructional program are organized in such a way that they may be meaningful to the learner. Planning permits maximum use of time, materials, and facilities available.

As we think through the evidences of planning in the several classrooms which we have visited, we can formulate five general principles of planning:

1. *Goals of instruction must be formulated.* They are set either by the teacher or by the teacher in cooperation with the learners.

2. *Content, materials, and activities must be selected.* They are chosen either by the teacher or by the teacher in cooperation with the learners.

3. *The content, materials, and activities selected should promote the goals of instruction and make best use of time, resources, and facilities available.*

4. *Ways of evaluating instruction must be devised.* They are devised by the teacher or by the teacher in cooperation with the learners.

5. *The learners should be encouraged to participate in the planning process to the extent of their competencies.* Opportunities for pupils to make decisions and suggestions should be provided by the teacher.

The question remains in our minds: How do teachers arrive at decisions on goals of instruction, selection of content, choice of materials, selection of activities, and choice of evaluative techniques? To consider this question we must examine the many kinds of planning that today's teachers do. For purposes of analysis we may categorize the teacher's endeavors in planning in respect to (a) levels of planning, (b) scope of planning, and (c) degree of shared responsibility.

LEVELS OF PLANNING

We may conceive of the levels of planning on which teachers work as a descending set of stairs. Schematically, we might depict our concept of levels as follows:

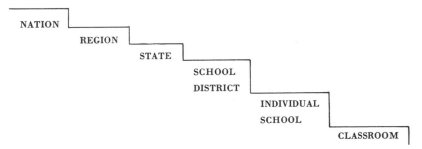

All classroom teachers are unavoidably concerned with planning at the classroom level. As we move up the stairs to each higher level the percentage of classroom teachers who are actively involved in planning is proportionately smaller, although, we hasten to add, countless teachers benefit by the planning done at each level.

On the national level teachers enter into planning of instructional programs, revision of materials, and studies of the curriculum. They may serve on study committees of their national professional organizations. They may participate in work sessions at national conferences. They may work with special national groups that are developing new and experimental programs.

Similarly, teachers participate, often as delegates of teachers' groups, to regional and state conferences of professional organizations.

Professional organizations have published materials that are helpful to classroom teachers in their planning. The professional organizations in the subject fields frequently give specific aids to teachers in planning for certain topics of study.

An outpouring of materials that help in classroom planning have come from regional, state, and district levels. Teachers have worked together to write curriculum guides that develop an entire sequence in a subject field. These curriculum guides show the scope or extent of a program and relative placement or sequence of topics. They suggest content, materials, and techniques.

Planning groups on the state, district, and individual school level are often engaged in the production of courses of study or syllabi, which detail the scope of a single course within a subject field.

In the individual classroom teachers are continuously involved in making plans for instruction of their own students. As a result of each effort in planning at each level teachers begin to make decisions on goals, content, materials, and techniques of instruction.

SCOPE OF PLANNING

The classroom teacher performs both long-range and short-range planning. He takes the long view when he asks himself: What will I teach in the sequence of courses in my subject field? What goals will I seek this year in this particular course? What should my students accomplish the first semester or the first six-week period?

When the teacher is involved in long-range planning, he attempts to visualize the over-all picture of his course. He uses all the instructional helps available to him and determines roughly the extent of his course in relation to the time available. He considers essential learnings which he feels he must cover in the scope of his course. He divides his program into rough segments and determines tentative goals, content, materials, and learning activities for each segment. He leaves considerable room for flexibility and change.

But he still knows where he is going and what he must teach. He knows also where he must include mandatory subject matter and where he may extend choice to pupils. He decides at what points he must himself plan and at what points pupils may join him in planning. When he has sketched his over-all plan, he turns to focus on short-range plans.

The teacher's short-range plans spell out what he hopes to achieve the next day, the next few days, the next week or two weeks. He may divide his subject matter into small components, perhaps using as his chief aid the basic textbook. He may organize his subject matter into unit form extending over the next week or two or possibly longer. In addition, he plans daily for each class. He prepares a lesson plan for each class period of the next day. As the classes proceed through their courses, the teacher continuously revises both his long-range and short-range plans.

SHARING OF RESPONSIBILITY

Reviewing our concept of levels of planning, we see that at all levels above the individual classroom teachers often share responsibilities in planning. Where teachers join together in team-teaching efforts they even share responsibilities of planning for instruction in the individual classrooms.

Teachers work together in their local faculties, planning for instruction and improving the school's program of studies. They work together on the district, state, regional, and national levels. In a sense, no teacher, even on the individual classroom level, works by himself in planning. He may draw up his own initial plans, but he often has assistance from pupils, other faculty members, administrators, and supervisors. He depends heavily on the work of others—authors of textbooks, curriculum guides, courses of study, and resource units.

Thus, if we repeat our question—How do teachers arrive at decisions on goals of instruction, selection of content, choice of materials, selection of activities, and choice of evaluative techniques?—we realize that teachers make their decisions using a variety of sources. They may find help in textbooks, programmed materials, curriculum guides, courses of study, even in state legislation which requires certain instruction. They select subject matter from our cultural heritage. They judge the needs of their learners. They consider their own strengths and weaknesses. All these factors enter into the intricate process of planning.

APPROACHES TO CLASSROOM PLANNING

The classroom teacher normally takes one of the following four general approaches to planning for his own instructional program. Although we shall draw the distinctions in these general approaches rather sharply, we must add that they are not mutually exclusive and that combinations of these approaches do obtain in many classrooms.

1. *The teacher plans for his classes using courses of study in the form of programmed materials that have been developed for him.* The teacher relies exclusively on the materials. No supplementary materials are deemed necessary. The programmed materials present the subject matter of the course in logical steps from the simplest element to the most complex. The goals, content, material, and learning activities are predetermined by the programmed materials themselves. The teacher's responsibilities in planning are limited. He may select from alternate programs on the market. He plans for use of facilities and time. As we have seen from our previous discussion of programmed instruction, the use of programmed materials is growing in our schools.

2. *The teacher plans for instruction using a single textbook.* He divides the content of the textbook into manageable segments. His instruction adheres closely to the textbook. His questions for class discussion are drawn from the text. Pupils are expected to supply answers given in the text. The teacher depends upon exercises that appear in the textbook or in a correlated workbook that accompanies the text.

3. *The teacher plans for instruction using a single textbook plus additional aids.* He divides the content of the textbook into portions. He departs from the textbook as the occasion warrants. He makes use of supplementary audio-visual aids, books, magazines, programmed materials, and exercises which he has created. The organizational structure of the textbook forms the backbone of the course, but the teacher injects a good deal of his own planning.

4. *The teacher plans for instruction around problems of the learner.* He makes his own organization of content and materials, using a wide variety of materials. His text is one of many aids. He may use several textbooks to present different points of view or different means of exposition of the content. He provides a variety of activities of differing levels of difficulty. The approach to planning which unifies intensive study of a problem or topic is commonly referred to as the unit method of teaching or simply, unit teaching.

In the first three approaches a considerable portion of the planning has been done for the teacher by the authors of the printed materials used. In the first two approaches and to a great extent in the third approach all students study the same materials. If any allowances are made for individual differences, they are made in the amount of content to be mastered by students or in the rate by which the content is mastered rather than in varied content. The fourth approach requires an original organization of the subject matter—a unit plan. It is to this fourth approach that we will devote more detailed attention.

WHAT IS A UNIT?

We may define a unit as an arrangement of materials and activities around a central topic. By unit teaching or the unit method of teaching we mean an instructional method followed by a teacher in a classroom when he uses units.

The reader will find in the literature references to a number of types of units. We shall focus on two principal types, the learning unit and the resource unit. "Instructional unit," "teaching unit," and "learning unit" are terms that convey essentially the same meaning. We shall use the last term in our discussion. A learning unit is a unit plan developed on a particular topic by the individual teacher with a specific class.

A resource unit, like the learning unit, is an arrangement of materials and activities around a particular topic or problem. It is much more comprehensive in nature than the learning unit and will be dealt with in the next chapter.

HOW DO WE CONSTRUCT LEARNING UNITS?

A learning unit should be constructed according to a pattern that will have meaning to the teacher who creates it. There is no single, "correct" way of constructing a learning unit. Any system which the teacher devises and which incorporates the salient features of a unit will prove satisfactory. Different authors of educational textbooks suggest different outlines which a teacher may follow. The outline used in the illustrative learning units that follow is a satisfactory outline for a learning unit in most subject fields of the high school curriculum. An experienced teacher will make modifications in his unit as he gains experience in unit construction. He will take short cuts which a beginning teacher should not attempt. A beginning teacher should follow an outline rather closely at first in constructing units. Once he has gained enough experience and insight as to where he can save time and effort, then he may modify the outline.

The reader will note that the seven units which make up this textbook are largely resource units. Many of the activities and much of the material have been used in learning units with the author's college classes. The basic units of this book serve a dual purpose as illustrations of units and as textual material.

We first show in its entirety the illustration of a learning unit for an English class, which we will refer to as Illustrative Learning Unit 1. We will proceed from that point to examine the construction of the component parts of a learning unit.

ILLUSTRATIVE LEARNING UNIT 1[1]

THE TWENTIETH CENTURY SPEAKS
THROUGH CARL SANDBURG

Twelfth-Grade English
Time: 2 weeks

A. Objectives

I. Teacher's Objectives

a. Understandings

1. To teach the understanding that Carl Sandburg was the poet of the common man confronted with the complexities of the new industrial civilization.

2. To teach the understanding that Carl Sandburg's diversified background better enabled him to write meaningful and genuine poetry.

3. To teach the understanding that Carl Sandburg fulfilled Whitman's prescription for a poet: That his country absorbs him as affectionately as he has absorbed it.

4. To teach the understanding that there are really two Carl Sandburgs—that he has two distinct styles of writing.

b. Appreciations

1. To develop an appreciation for contemporary poetry as exemplified by that of Carl Sandburg.

2. To develop an appreciation of the ways in which Carl Sandburg captures and combines the popular idiom and common idealism of the American people.

3. To develop an appreciation of both Carl Sandburgs: the heavy-hitting realist and the shadowy imagist.

c. Attitudes

1. To develop the attitude that poetry is for boys as well as for girls.

2. To develop the attitude that poetry can be as entertaining and enjoyable as any other form of literature.

3. To develop an attitude of respect for Carl Sandburg's ability to portray accurately the time in which he writes.

d. Special abilities and skills

1. To improve the student's ability to read out loud to an audience.

2. To improve the student's ability to read and comprehend poetry.

[1] Prepared by Beverly Tolan, 1958.

3. To teach the student to identify and define various mechanics of poetry.

4. To develop some skill on the part of the student in expressing himself in poetic form.

    e. Facts

        1. To achieve these facts about Carl Sandburg:

            a) At one time or another he held almost every conceivable job.

            b) His parents were from Sweden and he later spent some months there as a correspondent for the *Chicago Daily News.*

            c) He has been awarded the Pulitzer Prize plus many honorary degrees.

            d) He became known with the writing of *Chicago.*

            e) He is very devoted to his family.

            f) He has written prose biography, children's tales and lyrics, and American ballads, as well as poetry.

  II. Pupil's Objectives

    a. Why do authors write poetry instead of prose?

    b. Why did Carl Sandburg switch occupations so much?

    c. Is Carl Sandburg still living?

    d. Why does Carl Sandburg write with very few punctuation marks?

    e. What kind of boyhood did Carl Sandburg have?

    f. Isn't poetry sissified?

B. Overview

This unit covers the life and poetry of Carl Sandburg in such a manner as to give a well-rounded view of his personality and abilities. The unit is planned to develop a real understanding of the poet as a human being and poetry as a revealing and enjoyable pastime. Activities in the unit provide opportunities for extensive pupil participation which will bring them closer to the poet and to his writing.

C. Approaches

1. Make a bulletin-board display with an aerial view of the city of Chicago and a copy of Sandburg's poem "Chicago" beneath it.

2. Conduct a class discussion on the topic: Do you think poetry is just for girls? Follow the discussion with illustrations of poems that have a male appeal, such as "The Congo," "Invictus," and "The Charge of the Light Brigade."

D. Working Period

Learning Activities	*Desired Outcome*
1. Oral reports by students on:	1. To give students an opportunity
a. Several aspects of Sandburg's life	to present information to class.

Learning Activities (cont'd)

b. Sandburg's realistic poetry
c. Sandburg's imaginative poetry
d. The mechanics of Sandburg's poetry

2. Have each member of the class write a newspaper article about some event in Sandburg's life for a make-believe newspaper published at the time the event occurred.

3. Have a respected man from the community who is interested in poetry come to class and discuss the value of poetry.

4. Have various students read some of Sandburg's more well-known poems and have either piano or record background music. Recommended poems: "Cool Tombs" and ",The People, Yes."

5. Play the recording, "Sandburg Reads Sandburg."

6. Conduct a choral reading of the poem, "I Am the People, the Mob."

7. Have the class arrange appropriate pantomime actions to "Chicago." Stage a short musical act by playing a background record, having group interpretative actions, and the reading of the poem.

8. Hold a discussion and evaluation of several of Sandburg's poems, led by a member of the class.

9. Pass out copies of the following poems:
   "Chicago"

Desired Outcome (cont'd)

2. To make the event more meaningful by putting it into the present tense.

3. To show the pupils that poetry is not confined to the classroom.

4. To teach the pupils to identify moods in poetry.
To give oral reading practice.

5. To let students hear the real rhythm of Sandburg's work as read by the author himself.

6. To give more feeling to the poem by actually sounding like a group or mob.

7. To enhance the word pictures of the poem through interpretative actions.
To give practice in dramatic interpretation.

8. To teach the class how to judge the value of a piece of writing.
To give students a chance to lead a discussion.

9. To demonstrate how poetry has different meaning for different individuals.

Learning Activities (cont'd)

"A Fence"

"Washerwoman"

"Stars, Songs, Faces"

"I Am the People, the Mob"

Give three of these to every student. Ask students to look in magazines and newspapers and cut out a picture which best expresses the mood and theme of the poems. Bring to class for discussion.

10. Have various students bring samples to class of another contemporary poet and compare the themes, styles, and appeal of the other poet and Sandburg.

11. Discuss Sandburg's lack of conventional style and punctuation. Quote Sandburg's humorous poem about the centipede that tried so hard to think how to run that she couldn't run.

   Ask the students to tell how this is related to the problem of punctuation.

12. Have students write poems imitating as closely as possible Sandburg's style.

13. Have the class prepare a display of pictures and poems they have collected and original poems they have written during the two weeks of the unit.

Desired Outcome (cont'd)

10. To give the class a better perspective by which to place a value judgment on Sandburg's poetry.

11. To show the students that too much attention can be paid to mechanics.

   To show the students that originality and creativity are to be highly valued.

   To show the students that all poetry does not have to follow the same form.

12. To stimulate an interest in writing poetry.

   To provide opportunity for creative activity.

   To see if the students have grasped Sandburg's style.

13. To serve as a culminating activity, tying together various aspects of their study.

E. Evaluation Techniques

   1. Teacher observation of student performance such as effort and initiative in gathering materials, interest shown, and discussion.

   2. Teacher judgment of creative activity of the pupils in writing poems, dramatic interpretations, pantomimes, art work, etc.

3. Group evaluation of their own success in pursuing the topic. Class selection of best poems.

4. Tests to include:

a. High spots in Sandburg's life.

b. Identification of the more familiar lines of Sandburg's poetry.

c. Interpretation of some poem of Sandburg's not covered in class.

d. Comparison of one of Sandburg's poems with that of another contemporary author.

e. Oral reading of a few lines of Sandburg's poetry.

F. Bibliography

1. *a.* Books useful to the teacher

Hook, J. N. *The Teaching of High School English.* New York: Ronald Press, 1959. Chapter 7.

b. Magazine articles useful to the teacher

Corbin, Richard. "The Aesthetic Experiencing of a Poem," *The English Journal,* 46 (December 1957), 564–69.

2. *a.* Books useful to both the teacher and the pupils

Bradley, Sculley, Beatty, Richard, and Long, E. Hudson. *The American Tradition in Literature.* New York: W. W. Norton, 1957, pp. 681–89.

Foerster, Norman and Charvat, William, eds. *American Prose and Poetry.* New York: Houghton Mifflin, 1952, pp. 749–53.

Sandburg, Carl. *Always the Young Strangers.* New York: Harcourt, Brace and Co., 1953. 448 pp.

Sandburg, Carl. *Complete Poems.* New York: Harcourt, Brace and Co., 1951. 676 pp.

b. Magazine articles useful to both the teacher and the pupils

Emerson, William A., Jr. "At Home: All Brightness and Whiteness," *Newsweek,* 45 (February 14, 1955), 53.

"A Visit With Carl Sandburg," *Look Magazine,* 20 (July 10, 1956), 95–100.

McGill, Ralph. "The Most Unforgettable Character I've Met," *Reader's Digest,* 64 (May 1954), 109–13.

Sandburg, Carl. "Acquaintance with Death, Sit," *Colliers,* 138 (December 7, 1956), 31.

Waldrop, Evelyn Brock. "Carl Sandburg, the Musician," *Etude,* 73 (September 1955), 11, 41–43.

G. Instructional Aids and Sources
   1. Photographs of Carl Sandburg in:
     a. Américas, 6 (September 1954), 4.
     b. Look, 18 (September 7, 1954), 58.
     c. Look, 18 (November 30, 1954), 10.
     d. Newsweek, 43 (March 22, 1954), 104.
     e. Saturday Review, 36 (December 10, 1953), 10.
     f. Senior Scholastic, 65 (November 3, 1954), 17-T.
     g. Senior Scholastic, 69 (January 11, 1957), 25.

   2. Recording, *Carl Sandburg Reads the Poems of Carl Sandburg.*
Decca 9039. 12″ LP. $3.98.

   3. Frank J. Greene, 4113 N.W. 15th Street, local. Free-lance writer.
To speak on poetry.

The foregoing learning unit follows the suggested outline below.

SUGGESTED OUTLINE OF A LEARNING UNIT

TITLE OF UNIT

Grade level for which designed
Approximate time to be devoted to the unit.

A. Objectives
   I. Teacher's objectives
     a. Understandings
     b. Appreciations
     c. Attitudes
     d. Special abilities and skills
     e. Facts
   II. Pupils' objectives
B. Overview
C. Approaches
D. Working Period
E. Evaluation Techniques
F. Bibliography
G. Instructional Aids and Sources

This suggested outline can be readily used in most high school subjects.
Let us take a closer look at each of the parts of the outline of the learning
unit, explain what should be contained in each part, and illustrate each part
by referring to Illustrative Learning Unit 1.

TITLE

The title of the unit may be stated as a simple word or phrase such as "Conservation Practices in Utah" or may be written as a question such as "How Is the State of Utah Conserving Its Natural Resources?" Whatever the topic or problem, it should be specific enough to permit adequate study during the time allotted. All-encompassing themes such as "World Geography" or "The Literature of England" or "The History of Mankind" do not fit the concept of a learning unit. The topic must be narrow enough to give hope for study and progress toward solution or understanding during the brief time permitted.

The title of Illustrative Learning Unit 1 reads: "The Twentieth Century Speaks Through Carl Sandburg."

GRADE LEVEL

The grade level for which the unit is designed should be specifically mentioned on the title page of the unit. A teacher creates a unit for a specific class or at most for a specific grade level in a specific course. A learning unit on "Banking" for a seventh-grade class would differ from one made for a twelfth-grade class. Provided the unit incorporates a wide range of activities for students of varying abilities, it is possible and sensible to develop one unit for the teacher's grade level and use the same unit with appropriate adaptations in each of the teacher's sections of the same grade level.

Illustrative Learning Unit 1 has been prepared for twelfth-grade English.

TIME

The approximate time which the teacher wishes to devote to the topic should be estimated and stated. A unit should last a reasonable period of time. A project of two or three days' duration is not a unit in the usual sense of the term. Generally, units will run from one to three or four weeks, possibly longer, depending upon the scope of the unit, its relative importance in the course, needs of the students, and the material available.

The time allotted to Illustrative Learning Unit 1 is two weeks.

OBJECTIVES

By objectives we mean the outcomes or goals of a unit to be attained during its progress. It should be pointed out that the objectives given in the suggested outline include more than facts. The unit method insists on the setting up of specific understandings, appreciations, and attitudes as well as skills and facts.

Objectives are classified in two parts: (I) teacher's objectives, and (II) pupils' objectives. By teacher's objectives we mean the outcomes which the teacher plans in advance for the students to achieve. By pupils' objectives we mean the identification by the teacher of possible or probable pupil interests and questions. The section on pupils' objectives could conceivably be eliminated from a unit. However, preparing a section on pupils' objectives is a valuable way by which a teacher can project himself into the pupil's role and ask himself what things a pupil might ask about the topic. Pupils' objectives can be stated as questions that pupils might ask. This section can be validated by the teacher after he has heard the questions the pupils do ask. Close approximation to the pupil's actual questions will show the teacher that he is able to identify in advance the types of questions his students might raise. It is conceivable, probable, and in many cases desirable that the teacher's objectives and the pupils' objectives coincide.

TEACHER'S OBJECTIVES

There are five main types of teacher's objectives. These are:

a. *Understandings.* These learnings are intellectualized concepts or ideas, generalizations that can be drawn from the topic. In some ways the objectives of understandings resemble the objectives of facts. But an understanding does not detail specific data. It generalizes from the facts. Actually, an understanding is the type of learning that sticks with the individual longer than the specific facts.

Understandings may be stated in a number of ways. They must be clear and they should be consistent in form. One satisfactory formula for writing an understanding is: To teach the understanding that. . . . For example, we might write, "To teach the understanding that ancient Persia contributed much to the modern world." Or, the understanding may be written simply, "Ancient Persia contributed much to the modern world."

A variation in the pattern of wording understandings may be found in the form, "To teach the understanding of contributions of the ancient Persians to the modern world." The author would consider this an acceptable statement but not as direct or clear as in the paragraph above.

The use of the expression, "To teach the understanding of . . ." often leads to complications and lack of clarity. "To teach the understanding of war" would not be an acceptable statement of an understanding. Within that broad phrase could be a number of understandings which the teacher would need to specify. Does the teacher want the pupils to know that "war is hell," that war never solved anything, that men have fought wars since the dawn of history, that war has many causes, or that we have been at war with Germany twice in the first half of this century? Perhaps, the teacher wishes to convey all of these understandings to the pupils. If so, the understandings should be expressly stated in the unit.

"To teach democracy" or "To teach citizenship" are not suitable as statements of understandings. They have two serious weaknesses as objectives of a unit. They are far too remote for accomplishing in one unit. The school hopes that its clientele will have learned good traits of citizenship on completion of the entire curriculum. No single unit can possibly hope to accomplish such an ambitious goal. Secondly, these two objectives are impossible to evaluate with any degree of precision. Every objective that a teacher sets up should be capable of evaluation in some manner. If the objectives are too remote, too vague, or too abstract, they cannot be evaluated well. The teacher will be successful in writing these objectives if he will remember that he must clearly state the complete idea that he wishes the pupils to retain.

> The author of Illustrative Learning Unit 1 has decided upon four understandings, the first of which reads, "To teach the understanding that Carl Sandburg was the poet of the common man confronted with the complexities of the new industrial civilization."

b. Appreciations. Appreciations are value judgments, which are learning outcomes as important as any facts a student may learn. Appreciations, like understandings and attitudes, may be retained long after specific learnings are forgotten.

Appreciations may be stated in the form, "To develop an appreciation of (or for). . . ." For example, in a unit on "Technology in The United States" the teacher might desire students "To develop an appreciation of the high standard of living in this country." Other illustrations of statements of appreciations to be taught by various units might be "To develop an appreciation of the advanced stage of civilization among the Maya Indians," "To develop an appreciation for the depth of feeling in the poems of Browning," "To develop an appreciation of the calypso rhythms of the West Indies," "To develop an appreciation for the skill of Grandma Moses," and "To develop an appreciation of William Shakespeare's insight into human nature."

Statements such as "To appreciate art," "To appreciate music," "To appreciate literature," and "To appreciate Ernest Hemingway" should be avoided, since they are too vague and too broad. Further, statements of this kind cannot be evaluated well because of their all-inclusive nature.

> Three appreciations are sought in Illustrative Learning Unit 1. The second of these is stated, "To develop an appreciation of the ways in which Carl

Sandburg captures and combines the popular idiom and common idealism of the American people."

c. *Attitudes.* Attitudes are dispositions to action. Like appreciations they are emotional in nature. Attitudes are significant learnings that need to be specified. Attitudes, whether positive or negative, are types of learnings that often become permanent. It is the school's task throughout every course in its curriculum to inculcate positive attitudes that will be beneficial to our society.

Attitudes and appreciations and to some extent understandings are often referred to as "concomitant learnings." These are the learnings that accompany the usual subject matter. Concomitant learnings are often ignored in the teaching process. A student in geometry, for example, may be learning a number of theorems related to congruent triangles. He may be learning concomitantly to detest math (attitude), that this particular study has little application in everyday life (understanding), and that mathematics is hard work (appreciation). These are illustrations of negative concomitant learnings. Since positive learnings, especially attitudes toward work, toward other individuals, and toward citizenship, are so vital to life in a democracy, these outcomes cannot be left to chance. The teacher will seek to develop positive attitudes as objectives of his instruction in order to combat negative attitudes that might otherwise develop.

Attitudes may be stated in a unit as "To develop (or foster) the attitude of. . . ." For example, we might include "To develop the attitude of tolerance for other people's ideas." "To foster the attitude of cooperation when working in small groups," "To foster the attitude of persistence in seeking solutions to one's problems," and "To develop the attitude of acceptance of responsibility" are further illustrations of statements of attitudes.

An acceptable variant in the statement of attitudes is the expression, "To develop the attitude that. . . ." The teacher then goes on to state the specific attitude. For example, "To develop the attitude that it does make a difference what peoples of other countries think of us" is a clear statement of the teacher's objective. Other illustrations of this type are "To develop the attitude that eligible voters should vote in a democracy" and "To develop the attitude that every person behind the wheel of an automobile must act thoughtfully and courteously." Note that attitudes are usually normative in the way they are phrased. They often contain words like "should," "ought," and "must."

The source of all these objectives rests in the teacher's mind. It can readily be seen as we analyze the first three types of objectives—understandings, appreciations, and attitudes—that the objectives will differ considerably from teacher to teacher, depending on the learnings the individual teacher wishes to emphasize.

The first of the three attitudes found in Illustrative Learning Unit 1 is written: "To develop the attitude that poetry is for boys as well as for girls."

d. Special abilities and skills. Most teachers can readily identify abilities and skills as objectives of instruction. These are much more obvious aims than the foregoing types of objectives. Skill objectives may be stated in a variety of ways, such as: "To learn to make foul shots," "To learn to do the Australian crawl," "To improve sight reading and comprehension," "To achieve a basic Spanish vocabulary of 200 words," "To learn to trill an *r*," "To memorize Mark Antony's eulogy of Caesar in Shakespeare's *Julius Caesar*," "To reach a typing speed of 60 words per minute," "To learn to distinguish between good fabrics and cheap fabrics," "To learn to detect propaganda in the news," "To learn to hook electric lights in series," "To develop the skill of meeting people," "To learn the correct manner of introducing persons," and "To learn the skills of parliamentary procedure."

Along with the following category, facts, teachers have been most concerned with the learning outcomes of skills and facts.

The special abilities and skills sought in Illustrative Learning Unit 1 are: "To improve the student's ability to read out loud to an audience," "To improve the student's ability to read and comprehend poetry," "To teach the student to identify and define various mechanics of poetry," and "To develop some skill on the part of the student of expressing himself in poetic form."

e. Facts. In this section on objectives of the unit the teacher details the specific subject matter he wishes to include during the course of the unit. The section may be as simple or as detailed as the teacher wishes to make it. Since specifying every detail may be too comprehensive, the teacher can outline his subject matter if he desires rather than list every specific fact. Examples of statements of the specific subject matter are "To achieve a mastery of selected new words and their meanings" (list new words to be studied), "To achieve these facts about atomic energy" (list principal facts to be studied), "To learn these facts about the Revolutionary War" (list the principal facts), and "To learn the significant facts about the Middle East as outlined below" (outline).

Illustrative Learning Unit 1 outlines six facts about Carl Sandburg which the teacher wishes students to learn.

These five categories constitute the teacher's objectives. The teacher should include several statements under each category, if possible. The textbooks available will help the teacher in arriving at statements of understandings, skills, and facts. Statements of appreciations and attitudes, however, are not so quickly prepared, since textbooks frequently neglect these outcomes of learning. Statements of these last two types of objectives will require particular resourcefulness on the part of the creative teacher.

PUPILS' OBJECTIVES

In the unit's section on pupils' objectives the teacher should state in the terms a pupil would use probable questions pupils might ask about the topic. Let us illustrate this with a unit on "The Government of Our Town." The teacher must project himself into the role of the pupil in writing pupil objectives. With a unit of this nature pupils might ask:

a. Do we have a mayor?
b. Who is the mayor?
c. Where does the name of our town come from?
d. Who helps the mayor run the town?
e. Is the mayor paid?
f. How is the mayor elected?
g. Where do our taxes go?
h. Why are taxes so high?
i. How are taxes calculated?
j. What is an assessor?
k. What is the difference between a village and a town?
l. What do they do with the money from the parking meters?
m. Is it possible to fix a traffic ticket?
n. What does a Justice of the Peace do?
o. How could I get on the police force?

Pupils tend to ask specific questions of a concrete nature. They ask questions that may occur to them or their parents in daily life. By anticipating their questions the teacher can make the unit more interesting to the pupil and thereby motivate him to want to find out more about the topic. The teacher can lead through the concrete questions to greater understandings and broader learnings as he has planned for them in his section on teacher's objectives. One great value of the section on pupils' objectives is that it gives the teacher the opportunity to see if he is still able to visualize how those whom he is charged to teach actually think. The teacher will realize that as the students go up the ladder to the higher grades their questions will become more abstract, deeper, and broader. In writing pupils' objectives teachers will need to keep in mind the developmental level and experience of the students with whom he will be using the unit.

Illustrative Learning Unit 1 poses six questions in the section on pupils' objectives:

a. Why do authors write poetry instead of prose?
b. Why did Carl Sandburg switch occupations so much?
c. Is Carl Sandburg still living?
d. Why does Carl Sandburg write with very few punctuation marks?
e. What kind of boyhood did Carl Sandburg have?
f. Isn't poetry sissified?

OVERVIEW

The overview is a brief statement of the nature and scope of the unit. It can be written in narrative style or it can be outlined with the themes to be considered in the unit. It may contain justification for the unit and it may stress the value and importance of dealing with the particular topic. This section of the unit should not be extensive. A paragraph or two will often suffice.

The Overview of Illustrative Learning Unit 1 consists of three sentences: "This unit covers the life and poetry of Carl Sandburg in such a manner as to give a well-rounded view of his personality and abilities. The unit is planned to develop a real understanding of the poet as a human being and poetry as a revealing and enjoyable pastime. Activities in the unit provide opportunities for extensive pupil participation which will bring them closer to the poet and to his writing."

APPROACHES

The section on approaches should contain one or two ways of introducing the unit to the pupils. The approaches consist of activities which will engage the interests of the pupils so they will want to pursue the topic of the unit. A teacher with a flare for the dramatic will find that talent beneficial when it comes to stimulating a group of pupils to go to work on a particular topic. A unit might be started simply by taking a question a pupil has raised in class and opening the problem to class study. For example, a pupil's question on the Big Dipper might launch a seventh-grade class in science on a unit on astronomy. A comment on a television program such as the Columbia Broadcasting System's dramatization of *The Plot to Kill Stalin* might plunge a social studies class into a unit on totalitarianism.

If the teacher finds it necessary to spark interest himself, he might bring to class some tangible items connected with the topic he will propose for class study. A captured Nazi flag or a German Luger could kick off a unit on Naziism. The booming voice of John L. Lewis as transcribed on the record *I Can Hear It Now* could be used to introduce a unit on labor unions or labor-management relations. An attractive display of books and pictures about the life and times of Abraham Lincoln could stimulate interest in commencing work on a unit related to Lincoln. Some picture postcards or slides of Athens could serve as an approach to a unit on life in ancient Greece. A bulletin-board display of pictures and articles on flying saucers could be employed in physics class to introduce a unit on the phenomenon of light.

The possibilities are endless for ways to approach a unit. The means used will vary considerably from teacher to teacher. A technique as simple as reading from an article clipped from last night's newspaper may serve to begin a unit. The teacher should use a technique that will arouse curiosity. For example, the writing of an unfamiliar word or term on the blackboard is a technique used by some teachers to introduce a topic. Antidisestablishmentarianism is not only one of the longest words in the English language but it also provides a way of opening a discussion of the regime of William Gladstone in nineteenth-century England and church-state relations. "The woggly bird sat on the whango tree" could be used to inaugurate a unit on humorous literature or even on "Communicating Our Ideas Clearly." $E=mc^2$ can be placed on the board in the science class to start a unit on atomic energy.

It is advisable for the teacher to plan at least two approaches so that he may supplement the first approach, if necessary.

A word of caution in handling approaches to units should be given. There may be times when the teacher stimulates pupil interest in the topic for which he has made plans to teach. On the other hand, questions may arise related to topics which he did not plan to introduce immediately or on topics for which he had no unit planned. If a topic arises which he had not planned to introduce at that point but which fits into the scope of the course and can be appropriately introduced at that time, it would be more desirable to make fresh plans or a completely new unit on the topic raised than to try to force artificial interest in the topic which the teacher had in mind.

> Illustrative Learning Unit 1 uses two simple approaches: (1) a bulletin-board display with an aerial view of Chicago and a copy of Sandburg's poem, "Chicago," beneath the picture and (2) a class discussion on the topic: Do you think poetry is just for girls? The discussion is to be followed with illustrations of poems that have a male appeal.

WORKING PERIOD

The working period is the heart of the unit. The working period sets forth in some detail all of the activities that a teacher will use or may use with the class to pursue the topic of the unit. The term "activities" is used in this case in its broadest sense to mean anything the teacher or students do. Under this definition would come teacher lecture, class discussion, oral reports, debate, written reports, reading of textbooks, library research, art work, manual work, viewing of films and filmstrips, creative activity of all kinds, dramatizations, listening to records, field trips, use of community resources, use of resource persons, drill work, taking tests and other types of evaluation.

The activities in the working period are planned with a specific class in mind. The teacher should seek to provide enough types of activities of varying levels of difficulty to allow for individual differences in his class. Some flexibility will be needed to adapt the activities to class planning as the teacher goes along with the unit. The teacher will also want to be certain that he has enough worthwhile activities to carry the class through the time allotted to the unit.

Beginning and prospective teachers will find it desirable to give one or two possible objectives for each activity planned. For example, if the teacher lists "field trip to the local dairy" as an activity during the working period, possible outcomes for this activity might be "To develop the understanding that people are interdependent for their food supplies," "To develop an appreciation for the hard-working dairy farmer," "To learn how dairy products are transported, processed, and marketed," and "To learn the techniques of pasteurization." The types of outcomes listed with each activity can be drawn from any of the five categories of teacher objectives mentioned earlier in this discussion.

No activity planned in advance by the teacher should be considered so fixed that it is not subject to change when work has begun. Opportunities should be continually extended to the pupils to help in planning the various activities in which the class will participate during the course of the unit. The unit should be subject to continuous change as the situation requires. Some activities may have to be discarded, others added, and some revised. Opportunities for choice should be offered to the pupils. The unit under study should not be considered as solely the teacher's unit or as the pupils' unit but as a joint teacher-pupil enterprise.

Illustrative Learning Unit 1 makes use of a great variety of activities including:

> oral reports by students
> writing of newspaper articles
> resource person from the community
> individual oral readings
> listening to a record
> choral reading

pantomime
class discussion
clipping pictures from newspapers
writing original poems
display

Objectives sought appear with each activity.

EVALUATION TECHNIQUES

This part of the unit incorporates techniques used to determine whether or not the objectives of the unit have been realized. Tests are the most common form of evaluation in use in our schools. To written tests modern methods of evaluation would add teacher observation of students' behavior, evaluation of results of creative activity, rating scales of student performance, check lists, self-evaluation by the individual student, group evaluation of its own work, teacher evaluation of notebooks, diaries, and logs, and teacher-pupil evaluation of the successes and failures of the unit.

Most difficult of the categories of objectives to evaluate are appreciations and attitudes. It is doubtful if the achievement of these objectives can be measured by ordinary tests. The evaluation of appreciations and attitudes lies more in the direction of teacher observation and judgment, self-evaluation by the student, counseling of the student by the teacher, analysis of creative work, and observation of work habits and conversation of students inside and outside of class.

The teacher will need to evaluate student achievement and performance continuously during the progress of the unit rather than to give one large, all-inclusive written test at the end of the unit.

Illustrative Learning Unit 1 has provision for four evaluation techniques: teacher observation of student performance in relation to effort, initiative, interest, and discussion; teacher judgment of creative activity of pupils; group's evaluation of its success; and written tests.

BIBLIOGRAPHY

In this section the teacher will list all books and magazine references pertaining to the topic that are available either locally or by sending for them. It will prove helpful to break this bibliography into two major parts, books and magazines useful to the teacher for information and supplementary background, and books and magazines useful to the students for pursuing their study of the topic.

Books and magazines should be listed in an acceptable bibliographical form so that the reference may be readily found in the library or ordered from its source.

A number of styles are acceptable.[2] Whatever style the teacher uses, he should follow the same style throughout the section of the unit. References are listed in alphabetical order, author's last name first. Book and periodical references should be separated, with books listed first and then periodicals.

> Illustrative Learning Unit 1 lists in its bibliography one book useful to the teacher, one magazine article useful to the teacher, five books useful to both the teacher and the pupils, and five magazine articles useful to both the teacher and the pupils.

INSTRUCTIONAL AIDS AND SOURCES

The teacher should include in this last portion of a learning unit references to any aids and sources other than books and periodical references. This section would include references to charts, maps, photographs, records, tapes, films, filmstrips, slides, persons and places to visit, persons to invite to the classroom, and any other materials useful for the topic.

All references should be complete enough so the teacher will know exactly what the item is and where he can get it. If there is any cost for the item and the cost is known, this would be a helpful piece of information to include.

> Illustrative Learning Unit 1 includes three types of instructional aids and sources: photographs, recordings, and a resource person.

It will be noted that a considerable amount of planning has been done by the teacher in advance of the presentation of a unit in class. It will also be noted that subject matter remains the central focus of the unit. For this reason some teachers refer to the type of unit herein illustrated as a subject-matter unit.

Planning in advance does not rule out flexibility or pupil participation in planning. Although a considerable amount of planning has been done by the teacher, the unit should not be considered inviolate. Pupils can and should participate in refining the goals, choosing activities, selecting materials, and evaluating. Pupils may also make choices in selecting with the teacher alternates in equally desirable topics which they wish to study.

Following is Illustrative Learning Unit 2, prepared for a high school class in social studies. The two illustrative learning units should serve to

---

[2] See *National Education Association Style Manual for Writers and Editors* (Washington: National Education Association, 1962), and Kate L. Turabian, *A Manual For Writers of Term Papers, Theses, and Dissertations* (Chicago: University of Chicago Press, 1955).

give a picture of the type of planning that can be done by a teacher who has a little creativeness and imagination.

ILLUSTRATIVE LEARNING UNIT 2[3]

WORLD WAR II AND ITS IMPACT ON WORLD CONDITIONS

Twelfth-Grade Social Studies
Time: 2 weeks

A. Objectives

I. Teacher's objectives

  a. Understandings

1. To teach the understanding that the effects of World War II are still evident.

2. To teach the understanding that the United States played the major role in bringing victory over the Axis.

3. To teach the understanding that World War II was fought to preserve freedom.

4. To teach the understanding that World War II thrust world leadership on the United States.

5. To teach the understanding that the United States can never revert to isolationism.

6. To teach the understanding that appeasement does not pay.

  b. Appreciations

1. To develop an appreciation for the all-out effort of American industry and the American public.

2. To develop an appreciation of the sacrifices many of our American boys made.

3. To develop an appreciation of our American freedoms.

4. To develop an appreciation of the difficult job our statesmen now have in preserving the peace.

5. To develop an appreciation for the skill and courage of our armed services.

  c. Attitudes

1. To develop the attitude of repugnance for dictatorship in any form.

2. To develop the attitude of willingness and desire to protect our American liberties.

3. To develop the attitude of repugnance for the atrocities and devastations caused by World War II.

[3] Prepared by Marjorie Crittenden, 1958.

4. To develop an attitude of cooperation with other countries and other peoples.

5. To develop an attitude of sympathy for peoples who suffered from the war.

d. Special abilities and skills

1. To gain insight into the motives and aims of various countries of the world.

2. To improve the student's ability to read history with understanding.

3. To enable the student to detect the relationships between men and events.

e. Facts

1. Economic, social, and political causes of World War II.

2. Principal names, dates, and places.

3. Economic, social, and political problems left by World War II.

II. Pupils' objectives

1. What was a Nazi?

2. What kinds of men were Roosevelt, Churchill, and Stalin?

3. Who started the war?

4. Why did the Japanese bomb Pearl Harbor?

5. How many American soldiers were killed in the war?

6. Did we have atom bombs during the Second World War?

7. Whose side was Russia on?

8. Will we have another war?

B. Overview

The purpose of this unit is to teach the economic, social, and political causes of World War II. The unit takes up the progress of the war itself and the postwar complications. The main themes of the unit are (1) steps leading up to the war, (2) the war itself, and (3) postwar conditions, including efforts to prevent another war.

C. Approaches

1. Bring to class some war trophies from veterans in the community, such as a Samurai sword, a German pistol, a Japanese or Nazi flag.

2. Display interesting printed materials and pictures related to the war years.

D. Working Period

Learning Activities	*Desired Outcomes*
1. Textbook assignments Class discussion of assignments	1. To learn specific information about the prewar, war, and postwar years.

2. Prepare and give oral reports individually or in small groups. Possible topics include:
Roosevelt
Churchill
Hitler
Mussolini
Stalin
Tojo
The war in Europe
The war in the Pacific
The role of the U. S. Army
The role of the U. S. Air Force
The role of the U. S. Navy
The role of the U. S. Marines
Famous generals: Eisenhower, Marshall, Bradley, Patton, MacArthur, Arnold
Famous admirals: Halsey, Nimitz
Pearl Harbor
D-Day in Europe
Concentration camps
American industry in war
The atomic bomb
Lend-lease
Battle of Britain
Fall of France
Battle of the Bulge
The Marshall Plan and Foreign aid
The formation of the United Nations

3. Permit students to select a second topic from the list above and prepare a written report on it.

4. Show the films:
The World at War
Battle of Britain
Other excellent films as available.

5. Conduct debates on the following topics:

2. To give students opportunities for doing research.
To provide additional information on principal topics related to the war.
To give students opportunities to prepare oral reports.

3. To give students an opportunity for writing a research paper.
To supply added information.

4. To stimulate interest in pursuing the topic in greater detail.

5. To give students practice in debating.

Learning Activities (cont'd)

Should we have dropped the atomic bomb on Hiroshima?
Is foreign aid necessary?
Should the U. S. support the U. N.?

6. Conduct panel discussions on:
The meaning of Munich
Universal military training

7. Play the recordings:
"I Can Hear It Now," Vols. 1 and 2.
Recordings of music of the 1940's

8. Invite any of the following resource persons to speak to the class or to be interviewed by a committee of the class:
A local merchant to talk about rationing and shortages on the home front.
A member of the draft board to discuss how the draft operated.
A biology teacher to discuss Hitler's Aryan myth of the Master Race.
A health educator to discuss the high rate of rejections of men from service because of physical defects.

9. Creative work:
Keep a scrapbook of articles and pictures of the war.
Make charts classifying the policies of the U. S., Germany, Japan, Italy, Britain, France, and Russia at the outbreak of the war in 1939 and at the time of Pearl Harbor.

Desired Outcomes (cont'd)

To permit students to think through controversial problems.

6. To give practice in panel discussion.

7. To give students the opportunity to hear actual voices of many of the great persons of the era.
To stimulate interest in the topic and make it real to the students.
To acquaint students with music of the period.

8. To show the students that the war affected the lives of members of their community.
To show how democracy works in wartime.
To dispel the Master Race myth.
To seek solutions of the problem of poor health among our young people.

9. To apply visual education and creative activity to the study of the war.

Draw maps or sketches of some
of the major campaigns of the
war.

10. If located near enough, visit
United Nations Headquarters.

10. To see first-hand the nations of
the world discussing their problems.

E. Evaluation Techniques

1. Teacher observation of student participation in class discussion, research activities, and committee work.

2. Teacher judgment of student's performance on oral reports, papers, debates, panel discussions, etc.

3. Students' appraisal of their own work.

4. Tests

a. Written tests, both objective and essay type.

b. Map drill asking students to point out principal geographical locations.

c. Frequent short written or oral quizzes, as a name or two to identify, an issue to comment on.

F. Bibliography

1. Books useful to the teacher

a. Commager, Henry S., ed., *Story of the Second World War*. Boston: Little, Brown, 1945.

b. Hall, Walter Phelps. *World Wars and Revolutions*. New York: Appleton-Century-Crofts, 1952.

c. U. S. Department of State. *Our Foreign Policy*. Washington: U. S. Government Printing Office, annually. $0.25.

2. Books useful to the student

a. Faulkner, Harold, and Kepner, Tyler. *America, Its History and People*. New York: McGraw-Hill, 1950.

b. Muzzey, David S. *A History of Our Country*. Boston: Ginn and Co., 1950.

G. Instructional Aids and Sources

1. Films

The World at War. 45 min. Traces development of events from 1931 to Pearl Harbor. Washington: U. S. Office of Education.

The Battle of Britain. 5 reels. Shows the Luftwaffe's assault on Britain. From Association Films, 35 West 45th Street, New York 10017, New York.

2. Recordings

"I Can Hear It Now," Vol. 1. Columbia ML–4095. 12" LP. $3.98.

"I Can Hear It Now," Vol. 2. Columbia ML–4261. 12" LP. $3.98.

"Hits of the 40's." RCA Camden 398. 12" LP. $1.98

3. Resource Persons

Local merchant
Member of draft board
Biology teacher
Health educator
World War II veterans

4. Pamphlet

Let Freedom Ring. Department of State Publication 4443. General Foreign Policy Series 67. Division of Publications, Office of Public Affairs or Superintendent of Documents, U. S. Government Printing Office, Washington, D.C. $0.50.

THE APPLICABILITY OF UNIT TEACHING

Although the unit method of teaching is used in many subject fields, it lends itself particularly well to the social studies, the core curriculum, homemaking, science, and English classes. It is possible and desirable to organize the subject matter of these courses as a series of learning units, one leading into the other.

Although all subjects involve some instruction in skills, some high school courses concentrate to a greater extent and, in a few cases, exclusively on development of specific skills. Skill courses, i.e., those courses that stress development of manipulative, physical, and motor skills, do not as a rule incorporate the unit method as easily or as extensively as other subjects in the high school program of studies.

Courses or phases of courses that must be learned by repetition and drill are not necessarily best taught by use of full-fledged learning units. We would classify as skill subjects typing, bookkeeping, shorthand, phases of physical education (as calisthenics), construction activities in industrial arts, craft work, the audio-lingual skill stages of modern foreign languages, and phases of mathematics that require drill in application of mathematical principles.

In the skill subjects it may be found highly desirable to introduce from time to time units of the nature discussed in this section. "Cultural" units or units on civilization would be appropriate within the foreign language course. For example, a unit on the "Geography of South America" or the "Music of Spain" or the "French Parliamentary System" or the "Military Organization of Ancient Rome" are definitely suitable. Also, "Application of Numbers in Everyday Living" would be invaluable in a course in seventh-grade mathematics.

The use of learning units in the skill subjects would be more limited in both frequency and scope. Some teachers in the skill subjects, however,

do present a type of unit in their courses. In this way they speak of a
unit on "Bowling" in physical education, a unit on "Margins" in typing,
a unit on "Etching" in industrial arts, a unit on the "First Declension"
in Latin, or a unit on the "Binomial Theorem" in algebra.

Unit teaching is possible within all broad fields of the high school curriculum, though it would not necessarily be most applicable in all courses
within a field or in all instructional phases of a particular course. If we
browse through the educational literature and through some of the materials created in local school systems, however, we can find many illustrations of topics that have been developed into units. Let us look at the
titles of several learning units that have been created in each of the fields
normally found in the high school curriculum.[4]

Subject Fields	Titles of Units
English	The Twentieth Century Speaks Through Carl Sandburg*
	Shakespeare's England
	The Humor of Mark Twain
	Detecting Editorial Bias in the Newspaper
	How Do You Write a Letter of Application?
	How Do You Conduct a Public Meeting?
Social Studies	World War II and Its Impact on World Civilization*
	The French Revolution
	The Rise of Marxism
	What Should Be Our Policy in the Middle East?
	What Causes Juvenile Delinquency?
	What Have the Ancient Greeks Contributed to the Modern World?
Science	Heredity
	Evolution in Action
	Birds of California
	The Human Nervous System
	How Does Our City Get Electric Power?

[4] Titles marked with an asterisk appear as Illustrative Learning Units in the preceding discussion.

Subject Fields (cont'd)	*Titles of Units (cont'd)*
Science	What Plants Are Native to Our State?
Mathematics	Units of Measurement Using Arithmetic in Daily Life Using Algebra in Daily Life Geometric Shapes in Daily Living The Slide Rule Is the Metric System Superior to Our Units of Measurement?
Health, Physical Education, and Safety	Safety in the Home Safety on the Highways Do Cigarettes Cause Lung Cancer? Keeping Ourselves in Good Physical Condition Water Sports
Foreign Languages	English's Debt to Latin Spanish Holidays The Russian Revolution The French System of Education What Kinds of Foods Do the Germans Eat?
Music	Enjoying the Music of Beethoven The Instruments of the Orchestra Folk Dancing What Is Good Music? The Songs of the Early Pioneers
Art	The Genius of Michelangelo The French Impressionists The Spanish School of Painting Choosing and Blending Colors Is There Anything to Modern Art?
Industrial Arts	Buying Furniture Wisely Opportunities for My Chosen Vocation in Industry Planning the Home Shop What Should I Look For in Buying a House? What Is an Antique?

Homemaking

Good Grooming
Sewing Can Be Fun
Caring for the Baby
How Do You Prepare a Balanced
  Meal?
Are the Old Wives' Tales About Sex
  True?

Business Education

Investing in Stocks and Bonds
Advantages and Disadvantages of In-
  stallment Buying
What Is Insurance?
How Do I Figure My U. S. Income
  Tax?
Are All Advertisements True?

These titles suggest the possibility that the unit method of teaching may be applied in varying degrees within any subject field of the high school program.

The individual teacher develops learning units for his particular classes at a particular time. Assuming, however, that the topics or problems of his units are applicable to succeeding classes, the teacher may revise, edit, and recast his units as necessary for subsequent classes. Re-use of learning units with adequate revision will save a great deal of the teacher's time in planning. The teacher will also find that with a little practice units may be constructed without undue expenditure of time or effort.

CHAPTER 8

PLANNING A RESOURCE UNIT

WHAT IS A RESOURCE UNIT?

A resource unit, like the learning unit, is an arrangement of materials and activities around a particular topic or problem. The resource unit, however, is much more comprehensive than the learning unit. Resource units and learning units may bear exactly the same titles. For example, it is possible to have a resource unit on the topic, "The American Judicial System." A learning unit may be constructed with the same title. Aside from the fact that the resource unit is generally labeled as such, it can be identified by a number of special characteristics.

As the name implies, the resource unit is a source of information and ideas for teachers to use. Like the learning unit, the resource unit is created. It is not generally found in readily available form. Unlike the learning unit, which is normally constructed by one teacher for a particular class, the resource unit is usually made by a group of teachers who pool their talents to create units that will be of use to many teachers throughout the school system. Resource units are often preserved in some semipermanent fashion and filed for use as needed.

The major purpose of the resource unit is to provide ideas for a teacher who wishes to create his own learning unit on the same topic. The resource unit fills a need among teachers who wish to adopt the unit method of teaching but find themselves handicapped by lack of ideas and sources of information. The resource unit contains a wealth of suggestions and information which will aid the teacher in supplementing material found in the basic textbook. The resource unit shortens the busy teacher's planning time and simplifies his work in the construction of learning units for his classes.

Alberty lists eight purposes of a resource unit:

1. To furnish suggestions for materials, methods, activities, teaching aids, and evaluative procedures for building a learning unit.

2. To provide a means of helping the teacher to organize materials so that he can depart from the traditional use of the textbook as a guide in curriculum development.

3. To provide suggestions to the teacher for translating an educational philosophy into practice.

4. To serve as a guide in helping the teacher to include in the learning unit certain important values basic to education in a democracy.

5. To sensitize the teacher to all of the significant problems and issues that have a bearing on an area of living.

6. To utilize the personnel resources of the school appropriate to the cooperative pre-planning of a particular unit.

7. To conserve the time of the teacher.

8. To make it possible to have teaching materials available when needed.[1]

Modern schools are constantly concerned with the problem and necessity of curriculum change. To keep current with changing times the curriculum of the local school must be continuously subjected to systematic study by the local faculty. Physics, chemistry, biology, history, and other disciplines have moved ahead so rapidly in the last twenty-five years alone that it is difficult to keep pace with the changes.

One excellent way by which curriculum change and revision may be initiated is through the technique of the resource unit. Construction of a resource unit permits a group of teachers to work cooperatively, drawing together useful ideas and materials. The resource unit focuses attention on two aspects of curriculum change most in need of attention: the content of a course and the methods of presentation of material. Teachers working on resource units must, of necessity, consider how children learn, study the current needs of their young people, look into current information on the subject, use initiative and imagination in writing their units, use the group process in working together, exchange their problems, assist each other, and consider some of the newer developments in instruction.

Faculties should be encouraged to work together in heterogeneous groups made up of teachers in the various subject fields. Teachers will, no doubt, work a good deal within their own departments. But it is desirable that they have opportunities to work closely with teachers in other departments. It would be a valuable activity for a group of English teachers to work up a resource unit on a topic such as "The Elizabethan Era." The unit would be of even greater value, though, if a group composed of an English teacher, a social studies teacher, a science teacher, a music teacher, and an art teacher, for example, could work together on this topic. They

---

[1] Harold Alberty, *Reorganizing the High-School Curriculum* (New York: Macmillan, 1947), p. 272.

could pool their knowledge and skills to produce a really fine unit that brings various subject disciplines to bear on the topic under consideration.

By working together in small groups, teachers from the various departments of the school are able to understand more clearly some of the problems of other members of the faculty. Through this process unity and morale among the faculty are heightened and, as a result, the school is able to provide a better education for the young people in its charge.

HOW IS A RESOURCE UNIT CONSTRUCTED?

As with the learning unit, the teacher will find no single, fixed way of preparing a resource unit. Teachers may devise their own outlines or use any of a number of outlines that may be found in the educational literature or in sample resource units. Following is an illustration of a resource unit.

ILLUSTRATIVE RESOURCE UNIT[2]

THE UNITED NATIONS
A Resource Unit
Grades 10–12

A. Objectives

1. Understandings

a. To teach the understanding that the United Nations is man's most significant attempt so far to preserve peace.

b. To teach the understanding that the United States is officially committed to the support of the United Nations.

c. To teach the understanding that the United Nations has had a number of outstanding successes since its origin.

d. To teach the understanding that the organization of the United Nations is based upon democratic principles.

e. To teach the understanding that support of the United Nations does not mean that the United States gives up its own sovereignty.

f. To teach the understanding that all kinds of nations are represented in the United Nations.

g. To teach the understanding that the United Nations can help mankind.

h. To teach the understanding that nations in this day and age are interdependent.

i. To teach the understanding that isolationism is impossible for the United States.

[2] Prepared by David Blowers, William A. Edenfield, William Han, Jeanne Hullihan, and William Moon, 1957.

j. To teach the understanding that the free world looks to the United States for leadership.

2. Appreciations

a. To develop an appreciation of the complexity of the United Nations.

b. To develop an appreciation for United Nations' successes.

c. To develop an appreciation for the skill of the diplomats who come together for United Nations sessions.

d. To develop an appreciation for the many undertakings of the United Nations such as UNESCO, WHO, etc.

e. To develop an appreciation for the efficiency with which meetings are conducted in spite of the multiplicity of languages represented.

f. To develop an appreciation for the strong leadership the United States has given in the United Nations.

g. To develop an appreciation for the efforts of men of good will who are striving to preserve the peace.

3. Attitudes

a. To develop confidence in man's ability to cooperate for the peace and security of the world.

b. To develop a willingness on the part of the student to support the United Nations.

c. To develop a concern for all peoples of the world.

d. To develop an attitude of hope in spite of the difficulties facing the United Nations.

e. To develop an attitude of acceptance of customs that differ from our own.

f. To develop an attitude of patience with the processes of deliberation.

g. To develop an attitude of support for our United States delegation to the United Nations.

4. Special abilities and skills

a. To learn to detect the positions of the various countries on international problems.

b. To learn to detect blocs among the countries.

c. To learn to spot communist propaganda in United Nations' deliberations.

d. To improve students' abilities to carry on group discussion.

e. To improve students' basic skills of reading, writing, speaking, listening, and understanding.

5. Subject-matter outcomes

a. Members of the United Nations

b. Purposes for which the United Nations was created

c. Accomplishments of the United Nations

    d. Failures of the United Nations

    e. Criticisms against the United Nations

    f. Limitations of the United Nations

    g. Leading personalities of the United Nations

    h. Current issues before the United Nations

    i. History of the United Nations

    j. Comparison of the United Nations with the League of Nations

    k. Role of the United States as a member of the United Nations

    l. Organizations of the United Nations

    m. United Nations Headquarters

B. Overview

This resource unit is aimed at the attainment of a better understanding of a vital international organization, the United Nations. The teachers preparing this unit consider understanding and support of the United Nations essential to peace and security in the world. The unit is comprehensive in nature, dealing with the history, purposes, functions, organizations, activities, personnel, and problems of the United Nations.

A unit on the United Nations lends itself to the social studies curriculum for best placement in the high school program. Schools that have a general education or core program will find a unit on this topic especially suitable.

Teachers might find it desirable to begin a learning unit with their classes around October 24, United Nations Day. Or, they might wish to begin a unit before United Nations' Day and terminate the unit on that day with an exhibit or other culminating activity. It is possible that teachers may wish to draw a comparison between the role of the New World in the time of Columbus (Holiday: October 12) and the role of the United States in the twentieth century as shown by the U. S. President's proclamation of United Nations Day (Holiday: October 24). Changes in communications and transportation can be brought in to show how small the world has become.

C. Activities

    1. Assemble working library of information on the topic. This will include school and community libraries' materials; newspaper and magazine articles; books and pamphlets of materials.

    2. Write to United Nations Headquarters for general information.

    3. Small group reports, oral and written, on the following topics:

        a. Organization of the United Nations

        b. Purposes of the United Nations

        c. Accomplishments of the United Nations

        d. Activities of the United Nations throughout the world

        e. Problems of the United Nations

4. Panel discussions on the topics:

    a. Why should the U.S. support the U.N.?

    b. Why would another war imperil civilization?

    c. Should the U.S. stop testing H-bombs?

    d. How can education achieve international understanding?

    e. How can modern technology contribute to the solution of economic problems?

5. Have the class list as many members of the United Nations as they can think of and locate these countries on a large wall map of the world.

6. Follow in the newspapers the current problems before the General Assembly or the Security Council. Devote at least a few minutes of each period to discussion of latest developments at the United Nations.

7. Assign individual reports on prominent personages at the U.N. Include the Secretary-General, the President of the General Assembly, and principal ambassadors.

8. Assign as homework for the entire class the task of identifying the meaning of: The Summit, The Big Two, The Big Four, The Big Five, and the Council of Foreign Ministers.

9. Have students identify all the members of the U.N. which they would call (*a*) true democracies, (*b*) communist countries, (*c*) neutralist countries, and (*d*) dictatorships.

10. Role-play a session of the Security Council with students taking parts of the members of the Council. Select a controversial issue for them to debate, such as Resolved: That an international arms inspection team be set up with power to investigate anywhere in the world.

11. Role-play a session of the General Assembly with students taking parts of the members of the Assembly. Select a controversial issue for discussion, such as the admission of Red China to the United Nations.

12. Individual students may do research on a particular member of the U. N. in which they have a special interest. They should look up pertinent facts about the country. They may report to the class or they may prepare an interesting scrapbook about the country. Students may write to the embassy of the country in Washington or to tourist information centers for information about the country in addition to gathering material available locally.

13. Invite a person who has visited U.N. Headquarters to talk to the class about his trip. The talk should be supplemented with magazine and newspaper pictures or slides or photographs taken at U.N. Headquarters.

14. Permit students to look into opportunities to serve with the United Nations. Look up qualifications needed, duties, salaries, etc. Discuss the role of the international civil servant.

15. Assign small group reports on backgrounds, goals, and aspirations of regions of the world, such as Europe, Africa, Southeast Asia, the Middle East, the Far East, South America, and the Communist Bloc.

16. Interview persons in the community to determine their attitudes on the United Nations. Make sure both pro and con attitudes are uncovered.

17. Let students design or draw maps of the United Nations, flags of members of the United Nations, the flag of the United Nations, or sketches of prominent personalities.

18. Have a student of foreign languages translate some United Nations materials from the foreign language into English and vice versa.

19. Have a student of languages or electronics investigate the method by which simultaneous translations are carried to the delegates at the United Nations. A language student or a shop or physics student might rig up an experimental device simulating the system used at the U.N. and give a demonstration of how it is done.

20. Find articles in the newspapers and magazines which are very critical of the United Nations and its organizations. Discuss these criticisms in class.

21. Examine newspaper coverage of the United Nations. Have students distinguish between straight news, editorial comment, and columnists' interpretations.

22. Have a small group of students prepare a large chart showing major problems that have come before the United Nations, the actions taken by the U.N., and the success or failure of the action.

23. Investigate charges that UNESCO is subversive. Look into reasons why UNESCO materials were banned in some schools of the country.

24. Let homemaking students draw and/or make copies of unusual costumes worn by some of the delegates to the U.N.

25. Invite foreign students to come to class and talk about their countries and show native costumes.

26. Have a bulletin-board committee prepare an attractive exhibit for the classroom bulletin board.

27. Show any of the excellent films about the United Nations that are available or can be obtained. See Instructional Aids and Sources section of this resource unit.

28. Follow any television broadcasts from the United Nations.

29. Collect stamps from member nations and keep in stamp album.

30. Collect coins or paper money from member nations. Calculate the value of this foreign money in U.S. money. Let an interested student give a report on foreign exchange.

31. Study the budget of the United Nations and determine the sources of its revenue.

32. Have a student committee study the problems of underdeveloped areas of the world.

33. Have a student committee study the principal religions represented at the United Nations.

34. Prepare a final exhibit of all materials assembled on the United Nations.

D. Evaluation Techniques

1. Conduct a class discussion on the success of the unit.

2. Give an objective test asking students to identify principal persons, places, and events associated with the United Nations.

3. Give an essay test asking students to state their opinions on significant issues related to the United Nations.

4. Observe student effort and participation in class discussions.

5. Have students judge their own progress from the time the unit was started until the time the unit ended.

6. Have students write an answer to the essay question: How Does the United Nations Affect You?

7. Judge student reports and creative activities.

8. Attempt to evaluate attainment of desired attitudes by close observation of student behavior.

9. Look for special quality and initiative from the gifted youngsters of the group.

10. Look for group behavior that puts into practice the principles of democratic living.

E. Bibliography

Books

Adam, Thomas R. *Education for International Understanding.* New York: Institute of Adult Education, Teachers College, Columbia University, 1948.

American Association for the United Nations. *The United Nations and You.* New York: Education Department, American Association for the United Nations, 1947. 36 pp.

Arne, Sigrid. *United Nations Primer.* New York: Rinehart, 1948.

Beckel, Graham. *Workshops for the World: The Specialized Agencies of the United Nations.* New York: Abelard, 1954.

Carr, William Guy. *One World in the Making, the United Nations.* Boston: Ginn and Co., 1946. 100 pp.

Chase, Eugene Parker. *The United Nations in Action.* New York: McGraw-Hill, 1950.

Cory, Robert H. *Communicating Information and Ideas about the United Nations to the American People.* New York: Carnegie Endowment for International Peace, 1955.

Evatt, Herbert Vere. *United Nations.* Philadelphia: Saunders, 1948.

Fenichell, Stephen S. and Andrews, Phillip. *The United Nations, Blueprint for Peace.* Philadelphia: Winston, 1954.

Fisher, Dorothy Canfield. *A Fair World For All: The Meaning of The Declaration of Human Rights.* New York: McGraw-Hill, 1952.

Fisher, Lois. *You and the United Nations.* New York: Children's Press, 1947. 42 pp.

Frost, Frances, ed. *Legends of the United Nations.* New York: McGraw-Hill, 1943.

Galt, Thomas Franklin. *The Story of Peace and War.* New York: Crowell, 1952.

Lodge, Henry Cabot. *You and the United Nations.* U.S. Department of State Publication 6302. Washington: Superintendent of Documents, U. S. Government Printing Office, 1956.

National Education Association. *American Education and International Tension.* Washington: National Education Association, 1949. 54 pp.

National Education Association. *Education for International Understanding in American Schools.* Washington: National Education Association, 1948. 241 pp.

Reeves, Emery. *Anatomy of Peace.* New York: Harper, 1956.

Roosevelt, Eleanor. *Partners: The U. N. and Youth.* Garden City, N. Y.: Doubleday, 1950.

United Nations. *Structure of the United Nations.* United Nations, N. Y.: Department of Public Information, United Nations, 1955.

Periodicals

Dulles, John Foster. "Dulles Spells Out U.S. Foreign Policy," *U.S. News and World Report,* 37 (July 1, 1955), 82–85.

Dulles, John Foster. "Moral Foundations of the United Nations " *U.S. Department of State Bulletin,* 33 (July 6, 1955), 10–12.

Gelber, Lionel Morris. "U.N. in the Balance," *Saturday Review,* 39 (January 28, 1956), 22–23.

Hammarskjold, Dag. "Role of the United Nations in Work for Peace," *United Nations Bulletin,* 16 (May 1, 1954), 352–53.

Newsweek. "The United Nations on Trial—A Special International Report," *Newsweek,* 47 (April 23, 1956), 47–50.

Shotwell, James T. "United Nations 1956: Inventory," *Saturday Review,* 39 (January 28, 1956), 9–10.

United Nations Review. "Atoms for Peace, Health, and Prosperity," *United Nations Review,* 2 (June 1956), 47–49.

United Nations Review. "First Ten Years," *United Nations Review,* 1 (June 1955), 1–48.

United Nations Review. "International Pathways to Human Progress." *United Nations Review,* 3 (August 1956), 32–33.

F. Instructional Aids and Sources

1. Films

The following films may be rented from the United Nations Film Distribution Section, 10th Floor, 1600 Broadway, New York, New York 10019:

Article 55	10 min.
Battle for Bread	18 min.
Born Equal	10 min.
The Children	10 min.
Clearing the Way	20 min.
Defense of the Peace	10 min.
The Eternal Fight	18 min.
Fate of a Child	17 min.
First Steps	11 min.
For All the World's Children	30 min.
Grand Design	9 min.
Green Gold	22 min.
Help For Pakistan	10 min.
Indonesia Learns	10 min.
Lights That Never Fail	20 min.
Maps We Live By	17 min.
Of Human Rights	20 min.
The People's Charter	17 min.
The Sea, My Native Land	12 min.
Searchlight of the Nations	17 min.
Thailand's Streams of Life	10 min.
That All May Learn	19 min.
This Is the Challenge	10 min.
Tomorrow Begins Today	11 min.
U. N. at Work	17 min.
United Nations in Action	19 min.

All of the above films are with sound, in black and white.

Pattern for Peace-Charter of the U.N. Washington: British Information Service. 15 min. Sound. Black and white.

Watchtower over Tomorrow. New York: Teaching Film Custodians. 10 min. Sound. Black and white.

We, the People. New York: Young America Films. 8 min. Sound. Black and white.

Youth and the U.N. Audio-Visual Department, University of Minnesota. 30 min. Sound. Black and white.

2. Filmstrips

The following filmstrips may be obtained from United Nations Film Distribution Section, 10th Floor, 1600 Broadway, New York, N. Y. 10019:

Aims of the United Nations Charter
Atomic Energy—Problems of International Control
Economic and Social Council
Garden We Planted Together
International Convention on the Crime of Genocide
International Cooperation at Work
Non-Governmental Organizations and the United Nations
Sacred Trust
To Serve All Mankind
Universal Declaration of Human Rights
United Nations Reports
Visit to the United Nations
World Food Supply and the United Nations

For purposes of writing a resource unit the outline below may be followed.

SUGGESTED OUTLINE OF A RESOURCE UNIT

Title of the Resource Unit
A Resource Unit
Grade level
Body of the resource unit:
A. Objectives
B. Overview
C. Activities
D. Evaluation Techniques
E. Bibliography
F. Instructional Aids and Sources

The reader will notice the similarity between the outline of the resource unit and the outline of the learning unit. Only the section on approaches has been dropped, since that section of the learning unit is planned for a particular class.

TITLE PAGE

The title of the unit and the fact that it is a resource unit should be placed on the title page. The grade levels to which the unit is applicable should be indicated. Normally, a resource unit will be suitable for more than one grade level. Resource units may be created for junior high school or senior high school level or even for both junior and senior high school levels, depending on the nature of the topic and the difficulty of the content. Since the resource unit is used as source information and not as a teaching device, there is no mention of the element of time. Individual teachers will decide for themselves how much time they wish to spend on the particular topic. The names of the persons and the school system preparing the unit often appear on the title page so that recognition may be given for the work done. Teachers will find that some companies and organizations have published resource units and distributed them to the schools for teachers to use. The title page of these units will reveal their sources.

> The Illustrative Resource Unit presents its title, *The United Nations*, and indicates that it is a resource unit designed for grades ten through twelve.

OBJECTIVES

In this first part of the resource unit the teachers working on the unit will list all the objectives which they believe would be possible to realize if a teacher were to prepare a learning unit from the resource unit. This section may be limited to teachers' objectives. The responsibility for statement of pupils' objectives can be placed on the individual teacher who prepares a learning unit from the resource material. Teachers' objectives should be grouped into (*a*) understandings, (*b*) appreciations, (*c*) attitudes, (*d*) special abilities and skills, and (*e*) subject-matter outcomes (facts). Teachers preparing units should remember that ways to realize these objectives must be suggested in the activities section and ways to evaluate the attainment of these objectives must be suggested in the evaluation techniques section of the unit.

> The Illustrative Resource Unit specifies ten understandings, seven appreciations, seven attitudes, five special abilities and skills, and thirteen items of subject matter.

OVERVIEW

The overview is a brief summary of what is covered in the unit. It may be written in narrative style or it may be outlined. This section may include a statement of justification for the study of the topic as well as suggestions on how teachers may use the resource unit in various subject fields and at various grade levels. These suggestions should be considered as helpful hints to teachers rather than specific directions on how teachers must proceed.

> The overview of our Illustrative Resource Unit consists of three simple paragraphs. The overview states the aim and scope of the unit. It suggests the best placement for the unit in the high school program. It makes a few suggestions for teachers to consider when preparing a learning unit on the topic.

ACTIVITIES

The section on student activities is, perhaps, the most significant part of the resource unit. It sets forth possible ideas for teacher and student work. The ideas should be many and varied, including any and all types of activities from active to passive, from classroom to community, and from academic to manual. The activities should be broad enough to encompass the range of age levels for which the resource unit is planned and numerous enough to permit selection by the teacher who wishes to construct a specific learning unit. Since the list of activities is lengthy and the aims of individual teachers will vary, it is not necessary to specify a desired outcome with each activity as suggested in the learning unit.

The teachers preparing the Illustrative Resource Unit suggest thirty-four activities, which vary greatly in type and level of difficulty. There are enough activities to provide some valuable ideas for any teacher who wishes to develop a learning unit on the United Nations.

EVALUATION TECHNIQUES

The evaluation section includes many suggestions on how teachers may evaluate student performance on learning units made from the resource unit. Among the many varieties of evaluation techniques teachers should consider written tests, both teacher-made and standardized, oral tests, written and oral reports, anecdotal records, diaries and notebooks kept by students, reports by parents, student records, analysis of jobs undertaken by students, and observation of class participation. It is not expected that the teachers would compose for this section entire tests. The group constructing the unit might suggest types of test items and give an illustration of each type. The types of evaluation techniques used will vary from teacher to teacher and from class to class.

Ten evaluative techniques are suggested in the Illustrative Resource Unit.

BIBLIOGRAPHY

References useful to both teachers and students should be listed in alphabetical order in a suitable bibliographical style. References to books and references to periodicals should be grouped separately for easy identification.

The Illustrative Resource Unit includes a generous number of references to both books and periodicals.

INSTRUCTIONAL AIDS AND SOURCES

References to all types of aids and sources except books and periodicals may be listed in this last part of the unit. Among the items which might appear in this section are films, filmstrips, slides, pictures, charts, maps, kits, radio programs, tapes, recordings, television programs, resources available in the community, and resource persons.

A number of films and filmstrips are listed in the Instructional Aids and Sources section of the Illustrative Resource Unit.

Alberty would include two sections not given in the preceding outline.[3] These sections are (1) philosophy, which would come at the beginning of the outline, and (2) leads to other units, which would come at the end of the outline. These additional sections could be incorporated in the outline if teachers so desired. If teachers wished to add the section on philosophy, they would give a clear, short statement of the philosophy of education which they hold. Normally, a page or two will suffice to state the principal beliefs the teachers have about education in general and how this particular resource unit fits into their conception of a philosophy of education. If the teachers want to add the section on leads to other units, they may conclude the resource unit with suggestions of a few titles of possible units which may be derived from the resource unit under study. The suggested leads might be those for which future groups of teachers would wish to develop resource units. For example, a resource unit on "The New York Stock Exchange" might be followed by units on "The Federal Reserve System," "The History of Banking in America," "State and National Banks," "The Great Depression," and "Stocks and Bonds."

This author would consider the statement of philosophy and the section on leads to other units excellent, but optional. The statement of philosophy often results in an academic exercise. It has been the author's experience that these statements are generally very similar in nature from one group to another, including broad generalizations about modern education and theories of learning. There is some merit in sharpening one's views about education and learning. A more detailed statement of philosophy, needs of students, and needs of the school and community might be developed, however, as an in-service education project of evaluation of the school's total program. These statements might be developed in conjunction with a school's bid for accreditation by one of the regional accrediting associations. A project of this nature would be separate from the creation of resource units as an instrument of curriculum change.

[3] Alberty, *op. cit.*, pp. 277, 286.

CHAPTER 9

PLANNING A LESSON

WHAT IS A LESSON PLAN?

The lesson plan is the daily plan that a teacher prepares for instruction of his class. Lesson plans are generally made the day or night before the next day's class. One lesson plan is made for each class which the teacher instructs.

Nothing gives the beginning teacher more confidence and a greater sense of security than a well-made lesson plan. With a carefully prepared plan the beginning teacher can walk into a classroom knowing that he has put down in some organized form a sensible framework for the day's instruction. For this reason beginning teachers should expect to plan their daily lessons in considerable detail. There is no objection to the presence and use of a written plan by the teacher during the class period. Lesson plan are a visible sign of preparation on the part of the teacher. There can be no excuse for any teacher's appearance in his classroom without some evidence of previous preparation. Good planning admittedly requires time and skill. Yet, this is the central job of the teacher. Lesson planning is essentially the job of organizing the wealth of activities and materials available on a particular topic. Intelligent planning also divides these activities and materials into manageable portions for class periods.

As teachers gain in experience and have taught their courses a number of years, they may find short cuts to lesson planning as they did in unit construction. Experienced teachers do not require plans as detailed as those of inexperienced teachers. However, experienced teachers should not fall into the custom of using the same lesson plans year after year in class after class without change. No doubt, it is possible to use the same core of material for a lesson plan in a subject which a teacher has taught a number of times. But lesson plans must be tailored and changed for the particular class. No two classes are exactly the same. Further, the content of the course will change over the years. The objectives of the students, of the school, and of the teachers will change.

For these reasons lesson plans must be prepared afresh each day. They should be considered as a tentative outline of the class period. Teachers are well aware of the old saying that even the best-laid plans of mice and men often go astray. A carefully worked out lesson plan may have to be set aside entirely for a school assembly that has been called suddenly by the principal, or the teacher may have drawn up a five-point agenda for the day but only the first two items were considered. The teacher should expect this to be a natural situation. He must remain flexible. This is a further reason why lesson plans must be made out daily to adjust to the speed and progress of a particular class.

The lesson plan should provide for enough activities for the class period. The beginning teacher will find it more desirable to have planned too many activities than not to have planned enough. If he is flexible and does not insist on sticking exactly to his agenda, he may postpone until the next day activities that he and the pupils have not had time to use. The beginning teacher may find himself floundering around and the class out of control if his lesson plan is so brief that he has not provided enough activities to take up the class hour. Students can quickly detect when a teacher is bluffing his way through a lesson. Beginning teachers frequently find disciplinary problems developing as a result of poor planning.

HOW DO YOU CONSTRUCT A LESSON PLAN?

As with the learning unit and the resource unit, there is no single or best way of making a lesson plan. The teacher may and perhaps should devise his own system of lesson planning. The pragmatic test should determine the method that the teacher selects to use. If the plan works for him, then it is a suitable plan. Whatever form of lesson plan a teacher uses, the plan should be written out in intelligible style. This author is dubious about the assertions of some teachers who claim to keep their lesson plans "in their heads."

A word should be said about a type of plan that is referred to as a "lesson plan," but that does not fit our concept of a true lesson plan. Some administrators require teachers to maintain "lesson plans" for a week or more ahead of schedule. Schools often provide plan books that contain tiny blocks of space for recording "lesson plans" and require teachers to fill in these plan books and turn them in to the administrator for a week or so in advance. One reason these types of "plans" are required is to assist substitute teachers if the regular teacher becomes ill. In making plans of this type the teacher is able to give only the skeleton of the work he would hope to cover and can visualize over a period of time. He may designate certain pages or chapters or topics or exercises. Some administrators judge neat, well-kept notebooks of this nature as evidence of good planning. The plan books satisfy the administrator's need for organization, give him some indication of the content being covered in various courses, and set up routines that teachers must follow. These administrative requirements are not at all lesson plans in the concept of modern teaching. Merely as aids to substitute teachers these skeletal plans are justified. They allow, however, no provision for flexibility, for change, for detailed planning, and for providing for individual differences. They should not be used as a method of instructional supervision, nor should they take the place of more detailed plans.

The illustrative lesson plan that follows is the plan for one day of the previously illustrated learning unit for social studies, "World War II and Its Impact on World Conditions."

ILLUSTRATIVE LESSON PLAN 1

American History Class[1]

A. Objectives
    1. Teacher's objectives
      _a_. To teach the understanding that United States' entrance into World War II was inevitable.
      _b_. To teach the facts why the United States went to war.
    2. Pupils' objectives
      _a_. Why did the Japanese attack Pearl Harbor?
      _b_. Why didn't we keep out of foreign wars?
B. Activities
    1. Short objective test to review the past two days' work. This test should include the listing of major events up to the Pearl Harbor attack.

(10 min.)

    2. Group report on the activities of Hitler and the Third Reich.

(15 min.)

    3. Class discussion on the report and assigned materials.   (20 min.)
      What role did the United States play in world affairs at the time of Hitler?
      How important to the United States was the survival of Great Britain?
      What are the ideas of the United States regarding individual freedom?
      What are your own ideas about individual freedom?
C. Assignment
    1. Committee report on Churchill and Great Britain during World War II.
      Why is Churchill considered by many to be "The Man of the Twentieth Century"?
    2. Everyone read Muzzey, pp. 477–81, 591–602.

[1] Prepared by Marjorie Crittenden, 1958.

D. Evaluation Techniques

1. Teacher observation of students' preparation in class discussion and attentiveness to the report given in class.

2. Results of the short test.

E. Bibliography

1. Muzzey, *A History of Our Country*.

2. Thomas A. Bailey, *A Diplomatic History of the American People*.

F. Instructional Aids and Sources

A bulletin-board display of pictures and articles about *(a)* the training of German troops, *(b)* Hitler, *(c)* bombing of Britain, and *(d)* Pearl Harbor attack.

To assist beginning teachers, the following outline incorporates features of a good lesson plan. This is a general plan which will be found useful in most courses.

SUGGESTED OUTLINE OF A LESSON PLAN

A. Objectives
B. Activities
C. Assignment
D. Evaluation Techniques
E. Bibliography
F. Instructional Aids and Sources

OBJECTIVES

The teacher should briefly indicate the major aims of the daily plan. These goals must be specific enough for accomplishment during the class period. Teachers should consider outcomes, including understandings, appreciations, attitudes, special abilities and skills, and facts. Both teacher and pupil objectives should be included.

Illustrative Lesson Plan 1 aims for two teachers' objectives and two pupils' objectives, which should be possible of attainment in the one class period.

ACTIVITIES

In this section the teacher will list all the activities, materials, and content to be studied during the class hour. One of the best ways of maintaining pupil interest and preventing disciplinary problems is to provide a variety of activities and materials each class period. A single activity generally will not suffice to hold the interest of adolescents for a whole class hour. The younger the child, the shorter his span of attention. A variety of materials and activities will help the teacher toward meeting individual differences among pupils in his classroom. The teacher should make an estimate of the time to be allotted to each activity of the lesson plan. Some items to consider for inclusion in this section of the plan would be:

    a. Review of the previous lesson
    b. Provision of activities to meet individual differences
    c. Key questions for class discussion
    d. Important illustrations or anecdotes
    e. List of materials to be used
    f. Written exercises
    g. Summary

Illustrative Lesson Plan 1 contains a variety of activities: test, group report, and class discussion. It includes key questions for the class discussion. Estimates are made of the time needed for each activity.

ASSIGNMENT

The assignment for the next day should be clearly indicated in the lesson plan. Actually, the assignment might be considered as part of the activities of the class period. Time must be allotted to explanation of the assignment so that all students may clearly understand what is expected of them. Most authorities agree that there is no best time for giving the assignment. In practice, most teachers give their assignments at the end of the class hour. The assignment should be placed in the sequence of activities wherever it is appropriate for that class period. Sometimes the assignment may require only a few moments to give; at other times, if elaborate planning is required, the assignment could consume most of the class hour.

Illustrative Lesson Plan 1 indicates that all students will read two passages in the textbook and a committee will prepare a report for class. If no previous instruction has been given to the committee for its report, this portion of the assignment may take some time to explain.

EVALUATION TECHNIQUES

The teacher must make some provision for evaluating the success of pupils on the day's work. Among the many techniques possible are:

    a. Teacher observation
    b. Teacher's asking key questions in class discussion
    c. Teacher's asking pupils to summarize
    d. Written exercises: quiz, test, statements, essay, reports
    e. Comments from the pupils on their success

The teacher of Illustrative Lesson Plan 1 employs a short test and observation as evaluation techniques.

References to books and periodicals should be listed in this section of the lesson plan. For purposes of the lesson plan a short bibliographical listing of only those that have bearing on the immediate lesson should be sufficient.

Illustrative Lesson Plan 1 provides two bibliographical references.

INSTRUCTIONAL AIDS AND SOURCES

References to all aids and sources other than books and periodicals should be given in this final part of the lesson plan. The teacher should indicate only those aids and sources that have significance for the immediate lesson.

Illustrative Lesson Plan 1 outlines a bulletin-board display in this section.

In making lesson plans the teacher should avoid the common errors of (1) using too sketchy a plan, (2) being overcomplete, so that the plan is confusing and difficult to follow, and (3) using the same plans in exactly the same manner with all sections of a particular course.

The beginning teacher will find it a helpful practice to make a few evaluative notes on his lesson plans at the end of each day, commenting on the plan's effectiveness, its success, and particular difficulties he encountered in using the plan.

Following is an illustration of a lesson plan based on the learning unit in English presented earlier in this discussion. Additional illustrations of lesson plans may be found in the educational literature and in the files of teachers in school systems. In studying other teachers' lesson plans the reader should remember that different teachers use different outlines and forms in constructing their plans and may have completely different goals.

ILLUSTRATIVE LESSON PLAN 2

English Class[2]

A. Objectives

   1. Teacher's objectives

      a. To teach the understanding that form is not the only consideration in poetry.

      b. To teach the understanding that Sandburg began a new style of writing.

      c. To develop an appreciation of the spirit of Sandburg's poetry.

[2] Prepared by Beverly Tolan, 1958.

d. To prepare the way for the student to write in a free style later in the unit.

2. Pupils' objectives

a. Can we enjoy this poetry?

b. Why did Sandburg start a new style?

B. Activities

1. Read to students poem about the centipede who tried so hard to think how to run that she couldn't run.   (2 min.)

2. Class discussion of relation of poem to Sandburg.   (8 min.)

Is anyone puzzled by the way in which Sandburg seems to violate or ignore all poetic rules of writing?

3. Have students read aloud the poems:

"Chicago," with musical background of "Slaughter on Tenth Avenue."

"The People, Yes," with musical background of "What Is America to Me?"   (20 min.)

4. Class discussion: (10 min.)

What caused Sandburg to write as he did?

What suggestions do you have for musical background?

5. Teacher reads "Chicago."   (5 min.)

C. Assignment

Pass out dittoed copies of "Chicago," "A Fence," "Washerwoman," "Stars, Songs, Faces," and "I Am the People, the Mob." Read the poems, then find pictures in newspapers and magazines which they believe best tell what the poems are saying. Paste the pictures on paper with the poem; write a short explanation. Bring to class tomorrow.

D. Evaluation Techniques

1. Observation of the spirit with which the class undertakes the activities of the lesson.

2. Evaluation of students' comprehension of poems read.

3. Judgment of students' skill in reading poems.

4. Evaluation of participation of class members in discussion.

E. Bibliography

Bradley, Beatty, and Long, *The American Tradition in Literature,* pp. 681–89.

Foerster and Charvat, *American Prose and Poetry,* pp. 749–53.

Sandburg, *The Complete Poems of Carl Sandburg.*

F. Instructional Aids and Sources

Recordings of "Slaughter on Tenth Avenue" and "What Is America to Me?"

SUMMARY

In our discussion of planning for instruction we have stressed the need for careful planning; we have given attention to different approaches to planning; we have set forth principles of unit teaching and have discussed the advantages of the unit method of organizing subject matter; and we have learned how to recognize and construct (a) a learning unit, (b) a resource unit, and (c) a lesson plan.

We conceive of planning within the classroom as a highly individualized process that incorporates principles of learning, needs of the students, requirements of the subject matter, and the entity of the teacher.

CLASS AND EVALUATION ACTIVITIES

1. Pretest: Write your definitions of the terms "learning unit," "resource unit," and "lesson plan."

2. Discuss in class the question: What are the customary objectives that a teacher of (a) social studies, (b) English, (c) science, (d) mathematics, and (e) any other fields represented in class hopes his students will achieve? Follow this discussion with a discussion of the question: What objectives beyond the usual subject matter might be possible in each of these fields?

3. Visit five or six classrooms and decide whether the teacher is using the unit method of teaching or another method.

4. Interview a number of high school teachers in different fields and ask them the question: What is the place of the textbook in the high school classroom?

5. With several class members, visit on the same day teachers in two or more high schools who are teaching the same subject and same level of the subject, e.g., tenth-grade world history. Note differences in methods used by the teachers. Discuss with the teachers their goals of instruction and their techniques of planning.

6. Using a class committee, survey a local high school to determine how extensively the unit method of teaching is used in that school. Inter-

view a number of the teachers who use that method and record their reasons for using it. Interview a number of teachers who reject the method and record their reasons for rejecting it.

7. Observe at least one elementary school teacher who is known to use effectively the unit method of teaching.

8. Collect or borrow samples of learning units from teachers in various fields.

9. Collect or borrow samples of resource units from local schools.

10. Visit the curriculum center of a local school system to examine copies of materials that have been developed by local teachers.

11. Collect or borrow samples of lesson plans from teachers in various fields, particularly in your own field.

12. Construct a learning unit. The following suggestions may prove useful:

a. Construct a learning unit in your field on a topic that you feel fairly sure you will be called upon to teach.

b. Clear the topic with your instructor before you begin to work on the unit.

c. Unless you can devise a better outline, follow the one you will find in Chapter 7. If you use a different outline, make sure it incorporates all the essential characteristics of a good learning unit.

d. Consult samples of units from library files, local teachers, and files of the instructor for ideas and general information. Remember that not all authors use the same outlines.

e. Evaluate your own unit on the basis of the following criteria:

(1) The topic of the unit is appropriate for the grade level.

(2) The objectives of the unit are clearly stated and are consistent in form.

(3) There are several of each of the five types of objectives: understandings, appreciations, attitudes, special abilities and skills, and subject-matter outcomes (facts).

(4) The pupils' objectives show understanding of the way in which pupils at the grade level of the unit think.

(5) The overview is clear, complete, and brief.

(6) There are at least two approaches for starting the unit.

(7) The approaches are of a nature to stimulate the interests of the pupils for whom the unit is intended.

(8) Each activity is accompanied by a desired outcome.

(9) The activities are suitable for the grade level.

(10) There is a wide variety of activities.

(11) There is a range of difficulty in the activities planned.

(12) There are sufficient activities to last the time allotted to the unit.

(13) A variety of evaluation techniques is suggested.

(14) The evaluation techniques provide ways of judging attainment of the various types of objectives of the unit.

(15) Bibliography is adequate.

(16) Bibliography is in approved form.

(17) Bibliography contains references useful to teacher and pupils.

(18) A number of instructional aids and sources are included.

(19) Instructional aids and sources are listed in acceptable form.

(20) The unit as a whole shows effort and imagination.

(21) The unit as a whole is well organized.

(22) Attention has been paid to mechanics of English usage, including spelling, punctuation, grammar, etc.

13. Working in groups, construct a resource unit. The following suggestions may prove useful:

a. Divide into small groups of five to eight students. For purposes of this assignment it is desirable to have heterogeneous groups of students who are preparing to teach in various fields.

b. The groups should select a topic on which they wish to do a resource unit. The topic should be cleared with the instructor to assure its appropriateness and to avoid duplication among groups.

c. Groups should next decide upon subgroup assignments. Individuals and subgroups can work on various parts of the resource unit. A suggested outline of a resource unit is presented in Chapter 8. If groups vary in their outlines, they should be certain that their outlines contain all the essential characteristics of a good resource unit.

d. Groups should consult sample resource units in the library, in local schools, in the educational texts, and in the files of the instructor. Groups should remember that not all authors use the same sample outlines.

e. Groups should evaluate their own units on the basis of the following criteria:[1]

(1) The resource unit recognizes the needs and interests of the students.

(2) The resource unit suggests opportunities for student participation in planning, developing, and evaluating the work.

(3) The resource unit provides suitable materials to further the socialization of the students.

(4) The resource unit explores the resources of the community that may be utilized in developing the learning unit.

(5) The student activities that are suggested in the resource unit are based upon sound principles of learning.

(6) The various proposals included in the resource unit are practicable under prevailing school conditions.

[1] Criteria (1) through (13) are from Harold Alberty, *Reorganizing the High-School Curriculum* (New York: Macmillan 1947), pp. 273–76.

(7) The resource unit is constructed in such a way as to stimulate professional growth in democratic methods of working with students.

(8) The resource unit helps teachers to provide experiences for students which call for reflective thinking.

(9) The resource unit is based upon a definite educational philosophy.

(10) The resource unit is organized in such a way that it can be easily used by the teachers.

(11) The resource unit is developed by several teachers representing as many subject fields as possible.

(12) The resource unit contains many more suggestions than any class is likely to use.

(13) The resource unit is suited to the maturity of the students.

(14) The objectives are clearly stated and consistent in form.

(15) There are a number of each of the five types of objectives: understandings, appreciations, attitudes, special abilities and skills, and subject-matter outcomes (facts).

(16) The objectives are possible of realization.

(17) The overview is clear, complete, and brief.

(18) The evaluation techniques provide ways of judging attainment of the various types of objectives of the unit.

(19) The bibliography is copious.

(20) The bibliography is in approved form.

(21) Instructional aids and sources are listed in acceptable form.

(22) Instructional aids and sources are plentiful.

(23) The unit as a whole is well organized.

(24) The unit as a whole shows effort and imagination.

(25) Attention has been paid to mechanics of English usage, including spelling, punctuation, grammar, etc.

14. Prepare one lesson plan based on the learning unit that you have previously constructed. (If you have not constructed a learning unit, you may prepare a lesson plan based on material from a high school textbook in your field.) The following suggestions may prove useful:

a. Prepare a plan for one day's lesson, selecting any phase from your learning unit or textbook. Assume the class period to be fifty minutes in length.

b. Unless you can devise a better outline, use the outline of a lesson plan suggested in Chapter 9.

c. Your lesson plan should be fairly complete.

d. Evaluate your lesson plan on the basis of the following criteria:

(1) The objectives are clearly stated.

(2) The objectives are possible of realization during the class period.

(3) The activities planned are varied.

(4) An estimated time is allotted to each activity.

(5) The activities are suitable for the particular class.

(6) An assignment is planned and is clear.

(7) Sufficient evaluation techniques are planned.

(8) The evaluation techniques permit the teacher to find out if the students have attained the objectives set forth.

(9) Bibliographical references are given.

(10) Necessary instructional aids and sources are included.

(11) The lesson plan as a whole is well organized.

(12) The lesson plan is plausible for a class period.

(13) The lesson plan shows effort on the part of the teacher.

(14) Attention has been paid to mechanics of English usage, including spelling, punctuation, grammar, etc.

(15) The lesson plan is of sufficient length—not too brief, not too long.

15. Demonstrate your lesson plan in class. Let the class comment on the effectiveness of your plan and offer constructive suggestions for its improvement.

16. Questions for class discussion or written exercise:

a. Show how the unit method of teaching may be applied in teaching in your subject field.

b. On what philosophical, psychological, and sociological premises is the unit method of teaching based?

c. What features of the unit method of teaching do you like most? What features do you like least?

d. Show the interrelationships between a resource unit, a learning unit, and a lesson plan.

e. Show the relationship between the resource unit and curriculum improvement.

17. Find outlines of learning units, resource units, and lesson plans in the educational literature. Compare these outlines with the one given in your textbook. In what ways are they the same? In what ways are they different? Select (or create) an outline for a learning unit, a resource unit, and a lesson plan which you feel would suit you in teaching your subject.

SELECTED BIBLIOGRAPHICAL REFERENCES

1. Alberty, Harold. *Reorganizing the High-School Curriculum.* New York: Macmillan, 1953. Chapters 13, 14, and 15.

The author discusses and illustrates learning units in Chapter 13. Chapters 14 and 15 contain a detailed explanation of the resource unit in curriculum organization and procedures for developing resource units. This 1953 edition is a revision of his earlier 1947 edition, which is cited earlier in the footnotes.

2. Alcorn, Marvin D., Kinder, James S., and Schunert, Jim R. *Better Teaching in Secondary Schools.* Rev. ed. New York: Holt, Rinehart & Winston, 1964. Chapters 3, 4, and 5.

These chapters contain a helpful discussion on long-term planning, constructing teaching units, daily planning, and planning with students.

3. Alexander, William M. and Halverson, Paul M. *Effective Teaching in Secondary Schools.* New York: Holt, Rinehart & Winston, 1956. Chapters 14 and 15.

Chapter 14 considers planning the organization of instruction, developing statements of purposes of instruction, and planning units. Chapter 15 shows teachers how to plan from day to day, including planning class meetings, arranging physical facilities, and selecting resources.

4. Bossing, Nelson. *Teaching in Secondary School.* Englewood Cliffs, N. J.: Prentice-Hall, 1952. Chapter 3.

The author deals in this chapter with the development of teaching units.

5. Burton, William H. *The Guidance of Learning Activities.* New York: Appleton-Century-Crofts, 1952, pp. 388–479.

The author presents a thorough and detailed treatment of unit planning. He distinguishes between subject-matter units and experience units. He refers to resource units as "source units." See also the revised (3rd) edition of this book, 1962, Chapters 13, 14, and 15.

6. Grambs, Jean D., Iverson, William J. and Patterson, Franklin K. *Modern Methods in Secondary Education.* Rev. ed. New York: Holt, Rinehart & Winston, 1958. Chapter 6.

This is a readable chapter on planning for teaching and learning.

7. Hansen, Kenneth H. *High School Teaching.* Englewood Cliffs, N. J.: Prentice-Hall, 1957. Chapters 4 through 10.

The seven chapters, 4 through 10, include helpful material on a variety of phases of teaching and learning. Chapter 6 deals specifically with unit and lesson planning.

8. Klausmeier, Herbert J. *Teaching in the Secondary School.* New York: Harper & Row, 1958. Chapters 6 through 9.

The author presents in an attractive format material on unit and daily planning, developing activities, and evaluating progress in learning.

9. Mills, Hubert H. and Douglass, Harl R. *Teaching in High School.* 2nd ed. New York: Ronald Press, 1957. Chapters 10, 11, 14, and 15.

In these chapters the authors discuss the need for preliminary planning, sources of information for planning, long-range planning, daily planning, teaching instructional units, and selecting and using instructional materials.

10. Oliva, Peter F. and Scrafford, Ralph A. *Teaching in a Modern Secondary School.* Columbus: Charles E. Merrill Books, Inc., 1965. Chapter 2.

This chapter proposes methods of long-range planning, short-range planning, and involving pupils in planning.

11. Risk, Thomas M. *Principles and Practices of Teaching in Secondary Schools.* New York: American Book Co., 1958. Unit II.

The author in Unit II of this book considers means of planning courses, using unit plans, and planning daily activities.

12. Rivlin, Harry N. *Teaching Adolescents in Secondary Schools.* 2nd ed. New York: Appleton-Century-Crofts, 1961. Chapters 4 and 5.

In Chapter 4 the author discusses the characteristics of a unit of work and procedures for carrying out a unit. Chapter 5 focuses on developing a lesson plan and teaching a class lesson.

INSTRUCTIONAL AIDS AND SOURCES

1. Film: *The Broader Concept of Method, Part II: Teachers and Pupils Planning and Working Together.* 19 min. Sound. Black and white. New York: McGraw-Hill.

Guided by the teacher, the pupils plan and work together in groups to prepare a group report.

2. Resource persons: A panel of experienced teachers on the topic, "Planning For Instruction."

3. File of sample learning units, resource units, and lesson plans.

THE INSTRUCTIONAL PROCESS

OBJECTIVES OF UNIT IV

At the conclusion of his reading and correlated study-discussion activities the reader should

A. understand that

1. instructional practices are based to a large extent on learning theory;

2. planning, presentation, and evaluation are all parts of the instructional process;

3. the teacher's perception of himself as a teacher and as a person, his perception of others, and his perception of others' attitudes toward him affect the learning situation;

4. some theories of learning can be supported by experimental evidence; some theories are unsupported or have been disproved by experimental evidence;

5. teaching is a highly personalized and unique cluster of skills, concepts, and knowledge;

6. differences between effective teaching and ineffective teaching can be observed, although they are most difficult to measure;

7. there is no such person as "the born teacher";

8. actions of all humans, teacher and learners included, are colored by their previous experiences;

9. some of our beliefs about the ways human beings learn go back to antiquity;

10. conditioning is an ever-present phenomenon in our schools;

11. competition can be over emphasized;

12. the community can provide valuable educative experiences.

B. show appreciation for

1. the informed, knowledgeable teacher,

2. a smooth, well-organized presentation,

3. the teacher who skillfully employs many kinds of learning materials and activities,

4. the teacher who skillfully handles group instruction,

5. the teacher who can individualize instruction,

6. a mentally healthful, positive climate for learning,

7. the teacher who is a fully functioning personality.

C. adopt attitudes of

1. rejection of untenable psychological beliefs,

2. willingness to make application of supported psychological principles,

3. willingness to try out new techniques of instruction,

4. desire to perfect most frequently used techniques of instruction,

5. belief that change for the better is possible—in one's self, in pupils' selves, in one's teaching ability, in pupils' achievement,

6. concern for pupils' development of positive self-concepts,

7. avoidance of exaggerated claims for the value of one's specialty,

8. willingness to use educational experiences to be found in the community.

D. be able to demonstrate skill in

1. motivating students,

2. appraising oneself,

3. enhancing students' self-concepts,

4. conducting effective drill sessions,

5. utilizing classroom aids available,

6. questioning,

7. assignment-making,

8. handling classroom routines.

E. know the following:

1. general principles of:

  a. faculty psychology

  b. behaviorism

  c. experimentalism

  d. perceptual psychology

  e. gestalt psychology

2. distinctions between extrinsic and intrinsic motivation,

3. the meaning of the terms:

  a. self-concept

  b. fully functioning personality

  c. facilitating teacher

  d. individualized instruction

CHAPTER 10

THE NATURE OF EFFECTIVE TEACHING

WHAT IS EFFECTIVE TEACHING?

A plan for instruction, whether a lesson plan or unit plan, may appear excellent on paper. The plan may include ingenious, thoughtful objectives, provide for creative activities, and contain precise means of evaluation. The bibliography and instructional sources listed may be ample and pertinent. This fine plan, however, may prove a dud in the classroom when the teacher attempts to translate the plan into action. The objectives may not be realized. The activities may become disorganized. The teacher may not be able to evaluate the success of the plan. The resources planned for may not be available, or perhaps not be as pertinent to the topic as the teacher had previously believed.

The teacher may have spent many hours in planning for a classroom presentation. He may have followed his plan, made great effort in his presentation, waxed eloquent, utilized elaborate audio-visual aids, and, in spite of his heroic attempt to impart learning, been greeted by blank stares on the faces of his learners: in spite of careful planning the learners have not learned.

No plan can be considered successful unless it can be carried through effectively in the classroom. Neither planning nor presentation can be considered effective until such time as the planning and presentation have caused a change in behavior on the part of the learners. The effectiveness of instruction is revealed by sufficient demonstration that the pupils have learned, or realized the objectives of instruction.

EXAMPLES OF EFFECTIVE TEACHING

Let us, for a short time, assume the role of a general supervisor on the superintendent's staff. It shall be our mission to visit a large secondary school in our school district. Our major responsibility is to assist teachers in that school to improve the effectiveness of their instruction. We would undoubtedly be pleased as we discovered the following teaching situations on the day of our visit:

> Members of the physics class were seriously working with simple magnets and discussing elementary principles of magnetism.
>
> Members of the twelfth-grade English class were presenting a lively report on William Golding's *The Lord of the Flies.*
>
> The teacher in the problems of democracy class was conducting an interesting group discussion on the relationship between cigarettes and lung cancer.
>
> The teacher in the geometry course was explaining clearly to his group, using the blackboard, a point about set theory which apparently needed clarification.
>
> A student in the Latin class was indicating on a map of Ancient Europe Caesar's location as described in the passage the class was now reading.
>
> Pupils in a tenth-grade English class were, in an orderly fashion, asking the teacher questions about the next topic for study, which was the short story.
>
> The teacher in a homemaking class was moving from girl to girl offering assistance on a sewing project with which they were busy.
>
> The students in algebra class were busy with an examination on dittoed sheets which the teacher had just distributed to them.
>
> The walls of the room of a ninth-grade English teacher were covered with an exhibit of student compositions, charts, and pictures, which had been created and arranged by the students themselves.

In each of these classrooms was some clue to effective teaching. Interest appeared high in most of these situations. Pupil participation was encouraged. The teachers were making an effort to reach the students in terms they understood. There was evidence of control in each classroom. Teachers were emphasizing essentials and not trivialities. We might conclude that we had witnessed good teaching on this day. By good teaching we mean effective teaching. It is obvious in some situations that pupils are learning: We can see it in their faces. We can judge by their questions. We can gauge the manner in which pupils follow directions and go about assigned duties. We can observe the interchange of conversation in a classroom.

We should not, however, make the mistake of assuming that the effective teaching we had seen on that particular day in those particular classrooms would always occur. No teaching can be effective every period of every day. Some teachers are consistently more effective in their teaching than other teachers. When a teacher rather consistently produces positive, changed behavior in his pupils and it can be truly said that they have learned, that teacher can be labeled a good teacher. When a teacher's pupils rather consistently fail to learn, that teacher may be labeled a poor teacher or ineffective teacher.

EXAMPLES OF INEFFECTIVE TEACHING

Elements of ineffectiveness were in operation in the following classrooms on the same day of our visit:

The teacher in a tenth-grade world history class was shouting the next day's assignment over the din of bell and student chatter.

In a biology class the teacher was lecturing to a group on the paramecium, while pupils were talking in small cliques around the room.

The teacher in a general mathematics class was laboriously writing test questions on the board for pupils to answer.

In an American history class the teacher was asking pupils the most trivial, minute questions which she was drawing from the chapter of the textbook held open before her.

The same two students in a ninth-grade English class answered questions, made comments, and dominated the class session for at least one-half of the period.

The general science teacher was engaged in a conversation with one pupil at the front of the room while the other pupils were left to their own devices.

These teachers were not making maximum use of the instructional time. They were, perhaps, unaware that their teaching at these particular moments was less effective than it might have been. They did not realize, perhaps, that some modifications in their instructional techniques might have brought about a higher level of achievement on the part of the learners.

We would not generalize that the teachers in these latter classrooms were consistently poor or ineffective teachers. On the other hand, the incidents provide clues, which, if repeated, would indicate ineffective teaching.

As we reflect upon the teaching we have witnessed on our visits to various classrooms, we try to formulate in our mind answers to the perplexing questions: What is good teaching? Why were some of the teaching situations clearly demonstrations of good teaching? Why were others obviously inferior situations? Is it possible for a poor teacher to become a good teacher? For that matter, what is a good teacher? Are there such creatures as "born teachers?"

NO "BORN TEACHERS"

We should dispel immediately the notion that there is any such person as the "born teacher." There can no more be a "born teacher" than a "born lawyer" or a "born doctor" or "born musician." The subtle traits that go into the creation of a competent teacher are more the products of the environment into which the future teacher is born and in which he is reared than of his heredity.

Environmental conditions often confuse the layman and make it appear that certain individuals were destined for teaching. For one thing, many teachers come from families in which there have been several teachers throughout the years. The "born teacher" has been actually conditioned from earliest years by the presence of teachers in his family. He will be favorably disposed to teaching if the members of his family who are teachers are enthusiastic about their careers, if they find satisfaction in teaching, and if they encourage their children to look into teaching as a career. By the same token, prospective teachers are driven out of the profession by teacher-relatives who find low levels of satisfaction in teaching and who warn their children away from teaching.

The so-called "born teacher" often has personal qualities that would ensure success in a number of occupations. He likes people. He gets along well with others. He can live within the restrictions imposed by the profession. He speaks well. He enjoys appearing before groups.

The so-called "born teacher" is generally a person who enjoys books and has a respect for learning. He normally has an intense interest in some field of scholarship, such as history or mathematics or science.

We may conclude that the "born teacher" is a myth. Any teacher may become a better teacher, given a willingness to improve, certain basic personal traits, and sufficient preparation. There are some people who by reason of their personalities or of their lack of preparation or motivation should not be in the classroom. These teachers who may be called incompetent would constitute a small percentage of the teaching force. Given a desire to improve, wholesome fundamental personal traits, and the requisite preparation in both their subject fields and in pedagogy, even poor teachers can become better teachers—indeed, in some cases, good teachers.

CONCEPTS OF THE "GOOD" TEACHER

We should distinguish not only between the "good" teacher and the "born" teacher but we should distinguish between a good teacher whose pupils learn effectively and a teacher who is labeled good by certain partisans. For example, some administrators are prone to refer to strict disciplinarians as "good" teachers. As they walk through the halls they smile on the teachers whose classrooms are characterized by the complete absence of noise. Or they frown if they hear students talking during a class, whether the talking is pertinent to the subject or not. There are parents who label as "good" teachers who force their children to learn, who not only lead the children to water but make them drink as well. Or, they prize teachers whose harried students have achieved high scores on standardized achievement and scholarship tests regardless of factors of mental health and physical exhaustion. A few students believe "easy" teachers, ones who give few assignments, permit sloppy work, and give high grades, are "good" teachers. Fortunately, most students, administrators, and parents have a more balanced image of a "good" teacher.

We may describe the good or effective teacher as one who:

1. holds an adequate concept of himself;
2. understands basic principles of the learning process;
3. demonstrates effective techniques of instruction;
4. efficiently handles management of the classroom;
5. is fully prepared in his subject;
6. understands the role of the school in our society; and
7. possesses personal characteristics conducive to success in the classroom.

We have discussed the question of preparation in the subject field (item five above) in our first unit of this text, particularly as it bears on the certification of teachers. The role of the school in our society (item six above) forms a portion of our second unit. We shall deal with the personal characteristics of the teacher (item seven above) in our sixth unit, when we relate personality traits of the teacher to the problems of discipline and control. Now we shall consider the first four characteristics in our description of the effective teacher. Classroom management (item four above) is discussed in this unit as an integral part of techniques of instruction. In Unit VI we consider classroom management from the standpoint of discipline and control.

HOLDING AN ADEQUATE CONCEPT OF ONESELF

Except that it seems so abusive of the King's English to say, as do contemporary perceptual psychologists, "The effective person is one who holds an adequate concept of his self" we cannot overlook the relevance of modern psychology's studies of the "self" and the "self concept."

The self is the individuality of the person. It is derived from one's biological inheritance and all the past experiences of the individual. We have all undergone unique experiences. Some of these experiences have helped us to mature; some have hindered us and made us close up into our shells.

We have been and continue to be throughout life highly selective in the perception of elements in our environment. Our past experiences lead us to select from our environment elements with which we are familiar and to ignore or to be unaware of those environmental elements with which we have had little contact. As we walk down the street, we are aware of persons with whom we can identify. The ardent fisherman does not miss seeing a man who is carrying a large fish that didn't get away. Persons without contact with colored minorities may pass a Negro on the street and not know that he was actually there. When we read the newspapers, we select those articles that please us or are of special interest to us. We may begin with the news columns. We may turn to the sports page first and on the sports page we may look for the football news before we read about golf or boxing. We may turn to the comics first. Or we may read the advice to the lovelorn columns. If we had lived in France, we may scan the news for articles on France first of all.

The teen-ager perceives life in ways much different from the retired adult. As we grow older, we often tend to become more conservative in dress, manner, and our views on life. Our occupation determines to a great extent the elements of our environment with which we will have familiarity and the beliefs and values we will hold. The physician is concerned not only with saving lives and healing bodies but if he subscribes to the American Medical Association's views, he regards with abhorrence national health programs such as Medicare. The labor unionist and the industrialist have different views and interpretations of "featherbedding." The American and Russian differ fundamentally on the meaning of the word "democracy."

Those individuals who are satisfied with themselves, have a healthy outlook on life, can live with their limitations, are conscious of the world in which they live, value themselves, and see themselves as valued by others are "adequate" or "fully functioning" persons. Significantly, the self is shaped in relationship to others. We become what we are through the influence of others in our environment. We change our behavior as others assist us to change our behavior. Unfortunately, persons closest to us often have undergone experiences that have damaged their own personalities. Some children develop a contempt for books because their parents dislike books and ridicule "bookishness." Some children today are pushed too soon into social relationships with members of the opposite sex, since parents feel anxiously that their children must establish early heterosexual popularity.

On the other hand, children whose parents respect learning may themselves respect and want an education. Children whose parents expose them to the fine arts may wish to pursue some field of the fine arts. Children who associate with adults who value their relationship with other people may express a greater interest in others and more regard for the opinions of others. Children whose teachers encourage them to express themselves without fear of censure or ridicule or reprisal will be more open personalities. Children whose peers accept them and want their company are learning to become more adequate persons.

Persons whose unique experiences have enabled them to achieve self-fulfillment exemplify fully functioning personalities. Earl Kelley describes the characteristics of the fully functioning personality as follows:[1]

1. *The fully functioning personality thinks well of himself.* He likes himself. He knows his limitations but realizes there are limits to the capacities of all human beings. He believes himself capable of doing his chosen work.

2. *The fully functioning personality thinks well of others.* A person who regards himself as adequate tends to like other persons. He realizes that his own self-ness has been derived by association with other individuals. He sees others as helps to his own development and as companions and associates, rather than as threats to his existence.

3. *The fully functioning self sees his stake in others.* As Kelley puts it, "He has a selfish interest then in the quality of those around him and has responsibility in some degree for that quality. . . . He comes to see other people as opportunities, not for exploitation, but for the building of self."[2]

4. *The fully functioning self sees himself as a part of a world in movement—in process of becoming.* The fully functioning personality expects change and reacts positively to it. He knows that change is a fundamental law of nature. He knows that all life evolves and must evolve if improvements in living are to be made. The possibility of change can produce a positive outlook on the world, since one can hope for changes. The fully functioning self recognizes the fact that the old cliché, "You can't change human nature," is not and never was true. The fully functioning personality knows that he can improve, can become a fuller, more adequate personality. He knows that others may become fuller personalities, too. The fully functioning self has an optimistic view about life, never abandons hope that life and people can be better.

5. *The fully functioning self sees the value of mistakes.* The fully functioning self is not afraid to make mistakes. He is not afraid of what others may say about him if he takes a position contrary to common belief and practice. He knows full well that innovations will not always prove successful. But he knows that he must be willing to try out new ways and not be content that the status quo is the best way. Fortunately, many of our great men of letters and sciences have not been afraid to make mis-

---

[1] "The Fully Functioning Self," *Perceiving, Behaving, Becoming,* Ch. 2, 1962 Yearbook, Association for Supervision and Curriculum Development, (Washington: A.S.C.D., N.E.A., 1962), pp. 18–20.

[2] *Ibid.,* p. 18.

takes. They have experimented with new ideas, made mistakes, but wound up with essential truths.

6. *The fully functioning self develops and holds human values.* He values individuality and creativity. He believes that people are important. He views human values as more important than materialistic values. He realizes that others' values toward him as a human being and an individual are an integral part of his values toward others.

7. *The fully functioning self knows no other way to live except in keeping with his values.* "To thine own self be true" is a saying that well describes the fully functioning self. He knows the values he holds and strives to live within his pattern of values. He is honest and open. He has the essential ingredient of integrity.

8. *The fully functioning self is cast in a creative role.* He not only accepts and is aware of change but also enters into the process of effective change. He is not only unwilling to maintain the status quo but willing to help effect improvements in life. He contributes new ideas and energy. He derives a joy and zest from living.

RELEVANCE OF SELF-CONCEPT TO TEACHING

The self-concept has relevance for teachers and teaching in at least two respects: (1) the importance of the teacher's own development of a fully functioning self and (2) the necessity for the teacher to be concerned about the development of the pupils' selves.

We might substitute the word "teacher" in each of Kelley's statements about the fully functioning self. The fully functioning teacher is one who thinks well of himself. He thinks well of others. He sees his stake in others. He sees himself as a part of a world in movement—in the process of becoming. He sees the values of mistakes (not only his own, but his pupils'). He develops and holds human values. He knows no other way to live except in keeping with his values. He sees himself cast in a creative role. Teachers who exhibit these wholesome characteristics are fully functioning or, as some psychologists term it, "self-actualizing" personalities. They accept themselves and express themselves. They respect their profession. They see in it an opportunity for self-fulfillment. Teaching affords them an opportunity to express themselves creatively and to encourage others to express themselves. The self-actualizing person is free from impairing neuroses and psychoses.

Certainly, we have in the profession persons who do not possess fully functioning personalities, but, fortunately, the malfunctioning personality is found in only a minority of the teaching profession. That we are all less than fully self-actualizing personalities we would have to admit. But herein is one of the strengths of the self-concept. If we believe in change, we can believe that it is possible to improve, to become better than we are, to modify our ways of behaving. Provided that *(a)* we have some assistance from other self-actualizing persons, especially those in status positions such as the principal, and *(b)* we are not mentally ill, we can be less conforming, more courageous, less vindictive, less malicious, more informed, more understanding. The self unlike the body can grow as long as we live.

Arthur Combs, a perceptual psychologist, defines a "good teacher" as "one who has learned to use his unique self in effective ways." The good teacher has appraised himself. He knows his strengths and limitations. He sees his role clearly. He sees his place in the scheme of teaching and in the world. He sharpens the skills and competencies which he possesses. He knows that he is an individual who must find his own approaches to teaching. He also knows that the approaches he makes to teaching must be effective in that his pupils learn.

The good teacher has decided for himself what the real values of education are. He is aware of the attitudes of others in respect to objectives of education and approaches to learning. He realizes that he is not on a remote island by himself but is a part of a complex whole. He perceives of himself as an important individual, of teaching as a vital career, and of his subject matter as essential. He has confidence in his ability to present his subject and to make it intelligible to the learners. He knows how he evaluates himself and has a clear idea of how his colleagues, students, and others evaluate him.

The effective teacher must see himself as competent. He must see himself as a member of a competent team. He must feel that he is recognized as competent by his colleagues, superiors, and students.

While the fully functioning teacher is aware of the existence and development of the self, he is concerned at the same time that his learners develop adequate self-concepts. He knows that he is instrumental in helping them to develop a sense of adequacy. Teachers are often unaware of the tremendous impact they have on developing personalities. They are so preoccupied with their conceptions of their primary mission—to impart as much subject matter or book larnin' to as many pupils as possible in the shortest possible time—that they are blissfully unaware of the selves that go begging to be fed.

THE TEACHER AS FACILITATOR

The teacher who is conscious of the self plays a "facilitating" role. That is, he helps the learners to learn. He serves as a guide to learning rather than as a fountain of all authority. His classes are more democratic in nature than those of teachers imbued with an authoritarian outlook on life. He helps learners to become aware of themselves and each other. He provides experiences that give his pupils opportunities to develop confidence and to feel success. He establishes a classroom climate where pupils feel they belong, can make mistakes without reprisals, and can work cooperatively. The teacher who is conscious of the self seeks occasions for planning course work with the pupils. He recognizes that his primary mission is to help immature learners gain an adequate concept of the self.

The ASCD 1962 Yearbook clearly shows the role of the teacher in relation to the development of the self-concept:

> It is important, therefore, in working with students, that the feelings about self be given an important place in the classroom program. This does not call for units and assignments and lectures about how one should see himself. Rather, it grows out of the normal conditions of teaching. It is possible for a teacher to see his educational goals in terms broad enough to include the self concept while simultaneously achieving high academic standards.
>
> If a positive view of self is so important in the development of creative productive people, then the self must be admitted to the classroom and provision made for its development. Since teachers, like others, tend to behave in terms of what they consider to be important, the teacher who believes the self concepts of his charges are important will do something about them. Teachers who do not believe the self concept is important, or who are unaware of the nature of the self concept and its effects upon behavior, will be less likely to be effective in encouraging and assisting the development of more adequate selves.[3]

UNDERSTANDING BASIC PRINCIPLES
OF THE LEARNING PROCESS

Every act of the teacher in the classroom, every method or technique he employs, and every aspect of the curriculum is influenced to some extent by the teacher's conception of the nature of learning. As a result of his experience and preparation the teacher holds notions, some of which are erroneous and rigidly fixed, about the ways by which humans learn. Since we as teachers are concerned primarily that our learners do, in effect, learn, we must have some knowledge of the learning process. Intelligent application of the best we know about the complex and fascinating process of learning is a requisite of effective teaching.

All our beliefs and practices rest on some conceptions of learning. Some of these conceptions can be supported by ample research. Others are little more than myths or assertions of individual teachers or groups of teachers.

Some of our beliefs and practices are clearly disproved by psychological

[3] Association for Supervision and Curriculum Development, *Perceiving, Behaving, Becoming,* 1962 Yearbook (Washington: A.S.C.D., N.E.A., 1962), p. 95.

research but are perpetuated in the classroom and school in spite of scientific evidence which would negate them.

Some of our beliefs and practices can be clearly supported by psychological study. We know that human beings react better to praise than to blame. We know that all normal human beings seek recognition, approval, and success. We know that short drill periods are more effective and less exhausting than long drill sessions. We know that individuals differ in a variety of ways. We know that if an individual sees purpose in his learning he will more likely persist in his efforts to learn.

Some of our beliefs and practices cannot be supported by scientific evidence but appear to be sound on the basis of logic, previous experience, and limited success. It may be that a seven-period day has more merit than the six-period day. A seven-period day may provide interested students with additional opportunities for learning. It is highly probable that smaller classes produce better results than larger classes, but we have no evidence to indicate specifically how large a class should be for maximum effectiveness.

To help us determine which beliefs and practices can be defended we must turn to the realm of psychology.

CHAPTER 11

LEARNING THEORIES

In professional circles we often speak of "learning theory." Sometimes misinformed individuals use the term as if there were but one, single, fully proved theory which if followed to the letter would solve all our pedagogical ills. If we use the term "learning theory" at all, we should more accurately speak of "learning theories." There are some professional persons who would have us abandon the term "learning theory" and focus instead on "instructional theory." While we may eventually develop an adequate, well-synthesized, balanced instructional theory or theories, we will continue to hear and use in popular parlance the term "learning theory." In this chapter we use "learning theories" in reference to different schools of psychology and we use "learning theory" in a generalized way.

There have been through the centuries many theories as to the ways by which human beings learn. Some of the theories have been wild. Many have been untested. Over the years some of our erroneous notions about learning have been disproved by experimentation. Modern psychological studies have contributed a wealth of knowledge about the learner and the nature and process of learning.

We shall give our attention to three major theories and indicate the salient features of each. These are: (1) faculty psychology, (2) behaviorism, and (3) experimentalism. To these we add two companions of experimentalism: (4) gestalt psychology and (5) perceptual psychology. We have already made acquaintance with perceptual psychology in the preceding chapter of this unit where we introduced the self-concept. We shall discuss in the paragraphs that follow the other four theories.

In this discussion of learning theory it is our aim (1) to make the prospective and beginning teacher realize that every technique he uses, every task he assigns, every educational program he champions implies some conception about the way humans learn, (2) to make the prospective and beginning teacher familiar enough with some of the principal learning theories so that he may intelligently pursue further study of them, and (3) to illustrate ways by which these theories are applied in school situations.

FACULTY PSYCHOLOGY

Were it not for the fact that many teachers hold views of learning which smack of the elements of faculty psychology, we would omit any discussion of this theory from our text. It is in some ways unfortunate, though essential, that we must devote some time to consideration of a theory which no reputable psychologist on the current scene espouses. Although the principles of faculty psychology have been largely discredited by experimental evidence through the years, their melody lingers on. We hear the tune when teachers speak in the following manner:

Trigonometry teaches you to reason.

You should know the names of the capitals of each of the fifty states.

We'll repeat this list of spelling words until you have them all correct.

Every high school student should study foreign languages.

It doesn't matter if the course is uninteresting to the student.

They'd better learn this or else!

They want everything sugar-coated these days.

Let's cut out the fads and frills, and buckle down to solid subjects.

Who needs to use movies? I'm not entertaining them, I'm teaching them.

The exams should be longer and more difficult.

A high school diploma ought to *really* mean something.

Give 'em six subjects and keep 'em busy.

Pile on the homework.

We're losing the art of memorizing.

We could continue, but these commonly heard statements are sufficient to indicate that the authors of these statements hold some rather ancient, and unsupported, views on learning.

FORMAL DISCIPLINE

Faculty psychology is known to the profession in a number of guises. It is called "formal discipline," "mental discipline," and "mind-substance theory." We may use the names interchangeably. According to this theory the mind is a muscle which is made up of faculties. Among these faculties, each of which resides in a fixed portion of the brain, are reason, memory, observation, imagination, and will. The function of subject matter is to train the mind, exercising each of the faculties. The theory of formal discipline dates back at least to the time of Plato. Plato in *The Republic* concluded that the soul, composed of the elements of reason, spirit, and appetite, consisted also of the faculties of reason, faith, understanding, and knowledge of shadows.

In historical philosophy the mind was often equated or confused with the Christian soul. Wolff, an eighteenth-century German psychologist, identified faculties of memory, reason, and will as capacities of the soul. Another eighteenth-century German, the famed Immanuel Kant, separated mental processes into knowing, feeling, and willing.

The doctrine of formal discipline has long borne overtones of religious teaching, particularly the Calvinist doctrine of original sin. This outlook on life sees man as created in sin through the folly of Adam and Eve. Man is, then, essentially an evil creature. To overcome his sinfulness he must persist throughout life in unpleasant, disagreeable tasks to knock the sinfulness out of him. Persisting in disagreeable tasks is considered to be the best type of character training. This persistence strengthens and develops the will and leads the individual to strength of character and spirit.

With the mind-substance theory, subject matter itself is relatively unimportant. The task of the teacher is to identify suitable subject matter to train each of the faculties, the more rigorous, dull, uninteresting, and difficult the subject the better. To train the faculty of reason we might resort to geometry; for memory, spelling lists and dates; for observation, Latin with its many inflections; for imagination, classical literature. We might believe that science would be suitable for the development of reasoning and observation, but science was considered too mundane and too utilitarian for inclusion in the school curriculum until well into the eighteenth century. Nor did the English language fare much better until the same era. The classical languages and literature provided all the training in memory and imagination that any member of the intellectual aristocracy might want.

All of the faculties were valued as equally important. Consequently, the teacher should spend the same amount of time on each subject. Our high schools, by and large, in spite of the inroads being made by revolutionary practices, still subscribe to the practice of scheduling all subjects for one period a day, five days a week, to permit students to earn one Carnegie unit of credit. The 1894 Report of the Committee of Ten, mentioned in the previous unit, illustrated this point when it agreed with a group of ninety-eight teachers that:

> . . . every subject which is taught at all in a secondary school should be taught in the same way and to the same extent to every pupil so long as

he pursues it, no matter what the probable destination of the pupil may be, or at what point his education is to cease. Thus, for all pupils who study Latin, or history, or algebra, for example, the allotment of time and the method of instruction in a given school should be the same year by year. Not that all pupils should pursue every subject for the same number of years; but so long as they do pursue it, they should all be treated alike.[1]

DRILL

Drill is a key word in formal discipline. Pupils need plenty of drill. They should memorize whatever the teacher has selected for them to memorize: poetry, catechism, psalter, multiplication tables, postage rates. It matters not whether the drill has meaning to the learners. Drills should be frequent and difficult. While the learner is reciting, his character is being strengthened at the same time. We can all visualize the seventeenth-century schoolmaster standing over his charges, New England Primer in one hand and switch in the other, directing the rote-memorization of passages in the Primer. Fear of speedy punishment for not knowing or not doing the work was the motivating force. The overemphasis and malpractice in conduct of drill sessions have unfortunately given the very word "drill" a bad name in educational circles. If we have in mind rote-memorization of meaningless subject matter, drill deserves its bad reputation. If, on the other hand, we speak of meaningful practice through a variety of techniques until essential skills are built and habits formed, drill can hold an honored place in our repertoire of teaching techniques

TRANSFER OF TRAINING

The followers of faculty psychology are great believers in transfer of training. They believe that subject matter taught in school will transfer readily to life situations. If we do not transfer the skills or understandings learned in a course, we at least transfer habits of neatness, persistence, accuracy, and dependability. By developing our faculties in school we are made ready to transfer our training to out-of-school and future situations. The doctrine of formal discipline ignores the concept of individual differences. If there is any difference in intelligence, we need not concern ourselves too much. The slow student should receive more of the same rather than less or a different program. Or, he should not be permitted to continue in school at all, for school is the place where we train the mind. If a pupil does not have much of a mind to train, he would be better off hoeing potatoes or digging ditches or collecting garbage.

The formal disciplinarians grasped only half of the truth about transfer. Transfer of training is best realized when certain conditions obtain.

---

[1] National Education Association, *Report of the Committee of Ten on Secondary School Studies* (New York: American Book Co., 1894), p. 17.

Bright students transfer more frequently than do slower students. They see applications to situations not specified in their education. The brighter the learner, the greater the transfer. The more highly motivated the learner, the greater the transfer. Pupils who want to see applications of learning will more frequently do so. The learner will transfer more of his learning if the teacher consciously teaches for transfer. The teacher should point out possible applications of the learning in as many situations as possible. Students should know the conditions under which they will encounter and use their learnings. Transfer is greater when the learnings taught in school are most nearly like the situations which pupils will encounter out of school. For example, in the case of typing, the pupil learns to type in school and then utilizes the skills in office or college or home. The mathematics student who specializes in college in mathematics will transfer more of his learnings than will the mathematics student who ceases to use many of the mathematical skills he has learned in school.

THE FACULTY-PSYCHOLOGY CURRICULUM

The practitioners of the mind-substance theory, for the most part, scorn the necessity of appealing to individual interests. They regard interest on the part of the learner as inconsequential. They maintain that the individual can learn whether he is interested or not. If he were but a little less recalcitrant, he could apply himself. In fact, if he is not interested in the subject matter, it may do his mind or his soul more good. Johann Pestalozzi, to his eternal credit, though he believed that the learner possessed innate faculties, broke centuries of tradition when he instituted in the late eighteenth century a curriculum centered around interests of the learners and sought to permit young learners to make their own discoveries.

The curriculum of a school oriented to faculty psychology is largely bookish in nature. Vocational courses are lumped with extra-class activities, home economics, art, and music as frills. Elective courses are eliminated or minimized. The desire to reduce elective courses is heard in the derogatory phrase, "cafeteria courses," which suggests that there are too many choices offered to students, many of which are nonessential. The classroom teacher who stresses formal discipline maximizes drill, eliminates audio-visual aids, utilizes punishment rather frequently, emphasizes marks, conducts rigorous examinations, and enforces high teacher-set standards.

Efforts to localize the centers of mental faculties have not proved rewarding. Efforts to train the minds of numerous generations have been less than successful, since it is apparent that all of us who have been subjected to formal discipline would be far more learned had it been the rousing success it was supposed to be. Contemporary psychological research attempts to analyze intelligence in terms of primary mental abilities or differential aptitudes, which we consider at greater length in Unit V, "Guidance for the Classroom Teacher." We should not confuse these abilities with the so-called faculties of faculty psychology. Although reasoning and memory are identified as primary mental abilities, these differ from faculty psychology in a number of ways. Contemporary psychologists refer to these abilities as aspects of intelligence, rather than faculties of the mind. They do not localize these traits in specific portions of the brain, nor do they maintain that all of these traits can be developed equally by judicious selection of subject matter. Quite the opposite, contemporary psychologists maintain that some individuals excel others in respect to specific mental traits. One individual may rank high in verbal reasoning but low in numerical ability. No specific subject matter can be identified to develop specific mental traits. These mental traits or aptitudes may be developed through use of a variety of subject matters. Contemporary psychologists reject the notion that the mind is a muscle which can be trained by drill in selected subject matter.

There is great danger that in spite of the evidence to repudiate faculty psychology its doctrines can regain considerable strength in our schools. Some of our current practices in our frantic pursuit of scholarship on the part of all learners regardless of ability or purpose should be evaluated constantly. Are we not in our zeal to have more students learn more in a shorter time reverting to some of the archaic principles of formal discipline?

BEHAVIORISM

"Rat psychology" is the term that leaps to the minds of many undiscerning persons when we mention behaviorism. The term "rat psychology" is not only an oversimplification of a complex theory of learning but it is also a sarcastic means of decrying a theory which has considerable relevancy to instruction. If we had to choose those theories that have had the greatest impact on twentieth-century education, we would name behaviorism and experimentalism, which we will discuss next. It is true that a great deal of the psychological research of behaviorism has been conducted on animals. Granted that animals and human beings cannot be equated, we cannot escape the physical fact that human beings do belong to the animal kingdom and some of the principles of behavioristic theory do have implications for learning in the schools. We are treading the path of behaviorism when we hear teachers who say:

The important thing is to form proper habits.

Choose the right stimuli and you'll get the right response.

Always reinforce the right answer.

Let's have some awards for scholarship.

Objective tests are the best types of tests to use.

If you don't use your learning, you'll forget it.

The teacher must select the subject matter for the child.

Break your subject matter down into tiny pieces.

Teaching machines can teach anything.

Use marks as incentives.

We should give more standardized tests.

Instruction must always be teacher-centered and teacher-directed.

We place under the one canopy of behaviorism a number of related theories that contain minor doctrinal differences. Thus, we will speak of "association," "connectionism," and "conditioning" when we speak of behaviorism, since they all possess related elements and can be classified in the same family.

STIMULUS-RESPONSE

In essence, behavioristic theory holds that learning is the sum of all responses to specific stimuli. Learning can be explained in physiological terms as neural connections between the stimulus and the response, the S-R bond. A specific stimulus begets a specific response. Two plus two begets the answer four. We hear the French word "blanc" and we know, having been drilled on this by our teacher, that it means "white." The more responses we retain, the brighter or more intelligent we are. The mind is no longer a muscle as in the case of faculty psychology, but a totality of neural responses. We change the behavior of the individual, i.e., cause him to learn and to form habits, by carefully selecting and controlling the subject material. The teacher chooses the subject matter from the adult world on the basis of his decision as to what will be best for young, immature human beings to learn.

Instruction is largely a matter of drill. We repeat the subject matter, in different ways if you wish, whether it is history, foreign languages, science, or typing, until the student has made the subject matter a part of himself. The samovar concept of pouring knowledge into the head is not too far removed from behavioristic doctrine. We do a tremendous amount of pouring-in in our classrooms. We depart from the literal meaning of "education," which means "leading out or drawing out" of the learner. We prepackage the learning for the learner and present it to him in minute steps. The behaviorist plays down the role of the learner in figuring out his own answers or even in helping plan ways of attack to find those answers.

EXPERIENCE AND ASSOCIATION

Twentieth-century behaviorists owe a debt to their early forerunners, John Locke and Johann Herbart. Locke, whose political and psychological observations have had a strong influence in the Western world since the late seventeenth century, believed that we are all born into the world with our minds as blank as a white sheet of paper. Our experiences are written upon this blank paper. Locke believed that we learn through the process of association. For example, we encounter fire and by painful experience learn that fire burns us. We learn to avoid fire. We learn that a stove may contain fire and we ought not to touch it. On a more complex level we associate freedom with the good life. We learn to elect officials who will assure us of our freedom. If we experience life under one demagogue, we associate that unpleasant experience with all demagogues and reject others who aspire to power over us.

Herbart, a contemporary of Pestalozzi, regarded the mind as the organization of experiences. It became the teacher's task to organize experiences for the learner and present them to the learner in planned steps. These experiences come from outside the learner. From this thesis we gain a method of presentation referred to as the "Herbartian steps." By following these steps, essentially an inductive process, we can place the material in proper order for learning. The steps proposed are: (1) preparation, (2) presentation, (3) comparison and abstraction, (4) generalization, and (5) application. These steps are still rather widely followed in many classrooms. Both Locke and Herbart disagreed with Pestalozzi over the issue of innate faculties of the mind. Herbart, however, agreed with Pestalozzi that the interests of the learner are an important factor to consider. It is of interest to us to note how theories build on each other, how philosophers accept and reject portions of earlier theses, and how psychologies evolve.

AMERICAN BEHAVIORISTS

No recounting of the story of behaviorism would be complete without mentioning two twentieth-century American psychologists, John B. Watson and Edward L. Thorndike. Watson, behaviorist all the way, saw learning as a purely physiological process. All learning comes, according to Watson, from outside the individual. We learn by joining new responses to specific stimuli. It was Watson who believed that by carefully choosing the appropriate stimuli from the time of birth we could make an individual into anything we wished—scholar, musician, lawyer, or salesman. Thorndike, more properly classified as a connectionist, agreed with Watson that learning takes place through the connection of stimuli and their responses. Yet, he believed we respond in certain ways because we possess inherited tendencies to respond, a belief which Watson rejected. Thorndike is credited with the development of standardized tests of intelligence, achievement, and aptitude. It is Thorndike whom we credit or blame for the emphasis on objective tests. The objective test would be a natural by-product of a theory of learning which stresses mastery of subject matter in minute segments.

CONDITIONING

When we speak of stimulus and response, we speak, too, of a phenomenon of which we should be more aware than we frequently are, that is, the phenomenon of conditioning. The classic experiments in conditioning were performed by the Russian Ivan Pavlov in the late nineteenth and early twentieth century. Pavlov's experiments to condition a dog to salivate at the ringing of a bell have been so widely reported and talked about that sophisticated students of psychology now refer to Pavlov's subject as "that damn dog." Blessed dog or damn dog, Pavlov's work in the field of conditioning reveals implications for the instructional process.

Teachers need to be aware that some of the techniques we use in school are planned forms of conditioning. In one second grade pupils are taught to answer "Yes, ma'am" and "No, ma'am." When they come forth with the proper phrase, they are rewarded by the beaming smile of the teacher. We encourage good table manners by making the school cafeteria an attractive place in which to eat, with small tables, wall decorations, and piped-in music. We make books more appealing by supplying color, readable print, and attractive binding. We reward reading of books by presenting pupils with certificates for a certain number read. Or, we place tiny stars on a large wall chart for high performance in spelling. We are not far from Pavlov's dog when we waft the odors of a tantalizing lunch throughout the school, causing students to yearn for the lunch period. Nor are we far removed when we condition pupils to jump when the bell rings so they may pass to their next classes. The conditioning process can be used effectively. It can also be insidious. It can be a process whose effects we do not detect and whose strengths we cannot gauge. In instructing pupils in a subject teachers often condition them to detest the subject, an utter loss, since pupils may ever after refuse to have anything to do with the subject. By encouraging failure instead of success, by raising standards above the students' abilities to learn, by not heeding interests, by ignoring individual differences in ability and speed of learning, even by not presenting the material in intelligible form we can reap the by-products of conditioning.

We find teachers who employ negative techniques with the mistaken notion that they encourage learning. They threaten students with tests. They stand before the class with their grade books and jot down a numerical figure to be subtracted from the grade for every misbehavior in the classroom. They indulge favorites and penalize students they do not like. Pupils lose a zest for learning under these conditions and often cynically adjust to the idiocyncrasies of the teacher rather than jeopardize their standings in the class and their grades. The prevalence of conditioning in the school should be a topic of study by the faculty of the school. Some elements of conditioning are bound to exist in a school. A faculty should recognize these elements in operation and channel them to enhance rather than discourage learning.

The advertising world has spent millions in motivational research. By sight, sound, and smell, they seek to condition consumers to reach for the "right" product. We can recite from memory many little jingles that we have learned without knowing it. As teachers we must realize the perils in eliciting conditioned responses without the awareness of the learner. We might wish sometimes, however, that we could painlessly condition pupils to reach for a William Shakespeare or take a drink from the fountain of Aristotle or feel the triumphs of Alexander the Great or grasp eagerly the principles of Newton or rub themselves with the elixir of French or dress themselves in the knowledge of algebra or light up with an edition of *The Federalist*.

PROGRAMMED LEARNING

On the current scene B. L. Skinner and N. A. Crowder, advocates of programmed learning, continue the work of the behavioral psychologists. Dormant for a time while the theory of experimentalism was in its ascendancy, behaviorism has reasserted itself in the schools. Skinner and Crowder have helped to reinstitute behavioristic practices, particularly with the advent of programmed instruction. No current innovation in our schools illustrates the principles of behaviorism better than programmed learning, which we have discussed in Unit II of our text. With or without accompanying teaching machines, these materials provide content selected by adult experts in the subject. They offer the content in a step-by-step process. They eliminate failure, since students cannot proceed to the next step until they have mastered the present step. Reinforcement is provided throughout the program. The machine or program reinforces the right response by permitting the student to go on to the next step. The student knows immediately whether his responses are right or wrong. The program or machine says, in effect, "Good. That's right. Move on." The selected facts or skills are taught in sequence, easiest to most difficult. Along the way students take objective tests which are repetitions of material that has already been programmed.

Adherence to behavioristic practices is easily detectable in our schools. Our very courses are compartmentalized, isolated. Generally speaking, each subject is a separate entity with little planned efforts at integrating or correlating content. The material itself is fragmented and taught in bits and pieces, often from a single source or two. We rely on incentives to the learner, as scholarships, degrees, diplomas, certificates, letters, and prizes. Drill sessions are frequent and cramming is condoned, if not openly encouraged. We administer standardized tests of all shapes, sizes, and degrees of validity. We provide visual stimuli through television and teaching machines and oral stimuli through electronic equipment such as language laboratories, television, and stereo. There are some who say—an assertion which must be disputed—that we sugar-coat learning. Though it is difficult to find concrete evidence of sugar-coating, particularly in these times of scholastic zeal, if we did sugar-coat, we would be following behavioristic principles, i.e., conditioning the pupil to like learning.

The theory of behaviorism has many valid implications for teachers. Intelligent application of behavioristic principles can help the teacher realize success in learning.

EXPERIMENTALISM

More than any single group of philosophers and psychologists, the experimentalists succeeded in breaking the shackles of centuries of rigid tradition. The experimentalists were repelled by rote-memorization, drill without understanding, harsh punishments, lack of consideration for interests of the learners, absolute standards for all, choice of subject matter from the adult world, and passiveness on the part of the learner. They could not accept the thesis that the mind or intelligence consisted of separate faculties nor that it was a white sheet of paper which had to be filled in by adult teachers. They rejected the beliefs that thinking was a matter of exercising faculties of the mind, or a simple matter of applying habits that had been formed through drill. The experimentalists conceive of the mind as process, which process is called reflective thinking.

Experimentalism is known under a variety of names: pragmatism, instrumentalism, functionalism, progressivism, and organismic learning. Proponents of experimentalistic theory have been some of the best-known, and often highly controversial, figures on the American educational scene. There are few who have never heard of Charles Peirce or William James or William Heard Kilpatrick or Boyd Bode or John Dewey. Peirce and James are regarded as the originators of the philosophy of pragmatism, whose central thesis is that an idea proves true when it is borne out in practice. Following this premise we may discover that truth can often be a relative thing, depending on the circumstances in which it exists. For example, the ancients held it to be truth that the world was flat and that the sun revolved about the earth. The weight of constituted authority compelled these beliefs. The curious scientists, however, had reservations about these truths and through continual experimentation eventually upset many established doctrines.

APPEAL TO STUDENT INTERESTS

The pragmatists argue that humans learn as they interact with their environment. They must see, hear, feel, touch, and smell the elements of their environment. They postulate that learning must appeal to student interests. In this respect they could harken to Plato when he said: "Do not thou, excellent friend, compel boys in their learning; but train them up amusing themselves, that you may be better able to discern the way everyone's genius naturally tends."[2] If the learner sees a need in that which he is studying and if he has an interest in the subject, he will tend to pursue the subject. There will be less need of artificial incentives when the subject matter appeals to student interests. Motivation comes from within the learner when he wants to study, rather than from without when he is forced to study.

Humans learn more efficiently when they are actively involved in the process of learning. Thus we find students participating in planning, helping to carry out the work of a course, and evaluating results. Students' advice is sought and valued by the teacher. Students are made to feel a concern for sharing in the process of education. Instead of a teacher-knows-best attitude we find a teacher-pupil relationship that stresses the value of the learner's participation in the pursuit of learning.

PROBLEM-SOLVING

The experimentalists place emphasis on the technique of problem-solving or the scientific method. Learners are not supplied with ready-made, quick, pat answers but are encouraged to form hypotheses, gather data for these hypotheses, test and re-evaluate, finally forming conclusions. This, to the experimentalist, is the essence of thinking. Thinking becomes the process of solving problems, whether these problems exist in the world of mathematics or science or social studies or English. To solve our problems we must turn to a variety of materials and sources. We do not limit ourselves to one reference or one place. The world, in effect, becomes a laboratory for learning.

Drill takes a secondary role in experimentalist theory. Students who are involved in problem-solving apply their learnings as they go along. They put their knowledge to immediate use. They do not store up a series of facts to be called forth later when problems arise. They start with problems now and apply whatever facts are needed to the solution of the problems.

The experimentalist classroom is child-centered as opposed to teacher-centered. It is this feature of pragmatic thinking that has stirred up the

[2] Plato, *The Republic*, translated by H. Spens (New York: E. P. Dutton, 1932, Everyman's Library), p. 247.

passions of many educators. By extending and exaggerating the doctrines taught by men like Dewey, the child-centered classroom becomes a place where children do or say what they will. They work if they feel like it. There is no discipline. The children decide what they want to study, and if they wish to study at all. Such an exaggerated view is far from reality. Although some educators still decry what they misinterpret as "progressive education," it is virtually impossible to find any school anywhere in our nation which actually permits the students to decide for themselves what they will study, when, and how. Perhaps in the 1930's, in the heyday of progressive thought, there may have been some abuses in schools where teachers misinterpreted Dewey and his followers. But a reading of Dewey reveals clearly that he did not sanction complete freedom for youngsters to do as they wish nor did he espouse the idea that we must always appeal to child interests. Said Dewey:

> Apart from the question of the future, continually to appeal even in child-hood to the principle of interests is eternally to excite, that is, distract the child. Continuity of interest is destroyed. Everything is made play, amusement. This means overstimulation; it means dissipation of energy. Will is never called into action. The reliance is upon external attractions and amusements. Everything is sugar-coated for the child, and he soon learns to turn from everything that is not artificially surrounded with diverting circumstances.[3]

The experimentalists view learning as a cooperative endeavor, learners cooperating with the teacher and vice versa as well as cooperating with each other. The teacher is not removed from the picture. His role has changed from the source of all truth to an adult who intelligently guides young, immature learners to the solution of problems that are of real concern. This role also presupposes that the teacher will assist young people to identify these problems, to help them to reject the trivial, and to act as spokesman for the adult world and society as a whole.

CONCERN FOR INDIVIDUAL DIFFERENCES

A concern for individual differences of learners permeates experimentalist thought. They maintain that an individual can learn only in keeping with his capacity to learn. They can see little value in setting standards which are beyond the capacities of individuals. For this reason the pragmatist argues for flexible standards as opposed to absolute standards which all learners must meet. He is conscious of the fact also that learners possess different backgrounds, different aptitudes, different physical traits, and different levels of achievement. No learning can be truly effective, say the pragmatists, if we

[3] John Dewey, *Interest and Effort in Education* (Boston: Houghton Mifflin, 1913), pp. 4–5.

do not take into consideration the wide range of differences among learners.

Undergirding the psychological premises of experimentalism are the political and social theories of the pragmatists. More than any other group of theorists the pragmatists have shown concern for the democratic process. They claim that the school cannot legitimately be separated from the democratic mainstream of life in our country. The school must be a laboratory in democratic living. Pupils in the schools cannot learn democratic processes unless instruction is democratic in nature. The democratic process on an instructional level implies that the learners are partners in learning, not subjects of the school. The democratic process implies that freedom of the mind will be championed, that pupils will be permitted to read, analyze, draw conclusions of their own, rather than have presented to them packaged solutions to problems. In a democratic society we are cognizant of the worth of the individual. Each individual is important and has a right to be valued. An instructional process which ignores the value of individuals as individuals, which sees learners as parts of a gigantic mass, which is geared to an average level, which ignores variations in human capabilities, and which prohibits active involvement of the individual in the affairs most vital to him does not keep faith with the democratic process.

THE EFFECTS OF EXPERIMENTAL THEORY

Pragmatic philosophy swept like a fresh wind through the educational system of the nineteenth and twentieth century. It has acted as a liberating force in the instruction of our young people. Schools have sought positive approaches to learning rather than negative ones. Harsh, punitive measures have disappeared. Guidance programs have been instituted in most schools at all levels from elementary through university. Teachers look for ways of presenting material in terms young people can understand, drawing upon the past experiences of youngsters and appealing to their needs and interests. Teachers organize material into meaningful wholes in the form of units or topics or themes. In many schools teachers work together to correlate the subject matter of different courses. The use of audio-visual aids to stimulate learning is a prominent feature of modern instruction.

Teachers actively seek to cause students to like the subject they are taking. They see little value in forcing students to undergo disagreeable tasks simply for the sake of training their minds or character. If they are not able to create an active desire for learning on the part of students, they at least attempt to show pupils why they must study what they are studying. Drill is incorporated in the instructional program in a variety of meaningful ways. Pupils who need additional drill are offered opportunities for it while those who have mastered the material can go on to more advanced work. Ample electives provide for a variety of interests. Vocational courses have been inaugurated to supplement classical programs. Extra-class activities are recognized as valuable educational pursuits and means of releasing creative energies. Differentiation of instruction for bright, average, and fast learners is common practice in the schools because of the stress pragmatists have placed on individual differences. School libraries are stocked with a variety of books on many subjects with material at varying levels of difficulty. The materials of instruction themselves are more appealing. Grading systems recognize differences in ability. *Why?* is asked in many courses instead of a mere *what?* Pupils are encouraged to think rather than verbalize or parrot.

There has been some reaction against experimentalist theory today. It is unlikely, however, that the basic principles of subscribing to the scientific method, providing for individual differences, appealing to student needs and interests, stressing the democratic process, and involving pupils actively in the learning process will be abandoned.

GESTALT PSYCHOLOGY

We might sum up the tenets of Gestalt psychology in the following manner: (1) We perceive situations in terms of our past experiences. (2) We learn by wholes rather than parts. (3) Learning through insight replaces trial and error. (4) There are constantly in our environment many stimuli that predispose us to action. The corollary to this principle is that individuals often respond in different ways to the same stimulus. A given stimulus does not necessarily always produce the same response, as the behaviorists would have us believe.

Gestalt psychology is of German origin. The name itself, *gestalt*, is the German word for "field" or "configuration." From this we derive the term "field psychology." The Germans Max Wertheimer, Wolfgang Koehler, and Kurt Koffka were proponents of this theory of learning. Along with experimentalism, gestalt psychology has had a profound impact on instruction. We have classified this theory as a companion of experimentalism, for they are not mutually exclusive theories. Nor are perceptual psychology and Gestalt psychology separate entities: each bears elements of the other within it. They are, in a sense, compatible theories, which together provide insight into the manner by which learning takes place.

BUILDING ON EXPERIENCE

The author recently questioned a young man on how he liked the community where he was attending a university. The community itself is a small residential community of 40,000 in the interior of the state, where life is slow-paced, services are adequate but not excessive, and commercial entertainment is limited. The young man responded that he did not like the community. He came from Honolulu, a large city in tropical Hawaii, where he could pursue swimming, surfing, and sailing. His past experiences had not prepared him to enjoy the more limited pleasures of his university community. Contrast this attitude with the young person who comes to a city of 40,000 from a small village of 2,500. To this person the moderate-sized city is a metropolis. He may even feel lost at first. Or, take the case of a high school student who transfers from one high school to another. A bright student, he is placed in a course in new mathematics, which he has not been taking in his former high school. Or he is put into a course in foreign languages taught by an audio-lingual method which he had not been accustomed to in his previous high school. His previous experiences have not prepared him for the change and make it difficult for him to adjust to the new program.

We can learn only in relation to our previous experiences. We build on what we already know. A subject beyond our range of experiences has little or no meaning. When we use a term with which the learners are unfamiliar, we must make the term clear to them before we proceed. Teachers have all had the experience of delivering a fine lecture, in their estimation, only to discover at the end of it that the learners have not understood some of the simplest concepts which the teachers had assumed they would know. We can never take for granted that all learners understand without sufficient explanation presented to them, even when they have been through the same courses previously. Gestalt psychology tells us that students perceive content in various ways. They internalize content in their unique ways and in accordance with their unique abilities. In every class we always have a range of achievement. The learners may have been exposed to learning in previous courses, but they have most assuredly not all achieved the same level. We often make the mistake of assuming that learners have mastered all to which they have been exposed. The necessity for recognizing that learners have achieved at different levels has led to the recommended practice of "taking pupils from where they are." We begin at the point where the learners have left off, rather than at an arbitrary point where teachers would like them to be. It would make teaching much easier if we turned out a standard product at each grade level and at the conclusion of each course. Unfortunately, human beings have a stubborn individuality about them and cannot easily be turned into standardized products.

The novelist often expresses a concept in beautiful prose. Helen MacInness clearly illustrated the significance of one's past experiences when she wrote:

> He was thinking gloomily that the past was never over. As long as you lived, you carried it with you. It shaped your life: what you were, today, depended on all you had seen and felt and heard yesterday, and what you now accepted or rejected would mold your tomorrow. We are because of what we are. . . . Shall we be, because of what we are?[4]

LEARNING BY WHOLES

The Gestaltists have led us to see that learning by wholes is often more effective than learning by parts. This is the reverse of behavioristic practice,

[4] *The Venetian Affair* (New York: Harcourt, Brace & World, 1963), p. 55.

which breaks subject matter into minute, easily managed portions. The unit approach to planning, which we discussed previously, conforms to gestaltist principles. We start with a major unifying, general theme. We use whatever resources, materials, and activities we need to throw light on the central themes, attempting not to restrict our sphere of learning to a single subject area but to see the "big picture." We grasp the over-all situation and then analyze the parts, as opposed to scrutiny of the parts first to size up the over-all situation. We try to organize instruction into meaningful wholes so that learners may see the interrelationships therein. Learning under these conditions does not necessarily take place in a regulated, step-by-step process but by leaps and by insight. Too, we are conscious of the fact that the learner enters into the process in totality. We have coined a cliché, "the whole child," to designate this phenomenon. A child learns not only through the mental processes of his mind or brain or intelligence but also through his entire physical being. His health and emotions aid him or hinder him in learning. Students, like teachers, have their productive days and their off days. Education through the years has assumed a responsibility for aiding many aspects of growth, not only intellectual but also physical, social, and emotional. The gestaltists make us aware that we cannot divorce the mind from the body but must consider the whole organism.

LEARNING BY INSIGHT

Gestalt psychology spotlights learning by insight. The classic studies in this area have been conducted on apes. A banana is placed beyond the reach of an ape in a cage. The ape tries to reach it, fails, tries again, fails, and gives up the attempt. Into the cage are placed two sticks, which when joined together enable the ape to reach the banana. The ape studies the sticks, grasps the relationships between them and the banana, puts them together, and reaches out to draw in the tempting banana. The ape saw the relationship "in a flash." Many scientific discoveries have come about through a similar process of suddenly seeing relationships between stimuli and leaping to a fortuitous conclusion. It has not been necessary to try out every step before attaining the ends.

Learners who understand a principle can devise ingenious and novel ways of applying the principle. We can walk through a community and "size up" its attitude toward education. The mathematics student can frequently come up with new ways of solving a problem. The science student can discover the principles behind an experiment before he has carried out that experiment to its termination. In dealing with complex problems we often sift mentally through possible solutions and suddenly hit upon the answer we are certain is correct. Have we but guessed? Have we engaged in mental trial and error? Or have we by an intelligent process suddenly seen relationships between the elements with which we are dealing? The gestaltist believes that learners should be encouraged to use insight, that they should not always be given answers and steps to those answers, and that they should engage in the process of self-discovery. They should be encouraged to experience, as one school calls it, "eurekas," the joy of discovery.

PERCEPTUAL PSYCHOLOGY

The perceptual psychologist is concerned with the way a learner perceives his world, himself, and his relationship to the world about him. In our complex world we are assailed daily by many stimuli. As we drive our automobile we feel the wheel in our hands, we see other automobiles in front and behind us, we notice billboards of all shapes and sizes, we hear horns blowing, brakes squealing, people shouting, we smell the smoke of a nearby factory. It is almost impossible, even within the controlled environment of the classroom, to screen out stimuli. Many stimuli affect the responses pupils make. The teacher's voice, the rain outside the windows, the presence of the principal in the classroom, the patter of feet in the corridor, the tick of the clock, the interruption of the intercommunication system, the color of fellow students' clothing are part and parcel of the learning process.

VARIETY OF RESPONSE

It is not only virtually impossible to restrict stimuli so that only one stimulus strikes the learner, but it is also uncertain what responses individual learners will make to the given stimuli. We can assume that a given stimulus may often gain a dominant role provided the teacher forcefully and carefully provides the stimulus and minimizes extraneous distractions. But since we all perceive situations in our own ways, according to our own unique past experiences, we may react in differing ways to a given stimulus. Let us take, for example, a French class, where the teacher has written the word *pain* on the board. The teacher knows this word is translated into English as *bread*. If this were the first time the American learner had encountered the *-ain* nasal sound, he might easily pronounce the word "payn," as he pronounces the English word meaning "ache." After all, the two words look alike. The fact that they are from different language systems does not at first occur to the student. He uses the habits he has learned since childhood to solve his immediate problem. He finds out shortly from the teacher that the word should be pronounced "pɛ," containing a sound or phoneme for which there is no equivalent in his native tongue. The learner begins by applying phonemes that are part of his own behavior. Thus, we hear "pen," or "pan." Some students who have a sharp ear may readily detect the difference and immediately imitate the teacher's "pɛ." Others may not detect the difference until long after. In fact, the inability to discriminate sounds, though the teacher has provided the same stimulus for all, results in speaking the foreign language with an American accent.

On a cultural level the stimulus may evoke different responses. When a

Frenchman says *pain*, he has in mind a tasty long loaf of bread with a brown crust. When he goes to the store or bakery to buy bread, the grocer hands him one of a stack of unwrapped long loaves standing in the corner. He pays the requisite number of francs, tucks the unwrapped loaf under his arm, and carries it home. The American visualizes the loaves that he finds on any bread counter in any supermarket. To overcome this cultural difference the teacher has to provide additional stimuli, perhaps a picture of a loaf of French bread. Even a picture does not tell the full story. From a picture can we tell if the crust is hard or soft, the interior white or dark, the taste sweet or flat? The learner who has been to France and enjoyed French bread has little difficulty in knowing the true meaning of the word. It may not be until the teacher has actually provided a loaf of French bread for students to see, feel, smell, and taste that they can truly understand the difference between the American and French varieties.

Perhaps the distinctions between types of bread have not great importance. We can gain a general understanding that "bread" is "bread." But on a more complex level, what are students' perceptions of the words "stock market," "labor union," "the Renaissance?" What responses may be expected from all learners to a reproduction of the Mona Lisa or a photograph of Rodin's "Thinker"? What responses do we get from pictures of slums in our big cities: pathos, triumph, missionary zeal, satisfaction, guilt? Can we ever assume a particular response to a given stimulus? In terms of physical stimuli, it is likely that normal individuals will react in similar ways. But in terms of emotional and intellectual stimuli we cannot be certain of the responses. For this reason we must know as much as we can about learners—what their backgrounds are, what ambitions they have, what capacities, talents, and interests they possess. Only then can we be sure that learning is meaningful to the learner. We must constantly evaluate learning through a variety of techniques which assure us that students have understood what it is we have been trying to get across to them.

NO SINGLE THEORY OF LEARNING

We have stated briefly some of the principal tenets of a number of prominent theories of learning. We should point out in passing that philosophy and psychology are closely related fields. Many of our thinkers or philosophers have given their attention to the problem of learning. At times the hypotheses of the philosopher have been tested by the still-developing science of psychology. The ancient theory of faculty psychology, which originated with some of the ancient philosophers, has shown little validity in experimental studies. Pragmatism as a philosophy, on the other hand, has been demonstrated to possess some validity as a psychological theory.

With the exception of faculty psychology, all the theories of learning discussed in these pages have some significance for teaching. The teacher may be perplexed and ask himself, "Well, which is the true theory to follow?" Such a question misses the point. No single theory of learning is applicable to all human beings at all times and in all places. The search for a single theory of learning that will supply all the answers is akin to the search for a single methodology that will be effective with all teachers in all courses. Behaviorism, experimentalism, gestalt and perceptual psychology, each has its message for the instructor. Some principles will be applicable at all times—e.g., the self-concept, the relevance of past experiences of the learner, the concern for individual differences, and the effectiveness of reinforcement. Other principles may be applied at certain times—e.g., learning by wholes, learning in minute sequential steps, learning by insight, even learning by trial and error. The teacher may be eclectic in his approach. He can utilize effectively principles from each of the theories. He should not, for example, exclude programmed materials because he considers them behavioristic. If he lacks preparation in a subject he might do well to use good programmed materials. The goals of instruction and the nature of the learner must constantly be kept in mind. The philosophy, training, and experience of the teacher are important factors in the implementation of learning theory.

In the preceding pages of this unit we have set a psychological framework for the instructional process. If any learning theory is to have meaning, it must be translated into action in the classroom. As the teacher moves along the instructional continuum from planning to presentation, he is involved in the application of learning theory.

Chapter 12

IMPLICATIONS OF LEARNING THEORY FOR TECHNIQUES OF INSTRUCTION

THE MEANING OF MOTIVATION

The word "motivation" in educational terminology has taken on two meanings. The first and primary meaning of motivation as related to the process of learning is the disposition or desire of the learner to learn. This disposition to learn stems from sources that we call motives. Webster's New World Dictionary defines motive as "some inner drive, impulse, intention, etc. that causes a person to do something or act in a certain way . . . any impulse, emotion, or desire that moves one to action." Fear of disapproval or punishment, greed, and anger are motives that impel an individual to act. These are negative motives or forms of motivation. On a positive scale are the motives of curiosity, sense of accomplishment, pride in one's work, desire to please, desire to serve, and personal enjoyment. We find some students studying Latin, for example, because they desire to please their parents or because they feel a challenge in the strange language or because they fear disapproval of their parents or because they wish to copy their peers who are studying Latin or because they obtain satisfaction or enjoyment from the study of this language. The reasons for studying the language, that is, the sources of motivation, may be quite different with different students. A student may seek high grades because he wants to experience a sense of accomplishment or he dreads taking home a poor report card. The most effective form of motivation, perhaps the only form of motivation in its true meaning, is that desire which lives within the learner. The ultimate goal of the learning process is the arousing of this desire within the learner to modify his behavior through learning.

In popular usage we call motivation those actions which the teacher takes to arouse a desire of the learner to learn. We often hear teachers say, "I wish I could motivate him." In this usage the word "motivation" signifies the techniques or stimuli which originate from without the learner but which seek to encourage him to desire to learn. Parents motivate their children when they encourage them to study, when they show approval for their children's accomplishment, and when they express disapproval over poor work. Siblings serve as sources of motivation, sometimes positive, sometimes negative. One child desires to emulate a sibling he admires. Or he becomes discouraged with attempting to live up to an enviable record made by his older brother or sister in school. Nothing is more deadening to the pupil than to hear, as countless thousands hear from their teachers, remarks such as: "Oh, I am disappointed in your work. Your sister was a such a good student when I had her in class two years ago." In that remark, intended to stimulate the pupil to better performance, the teacher may well have killed motivation.

When a teacher seeks to motivate students, he plans and carries out learning experiences that he hopefully believes will lead the students to a desire to learn. Since there is some confusion in this dual use of the term "motivation," it would help if we had two separate terms. But since we do not have separate terms, we use the word "motivation" to signify both the internal desire of the learner to learn and those techniques which the teacher uses to stimulate the desire to learn. We shall recognize the distinction in meaning in the context of the discussion.

THE CHARACTERISTICS OF MOTIVATED LEARNERS

It is not difficult to observe the presence or absence of motivation in the classroom, library, assembly, or study hall. In some classrooms students look alert, respond quickly, show enthusiasm for what they are doing. Look in on a study hall and you are bound to find pupils who in bored fashion gaze at the pages of an open book without reading, without any apparent interest. Drop into the library and you will find some pupils working in an efficient manner on a research paper while others indifferently thumb through magazines, possibly looking at pictures now and then. Some students watch the clock, impatient for the end of the hour or the end of the day when they will be released to take part in activities which they enjoy or in which they can experience success. There are degrees of interest among learners from intensity to complete apathy. The highly motivated learner actively participates in class. He tackles his problems with enthusiasm. He is persistent. He sees purpose in what he is doing. He feels himself able to accomplish the tasks before him. He is willing to pursue even difficult tasks when he knows the tasks are important and when he realizes that he has the competence to fulfill them. The highly motivated pupil can do with less direction than the less motivated. He listens and tries his best to perform well. The highly motivated pupil draws upon his own sense of pride and satisfaction while the less motivated must be cajoled, pushed, and even ordered to do his work. The positive motives are operant more often in the highly motivated student than negative motives. He is both interested and interesting.

If the teacher could but have a roomful of such learners every period of the day, he would feel that he had reached nirvana.

The highly motivated learner enjoys school and learning. More often than not he is a good reader, can handle abstractions, possesses verbal aptitude (since this is the essence of a high school program of studies), and is intelligent. This is not to say that all intelligent pupils are highly motivated. Far from it. One of the tragedies of the modern high school is the phenomenon of intelligent pupils who are not at all motivated. They slop through their work, doing a minimum to get by. They see little purpose in what they are doing. They may be so bright that the high school curriculum offers them no challenge and they are bored. Creative minds are often squelched with the formalism of high school education and do not show interest in their schooling. It is possible also, as in the case of highly creative individuals, to be so preoccupied with one interest, be it mathematics or science or chess, that they show interest in only this one field and ignore all other fields. At the other end of the spectrum we can find slow learners struggling to learn, plugging along, giving their studies all they have. Nothing is so heart-warming to the dedicated teacher as to see achievement from highly motivated slow learners.

In our evident pleasure with achievement, usually of a scholastic nature, we as teachers seek to distinguish between achievement that comes from positive, healthy motivation and achievement that comes from negative, destructive motivation. We should be aware of intense pressures brought on many adolescents to learn, to achieve, to perform, to get to the top. We must know if anxious parents are pushing their children beyond their levels of endurance. We should not settle for scholastic results alone. We should work toward the achievement of postive attitudes, values, and mental health. High motivation, if forced and pressured, may result in short-term scholastic gains but disastrous long-range effects in mental illness.

THE CONDITIONS OF MOTIVATION

Learners are motivated when they conceive of themselves as capable individuals. They feel that their peers, teachers, and others in their environment recognize them as able to achieve. Learners possess the desire to learn when they are dealing with materials which they understand and which are geared to their level. They are motivated when they see purpose in their activities and study. They show interest when they regard their studies as important. Parenthetically, we might add at this point that students are often willing to take easy paths, sometimes grumble if the path is difficult, but end up respecting their education if they have been made to feel they have undergone a valuable learning experience. We can go to extremes at any level of education by providing experiences so trivial and easy as to insult the intelligence of the learner or so difficult as to frustrate him.

Learners are motivated if they live in a secure environment. The teacher should be receptive. Learners are motivated if they have opportunities to satisfy their psychological needs of success, recognition, and approval and can make mistakes without punishment. Students must feel that the learning experiences are for them, not for the teacher. For this reason they need to understand why the subject matter is important, what application it may have in daily life, and why the subject matter they are studying should have precedence over other matter which they might feel to be important.

Learners are motivated when the subject matter itself is interesting. When the subject matter is dull, they will call it "dry" and involve themselves only half-heartedly. An intrinsically dull subject, if such a thing exists, calls for all the ingenuity of the teacher to make it live. The teacher should not make the error of assuming that a subject interesting to him will necessarily be of interest to the learners. The history teacher has dedicated his life to the study and teaching of history. The student who is required to take history during his short span of high school years may not feel the keen satisfaction in studying history that his teacher does. When we speak of interest of the learner, we would not be so optimistic as to believe that all students will be highly motivated in all courses. Students vary in their interests. Some will love history. Some will detest it. Cultural factors have been operant for many years to lead the learner to a favorable disposition to some subjects and an unfavorable disposition to others. Our culture, for example, has encouraged boys to excel at mathematics and science, while girls often achieve higher results than boys in reading and art. Boys are guided into pursuits which our culture has designated as manly and girls into activities which are feminine. Teachers have an uphill fight to motivate boys to enjoy poetry and girls to excel in trigonometry.

Learners are motivated when they have some opportunities for decision-making. When they can enter into the process of planning and feel some responsibility for participating, they are more likely to feel a desire to learn.

Learners are motivated when they experience success more often than failure. If the learner begins to believe that he is incapable of success, he will give up. No individual can maintain an interest in a task that he fails time and time again. Classroom and school conditions that permit learners to realize their potentialities will encourage the development of motivation.

TECHNIQUES OF MOTIVATION

It would be fortunate if we could prescribe a bag of tricks which would be surefire means of motivation. But impelling motives differ from person to person. Consequently, the techniques that work with one individual or one group may not work with other individuals or other groups. We should not be surprised or discouraged if we cannot arouse enthusiasm and interest on the part of all learners at all times. Boredom is bound to creep in from time to time. The conditions for learning may not always be optimal. The teacher may turn in a poor performance on a certain day. The students may be tired after a big game the preceding evening. Some national or international crisis may have leaped to the front pages to shut out all attempts at school studies. The best a teacher can hope for is that he may reach most of his learners most of the time. Though we may not be highly successful in motivating all learners at all times, there are some principles and practices related to motivation which experienced teachers have found generally effective. Following these principles and practices, the teacher has a better than average chance of stimulating pupils to learn:

1. *Motivation is enhanced when the content is adjusted to the learner, rather than vice versa.* Materials must be provided at the level of the learners. This problem is particularly acute in heterogeneous groups where there is a wide range of ability. Some teachers resort to the use of multiple texts, written at different reading levels. If they use a single text, they often supplement it with materials at graded levels of difficulty. The learner is more likely to respond favorably when he deals with materials he can understand. He will develop a positive attitude in his subject when he considers himself competent to succeed. Successful students are motivated students. Unsuccessful students lose their zeal in situations where they experience failure. If the materials are too difficult, if the content is too advanced, if the standards of expected performance are too high, motivation dies. Motivation is killed, too, if the standards are too low for a group of learners, if content is too elementary, and if materials are too easy. The teacher must determine the range of abilities and interests in his classes and seek to provide kinds of experiences which relate to these abilities and interests.

2. *The content of instruction should be as close to student interests as it is possible to make it.* Content which has meaning in the on-going life of the pupil will be received with greater interest than content which appears remote. Motivation is higher when the subject matter seems related to the learner's past experiences. When content cannot be demonstrated to be close to the more immediate life of the students, the teacher should set the stage for study by showing pupils the reasons why the study is important. He should attempt to show them applications of the study in our society, pointing out to them that though they may not feel an immediate need for the study, they will definitely have need for it in the future.

3. *Motivation is increased through the use of audio-visual aids.* Audio-visual materials appeal to student interest as no other means can. An illustrated talk on science or geography or history can evoke interest well beyond that which might arise from a straight, unillustrated lecture. Pictures,

charts, models, records, and the like can do much to give an accurate portrayal of some aspects of a subject. No word picture can describe the United States Capitol building as clearly as a photograph of it. No lecture can recall the meaning of war as vividly as the military films of the Normandy landing, Iwo Jima, the liberation of Paris, and the North African campaign. Not only do audio-visual materials aid in instruction, they liven up the classroom. They add color and zip to an otherwise drab atmosphere. Audio-visual materials which the students prepare themselves, such as art displays and bulletin board exhibits, help learners feel a sense of identity with the subject matter.

4. *Variety is a key to motivation.* Each lesson plan should provide a number of activities for motivational purposes. Students lose interest when they must confine themselves to one activity during an entire period, such as listening to a lecture. Some lecturing, some class discussion, student reports, and the use of audio-visual aids when applicable help to keep interest from lagging. When drill sessions are required, the manner of drilling should be varied. Drill can be oral or written. The teacher can have pupils do drill exercises at their seats or at the blackboard. Drill sessions can be conducted by the teacher or by the students. Visual devices, such as flash cards, lighten the dulling effects of drill. Students eagerly participate in classroom games in which the class is divided into teams. Variety has a powerful motivational effect on students.

5. *Resumés and review sessions can help pupils to gain a better knowledge of their subject and therefore to want to continue their studies.* It is good practice for teachers to begin the daily lesson with a short resumé of the last class period. Even this technique may be varied. The teacher may sometimes summarize the work covered during the last class period. He can ask judicious questions which bring out the salient points of prior study. He can ask pupils to give a summary of the work they have been doing. He can give a brief oral or written quiz to see if students have learned their lessons well. The resumé may take only a few minutes at the beginning of the period. It can set the stage for the activities to be carried out during the present class period.

6. *A summarization or other evaluative technique at the end of the class period will help students to achieve better results.* Varied evaluative devices are possible. The teacher may ask students to respond to significant questions that recapitulate the day's lesson. He may tie together the day's work with a brief lecture. He may review with the pupils salient points, jotting some of these points down on the blackboard as he goes along. The review technique is used by many teachers who realize that adolescents do not always learn

thoroughly the subject matter the first time around. Some teachers conduct extensive review sessions, particularly prior to a major test. There is no objection in providing for a review session, as long as the techniques utilized do more than encourage recitation, rote-memorization, and cramming. Students are usually appreciative of review sessions. This appreciation can lead to higher motivation.

7. *The alert teacher looks for timely events which affect the lives of members of his class.* By capitalizing on some of these events he can enhance motivation. A student's older brother, for example, has been sent to Vietnam. Suddenly, the war in Southeast Asia has taken on a new and personal dimension. A government report on the perils of cigarette smoking can intimately involve teen-agers, some of whom have the habit. A new student joins the class from another state or a foreign country. A member of the class has won a significant prize in the community. Some of the timely events will fit neatly into the instructional program. At times events occur that seem more appropriate to topics which will be studied later in the year. A flexible teacher will recognize the timely event as an opportunity for capturing interest and will revise his teaching schedule accordingly.

8. *The kinds of assignments a teacher gives have a bearing on the motivational level of learners.* If they see the need for an assignment, pupils will be more disposed to do their homework. If they regard the assignments as busy-work, they will show little interest and do them, if they do them at all, in a perfunctory way. We shall discuss the technique of making assignments further on in this unit.

9. *The teacher may resort to extrinsic forms of motivation of a positive nature.* The purpose of all extrinsic forms, i.e., those which originate outside the learner, is to encourage development of intrinsic motivation, i.e., that which comes from within the learner. The teacher may post on the bulletin boards samples of effective student work. He should be generous with praise for deserving accomplishments. Students who do well in their studies may be rewarded for their efforts with special privileges—for example, opportunities for independent study, exemption from certain tests, and opportunities to help fellow students who are having difficulties.

10. *The creative, imaginative teacher will experience greater success in stimulating pupils to learn than will the pedestrian, unimaginative teacher.* The teacher who cares about pupils and whose pupils know he cares will be more successful in helping pupils to develop interest in a subject. If the teacher is never available for conferences and extra help, if he does not seem to enjoy his subject or teaching, if he races the students to the door at the end of the day, and if he is unwilling or unable to entertain questions pupils pose, he can little hope for highly motivated learners.

THE EFFECTS OF COMPETITION

For generations competition among individual learners has been a part of our instructional process. Students compete with each other for standings in the class, marks, position on the honor roll, and approval by the teacher and their peers. Teachers maintain an absolute set of standards to which all learners must aspire regardless of their individual abilities and interests. Students are marked in relationship to each other, so that a student who obtains an *A* knows that he is "better" in that class than the student who receives a *C*. Standardized tests inform students how they rate in relation to thousands of other students who have taken the test. The competitive factor is particularly acute in heterogeneous classes where there are students with varying abilities. The bright students set a pace difficult for the average and slower students to follow.

OUR COMPETITIVE SOCIETY

Teachers often justify competition on the basis of the presence of competition in our society. Since the school reflects our culture and since we are preparing students to be citizens of that culture, they say, we should expose them to the harsh realities of the competitive way of life. Such reasoning misses one fundamental aspect of our competitive society. Individuals do not compete across the board. We are not in competition with every other individual in our society. Unless we descend to a starvation economy, we shall never have this across-the-board type of competition. We compete on levels. Within well-defined spheres individuals compete with each other. Teachers may compete for teaching positions. The bright compete with the bright, the unskilled with the unskilled. The unskilled laborer does not seek to compete with the highly trained surgeon. The competitive way of life considers the differences in ability, a factor often overlooked in the competitive classroom.

If competition is a part of our free enterprise system, cooperation is another undercurrent in the democratic way of life. Cooperation is also one of the great tenets of our Judaic-Christian heritage. We teach our young people in churches as well as in schools that they should help one another.

Competition in itself may be both a salutary and a destructive element. The difference in effect of competition in school will depend to a great extent on how the teacher utilizes it. A little competition goes a long way. Competition may be a motivating influence if students who are urged to compete have the competencies to do so. It is patently unsound to expect a child who ranks at the 40th percentile in intelligence to compete scholastically with a child who ranks at the 99th percentile. Nor should we ask the skinny, underweight boy to compete on the football field with a bruiser of 170 pounds. The pupil with a low quantitative aptitude should not be expected to compete on equal terms with a mathematical whiz. As adults we know our own limitations. Unless we can meet individuals on even terms, we do not seek competition with, for example, Arnold Palmer in golf, Robert Oppenheimer in nuclear physics, or Van Cliburn on the piano. Students with relatively similar abilities will enjoy the stimulation of limited competition. Motivation can be stifled if students of unequal abilities are required to compete. The less favored individual may try to compete, but failing, become frustrated, or he may withdraw, leaving the scene of battle entirely.

COMPETING IN GROUPS

Homogeneous groups have reduced the range of abilities so that students may more nearly compete with each other. But even in classes grouped by ability there will be a range of differences which should act as a brake on intense competition. One of the values of homogeneous grouping lies in the fact that the slow students do not have to experience the frustration of having to compete with the faster students.

Competition is more effective if students are permitted to compete as groups rather than as individuals. Well-balanced groups derive pleasure from competition. This kind of competition can serve to develop teamwork toward mutually shared goals. Competition used in this manner can become a motivating force.

Since competition can have a deleterious effect on students who do not have the skills required to compete on an equal level, an evaluation system should make allowances for differences and consider the individual abilities of the learners. As we shall see in our discussion of evaluation in Unit VII, a marking system should consider the unique abilities of learners. Students should be encouraged more often to compete with themselves, with their past records, than with each other. The motive of personal satisfaction can come from improvement in one's own record. The individual's self concept is strengthened when he can see progress in relation to his own ability.

When we liken competition in the schoolroom to competition in other life situations, we are equating immature learners with mature adults. Adults compete at their levels for pay and prestige. Learners are often expected to compete for grades. We forget that the learner is in a period of preparation. The grade is supposed to represent his progress toward educational goals. He is not demonstrating efficiency on the job. He has not perfected his vocational skills. The teacher is not the boss who rewards him with a pay envelope. The teacher is the individual who is helping him to develop his own civic, social, and vocational skills so that when he reaches maturity, he will have enough confidence and competence to be a productive citizen.

BROADENING THE LEARNING BASE

The teacher can broaden the learning base by reaching beyond the adopted text materials. Magazines and newspapers furnish plentiful sources for pictorial and descriptive materials. The teacher can make effective use of all library resources in the community, including the public library if there is one. It is helpful for the teacher to go into the public library, discover the extent of resources, and establish a working relationship with the public librarian. He should make it a point when he first enters a community as a teacher to find out what audio-visual aids are owned by the local school system, what aids can be obtained from state sources, and what supplementary budget is available for purchase and rental of audio-visual aids.

USE OF TELEVISION

Today's teacher should make it a habit to check the week's programs on both commercial and educational television. Not only can some of the programs supplement the course of study, but pupils can be taught to be discriminating in their choice of programs. Such programs as "The Twentieth Century," special newscasts, productions of outstanding plays, and science programs often provide valuable learning experiences. When they can be incorporated into the class's planning, the values to be derived from them are greater than can be realized from mere casual viewing.

The teacher should know what programs are to be telecast on local, open-circuit educational television. If the school is equipped with television receivers, he may also take advantage of both closed-circuit and open-circuit instructional television.

FREE AND INEXPENSIVE MATERIALS

The teacher should be on the lookout for free and inexpensive materials. Various publishers issue periodically catalogues of free and inexpensive aids.[1] One word of caution should be given about these materials: many of them incorporate a message from a commercial source. Many companies distribute materials to the schools in order to advertise their wares. The teacher wants to make sure that the claims of the manufacturers who do this

---

[1] For free and inexpensive aids consult the following: *Educators' Index of Free Materials* (Randolph, Wisconsin: Educators' Progress Service); *Sources of Free and Inexpensive Aids* (Chicago: Field Enterprises Educational Corporation, 1958); Division of Surveys and Field Services, *Free and Inexpensive Learning Materials* (Nashville, Tenn.: George Peabody College for Teachers); Thomas J. Pepe, *Free and Inexpensive Educational Aids* (New York: Dover Publications, 1962); Robert L. Schain and Murray Polner, *Where to Get and How to Use Free and Inexpensive Teaching Aids* (New York: Teachers' Practical Press; distributed by Prentice-Hall, Englewood Cliffs, N. J., 1963).

are not exaggerated. The teacher can use the materials, even though they may incorporate an advertisement, as long as the advertisement is truthful and not overdone. The teacher can offset propaganda with additional information about reliable products. Of course, he should not use materials, no matter how good they are, if the commercials included are untruthful or inappropriate for his learners.

USING COMMUNITY RESOURCES

The teacher should reach out into the community and tap the resources available there. He should encourage qualified resource people from the community to come to class as needed. Pupils can profit from studying at first hand phases of community life. We should not neglect cultural advantages such as museums, botanical gardens, art museums, theaters, and zoological gardens. Not only are these features of progressive communities enjoyable, but their instructional values are significant.

Field trips can be beneficial, if properly planned. Students should know in advance what they are to look for, why they are going to a particular place. Contacts should be made beforehand so that trips can be scheduled with a minimum of lost time. Field trips should provide instruction that cannot be obtained as effectively in the confines of the classroom. A field trip should be scheduled only when it clearly enriches the educational program. Students should appraise the field trip when it has been completed, evaluating very carefully what they have learned from it, deciding whether they have learned those things which they set out to learn.

New York City has taken a close look at the educational values to be derived from community resources in its famed Higher Horizons Program.[2] This program was begun in 1956 in two educationally disadvantaged (i.e., low socioeconomic level) secondary schools: George Washington High School and its feeder school, Junior High School 43 in Manhattan. Significantly, the original program was known as the Demonstration Guidance Project. Through special instruction, counseling, and enriched curriculum it was hoped that students in the Demonstration Guidance Project schools would achieve more scholastically and aspire to higher educational and vocational levels. In addition to receiving special help and counseling in school, pupils were afforded cultural opportunities which were heretofore beyond their sphere of experiences. They were taken to theaters, museums, art galleries, concerts, and libraries. Scholastic improvements in the records of students in the project have been noted. The students showed growth in reading achievement. A sizeable percentage of them raised their IQ scores, a further demonstration of the effect of culture and reading ability on IQ test scores. The

[2] Information on the Higher Horizons Program may be obtained from the Coordinator of Higher Horizons, New York City Board of Education, 110 Livingston Street, Brooklyn, New York 11201.

dropout rate of students going on to senior high school was cut dramatically. Students who never aspired to college have begun to consider higher education as a live option for them.

The Higher Horizons Program has yielded sufficient results to cause its expansion to other schools. What started as an effort to "identify, stimulate, and guide into college channels able students from low socioeconomic status homes" has expanded to include "raising the educational level of all pupils" in the Higher Horizons schools. In 1963 the Higher Horizons Program included 33,500 pupils in fifty-two elementary schools, 19,500 pupils in thirteen junior high schools, and 11,000 pupils in eleven senior high schools.

Even in communities that do not have the rich resources of New York City, the alert teacher can find many educational opportunities. The world of science is all around us. A wooded field, for example, is an ideal botanical laboratory. Community landmarks and scenic spots offer opportunities for creative writing, art, photography, and journalism. The community serves the social studies teacher as a source of local history, local customs, and local government. Vocational agriculture, distributive education, and the diversified cooperative training programs have long ago tapped the educational benefits to be found in the community.

The use of the community in the instructional process helps to remove some of the barriers which have traditionally been built around the school. Modern educators believe that the school should be considered an integral part of the community. Perhaps when we speak of school-community relationships we think first of local citizens' attendance at sports events, the senior play, and occasional back-to-school nights for parents. The school-community concept extends well beyond this to include a deliberative search for ways by which the two social institutions can mutually aid each other.

CREATING A POSITIVE CLIMATE FOR LEARNING

The teacher can create a positive climate for learning. In a climate of this kind pupils feel accepted. The teacher permits, even encourages, curiosity and exploration. He is ready and willing to provide suggestion and help. He maintains none of the unhealthy types of group climate which we discuss in Unit VI on discipline and control. The climate is a mentally and physically healthy one, aimed at developing the inquiring mind. The teacher avoids harsh, punitive measures. He rejects fear, sarcasm, and threats as tools which he knows to be destructive. In a positive climate pupils succeed more often than fail. There is opportunity for each pupil, regardless of his ability, to achieve satisfactory results. The teacher actively tries to create an interest in the subject he teaches.

The classroom itself is an attractive place. Students and teacher both feel that this is their learning center. The teacher enlists the aid of students to keep the schoolroom neat and attractive. In a healthy climate of learning the teacher has achieved a high degree of rapport with students.

PERFECTING TECHNIQUES OF INSTRUCTION

The teacher can improve the learning period by perfecting some of the more universally and frequently used techniques of instruction. What we are saying here is similar to the remark of the farmer to whom a friend was suggesting a number of techniques that were bound to improve his farming, "But I already know how to farm twice as good as I do." Teachers often know how to teach better than they actually do. A few reminders and constant self-evaluation should call to mind ways to improve instruction. Improvements can often be made in the following instructional techniques.

USING THE BLACKBOARD

The teacher should make effective use of those tools which he has, not the least of which is the blackboard or chalkboard. It is an incredible fact that teachers who have blackboards covering the walls of the room often fail to put them to use. They can effectively use the boards for mass drills, moving students out of their seats to take positions at the board for practice exercises. They can put the boards to use with classroom games. The teacher will find it a helpful technique to form the habit of writing on the board new words or difficult words so pupils can see them as well as hear them. The boards can be used for art work, charts, diagrams, and graphs, which may frequently be drawn after class hours. The technique of the chalk talk, an illustrated lecture, carries across a message more effectively than oral presentation alone. The blackboard may be used to supplement assignment-making. It is good practice for the teacher to have placed on the board where all may see a summarization of the assignment for the next day. Paradoxically, blackboards which go unused most of the time are sometimes put to use in a most time-wasting manner. We find teachers who laboriously write their tests on the blackboard. In this day with the modern duplicating machine there is little reason for the inefficient process of writing tests on the blackboard.

USING THE BULLETIN BOARD

The bulletin board is another tool which is taken for granted in most classrooms but used improperly or infrequently by many teachers. The reader of these pages can go into a school almost at will, stop in the classrooms, and find examples of ineffective use of bulletin boards. We will wager that he will find blank, unused bulletin boards. The teacher has not considered them worth the bother, though the taxpayers have footed the bill for their installation. The observer will find bulletin boards cluttered with announcements of the principal, yesterday's lunch menu, and memos from the superintendent. He will find bulletin boards that look like used table-cloths. Wrinkled papers, yellowed articles, and outdated publications whip around in the breeze.

The teacher can make most efficient use of this valuable tool if he accepts it as an instructional device. Bulletin-board displays should be changed frequently. A week is certainly long enough for any display. The bulletin board should often reflect timely and significant news which is of concern to the class. If the bulletin board is used primarily for instruction, samples of students' work should always be visible. Posting of fine work serves as an incentive to pupils to do good work. We like others to recognize our achievements. The bulletin board helps to promote satisfaction of the need for recognition.

The teacher should make the bulletin board serve the needs of as many students as possible. He should not choose to post always the work of the same students. If the teacher is making the choice of student work to post, he should find occasions for posting some of the best work of the poorer students as well as the good work of the better students. The teacher may assure greater utilization of the bulletin board if he assigns committees the responsibility for preparing displays. A mistake teachers frequently make in using bulletin boards is to select all the items to be displayed and to arrange the displays themselves. These are often the fastidious teachers who must arrange the displays just so. Pupils scarcely pay heed to the teacher's display. Active involvement of the learner pays off in the instructional process. Students gain more from displays which they have planned and arranged themselves.

The teacher should sensitize pupils to be on the lookout in their reading for articles and pictures which would be suitable for the class bulletin board. He can accumulate a file of useful items that committees might wish to include in their displays. Attractive bulletin-board displays lend color to the classroom, stimulate pupil interest, and contribute to students' learning experiences.

THE OVERHEAD PROJECTOR

One of the newest devices to aid teachers is the overhead projector. This instrument permits the teacher to present material with clarity to a large group of learners. The teacher faces his audience and the projector. He places his material in the form of transparencies on the illuminated surface of the projector. A large, clear image is projected over the teacher's head and behind him to a screen or blank wall surface. The teacher may write on the transparencies and accomplish the same purposes he would in a chalk talk. The overhead projector has advantages over the chalkboard in that the images are large and clear and the teacher never has to turn his back to the audience. With the projector he may reach larger than average groups. For this reason the overhead projector has become a standard fixture in team-teaching situations for presentation of material to large groups. This piece of equipment is rapidly becoming as common in the classroom as tape recorders and record players. The transparencies required for use with this instrument can be reused time after time. Teachers can prepare outlines of their talks, sketches, and charts on the transparencies. If a school owns one of the modern duplicating machines, copies of pages of texts, maps, and other pictorial material can be placed directly on the transparencies themselves, saving the teacher valuable time. The teacher can introduce a great deal of supplementary material which he might not use if he had to reproduce it laboriously by hand. The teacher should take full advantage of those instructional aids that he does have.

THE ART OF QUESTIONING

The teacher can perfect the art of questioning. Teachers spend a considerable portion of their academic year firing oral questions at pupils. Some of the questions provoke thought; others elicit brief bits of information. Some questions induce thinking; others parrot the material in the textbook. Some have been thoughtfully prepared in advance; others are taken "off the top of the head" as the spirit moves the teacher. Questioning is a more complex skill than would seem on superficial examination. It is a skill so universally used by instructors that special training should be given in teacher preparation programs.

We often assume that questioning, like marking, is a competency that develops naturally without need for special study and practice. This false assumption has led to learners' suffering through thousands of inconsequential, trivial questions, designed more to consume the learning hour than to bring out understandings and to stimulate thought. Some of the questions to which pupils must respond might be classified as the who-is-buried-in-Grant's-Tomb? variety. If we were to make an analysis of questions that teachers ask pupils, we would generally find a preponderance of Who?, What?, Where?, and When? types. We would find fewer Why? and How? types. The Who?, What?, Where?, and When? varieties are derived from the ancient concept of the teacher's role as the imparter of information and the school's mission as the transmission of the cultural heritage. The Why? and How? types of questions emphasize the teacher's role as a guide in learning and the school's mission as the development of the ability to think critically.

The Who? What? Where? and When? questions focus on the learning outcomes of facts, abilities, and skills. The Why? and How? questions aim at development of understandings or concepts, appreciations, and attitudes. Who? What? When? and Where? skim the surface, whereas Why? and How? probe more deeply. This is not to say that both types of questioning do not have a place in the school. It is to say, however, that more of the Why? and How? questions have a place in the curriculum. When we fire a barrage of questions at the learner, we might stop now and then and ask ourselves the purposes of questioning. Why do we use this time-honored technique, which we can trace back to Socrates?

A question elicits information from pupils. It emphasizes particular aspects of the subject which the teacher deems important. Questioning is an evaluation technique, which can be used by the teacher to judge daily achievement and progress. Questions provide a means of reviewing and drilling material. Questions are opportunities for developing creative thinking, bringing forth appreciations, values, and attitudes. Questioning is a two-way street. We think first of the teacher's task as interrogator. The teacher poses the questions. The pupils answer. Yet, questioning can be a sharper tool if we encourage pupils to raise questions, not only of the teacher but also of each other. By the questions pupils raise the teacher gains insight into their thinking. It can be a greater demonstration of the intelligence of the learner when he knows enough to raise further questions. The giving of a brief response to a factual question does not rank on the same level of intelligence as the asking of a probing question. Bright pupils often raise profound questions that the teacher had never considered, sometimes to his chagrin.

The teacher who is desirous of polishing his questioning technique might implement the following guidelines:

1. *Key questions, that is, those which are so important to the lesson that they must not be omitted, should be noted in the lesson plan.* Our memories are fallible. We cannot trust that we will remember to bring out the essential points of a lesson unless we make some annotation to remind us. We should include in our lesson plans those questions which we feel bound to bring up in class.

2. *Questions should be clearly stated.* They should be brief and to the point. The teacher should avoid a vagueness that confuses pupils. The teacher should use language that the pupils understand.

3. *The teacher should not ask questions which yield a simple "Yes" or "No" answer.* Very little information or thought is required to answer a question "Yes" or "No." The pupil has a fifty-fifty chance of guessing the right answer even if he has no idea of the nature of the question.

4. *Questions should be distributed among pupils in varying degrees of*

difficulty. The bright pupils should be expected to respond to more difficult questions than the slow pupils. All pupils should be given opportunities to respond.

5. *Since students must be taught to listen as well as to speak, it is a good general rule to avoid repeating questions and answers.* How many teachers parrot the answers given by students because they are fearful the others in the class have missed the correct answer! This practice is wasteful of class time and poor training in listening habits. If teacher and students both speak loud and clear, questions and answers do not have to be repeated.

6. *Questioning ought to amplify and clarify the textbook, not repeat the textbook material.* It is not uncommon to find the teacher who stands with textbook open, picking questions out of the textbook, often in the textbook language itself. Good questions supplement the text, bring out generalizations, take issue with the author, and raise further questions not covered by the author of the text.

7. *Questions should be significant.* Some learners will regard questions as a challenge if they deal with a subject of consequence. Questions may provide a motivating factor in the learning situation.

8. *The technique of questioning can be used frequently,* but it should not be overdone. The author of this text recently sat through a fifty-minute period of a student teacher in social studies who bombarded her class with minute questions drawn from the text for a full period. Boredom can ensue from the overuse of any single technique.

9. *Questioning can be given a pleasant twist by adapting it to instructional games, such as "question bees," "twenty questions," and "baseball."*

10. *Questions should not be used to furnish daily marks.* Questions provide a means of evaluating pupils' daily progress but this does not mean that the teacher must record a symbol for every response a pupil makes. The teacher stifles responses and thinking when pupils must respond for purposes of a mark. Teachers here and there feel compelled to place a daily recitation mark in their grade books. These marks are often based on whether a pupil has responded correctly to a single oral question in class!

11. *The teacher may use the technique of questioning to maintain what we refer to in Unit VI on discipline and control as "simple control."* There is no harm in the teacher's throwing a question to pupils who obviously are inattentive. Pupils learn through this technique that they are expected to pay attention. When an inattentive pupil has not heard the question, the teacher may give it to an attentive student, with the admonition to the inat-

tentive one to pay closer attention. As a general practice, most teachers state the question first for all, then call on an individual pupil after they have all had the opportunity to think over a response. Questions offer opportunities not only for evaluation of learning, for stimulating thinking, and for eliciting information, but also for development of oral skills on the part of the learners. Each answer a student makes gives him a chance to express his thoughts. Students whose oral skills are poor can be aided through judicious questioning to improve.

12. *The teacher should encourage tolerance of one another's answers in relation to both accuracy of response and manner of response.* Students should feel free to make mistakes without being ridiculed either by the teacher or by his classmates. If the question calls for an opinion, each individual's opinion should be valued if expressed with sincerity and conviction. The teacher should encourage good manners in pupils' answering of questions. A question-and-answer period is an additional opportunity in perfecting civic skills. The teacher should not permit some individuals to dominate a question-and-answer period. It is easy to allow the enthusiastic, the aggressive, the informed, and the hand-wavers to take over a questioning session. The teacher need not wait for pupils to volunteer answers. He may direct answers to individual pupils as he deems wise.

13. *Questions from the students should be encouraged.* Students need instruction to discriminate good questions and poor questions. They often need help to prevent them from digressing from the topic. When questions are obviously designed to sidetrack the teacher or are not appropriate to the subject under discussion, the teacher should so state and move on. If students raise questions to which no one, including the teacher, can reply, the teacher should admit that he does not know and promise to find out if he can. The teacher need not feel apologetic for not knowing all the answers to all the questions students will ask. With the explosion of knowledge it is next to impossible for teachers to know everything about every aspect of their subject, but they should know where to locate further information. They may have to call on specialized help in the community for answers to difficult questions. The teacher should not feel threatened when he realizes that he has in his classes some pupils who are more intelligent than he is. He should consider it a source of personal stimulation to be challenged by inquiring minds. An intellectual give-and-take is an intensely motivating experience for both the teacher and students. Students should be able to question the teacher's position on topics discussed. No student should be forced to accept the teacher's opinion as gospel truth. A little skepticism is a healthy ingredient in a democracy. Too ready an acceptance of every opinion as the truth leads a citizenry into the danger of the loss of its freedom.

14. *Questions should be asked which probe deeply and which call for thinking.* Questions should allow pupils to *(a)* express their own positions on a topic, *(b)* decide what additional data are necessary for solving a problem, *(c)* compare and contrast situations and events, *(d)* cite examples of some principle or phenomenon in operation, *(e)* suggest new ways of solving a problem, *(f)* summarize data, *(g)* draw conclusions and generalizations from the data, *(h)* explain how or why an event took place or something works as it does, *(i)* place themselves in a particular role and decide what they would do under similar conditions, *(j)* find biases in data, and *(k)* show relationships between aspects of a situation.

15. *Creative thinking can be stimulated by the technique of brainstorming.* The teacher throws out a broad question on some unresolved problem, for example, "What can be done to remedy the unemployment situation in the United States?" There are no pat answers to this question. Pupils are given free rein to suggest possible solutions to the complex problem. This is a process in group thinking. Questioning should not be viewed as a dialogue between the teacher and an individual student. It is a technique that develops group skills and requires group action. Pupils assume different roles: as active responder, as active questioner, as passive listener. Discussion and summarization of the pupils' solutions to the problems may lead to further study.

Means to sharpen the technique of questioning deserve the teacher's time and study.

THE TEACHER AS GROUP LEADER

The teacher should recognize his function as a group leader. Instruction is to a considerable degree a problem of skillful handling of groups, some of them very large groups in modern schools. The teacher not only works with a collection of individuals but also releases the potential of a group which shares common living and learning experiences during the course of an academic year. He seeks to develop a solidarity, a unity, a spirit of cooperation. He makes pupils conscious of the fact that their learning tasks are as much a concern to the total group as to the individual members. Keys to effective group leadership include the following:

1. *The teacher's role in group instruction varies from time to time.* At all times the teacher is the personification of the authority of society. He is the representative of the adult world, of mature society, whose task it is to guide young people toward maturity. At times he is the imparter of knowledge, the fountain of information, the expert. At other times he plays the roles of reinforcer, listener, coordinator, giver of advice and counsel, judge, mediator, and tester. He continuously helps his groups to define

their goals, devise ways of proceeding in their instructional tasks, and evaluate the results of study. The teacher assumes a variety of roles in the instructional process.

2. *The teacher should know intimately the composition of his group.* He should have a special awareness of learners who fail to assume their responsibilities for class progress or who interfere with class progress. As we work with groups we discover pupils too timid to participate, pupils fearful or self-conscious, and pupils so aggressive as to disrupt group efforts. We find pupils who demand the teacher's attention to the exclusion of others, pupils who are highly critical of their classmates, pupils who are struggling for acceptance by their peers, and pupils who are recognized by their peers as leaders. The sensitive teacher attempts to bring out the latent abilities of the shy and to teach the aggressive, domineering student to channel his energies into socially acceptable behavior. Each class period is not only an experience in contact with the subject matter, it is also an experience in group living. Every group discussion gives learners the chance to develop skills they will need in adult society. Pupils, like the teacher, learn to assume varying roles determined by the group's needs.

3. *Participation should be universally distributed.* No student should be consistently overlooked in the class activities. All students need the opportunities to respond to questions, to express their thoughts, and to feel that their talents are valued. The extent of participation and leadership may be determined by the abilities of the pupil; but an honest effort, no matter how limited it may be, should bring acceptance and approval. Participation implies experiences in self-evaluation. It means further that students should enter into the process of making decisions that affect them.

Leadership responsibilities, a significant phase of pupil participation, should be widely shared. We can fall into the habit of aiding the "natural" leaders to become even better leaders, while we fail to draw out latent leadership talents of many students. Our "natural" leaders are often those who have had numerous opportunities to develop their talents. They are self-confident individuals and often extroverted. The school may be the only place where the less confident, the introverted, and the shy pupil will have a chance to demonstrate any leadership potential. If some students are constantly pushed into the background, they readily convince themselves that they have no capabilities of leadership. Yet, they might fulfill well many leadership roles.

We do not confine our definition of leadership to exalted positions, such as the president of the class or the leading role in the senior play or the star quarterback. The chairman of a small student group has a chance to demonstrate leadership. The student who takes the responsibility to serve as a host to visitors is exercising leadership. The pupil who gives a thoughtful answer to a question enters into the role of leader. The tendency to label individuals as either "leaders" or "followers" misses a central point in a democratic society. We are all both leaders and followers. We lead on some occasions; at other times we follow. We serve in varying leadership capacities in civic, social, and religious groups. Democracy can function more efficiently if its citizens know when to accept responsibility of leadership and when to serve in the capacity of follower. Nothing could so hinder our society as to condemn a segment of the population to followership. No one will deny that individuals possess varying degrees of leadership ability. Drive and motivation differ from individual to individual. An intense desire for achievement, for recognition, for rewards of material or other gain bring forth leadership. Obviously, not all individuals can become President of the United States, or governor of the state, or superintendent of schools. In a purely figurative sense we can all aspire to high office. This is a part of the American dream. On a more realistic plane, however, leadership potential should be developed to the fullest extent of an individual's capacity. We simply do not know the potential of an individual unless we give him opportunities to show his ability.

ASSIGNMENT-MAKING

The teacher should give more than cursory attention to assignment-making. Pupils spend many hours of the academic year fulfilling tasks set for them by a host of teachers. There is a tendency on the part of some teachers to treat the matter of making assignments in a rather cavalier fashion. Assignments for home study are appended to the lesson, sometimes hastily at the last minute. It is not uncommon to see a teacher shouting the assignment to a group of confused students as the bell rings. A technique of such scope and frequency as assignment-making deserves serious consideration. Some of the guiding principles for teachers who wish to perfect this technique include the following:

1. *The assignment should be considered an integral part of the instructional process.* Provision should be made in each lesson plan for the assignment, if there is to be one. The assignment should not be an appendage tacked on as an afterthought.

2. *The assignment should be necessary.* Pupils and parents will attest to some assignments which are in essence busy-work. Unless the assignment fulfills some specific purpose which can be accomplished in no other way it should not be given. Teachers assign homework for a number of reasons. Some feel that the work of a course cannot be adequately covered in the brief time allowed during the school period. Some teachers assign homework because it appears the thing to do. They reason that with

the emphasis on scholarship and excellence assignments are essential; they equate quantity of study with quality of instruction. Some feel that parents demand homework and they must oblige. This is often a rationalization for busy-work. Parents generally desire that their young people have some home assignments but they object to overloading students and to nonessential tasks. If the assignments are pertinent, neither parents nor students should object.

3. *Assignments should be clear.* The teacher, when he gives an assignment, should put himself in the student's place and try to anticipate problems the student might have in tackling the homework. In order to assure clarity it is a useful technique to give the assignment both orally and in written form. The teacher can explain orally in detail what is expected. He may supplement this with a written summary of the assignment on the blackboard for students to copy. It is a desirable practice to train students to copy assignments in their notebooks or in their assignment pads, rather than permit them to trust to memory what they are to do. If the teacher starts this practice at the beginning of the year, pupils will soon make it a habit to write down their assignments.

The teacher should explain the assignment at sufficient length so that pupils know exactly how to proceed. It is doubtful if common assignments such as "Read the next chapter" or "Work the next ten problems" produce the best results. The teacher may suggest items to look for in the next chapter. He may anticipate problems the pupils may encounter and show them ways to go about solving these problems. He may supplement his assignment with questions to which pupils may find the answers. He may summarize or give pupils an overview of what they will encounter in their assignment. It is a helpful practice to have the class look over the chapter to be read or to begin work on the assigned study in class so the teacher may see if the students know how to do the assigned work.

4. *Sufficient time should be allowed for making the assignment.* The teacher should budget his time in such a way that he is able to give complete details of what he expects the students to do. The length of time will vary depending upon the type of assignment to be given. The assignment can be made at any convenient time during the period. If assignments of a long-term nature are to be made, a large portion of the class hour or perhaps on some occasions a whole class hour may be devoted to making assignments.

5. *When long-term assignments are given, pupils should be allowed sufficient time to prepare the assignments.* The teacher should be available for help as pupils proceed in their assignments and reminders should be given periodically. Teachers should make allowances for the adolescents'

lack of maturity by giving them sufficient warnings that assigned work is due.

6. *Resources for the assigned work should be readily available.* The teacher should know that the resources are available and should indicate places where information can be obtained if needed. As a general rule, resources should be available in the school or within easy access to students' use. It has become increasingly apparent that a sizeable number of teachers are teaching high school courses under the assumption that all pupils have unlimited resources and facilities at home. It is not uncommon, for example, to find social studies teachers who take for granted that pupils have a set of encyclopedias in the home, typing teachers who assume students have typewriters in their homes, homemaking teachers who assume students have sewing machines at home. No assignment should be given unless resources are available to the students who must perform the assignments. If assignments are given in typing and home economics, for example, which require work out of class hours, the school and teacher are obligated to make school facilities available for this work. This means that the teacher will be available before school hours or after school hours or during scheduled periods of the day. Unless the school can provide facilities, time, and supervision for assignments of this nature, the teacher should restructure his program in such a way that out-of-school work is not assigned. The assumption that all homes have the resources demanded by modern programs of education is untenable. Many homes lack even a single newspaper, let alone a set of encyclopedias. It is the teacher's responsibility, rather than the student's, to ascertain whether resources and facilities are available either within the school or within easy reach of the students before assignments are made.

7. *Assignments should be differentiated according to the ability and interest of the students.* This means that a blanket assignment should not habitually be given to all members of the class. The blanket assignment is the simplest technique, but not the most effective. Students need some element of choice, if it is possible to extend that choice. If they may choose between equally suitable topics, books, and other materials, the opportunity for choice should be granted them. Some teachers use the technique of making a minimal blanket assignment, then supplementing it with "bonus" questions for those who wish to try them on a voluntary basis. The teacher may make some distinctions in assignments for bright, average, and slow pupils. He may tactfully suggest more complicated topics and materials to the faster students. He may make allowance for less quantity and quality of assigned work for slower pupils. He may suggest simpler reading materials for students who have difficulty with reading. He may even exempt pupils from certain assignments when they have demonstrated that they have the competencies which the assignments are designed to bring

out. There is no point in requiring a pupil who has mastered certain material to go over the same ground ad nauseam. Every device that the teacher can create to tailor assignments to the abilities and interests of the learners should be employed.

8. *Assignments should be reasonable in length.* If assignments are given daily, it is questionable whether they should average over one-half hour of home study per course. With an increase in number of subjects carried, pupils now average five or six academic subjects per day. Many high schools have abandoned study halls, so pupils have no periods scheduled during the day when they might do their homework. Further, many teachers do not allow time in the class hour to begin assignments for the next day. If the student carries five academic courses and is expected to do a half-hour's homework for each, he will be occupied two and one-half hours in study time, which is certainly sufficient for growing adolescents. The overloading of students with homework causes consternation in the families of those who care about education. Overloading can cut down on other outside activities of young people, which may be as beneficial as the required school work. It can also interfere with the maintenance of a healthy, happy family life.

The faculty should periodically examine its policies on homework to make sure that assignments are kept to a reasonable length. Some faculties have gone to the extent of permitting teachers in specified courses to schedule homework only on certain days of the week. Teachers should generally refrain from assigning homework on the eve of important school events and during major school vacation periods. An occasional messianic teacher feels his own subject is so important that other events may interfere with it, even Christmas or Easter. Such a teacher may have to be restrained by school policy or by a firm school principal.

9. *Some check should be made on all assignments.* This does not mean that a teacher should take on the herculean task of correcting and grading all homework. But he should check to see that assignments have been done. He may often spot-check homework papers to see if students appear to be doing the work properly. He must convey to pupils the idea that homework is important. If the teacher does not collect homework papers or collects them and tosses them in the basket, pupils will develop slovenly habits and attitudes toward homework. If homework is important enough to be assigned, it is important enough to check. In fact, the successful completion of homework assignments should be reflected in the mark a teacher gives at the end of a marking period.

10. *Students who miss a required assignment for a legitimate reason should be given adequate opportunity to make up the work.* Students who fail to do an assignment or are absent from class without a legitimate reason should not receive credit for that assignment.

11. *As a general rule, assignments should be given only on material which has been fully explained in class.* If the teacher assigns advanced work which he has not explained beforehand, the student may do the work wrong and thereby learn incorrect habits. The teacher will then have to face the problem of unlearning wrong procedures. Assignments should be made only after pupils have the required skills and background to go about the work correctly.

Assignment-making is a skill that the teacher should seek to perfect. It is a technique which he will use repeatedly and which can result in better learning on the part of the students. It is a technique which can also be used ineffectively and abused.

ACTION RESEARCH

The teacher should try out new ideas, methods, and approaches. He should conduct periodically what is known in the profession as "action research." He may, for example, try a new technique he has learned at a professional meeting or has read about in a professional journal. He may set two of his classes to work at a particular task using different approaches and make some judgments on the efficacy of each approach. He might, by way of illustration, attempt to teach one of his classes using daily homework. He might teach another class using supervised study during the class period instead of assigning homework. After a period of time with both methods he judges the results by means of various evaluative instruments. Research of this nature is not pretentious. It is not stringently controlled. Results point directions but do not yield conclusive answers. Action research helps a teacher to vary his program and to grow professionally. Trying out new ways of teaching, the teacher does not grow stagnant. In the process of action research he may discover new and better ways of stimulating the achievement of learners.

We are mindful, in suggesting means of improving techniques of instruction, that successful teaching is a unique cluster of skills, knowledge, concepts, and attitudes varying from teacher to teacher. The individual teacher's success in utilizing specific techniques will depend upon his perception of the purposes, effectiveness, and applicability of the techniques. Teachers will meet with varying degrees of success in the use of particular techniques. What may work for one teacher with his unique personality and approach to teaching may be totally ineffective for another teacher. Each teacher should be encouraged to find techniques and approaches to instruction which are compatible to him and which meet with success as demonstrated in the behavior of the learners.

SUMMARY

A number of factors enter into the instructional process. In this unit we have analyzed three of the factors that make for better teaching. We have described the effective teacher as one who (1) holds an adequate self-concept, (2) understands basic principles of the learning process, and (3) uses efficient techniques of instruction. The techniques that the teacher uses in the classroom are directly related to the psychological framework for learning.

CLASS AND EVALUATION ACTIVITIES

1. Visit several classrooms and apply the check list on page 266 to the teaching you observe.

2. List traits you like in a teacher. Rank in order of importance to you. List and rank traits you dislike in a teacher.

3. Define "drill." To what extent is drill necessary in your subject?

4. Show the relationship of the following to motivation:
   a. teacher's goals
   b. pupils' goals
   c. rewards
   d. interest on the part of the learner
   e. learner's ability
   f. climate for learning in the classroom
   g. variety in instructional program
   h. difficulty of material

5. Evaluate a number of commonly used awards, rewards, and prizes in schools.

6. Observe and evaluate the use of programmed materials. If you can find none in use, obtain and examine some programs especially in your subject.

7. Evaluate several teachers' use of blackboard, bulletin boards, and display cases in their instruction.

8. Evaluate several homework assignments given by several teachers,

Key to ratings: 1. Unsatisfactory   Teacher ....
                 2. Poor   Subject ....
                 3. Fair   Period ....
                 4. Good   School ....
                 5. Superior   Date ....

	1	2	3	4	5	Notes
Relationships with Students						
Learning atmosphere in classroom						
Interest in children						
Understanding of children						
Personal relationships; rapport						
Discipline						
Attention to individual differences						
Teaching Techniques						
Aims apparent						
Planning apparent						
Variety of activities						
Pupil participation						
Skill in oral expression						
Skill in oral questioning						
Skill in written expression						
Utilization of materials and aids						
Efficient use of class time						
Assignment-making						
Review and practice						
Evaluation of pupils' work						
Personal Qualities						
Professional behavior						
Mature behavior; emotional stability						
Voice (audible; free from monotony)						
Correct language usage						
Tact						
Poise						
Appropriate grooming and dress						
Fairmindedness						
Physical stamina						
Efficiency						
Resourcefulness						
Sense of humor						
Academic preparation						

266

including several in your subject, as to length of assignment, time required, quality of assignment, necessity for assignment, purpose, and disposition of the completed assignment.

9. Topics for group discussion:

a. What is effective teaching?

b. What is the mind? the self? the soul? intelligence? scholastic aptitude?

c. Does it matter whether students like a subject? Why? Must they like a subject in order to succeed?

d. Have you ever persisted in a disagreeable task? Why?

e. Some persons believe that no person can teach another person to teach. Evaluate this belief. If this be true, what are the implications for instruction?

10. Conduct panel discussions on:

a. How would you develop leadership in the classroom?

b. How do people learn?

11. Explain to the class how you would go about teaching students to think in your subject.

12. Evaluate this statement: Mathematics makes you think. Change the subject to any other you wish.

13. Prepare a short report for the class on the learning theories of:

a. John B. Watson

b. Edward L. Thorndike

c. John Locke

d. Johann Pestalozzi

e. Johann Herbart

f. Ivan Pavlov

g. Charles Peirce

h. William James

i. John Dewey

j. Boyd Bode

k. B. L. Skinner

l. N. A. Crowder

14. Evaluate the principle: We learn by doing. How can this be implemented? When can it not be? Of what value are vicarious experiences?

15. Report on the "scientific method." Show whether it is applicable to your subject.

16. Observe several classrooms. Did they have a good climate for learning? Why?

17. Show an abstract painting and ask students to write their reactions to it. Compare the reactions. Why do students react in different ways to the same painting?

18. Play a piece of mood music on a record player. Ask students to

describe their feelings about the music. Read some of the statements. Why do students describe different reactions?

19. Perform the following experiment on the effects of competition in the classroom: Take a student from the class or from elsewhere who is top-notch in mathematics. Prepare a series of simple mathematics problems and let as many students challenge the math expert as wish to do so. Record the time it takes to solve each problem in the series. The winner is the person who solves each problem in the shortest time. As the math expert solves each problem in shorter time than others, see if volunteers to challenge him decrease in number. Why should this be true?

20. Have a single girl and a married boy in class explain to the group their views on campus problems. Account for differences in their views.

21. Observe several teachers
   a. starting a class
   b. closing a class
   c. distributing materials
   d. taking care of routine details such as sharpening pencils, ventilation, light, etc.
   e. taking attendance

Evaluate their methods. How would you make improvements in these?

22. Investigate a school's procedures in such matters as:
   a. reporting absences and tardiness
   b. filing excuses for absence
   c. keeping attendance registers
   d. keeping other records

23. Find, if you can, any illustrations of action research in progress, recently completed, or to be conducted shortly.

24. Find illustrations of practices in schools which you would attribute to the teachers' adherence to (1) behavioristic psychology and (2) experimentalist psychology.

25. Cite illustrations of conditioning in schools.

26. Suggest several measures you would use to prevent pupils from disliking your subject.

27. Explain how you would go about developing (1) ability to think or reason and (2) memory.

28. Show the transfer value of your subject.

29. Privately evaluate yourself: Would you classify yourself as a fully functioning personality? Why?

30. A pupil is having difficulty with fractions. How would a proponent of faculty psychology remedy this? a behaviorist? an experimentalist?

31. What significance does perceptual psychology have in the case of students who say: "I'm no good at math." "I can't draw a straight line." "I can't speak in front of a group"?

32. Mention several ways you could individualize instruction in your subject.

33. Prepare an instrument, e.g., a check list, to evaluate (1) assignment-making and (2) oral questioning.

34. Formulate several generalizations on group dynamics or the group process which may help a teacher.

35. Give illustrations of positive forms of motivation used by teachers; negative forms used by teachers.

36. How would you use community resources in your subject? What resources would ordinarily be available?

37. Formulate ten questions which you could use in a lesson in your subject. Students in the same subject field can prepare questions on the same topic. Work in small groups after preparing the questions; compare and discuss the questions. Members of the group may try out their questions on each other.

38. Prepare an assignment for a lesson plan in your subject. Work in small subject-matter groups and discuss each assignment prepared.

39. Give as many generalizations as you can in regard to learning, which you believe can be substantiated.

SELECTED BIBLIOGRAPHICAL REFERENCES

1. Association for Supervision and Curriculum Development. *Perceiving, Behaving, Becoming.* Yearbook 1962. Washington: Association for Supervision and Curriculum Development, N.E.A., 1962. 256 pp.

    Insightful work on psychological foundations of education with implications for instruction. Emphasis on the development of the self-concept. Basic papers by psychologists Arthur Combs, Earl Kelley, A. H. Maslow, and Carl Rogers.

2. Association for Supervision and Curriculum Development. *Individualizing Instruction.* Yearbook 1964. Washington: Association for Supervision and Curriculum Development, N.E.A., 1964. 174 pp.

    Focuses on personal relationships between teacher and student. Describes ways to discover and release human potential.

3. Bode, Boyd H. *How We Learn.* Boston: D. C. Heath, 1940. 308 pp.

    Old but still valuable discussion of four theories of mind and learning.

4. Cole, Lawrence E., and Bruce, William F. *Educational Psychology.* Rev. ed. New York: Harcourt, Brace & World, 1958. 701 pp.

Comprehensive text which includes excellent material on the development of personality, the psychology of learning, and applications in the schools.

5. Murphy, Gardner. *Historical Introduction to Modern Psychology*. Rev. ed. New York: Harcourt, Brace & World, 1949. 466 pp.

Interesting and informative history of psychology from ancient times to the present.

6. National Society for the Study of Education. *Individualizing Instruction*. 61st Yearbook. Part I. Chicago: The University of Chicago Press, 1962. 337 pp.

Helpful volume which includes among its four sections illustrations of individual differences and analyses of current school practices for individualizing instruction.

7. Thayer, V. T. *The Role of the School in American Society*. New York: Dodd, Mead and Co., 1960. Part III.

Interesting and readable account of conceptions of learning in their cultural setting. Shows interrelationships between psychological theories and sociological conditions and philosophical tenets.

INSTRUCTIONAL AIDS AND SOURCES

1. Films

a. Audio-Visual Aids to Learning. 13 min. Sound. Black and white. U.S. Army.

This film shows an eighth-grade social studies teacher developing a unit on Japan with the help of a variety of audio-visual aids.

b. Bulletin Boards: An Effective Teaching Device. 11 min. Sound. Color. Bailey.

This film shows how to plan and organize bulletin-board displays.

c. Chalkboard Utilization. 16 min. Sound. Black and white. Young America.

This film depicts ways to use the classroom chalkboard effectively.

d. Motivating the Class. 19 min. Sound. Black and white. McGraw-Hill.

A young student teacher of mathematics learns that adequate motivation is basic to all good teaching and is obtained by translating the values of the subject matter into terms the pupils can understand.

e. Near Home. 25 min. Sound. Black and white. International Film Bureau.

This British film tells the story of a class engaged in the study of local history. It shows the effective use of field trips and community resources.

f. Overhead Projector. 16 min. Sound. Black and white. Iowa State University.

This film shows how to use the overhead projector, including the process of making transparencies.

g. Using the Classroom Film. 21 min. Sound. Black and white. Encyclopedia Britannica Films.

This film shows how to select, preview, and use classroom films.

2. Tapes

a. Combs, Arthur. *Seeing Is Behaving.* Tape of talk given at the Association for Supervision and Curriculum Development conference, March, 1958 at Seattle, Washington. Interesting and informative presentation of perceptual psychology. Available from Educational Media Department, College of Education, University of Florida, Gainesville, Florida.

GUIDANCE FOR THE CLASSROOM TEACHER

OBJECTIVES OF UNIT V

At the conclusion of his reading and correlated study-discussion activities the reader should

A. understand that

1. guidance in the schools is an essential feature of a system of universal public education;

2. every teacher has responsibilities for guiding pupils;

3. the classroom teacher is in a strategic position to fulfill certain guidance responsibilities;

4. a great part of the task of guidance falls upon the classroom teacher;

5. the term "guidance" implies counseling of the student on all kinds of problems;

6. American adolescents have many needs in common;

7. all students are in need of some type of guidance;

8. tests have their place in the guidance program but are not infallible nor the only technique for gathering information.

B. show appreciation for

1. a well-planned school-wide guidance program,

2. an efficient and up-to-date system of keeping guidance records,

3. the usefulness of certain guidance techniques, including testing,

4. the services of specialists in personnel work.

C. adopt attitudes of

1. willingness to accept guidance responsibilities,

2. willingness to use certain guidance techniques,

3. willingness to maintain the necessary records;

4. willingness to recognize the hazards and limitations of certain guidance techniques.

D. be able to demonstrate skill in

1. gathering data about the individual pupil,

2. using the resources available for counseling,

3. interviewing,

4. interpreting test results.

E. be familiar with the following:

1. the needs and interests of American adolescents:

   a. developmental tasks of adolescence,

   b. the ten imperative needs of youth;

2. the types of information which should be obtained about individual pupils;

3. techniques used in studying and handling groups for guidance purposes;

4. certain guidance techniques:
   - *a*. standardized tests
   - *b*. interview
   - *c*. case study
   - *d*. autobiography
   - *e*. records and forms
     - (1) the cumulative record
     - (2) questionnaire
     - (3) high school program plans
     - (4) anecdotal record

5. basic guidance materials, including tests and reference materials.

CHAPTER 13

THE NEEDS AND INTERESTS OF
ADOLESCENTS IN OUR CULTURE

Over a period of years the term "guidance" has taken on new and broader meaning. Guidance in today's schools means the advisement of young people on a wide range of personal problems, including vocational, educational, social, and emotional problems. The many facets of guidance are now included in the more comprehensive term "pupil personnel services."

Guidance in the public schools is a normal outgrowth of the American commitment to universal public education. To carry out this commitment every teacher assumes certain guidance responsibilities. Recent years have seen a shift from the concept of guidance as a function solely of an expert to the concept of guidance as a function of both the expert and the classroom teacher.

This discussion of the field of guidance emphasizes the understandings and attitudes which the classroom teacher should know and use. In fulfilling his function as a pupil personnel worker the classroom teacher must have:

1. a knowledge of the needs and interests of adolescents in our culture

2. a knowledge of the needs and interests of the individual pupil

3. a knowledge of the needs and interests of the group or groups to which the individual pupil belongs

4. a knowledge of and ability to use certain guidance techniques

In order to deal with the problems of an individual pupil the teacher must know whether or not the problem is typical of American adolescents in general. The teacher must have some knowledge of the patterns of growth and development of boys and girls. He must have a background in sociology in order to place student behavior in its social setting. He must be aware of factors in the culture which shape pupil behavior. He must know the common needs of boys and girls in our society.

Recognition of the developmental tasks of the adolescent period and of the imperative needs of adolescent youth constitutes a beginning phase of guidance.

DEVELOPMENTAL TASKS

At various periods in the growth of the human being varying types of behavior must be learned. That behavior which must be mastered at a particular stage in the development of the human being is referred to as a "developmental task." Psychologists, through intensive study of the human organism, have identified specific tasks that must be learned at childhood, adolescence, and old age. These tasks must be learned in sequence. The child learns to walk before he learns to talk. He learns to talk before he learns to read.

At the adolescent stage, developmental tasks are primarily social and emotional in nature. Havighurst defines the nine developmental tasks of adolescence.[1]

1. *The adolescent must learn to accept his own physique.* Psychologists refer to the importance of self-concept, meaning that much of our behavior is influenced by the manner in which we perceive ourselves. Adolescents do not want to appear different in any way from other members of their group. Differences in stature may cause an adolescent to feel out of contact with his group, or the appearance of secondary sex characteristics may cause him or her embarrassment and worry. Counseling seeks to point out to young people the wide range in growth patterns of adolescents. The counselor will assure the individual that his pattern of growth is perfectly normal and that many adolescents share the same problems and worries. The counselor will interpret to the individual the bodily changes that occur during the adolescent period. He will also assist the adolescent to make the best use of whatever talents he has.

The adolescent must also learn to accept the masculine or feminine role. The roles which boys and girls must play in our society are culturally determined. The differences in sex roles find expression in adolescent behavior. Boys in our culture are expected to be daring and aggressive; girls are expected to be neat and orderly, more docile and less aggressive than boys. The boy who deviates from the culturally approved patterns is branded as a "sissy" or "odd-ball"; the girl who strays from the approved path is a "tomboy." These labels are terms by which society expresses its disapproval of deviation from expected roles. The counselor will assist the

---

[1] Robert J. Havighurst, *Developmental Tasks and Education* (New York: David McKay Company, Inc., 1952).

individual to live up to his expected masculine or her feminine role. Unless the individual accomplishes this developmental task, he will encounter severe adjustment problems.

2. *The adolescent must establish new relations with age-mates of both sexes.* Adolescents are concerned not only with maintaining good relationships with members of their own sex but also with establishing good relationships with members of the opposite sex. Adolescents feel the need for learning appropriate social behavior. Dating becomes an accepted and important practice. Rejection of an individual by members of the opposite sex can cause great anguish.

Both parents and teachers are seriously concerned these days with the fact that youngsters start "going steady" at such an early age. Going steady is an accepted practice in senior high schools and in many junior high schools of the country.

Counselors will assist young people to establish healthy relationships, explain proper behavior to them, and provide opportunities in the school curriculum for learning suitable relationships. Effort may be made to explain the disadvantages of going steady, but it is doubtful if sermonizing against the evils of going steady or outright prohibition will dissuade young people from the practice. The use of force to prevent boys and girls from going steady is interpreted by young people as a further lack of understanding of their problems. The teacher and parent can take comfort from the fact that most of the "steady" couples break up, some of them after a very brief period of time. For young people, going steady fulfills a precourtship type of learning experience and helps satisfy adolescent needs for security and belonging. Young people themselves are concerned about the practice of going steady, since they are constantly questioning themselves and others about its propriety. Discontinuance of the custom must come from the inner desires of the adolescent rather than from the preachments of the counselor or other adult.

3. *The adolescent must attain emotional independence from parents and other adults.* The desire for independence accounts for the general rebellious nature attributed to adolescents. During this period they must learn to stand on their own feet. Parents who deny their adolescents the opportunities to make their own decisions and to achieve some measure of independence are delaying the young persons' development and thwarting achievement of this developmental task. Truly pitiful is the adult who has not learned independence in adolescence and who is still emotionally dependent upon his parents. It is the contention of some writers like Philip Wylie that "momism," complete dependence on the parent, is a great threat to our society. A counselor who understands this phase of adolescent development can interpret the causes of rebelliousness to parents

and thereby eliminate some of the frictions that might otherwise arise. The counselor can interpret to the adolescent his behavior so that the adolescent may learn why he acts as he does and may understand his parents' attempts to restrict his behavior.

4. *The adolescent must achieve assurance of economic independence.* He must be enrolled in courses which will ultimately lead to a vocation, after either high school or college. Emotionally desiring independence, the adolescent must seek ways of attaining at least partial economic independence. Part-time work will help satisfy this task. The adolescent needs to feel that he can help provide for himself, at least to the point of earning some of his own spending money. The counselor should encourage and assist the student in obtaining part-time and summer employment so he can gain some sense of economic independence. The adolescent has an uphill fight in accomplishing this developmental task since opportunities for part-time employment are often very limited, especially in depressed areas where unemployment of adults is a critical problem.

5. *The adolescent must select and prepare for an occupation.* Far-reaching decisions must be made during the high school career. The student has to choose between various curricula. He needs help in appraising his vocational interests and aptitudes. He needs help in electing courses that will be in line with his interests and aptitudes. He needs help also in examining the myriad opportunities in the world of work for persons with his abilities.

6. *The adolescent must develop intellectual skills and concepts necessary for civic competence.* Every attempt must be made to encourage the highest degree of scholarship of which the student is capable. For those with deficiencies remedial instruction must be provided.

7. *The adolescent must achieve socially responsible behavior.* In spite of the lurid headlines that feature adolescent misbehavior, the majority of boys and girls want to become socially responsible citizens. In order to attain this goal they must have opportunities during their school careers to learn the skills of self-discipline. The counselor has the responsibility of pointing out to the irresponsible youth the social hazards of his conduct.

8. *The adolescent must prepare for marriage and family life.* Many young people will marry directly after graduation from high school. Some instruction preparing them to take their places in society as responsible family members should be a part of the high school curriculum. Included in this discussion should be elements of sex education. The counselor who is trusted and respected by young people will be able to help them with the many questions and problems that are of serious concern to them in this area.

9. *The adolescent needs to build conscious values in harmony with an adequate scientific word-picture.* The young person of today is confronted with conflicting values. He is unsure of himself and cannot know how to make value judgments without the guidance of sympathetic adults. He needs to become familiar with the world of science in which we live. He needs to be aware of the problems we face in this age of science. He needs help in applying the scientific method to analysis of problems he will meet. Through the instructional program and through counseling he can be helped to formulate his own values, to see how they are related to the society in which he lives, and to translate these values into socially acceptable behavior.

Should the adolescent not complete any of these developmental tasks, he will find himself handicapped in achieving the next set of developmental tasks which he will meet as he grows older. Unless social and emotional tasks are accomplished, the intellectual learnings that the school is attempting to instill in adolescents will be meaningless. Although we, as teachers, would desire the student to be more concerned with the academic phase of his development, social and emotional difficulties must be resolved before he can concentrate on the intellectual tasks before him. Thus, the need for a continuous program of individual guidance is apparent.

THE TEN IMPERATIVE NEEDS OF YOUTH

All adolescents have specific educational needs. A teacher who is seeking knowledge of the needs and interests of adolescents in our culture should study at length the statement of the Educational Policies Commission of the National Education Association, *Education for All American Youth,* which first discussed "the ten imperative needs of youth."[2] The National Association of Secondary School Principals has widely publicized these ten imperative needs.[3] Suffice it for purposes of our discussion to outline the ten imperative needs of youth.

1. All youth need to develop salable skills.

2. All youth need to develop and maintain good health, physical fitness, and mental health.

3. All youth need to understand the rights and duties of the citizen of a democratic society.

4. All youth need to understand the significance of the family.

2 (Washington: National Education Association, 1944.) Also see the Commission's *Education for All American Youth, A Further Look* (1952), p. 216.

3 *Planning for American Youth* (Washington: National Association of Secondary School Principals, 1951).

5. All youth need to know how to purchase and use goods and services intelligently.

6. All youth need to understand the methods of science.

7. All youth need opportunities to develop their capacities to appreciate beauty in literature, art, music, and nature.

8. All youth need to be able to use their leisure time well.

9. All youth need to develop respect for other people, to grow in their insight into ethical values and principles, to be able to live and work cooperatively with others, and to grow in the moral and spiritual values of life.

10. All youth need to grow in their ability to think rationally, to express their thoughts clearly, and to read and listen with understanding.

When the teacher has secured a knowledge of the common needs and interests of boys and girls in American society, he can move to the next step, attaining a knowledge of the needs and interests of an individual pupil.

UNDERSTANDING THE NEEDS OF THE INDIVIDUAL PUPIL

The classroom teacher will find it necessary to gather certain pertinent data about each of the pupils in his charge. The following data are essential to the understanding of the pupil. Examples drawn from actual guidance records are given to demonstrate the need for the data.

1. *The teacher will seek general information about the background of the pupil, such as full name, nickname, age, etc.* Need for these data is shown in Case 1 below.

> *Case 1.* C., a sixteen-year-old boy, was in the sixth grade. He was repeating the grade. At mid-term he quit school.

A significant factor in this case is the discrepancy between his chronological age and his grade placement. It is possible that by giving serious consideration to this discrepancy the teacher might have worked with the boy to prevent his dropping out of school. The teacher would seek opportunities to help him accomplish his sixth-grade tasks. He would diagnose, through testing, if necessary, scholastic difficulties and give the boy opportunities for remedial instruction. In some cases a conditional promotion might provide a satisfactory solution. If the boy was utterly incapable of seventh-grade work and had to be retained in the sixth grade, the sixth-grade teacher would seek to minimize the age discrepancy by giving the boy opportunities to assist with the work of the course, to help younger members of the class, and to develop some sense of responsibility. The author makes the assumption that the more education a boy or girl gets, the better. This is contrary to the thinking of a sizable group of present-day critics of public education who feel that boys and girls such as those cited in Case 1 should be permitted, indeed encouraged, to leave school.

2. *The teacher will find out all he can about the student's previous school history.* He will want to know the child's rate of progress through the grades, and instances of acceleration or retardation. He will want to know what subjects the child has taken. He will find useful the pupil's statement of his favorite subjects and his least-liked subjects. The teacher will examine marks given in subjects in the previous grades to get an over-all picture of the academic history of the student. The necessity of knowing this type of information can be found in Case 2 below.

> *Case 2.* B., a freshman girl, was experiencing difficulty in ninth-grade science. A check of her school history revealed that she came into the public high school from a parochial school where science was not taught in the junior high school grades. Her ninth-grade science course was taught with the assumption that all pupils had some foundation in science in the junior high school.

Having this type of information should evoke some means of providing pupils like this girl with additional help in the subject matter. Failing marks in a subject may indicate a lack of intelligence, scholastic aptitude, or preparation in the particular subject. Failing grades may call for intensified effort on the part of the pupil, a change in methods of instruction, a change of program or selection of another course if the course is not a required one. Failure may also be symptomatic of indifference or dislike for the subject matter.

3. *The teacher will seek information about the pupil's family history and background.* A determined effort to encourage the boy described in the case below might have enabled him to continue with his schooling.

> *Case 3.* Both of E.'s parents were dead. He lived with relatives who had little interest in him or in his schooling and were anxious for him to finish school in order to start earning money. He later dropped out of school and enlisted in the Navy.

Analysis of the home environment will give the counselor clues by which he can understand the pupil's actions and by which he can assist the pupil. The counselor of the boy above, had he known something of the family background of the boy, might have helped him to find part-time work after school, might have shown the boy reasons for staying in school, and might have worked with relatives to persuade them to urge the boy to complete his schooling.

Pertinent data about a student's family background would include the names of the parents or guardians, brothers, and sisters; ages of members of the family; schooling of members of the family; occupational and church affiliation; relationships between members of the family; ambitions that parents have for their children; and parents' attitudes toward school. Adequate counseling is impossible without knowledge of the family background of the pupil.

4. *The teacher will want to learn whatever he can about group, neighborhood, and community influences which impinge upon the behavior of the pupil.* Following is a simple case where outside influences affected a high school student.

> *Case 4.* M., a junior girl not of college ability, was enrolled in a college preparatory course in order to keep up with her girl friends who were college bound. She was failing several of her courses and was very unhappy.

The counselor in this case would recognize the situation as an instance of "keeping up with the Joneses," a phenomenon which often results in maladjustment. The peer group, the neighborhood environment, and community attitudes and mores affect a student's behavior. Teachers in consolidated or centralized schools are conscious of significant differences in pupils of the various communities from which the students come.

Youth groups, gangs, church groups, cliques, the family's circle of friends, and boy-girl relationships are all significant factors concerning which the counselor should have information. By knowing the friends with whom the girl in the case above associated, the counselor might surmise the reason why the girl is misplaced in the school curriculum. By discussing with the girl her strengths, weaknesses, and interests, the counselor might work out with her a more suitable program.

5. *The medical history of the pupil is a necessary piece of information.* The importance of knowing about the pupil's medical history is shown in the case below.

> *Case 5.* E., a senior boy, was experiencing difficulty in all his courses. He was branded by a teacher as "lazy." Medical records showed that he had had rheumatic fever as a boy. He tired easily and was unable to do all his homework assignments.

Knowledge of the physical condition of the student will enable the counselor to make a more accurate appraisal of pupil difficulty. It is unfortunate that many schools are unable to provide the services of a nurse to assist teachers in spotting children with health problems. Few schools in the country provide the services of a school physician beyond the most cursory attention. A minority of school systems offer the services of a dental hygienist.

In those schools where the services of a nurse and physician are not provided the teacher must be extra cautious that he does not attribute to other sources the causes of problems which are physical in nature. The counselor should advise parents to have each child checked thoroughly by the doctor at least once a year. Medical records should be available in the school so that the counselor can learn the student's history of child-hood diseases, accidents, handicaps, and medical treatment. Vision and hearing tests should be conducted in all schools. It is possible for the teacher himself to conduct simple vision and hearing tests where schools do not provide such a testing program. A teacher who is aware of a student's physical handicaps will make special provision for him. He may find it necessary to make adjustments in the child's schedule, in the quantity and quality of work that can be expected of him, in physical arrangements within the classroom, in time allowances for completion of assignments, and in giving special help.

6. *The teacher must obtain evidence of the student's mental ability.* By and large, schools administer standardized tests of intelligence. Differences in mental abilities of pupils show up as in the common case below.

> *Case 6.* E., a tenth-grade boy, was enrolled in biology, a course required of all pupils in the tenth grade. Standardized tests showed him to be well below average in mental ability. He was also repeating ninth-grade algebra, another course required of all pupils in the school.

In the case above, the small school, conforming to state requirements to offer a year of mathematics and a year of science, provided only college preparatory mathematics and science. No differentiation in course content was made for the noncollege-bound students who constituted two-thirds of the student body. If the doctrine of individual differences means anything at all, it means differentiation of the objectives, methods, and materials to meet the needs of the learner.

The counselor can compare a student's grades with his scores on a mental ability test. Where there is great and consistent discrepancy between the teacher-grades and scores on a standardized test of intelligence, the counselor will call for a repetition of the standardized test, making certain that the pupil is in the best possible condition to take the test. The teacher will seek out the bright pupil and give him every opportunity to progress as far as he can. He will work with the slow pupil to help him overcome deficiencies. Some schools feel that homogeneous grouping is a solution to the problem of providing for differences among levels of learners. Further along in this unit we will discuss at some length the practice of ability grouping.

7. *The teacher will want to learn as much as he can about the emotional and social state of the student.* The boy in the case below was severely reprimanded by the teacher for his deviant behavior.

> *Case 7.* R.'s work as a freshman was extremely poor. His IQ was above normal. Psychiatric examination disclosed tendencies of fantasy, day-dreaming, reading of adult erotic literature, and possible latent homo-sexuality.

No teacher could work intelligently with this boy without insight into the emotional make-up of the student. It is indeed possible and highly probable that even with the knowledge of the boy's condition the teacher would find solution of the pupil's problem difficult. Yet, the important consideration here is that the teacher would have a different attitude toward the boy when he realized that the student had deep-seated psychological disturbances. Detection of the presence of some disturbance would, in itself, be an important first step. The counselor, if he found the problem of such a nature that he could not handle it, would refer the student for assistance to specialists equipped to deal with the problem. Included in the category of behavior which might be referred are antisocial, delinquent, incorrigible, psychotic, and sexually deviant forms of behavior.

8. *The teacher should make a careful study of the vocational and educational interests and goals of the student.* A sympathetic teacher will realize the dilemma of students like the boy in the case below.

> *Case 8.* G. was following, with little success, a college entrance course, though his interests lay in industrial arts. A conference with the student's mother evoked the statement from her, "Well, he'll have to pass geometry if he has to stay in school forever."

The boy's program of study was clearly out of line with his vocational aims and abilities. The counselor in this case will need to work with the parent so that she will understand the problem her son is facing. Every effort must be made to provide a curriculum which will be in line with the student's talents and ambitions. The teacher will use whatever techniques he knows to uncover the talents of gifted pupils and to take every opportunity to capitalize on these talents.

High schools, through organized guidance programs, have assisted teachers in gathering, recording, and interpreting data that the teachers need in counseling pupils. Many schools provide the services of guidance specialists. Where no organized guidance program is in operation in a school system, the teacher's job in the area of guidance will be more difficult, but not impossible. The latter part of this unit will concern itself with techniques that can be used to obtain various kinds of data and with the interpretation of the information gathered.

CHAPTER 14

GROUP NEEDS AND INTERESTS

Every group with which a teacher works has a personality of its own. The typical secondary school teacher will have responsibilities for a homeroom group, one or more extra-class groups, and sometimes a study hall as well as his classes.

Every group to which the student belongs has its effect on the development of that pupil. Groups that influence the development of the student are his classes, the family, the neighborhood, the student's close circle of friends, his social organizations, and his community as a whole.

In the unit on discipline and control, which follows this unit, we will take up in greater detail the effects of various groups upon the behavior of the individual. Some understanding of the dynamics of the groups in the following instances would help the teacher who attempts to work with an individual pupil.

Interpersonal relationships in the class have had an effect upon the girl in the following case:

> *Case 9.* C., a ninth-grade student, is new to the school this year. She has found it difficult to make friends in her homeroom class. As a result, she is an unhappy girl. The homeroom class consists of a highly cohesive group which has been promoted as a group and kept together since the students were in fourth grade. The high degree of cohesiveness makes it difficult for newcomers to gain acceptance.

The family as a unit exerts influence on the individual, as in the case below:

> *Case 10.* D., a twelfth-grade boy, has no doubts about his occupational goal. He wants to become a high school mathematics teacher. His father is a high school principal. His mother is an elementary school teacher. His older sister is currently in college preparing for teaching. There have been school teachers in D.'s family for generations. He has scarcely ever con-

sidered any other line of work. The spirit of teaching has permeated the life of this family.

Social groups to which youth belong have both negative and positive effects upon the development of the individual. The following case illustrates the negative influence:

> *Case 11.* When they have nothing more constructive to do, E., a tenth-grader, and his buddies, a group of five or six boys living in the same neighborhood, prowl around town at night hunting for cars with keys left in the ignition switch. Finding a car with keys, they hop in, take a brief joy ride, and leave the car at some out-of-the-way spot.

The following case shows the positive influence of social organizations:

> *Case 12.* R., sixteen years of age, has just received his Eagle Scout award at a Court of Honor. For four years, since his admission to the Boy Scouts, R. has taken his scout work seriously. He has attempted to implement in his own living the noble ambitions subscribed to by the Boy Scouts.

Group mores are operant in the case below:

> *Case 13.* F., a white senior high school boy, joined a group of other white boys and girls to jeer at several Negro students who were recently admitted to their formerly all-white high school.

The teacher in working with groups and in studying the effects of the group on the individual will be concerned with at least three techniques: (1) analysis of the groups to which the student belongs, (2) techniques of group guidance, (3) homogeneous grouping. Let us consider each of these techniques individually.

ANALYSIS OF THE GROUPS
TO WHICH THE STUDENT BELONGS

The teacher should discover as rapidly as possible the goals of the group as a whole as well as the goals of the individual members of the group. Homogeneity or the lack of it will affect the goals of the group. The teacher will ordinarily find within his classes, particularly in the required courses, subgroupings with varying purposes. A portion of the class may be college-bound. Others in the class may be headed for particular vocations. Among the purposes of a junior high school group may be admission to a particular high school in the area. Several pupils may have the improvement of the skills of reading as their immediate goal. Others may need to enhance their skills with numbers. A senior high school group may be concerned with completing successfully state achievement examinations either for admission to college or for state diplomas. As the teacher gets to know his class, he can discern the general purposes of the group and detect purposes of subgroups within the class.

SOCIOMETRIC STUDY

The teacher will want to study carefully the composition of the group to learn the inner working of the group which some people refer to as "group dynamics." The study of the composition of the group is referred to in the professional literature as "sociometry." Sociometric study is a method of discovering the pupils whom the group recognizes as the leaders, those pupils who have not been accepted by other members of the group, those who are mutual friends, and those who form the cliques. The teacher may be amazed at the results a sociometric study of a group reveals. Students do not always respond in ways a teacher might have anticipated.

Every teacher ought to attempt the sociometric study of at least one of his groups to see what sort of information this technique of group analysis discloses. It might be well for a teacher to select for sociometric analysis a group with which he is having some difficulty.

To begin the sociometric analysis of a group the teacher may announce that the class will be working on a project in the near future which will require the formation of a number of committees. The teacher may then ask the students to write down on a piece of paper the names of three persons with whom they would most like to work. The teacher tells his students that the information will be used to help him set up the committees. The teacher attempting a sociometric analysis should not disclose the fact that he intends to study the composition of the group.

By inspecting, tabulating, or charting the data, the teacher can determine which students are the most popular with their classmates and which are the least popular. He can discover which students wield influence over their peers.

The results of a sociometric study of a group can provide the teacher with information he may use to (1) counsel pupils who have not gained acceptance by their peers (the "isolates"), (2) make use of the recognized leaders of the group (the "stars"), (3) detect sources of trouble which may lie in antisocial subgroups, (4) learn the associates of individuals within the group, (5) discover whether or not pupils are accepted by members of the opposite sex, and (6) adapt instructional techniques to the group and its subgroups.

GROUP GUIDANCE

General problems which are of concern to all boys and girls may be studied through a program of group guidance. The term "group guidance" has varied connotations. In our discussion the term refers not only to the dissemination of information to groups of students but also to group deliberation of problems pertinent to the group. In a program of this nature students and teachers select topics of interest to them and subject these topics to group study and discussion. Since many of the problems of adolescents and preadolescents are encountered by the majority of boys and girls, it is possible to give generalized treatment to these problems through group procedures. It is understood, however, that students still must have available to them counseling facilities of an individual nature.

Among the problems of frequent and persistent concern to adolescents are (1) personal problems of boys and girls: personal health, grooming, boy-girl relationships, understanding oneself, identifying interests and aptitudes; (2) problems related to the school: how to study, budgeting time, choice of curriculum, choice of activities, preparing for college, reasons for staying in school; (3) problems related to the home: getting along with parents, building a home, beautifying the home, buying wisely; (4) problems related to work: choice of occupation, how to get a job, how to hold a job, developing skills for work; (5) problems related to moral values: developing spiritual values, ethics, tolerance, understanding others; and (6) problems related to the community and society: the nature of democracy, social problems, knowing the community, problems of an industrial society, governmental processes, the responsibilities of citizens in a democracy.

ALLOCATION OF GUIDANCE TOPICS

Topics of a guidance nature, such as those mentioned above, may be placed in a well-developed homeroom program or spaced throughout the courses that already exist. Schools that have only a brief homeroom period will find it necessary to lengthen the period if they wish to make the homeroom the center of the group guidance program. A suitable homeroom period would be no less than thirty minutes in length and, preferably, one full period. Topics consistently of interest to boys and girls of the school can be placed in the homeroom program in such a way that different topics are considered at each grade level from the seventh through the twelfth grades. Topics discussed at each grade level should be reviewed by faculty and students of that grade level annually to see if they continue to meet the interests and needs of the current groups. If we were to assume that the school would devote only one homeroom period per month to group guidance, this would mean about nine topics for general group discussion per year. In the course of the six years of junior and senior high school some fifty-four topics would have been explored. By this plan many of the questions that nag boys and girls can be answered before they become difficult problems to them. It would not be an unbearable burden on any school or faculty to provide one period per month to make the homeroom do what it was originally created to do—provide guidance for boys and girls.

Lacking an effective homeroom program or, perhaps, supporting the homeroom program, a school can incorporate units of a guidance nature in the existing curriculum. The topics of the units to be incorporated should be those that apply most closely to the course. Physical education, for example, could profitably assume units related to personal and public health. These topics could provide the material for a suitable series of rainy-day programs, if desired. The social studies (or core) program can adopt units related to community life. Homemaking, industrial arts, and business education can provide discussion of problems related to family life, occupations, and finances. The English curriculum could reserve space for study of the problems of preparation for college, improving school work, and the social amenities and manners. Once the topics for discussion have been chosen by the students and faculty, the school should not find placement of the topics too great a problem. Kimball Wiles' proposal for Analysis Groups[1] would serve to fulfill some functions of guidance.

Group guidance in either the homeroom plan or the plan wherein units are placed within the courses must be considered a responsibility of the classroom teacher. No guidance director or counselor could handle alone a program as broad as this. A classroom teacher, accepting responsibilities for a program of group guidance, will seek to develop an understanding of the problems his students have, will do his best to locate materials which will be useful in discussion of the various topics, and will seek to develop a permissive group climate, so students will be willing to state their views and concerns frankly. During discussion of the different topics the classroom teacher will watch carefully for evidences of particular difficulties on the part of individual pupils. Detecting these difficulties, the teacher will want to counsel the student individually or refer him for counseling.

SPECIAL GUIDANCE PROGRAMS

A school imbued with the guidance philosophy can supplement the classroom and homeroom programs with assemblies which are carefully selected and planned for the entire student body. The school may also sponsor Career Days, at which time it invites representatives of various occupations to talk to students about requirements for their occupations, training needed, job opportunities, and financial prospects. The school may reserve a whole day

---

[1] *The Changing Curriculum of the American High School.* (Englewood Cliffs, N. J.: Prentice-Hall, 1963), pp. 301–2.

during which students may attend talks of a number of representatives of vocations in which they have an interest.

Similar to the Career Day is the College Day or College Night when representatives of various colleges and institutions of higher learning are invited to come to talk with students and parents. Schools normally invite representatives of colleges to which graduates of those schools usually go. Although there are some objections to Career and College Days, the author feels that this method of providing occupational and educational information is superior to permitting a number of interruptions in the school schedule. If representatives of colleges simply drop in at a school and offer to talk with students who may be interested in the colleges they represent, the students must be pulled out of their classes. Interruptions of this kind tend to disturb teachers and students. An organized program such as the Career Day or College Night eliminates the necessity for periodic interruptions.

HOMOGENEOUS GROUPING

Over the past thirty years the question of homogeneous grouping, i.e., sectioning of students into groups on the basis of mental ability or other criteria, has been argued at considerable length in educational circles. In general, the weight of opinion among professional educators until recent years has been opposed to homogeneous grouping.

Homogeneous grouping was in vogue in our schools in the 1930's. Gradually, schools moved away from this practice. The separation of pupils on the elementary school level into slow, average, and fast classes met with disfavor from the parents and teachers. Ability grouping of this type was discarded in the elementary school in favor of subgrouping within elementary classes. It is common now to find in the elementary school classroom subgroups at varying stages of progress in reading and arithmetic.

To some extent teachers on the secondary school level have attempted the technique of subgrouping within their classes. But with an average load of five classes of thirty or forty boys and girls per day, teachers generally find subgrouping burdensome and difficult. Consequently, the demand for homogeneous grouping has increased in recent years, especially in the light of demands for higher scholastic achievement.

No debate on homogeneous grouping can fail to evoke the following arguments against ability grouping:

1. We have no accurate measures of a student's true ability. We cannot, therefore, group accurately. Since we cannot group accurately, we should not group at all.

2. Even if we section classes using the measuring instruments we now

have, such as intelligence tests and achievement tests, there will still be within each group differences necessitating individual attention.

3. Homogeneous grouping does not present a real-life situation. People are not grouped homogeneously in life situations.

4. Homogeneous grouping is undemocratic. Any form of segregation of groups is not democratic.

5. Slow pupils placed in slow groups feel frustrated and discouraged, since they bear the stigma of being classed as "stupid."

6. Fast pupils placed in fast groups become snobbish.

7. The slow group becomes the dumping ground for all kinds of misfits.

8. Parents are dissatisfied with homogeneous grouping, particularly those parents whose children are in the slow groups.

9. Teachers do not enjoy teaching the slow groups.

10. Teachers are not trained to handle slow and fast groups separately.

11. Homogeneous grouping is too difficult for administrators to schedule.

12. Homogeneous grouping denies the bright student the opportunity to inspire and help the slow student.

There is some research on ability grouping to indicate that ability grouping on the secondary school level does not have all the horrors which educators once thought it had.[2] Studies of student achievement indicate that students attain higher scholastic results when grouped homogeneously. Studies further indicate that worries about the undemocratic nature of homogeneous grouping are not borne out in practice. Students in schools that have sectioned classes by ability do not inevitably adopt the predicted attitudes of frustration, resentment, or superiority.

Further on the positive side, ability grouping has freed the teacher to give more attention to individual differences than he has been able to in the heterogeneous groups. Ability grouping has permitted the slow student to work to his capacity while freeing the bright child to move ahead without being held back by the slower pupils. Grouping eliminates the necessity for the slow pupils' competing with the fast pupils for academic success and marks. By grouping students according to ability, discipline and control are improved. In heterogeneous groups it is a common occurrence for both the slow child and the bright child to become behavior problems, since in-

[2] Miriam L. Goldberg, "Recent Research on the Talented," *Teachers College Record*, 60 (December 1958), 150-63.

struction is largely geared to the average child. The author feels that homogeneous grouping on the secondary school level is desirable under the following conditions:

1. *The approval of the community should be secured before the practice is put into operation.*

2. *Groups should be determined by a variety of measuring instruments and techniques,* including standardized tests of achievement and intelligence plus teachers' grades and judgment.

3. *Groups should be scheduled on a subject-matter basis rather than on a grade-level basis.* Students with high achievement in one subject should be placed in the fast section of that subject, while they may be placed in an average or slow group in other subjects in which they have low achievement. Provision should also be made for moving a student from a slower section to a faster section whenever it is apparent the student should be moved. Initial grouping should be carefully done so that pupils will not have to be moved downward from faster sections to slower sections. A movement downward can have a negative and demoralizing effect upon the student.

4. *There must be opportunities in the school day for pupils to come together for instruction.* This may be achieved through the physical education program, through clubs, or through part of the academic program. Some schools have found an intermediate method of grouping satisfactory. In this plan students are grouped for certain classes such as science and mathematics but are kept in heterogeneous groups in the required subjects such as English and social studies. There is a body of opinion to the effect that students should be grouped homogeneously for specialized education and heterogeneously for general education courses.[3]

5. *The school must be large enough to permit the formation of homogeneous groups.* In the tiny high schools of our country where we have as few as 100 students, homogeneous grouping is not possible. It is doubtful if homogeneous grouping can be practiced in schools of less than 500 to 1,000 student enrollment. One of the greatest selling jobs educators must do in future years is to convince the public that the small high schools operated in many communities are inefficient and uneconomical. It must be demonstrated to the public that boys and girls enrolled in these small schools are being cheated, since they are receiving an inferior education.

6. *If the faculty and parents are agreed on homogeneous grouping and the school system adopts the practice, the teachers must make distinctions in*

[3] Kimball Wiles and Franklin Patterson, *The High School We Need* (Washington: Association for Supervision and Curriculum Development, N. E. A., 1959), pp. 14–15.

objectives, materials, methods, and marking practices in each group. Too often homogeneous grouping has "failed" because teachers have set up the same objectives, used the same materials, and employed the same methods in slow, average, and fast groups alike. They have further restricted the high marks to the fast group, the middle marks to the average group, and the low or failing marks to the slow group. Unless the teacher is willing to handle each of the groups differently, there is no point in homogeneous grouping in the first place.

James B. Conant has recommended in regard to ability grouping:

> In the required subjects and those elected by students with a wide range of ability, the student should be grouped according to ability, subject by subject. For example, in English, American history, ninth-grade algebra, biology, and physical science, there should be at least three types of classes—one for the more able in the subject, another for the large group whose ability is about average, and another for the very slow readers who should be handled by special teachers. The middle group might be divided into two or three sections according to the students' abilities in the subject in question. This type of grouping is not to be confused with across-the-board grouping according to which a given student is placed in a particular section in all courses. Under the scheme here recommended, for example, a student may be in the top section in English but the middle section in history or ninth-grade algebra.[4]

Conant makes the assumption that the high school must be large enough for this practice. He advocates consolidation of high schools so that no high school has fewer than a hundred students in its graduating class.

To summarize, the classroom teacher pursues his guidance responsibilities by attaining a knowledge of his groups' needs and interests, by analyzing the composition of his groups, by instituting an effective program of group guidance, and by grouping students under specified conditions.

---

[4] Conant, *The American High School Today* (New York: McGraw-Hill, 1959), p. 49. By permission of A Study of American Education, Princeton, N.J.

CHAPTER 15

SELECTED GUIDANCE TECHNIQUES

Among the guidance techniques with which a classroom teacher should be familiar are (1) standardized testing, including interpretation of test results, (2) the teacher-student conference, (3) the case study, (4) the autobiography, (5) the use of records and forms, and (6) the referral.

In an organized guidance program standardized testing may be done through the special guidance department, through the principal's office, by the classroom teacher, or by the homeroom teacher. Insofar as possible the classroom teacher should have test data on a student's (*a*) intelligence, (*b*) achievement, (*c*) interests, and (*d*) aptitudes. Whether or not the classroom teacher has the responsibility of selecting, administering, and scoring standardized tests, he must have the ability to interpret and use the test results.

STATISTICAL TERMS

For purposes of our discussion we shall first explain a number of the common statistical terms which a teacher must know in order to make intelligent use of test results. We shall then proceed to a brief discussion of each of the major types of standardized tests available. Among the common statistical terms which a teacher should understand are the following:

NORMS

To the test user norms are a set of statistics found in the table of norms given in the test manual. The table of norms shows the distribution of scores of the group or groups to whom the standardized test was administered. By use of norms we may determine how an individual ranks in comparison with other individuals who took the same standardized test. Norms are based on samplings of the population to whom the standardized test has been administered.

When we deal with standardized tests, we use national norms, that is, norms based upon results attained by students throughout the country. We should state that norms which are supposedly national norms are not always truly national in scope, since some tests are standardized on a population of a particular region of the country, for example, the northeastern states. Test results may be more meaningful if regional, state, and local norms are established. It is most helpful if the teacher has local norms that have been accumulated over a period of years so that he can compare performance of pupils currently in class with performance of pupils in the same school in previous years. The teacher will be interested in how his students compare with national, regional and state norms, but performance of pupils in relation to local norms may be the most meaningful of all. Unfortunately, local norms for standardized tests are not usually available. Someone must take the time to compile test scores made by local students over a period of years in order to establish local norms.

Norms are of varying kinds, including the IQ, the percentile rank, age norms, and grade norms.

THE IQ

Of all the statistical concepts related to standardized testing the IQ, or Intelligence Quotient, is the most widely known. The IQ is the figure obtained by dividing a child's mental age (determined by a standardized test) by his chronological age and multiplying the quotient by 100. Thus, if a child's mental age is determined to be 11 years and if his chronological age is 10 years, the child's IQ is 110.

$$11/_{10} \times 100 = 110$$

110 is considered to be above average, since a figure of 100 would represent "average" intelligence. A child with a mental age of 9 years and a chronological age of 10 years would be said to have an IQ of 90 or below average. The following may be considered rough equivalents to IQ scores:

```
    140 up   – genius
    130-140  – gifted
    110-130  – academically talented
    90-110   – normal intelligence
    70-90    – subnormal
    50-70    – moron
    25-50    – imbecile
under  25    – idiot
```

The IQ indicates a student's potential rather than his achievement. Teachers are well aware that many students do not live up to their potential. Conversely, some students, through great effort and motivation, come close to realizing their potential. It should be emphasized that it is not possible to determine exactly a person's true intelligence with the measuring instruments we have today. In using IQ figures the teacher must be cautious. Although a student's IQ generally remains stable during the school years, it does not necessarily remain constant. A person's true intelligence will remain constant. The IQ, however, is determined by measuring instruments which render only an approximation of a person's intelligence. There is a measure of error in every test constructed.

The IQ of a student may change when the test is administered to him a second time. This may be attributed to a number of reasons. The student may feel better physically or mentally when he takes the test a second time. The test directions may be clearer to him. The practice effect from having taken the test before will affect his score on the second testing. Test bureaus can affirm that test scores on standardized tests administered nationally to college aspirants have been rising continuously. Although some of the increase in levels of scores may be credited to the identification of greater talent among boys and girls, to improved curriculum and methods of instruction, part of the rise in scores may be attributed to savvy on the part of test-wise students. Some high schools even resort to conducting test practice classes for its many students who are determined to get into college.

Different intelligence tests may yield different IQ results. A student who obtains a 120 IQ on the test of one publisher will not necessarily obtain a 120 IQ on the test of a second publisher. The teacher, in interpreting test results, must make allowances for the differences in scores caused by differences in the construction of the tests.

A student's home environment will definitely affect the scores he obtains on standardized tests. Students with nutritional defects will tend to score lower than healthy students. Students who have been exposed to cultural advantages such as books, travel, and science in the home and community will tend to score higher on standardized tests. Intelligence-test makers write items which are meant to be in the general cultural experience of the pupils of the age level to be tested. Some test items which slip into a test, however, can be identified or understood by only a limited number of individuals who take the test. To illustrate, the Hawaiian youngster may be expected to recognize a field of pineapples growing. This would not be an appropriate test item on a test of general intelligence for most students in the continental United States. Items that are in the general cultural range of white boys and girls do not come within the range of many Negro boys and girls. Consequently, students who have had exposure to cultural items that appear on standardized tests will score higher than students who have not been so exposed. This is particularly noticeable in relation to verbal ability. Students who have high verbal ability tend to make higher scores on intelligence tests. These students read faster, understand the questions better, and have a larger vocabulary than do students with low verbal ability. Standardized tests of intelligence often place a premium on verbal ability by their very construction.

The teacher must be on guard against intelligence tests or test items that favor a selected group of the population. Where he has doubts about the student's cultural advantages or lack of them, he must analyze the student's responses to test items. When he knows the student is a poor reader, he must take this into consideration in judging the student's intellectual ability. There are times when the test scores should be discounted or thrown out entirely. The teacher must always realize that the IQ is only an approximation of intelligence. It is a mathematical concept that is subject to error.

The public has become familiar with the term "IQ." The public understands the general connotation that the higher the IQ, the brighter the pupil. It is doubtful, though, whether actual figures should be released to students or to parents. The author inclines to the practice of using descriptive terms, "gifted," "well above average," "average," "below average," and "unable to profit from instruction."

Psychologists are moving away from the use of the IQ figure. They have found that a single quotient or global score is not an accurate indication of a student's intelligence. Research has demonstrated that intelligence consists of multiple mental traits and that persons may differ in respect to any of these traits.

THE PERCENTILE RANK

A table of percentile ranks constitutes one type of norm. The percentile rank shows an individual's rank in relation to others who have taken the test, i.e., the percentage of persons whom the individual surpasses on a particular test. For example, a student who ranks at the 90th percentile on a given test has surpassed 90 per cent of the population, calculated on the sample that took the test. He is exceeded by only 10 per cent, i.e., he is in the top 10 per cent of the group. Tests of intelligence may render a percentile rank for the verbal score of a test, a percentile rank for a nonverbal score of a test, and a percentile rank for the combined scores. For example, a student may be at the 89th percentile in the verbal or linguistic part of an intelligence test, at the 65th percentile in the nonverbal or quantitative part of the test, and at the 80th percentile for the combined scores. We should note that the percentile rank for the composite score is not necessarily the arithmetical average of the percentile ranks of the separate scores. Tests which break intelligence into its component primary mental abilities (linguistic, perceptual, quantitative, reasoning, and spatial relations) would yield separate percentiles in each ability plus a percentile rank for the combined scores.

THE AGE NORM

The age norm shows the relative chronological position of a child in respect to the trait or traits measured by a standardized test. It may be said, for example, that the age of a student as determined by a standardized test of reading is 12—3. For this norm to have meaning it must be considered in the light of a child's chronological age. If the child reads at the level of 12 years, 3 months and is 11 years, 0 months of age chronologically, he is exceeding normal expectations for his chronological age. Thus, he is a good reader. On the other hand, if he is 16 years, 0 months of age chronologically and he is reading at the level of a child of 12 years, 3 months, he is reading below the standard which might normally be expected of a child of his chronological age. Age norms are commonly used with standardized tests of achievement.

THE GRADE NORM

The grade norm is very similar to the age norm except that figures for these norms are given in respect to the grade in school, rather than chronological age. A child in the beginning of the fifth grade (5.0) may take a standardized test in arithmetic and place at the 4.5 grade norm. This indicates that the child has placed at the middle of the fourth grade as far as his skill in arithmetic is concerned. He is thus behind his grade placement in arithmetic. On the other hand, if he were to score at the grade norm 6.9, he would demonstrate skill in arithmetic at the level of a sixth-grader who is at the ninth month of the sixth grade. By convention grade norms are written with decimals, while age norms are written with dashes.

Standardized tests generally give all norms in table form in the manual that accompanies a test. The teacher has but to read through the manual and select the table of norms corresponding to the specifications of the group to whom the test is administered.

MEDIAN, MEAN, AND MODE

The median is the 50th percentile. The student who ranks at the 50th percentile on a standardized test is "average" in the trait measured by the test. He excels 50 per cent of the population in respect to this trait and is, in turn, excelled by 50 per cent. It is unfortunate that the term "average" has so many meanings. Two other concepts of "average" should be mentioned in passing.

The *mean* refers to the arithmetical average, i.e., the sum of all scores divided by the number of scores. When the layman speaks of "average," he usually wishes to imply the mean. The mean is a useful figure, but it is subject to gross misinterpretation. To say that the mean temperature of Gainesville, Florida, is 65 degrees implies to the undiscerning that the "average" or customary temperature in Gainesville is warm the year round. On the contrary, to compensate for the days of 90- and 80-degree weather in the summer, there are many days of cold weather in the winter. The temperature drops often to 20 and 30 degrees and sometimes below. So the use of the term "mean" in this case is deceptive.

Another term used to signify "average" is the *mode*. This is the score that appears most frequently in a test administered to a group. As an "average" the mode is not reliable. It may very well be that on a test whose scores range from 75 to 35 the score of 38 appears most frequently, even though only 3 or 4 students received the score of 38. Or let us assume that a number of students achieved the score of 74 on the high end of the scale. You can easily see the distortion involved in the use of the mode. To say that 38 or 74 was the "average" score would be misleading.

Consequently, for statistical purposes the median is the most satisfactory concept of "average." The teacher may apply this same concept in relation not only to standardized tests but also to his own teacher-made tests. In order to determine the median grade on any exam, he can simply stack his examination papers in order, highest score on top (or lowest, no matter). He counts the number of examination papers, then counts down exactly halfway. The middle paper reveals the median score on that test.

RELIABILITY

The term "reliability" indicates the consistency with which a test measures what it is created to measure. A reliable test will render similar results when administered repeatedly. Since no test is 100 per cent reliable, it is not to be expected that exactly the same score will be obtained on repeated administrations of the test. Reliability is expressed mathematically in terms of a coefficient of correlation, or r. Coefficients could run from .00 (no consistent relationship) to 1.00 (perfect consistency). A correlation coefficient of .85 is high and means that the test is reliable. Consistent results may be expected from this test, assuming that the reliability coefficient is accurate. A low reliability coefficient of .34 means that the test has not been demonstrated to be reliable. The coefficient of reliability is given by the test maker in the test manual.

VALIDITY

The term "validity" indicates the truthfulness with which a test measures what it is created to measure. With a valid test of intelligence, for example, the test user knows the test is actually measuring intelligence, or rather that which the test maker has defined as intelligence. No test is 100 per cent valid. Validity is expressed mathematically in terms of a coefficient or r, ranging from .00 to 1.00. A coefficient of .50 means that the test has moderate validity. A low coefficient of .30 means that the test has low validity. The coefficient of validity may be found in the test manual.

THE NORMAL CURVE

The normal curve is a widely used, often abused, mathematical concept. In essence, it is a particular bell-shaped representation of the distribution of a trait, such as intelligence, throughout the population. A normal curve would appear as shown in Figure 1.

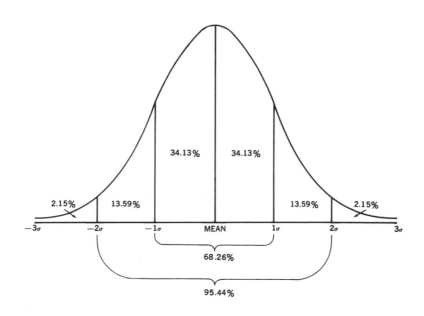

FIGURE 1

The mid-point of a normal distribution is shown by the tallest of the vertical lines. This line, which runs from the middle of the base to the peak of the curve, represents the mean. In a normal distribution the mean and the median coincide. By convention, scores that are greater than the mean score fall to the right of the mean. Scores that are smaller than the mean score fall to the left of the mean.

Vertical lines to the right and left of the mean represent units of standard deviation as measured from the mean. Statisticians refer to the standard deviation as sigma, σ. The sketch above shows three standard deviations either side of the mean. Percentages of scores which may be expected to fall within one, two, or three standard deviations from the mean are written on the sketch above. We can interpret these percentages to indicate that 68.26 per cent, or roughly two-thirds, of the scores of a normal distribution will fall within one standard deviation either side of the mean. 95.44 per cent of the scores will come within two standard deviations. 99.74 per cent of the scores will fall within three standard deviations.

Many traits, such as intelligence, are distributed normally throughout the general population. Small groups (e.g., classes) do not conform to a normal distribution. It is not mathematically sound, therefore, to conclude that 68 per cent of your students must make C's, 14 per cent B's, 2 per cent A's, 14 per cent D's, and 2 per cent F's. One of the most serious mistakes a teacher can make is to base marks on the concept of a normal distribution when, in fact, his students are usually a small, selected grouping. The normal curve is a useful concept, provided its limitations are known.

TYPES OF STANDARDIZED TESTS

At this point let us turn our attention to the principal types of standardized tests that are available. We will comment on their major characteristics, purposes, and usefulness.

INTELLIGENCE TESTS

Intelligence tests are standardized tests of a student's ability to learn. These tests ordinarily render a Mental Age, an IQ, or a percentile rank. Intelligence tests may be administered to a group or to an individual. Usually, the classroom teacher will be most concerned with group tests. These tests may be of the paper-and-pencil variety or performance type. In general, the group tests are written while the individual tests are manipulative or performance type.

Some tests yield a linguistic or verbal score, a quantitative or nonverbal score, and a combined or total score. A few tests or batteries of tests yield scores on primary mental abilities or differential aptitudes, including verbal reasoning, numerical ability, spatial relations, abstract reasoning, memory, and language usage.

If used with discretion, an intelligence test can be a most useful tool. The IQ or percentile rank should be corroborated with repeated testing during a student's academic career. Where the results obtained by a student on a group test are subject to doubt, an individual test should be administered. Where the results obtained by a student on a verbal test are subject to doubt, a nonverbal test should be administered. Though tests may not be as refined as might be desired, they are superior to individual teacher judgment. The teacher's judgment of a student's ability is often colored by the personality of the pupil and by the expectations of the teacher.

The teacher should note that the test makers employ the terms "intelligence test," " psychological test," and "test of scholastic aptitude" to refer to tests that attempt to measure a student's capacity to learn. It is true that "scholastic aptitude" and "intelligence" are not identical. Scholastic aptitude implies the ability to learn in the academic field. Nevertheless, in common practice high school students who achieve high scores on tests of scholastic aptitude, which are partially tests of intelligence, partially tests of achievement, and partially tests of aptitude, are referred to as "bright" or "intelligent."

ACHIEVEMENT TESTS

Achievement tests are examinations of a student's attainment in a particular subject or in a number of subjects. Achievement tests may be used for diagnostic purposes to reveal deficiencies in the students' attainment, to compare a local group with national norms, to test the effectiveness of teaching, and to check on the effectiveness of various phases of the school's curriculum.

Norms of achievement tests may be reported in percentiles or age norms or grade norms. By administering an intelligence test to find out a student's capacity to learn and a number of achievement tests to discover a student's actual attainment, the classroom teacher can see how closely the student is living up to his academic potential. Students who have high potential but are underachieving will require immediate counseling. Students who reveal deficiencies will require immediate remedial work. Groups which as a whole do poorly on standardized tests of achievement need study to determine if the course content and methods of teaching are suitable.

Achievement tests are available in any of the subject fields of the high school curriculum. Tests in specific fields may be located by consulting the catalogues of the test publishers, *Tests in Print,* and *The Mental Measurements Yearbook.*[1]

The latter reference reviews most of the major standardized tests on the market. Each review, written by an expert in the field, discusses the nature of the test, the adequacy of the norms, types of norms used, reliability and validity, administration of the test, scoring, and prices. The reviews objectively and critically discuss the claims made by the test publishers.

INTEREST INVENTORIES

Interest inventories are instruments created for the purpose of surveying a student's interests in various fields. The term "inventory" is preferred to the term "test," since the student's interests are not being subjected to testing as such. Interest inventories assist the teacher in identifying pupil interests. Perhaps more important, they assist the student in identifying his own interests. Students are often uncertain about their own interests and about their choice of occupation. This state of confusion is plainly visible even on the college level, where many students drift along without identifying their life's work until late in their college programs.

A standardized interest inventory may be used profitably in the high school program. It may be administered in the homeroom or in a special

[1] Oscar K. Buros, ed., *Tests in Print* (Highland Park, N. J.: The Gryphon Press, 1961), and *The Sixth Mental Measurements Yearbook* (Highland Park, N.J.: The Gryphon Press, 1965), 1714 pp.

testing session. It can be made part of a unit on occupations, for example, in social studies, English, core, homemaking, industrial arts, or business education. Students, as a rule, find taking interest inventories a pleasant experience. They are strongly motivated to discover in what areas their interests prove high.

An inventory used very frequently in the high school and junior high school is the Kuder Preference Record.[2] This inventory is composed of a series of items from which the student selects the items he likes best and the items he likes least. The student takes the inventory by punching holes with a pin into an answer sheet. He scores his own inventory. Then he may construct his own profile of interests in the form of a bar graph, which reveals the student's high and low interests. The teacher and the student study the student's pattern of interests and then consult the inventory's manual, which suggests possible occupations for the student to explore. It is desirable to administer an interest inventory in the junior high school and repeat it in the later years of high school to reveal changing interests as well as continuing interests.

Results of interest inventories must be coupled with the knowledge of the student's intelligence, achievement, and aptitude.

APTITUDE TESTS

Aptitude tests measure a student's potential in certain skills or for certain occupations. Aptitude tests may be of the paper-and-pencil, group variety or of the individual, performance variety. Tests are available which measure aptitude in a number of occupations and professions. Commonly measured are clerical, manual, and mechanical aptitudes. High scores on aptitude tests would point to the types of training pupils should have to develop their potential. Aptitude or potential should be distinguished from achievement and interest, although there is certain to be some achievement and some interest present in a high aptitude score.

PERSONALITY TESTS

Of all the standardized tests on the market, personality tests or inventories which attempt to measure personal traits of an individual are the most subject to controversy, most difficult to interpret, and most dangerous to use. After several years' experience with group tests of personality, the author is forced to the conclusion that personality tests should not be administered or used by the classroom teacher. The following reasons may be cited for this conclusion.

1. *The reliability and validity of some of these tests are often subject to question.* Since most tests purport to measure emotional difficulties, personality disturbances, mental and physical problems, students can and do fake

2 *Kuder Preference Record,* Science Research Associates, Chicago, Illinois.

the results. How many young people will respond truthfully, knowing their answers will be preserved, to such questions as "Do you love your father?" or "Are you afraid of the dark?" A student who is intelligent will know the expected responses and will often give the responses he believes the teacher expects or society expects rather than his own truthful responses.

2. *There is too great reliance placed on the scores made on these tests.* Scores are compared with the norms supplied by the test maker. The norms themselves are not and should not be greatly significant. What is "normal" or "abnormal" depends to a large extent on the values held by the test maker and by the sample of the population who took the test. The personality test often makes the assumption that the values or traits held by most persons in the group are the values or traits that an individual should possess. As a result, a high premium is placed on results which show a high standard of conformity. Within a broad framework the individual in our society should be free to grow and develop without needless strictures placed on him by group standards. If we are to test for values, shall we require, for example, that all individuals measure up to middle-class, Yankee, white, Protestant values? Or does our society have room for the development of many values within our democratic structure?

3. *Results of personality tests too frequently become the common knowledge of too many individuals.* Unwise discussion about a student's responses on a test of this nature can cause irreparable harm.

4. *The results of personality tests are difficult to interpret.* The results are difficult to put to use. Using the results with the student, as in an interview, may be harmful. Unless the teacher is thoroughly versed in the use of these tests, he may destroy his own rapport with the student and may create psychological problems which did not exist before.

William H. Whyte, Jr., in *The Organization Man* has devastatingly attacked "the mass testing of 'personality.'" Some of his comments are pertinent to our discussion of personality tests. Says Whyte:

> These curious inquisitions into the psyche are becoming a regular feature of organization life, and, before long, of U.S. life in general . . . more than any other current development these tests dovetail the twin strands of scientism and the total integration of the individual. . . . They are not, I hope to demonstrate, objective. They do not respect individual difference. They are not science, only the illusion of it. [pp. 189–90]

> What I am examining is not the use of tests as guides in clinical work with disturbed people, or their use in counseling when the individual himself seeks counseling. . . . What I am addressing myself to is the standard use of tests by organizations as a gauge of the "normal" individual. . . . [pp. 201–2]

Who is "normal"? All of us to some degree have a built-in urge to adjust to what we conceive as the norm, and in our search we can come to feel that in the vast ocean of normality that surrounds us only we are different. . . . Are the people who don't score well necessarily the misfits? Almost by definition the dynamic person is an exception—and where aptitude tests reward, personality tests often punish him. Look at a cross section of profiles and you will see three denominators shining through: extroversion, disinterest in the arts, and a cheerful acceptance of the status quo. Test scoring keys reveal the same bias. [pp. 216–17][3]

In his provocative book, Whyte includes a chapter on "How to Cheat on Personality Tests." It is Whyte's contention that to preserve his self-respect the person taking a personality test not only *can* cheat but *must* cheat. He suggests in this chapter ways to score well on personality tests.

Two other books, *The Brain Watchers* by Martin L. Gross and *The Tyranny of Testing* by Banesh Hoffman, have emphasized the dangers of mass testing.[4] *The Brain Watchers* stresses dangers in personality testing, which Gross refers to as "brain watching." Hoffman's book makes a cogent presentation of the perils of testing, specifically standardized multiple-choice tests.

Personality tests, either of the group test variety or of the projective variety such as the Rohrschach, should be used only by trained school and clinical psychologists. Aberrant behavior at the level with which a teacher must contend may be detected by careful observation. When such behavior is detected, the student should be referred to the psychologist or psychiatrist for help.

In summary, the high school testing program should consist of intelligence, achievement, and aptitude tests plus interest inventories. Personality tests should be reserved for clinical work.

THE TEACHER-STUDENT CONFERENCE

The conference is the heart of the counseling process. It is the face-to-face interview between a sympathetic teacher-counselor and a student. The purpose of the interview is to help the pupil with any problem he has, be it major or minor. A simple, informal chat with the teacher does not fit our definition of an interview. Nor does a conference between the pupil, teacher, and one or more other parties (principal, parent, etc.) fit the definition as we are using it.

The teacher should study all the available information about the pupil prior to the interview. The interview should be scheduled at a time mutually convenient for the pupil and the teacher. Some schools provide conference

[3] New York: Simon and Schuster, 1956; Garden City, N.Y.: Doubleday (Anchor Books), 1957.

[4] Martin L. Gross, *The Brain Watchers* (New York: Random House, 1962). Banesh Hoffman, *The Tyranny of Testing* (New York: Crowell-Collier Press, 1962).

periods. In other schools interviews must be conducted before or after school. It is not a wise or effective procedure to sandwich interviews in between periods or at odd moments. The conference must be long enough for full discussion of the problems under consideration.

The school must make provision so that every pupil can find at least one counselor congenial to him somewhere on the faculty. In many cases the counselor will be the homeroom teacher. In other cases the counselor may be a particular teacher whom the student finds interested in him. The teacher may be doing a great deal for the pupil by just giving him the assurance that there is a sympathetic adult who is willing to take time to sit down and talk with him about his problems.

As an aid in conducting an interview with a pupil, the following suggestions may guide the teacher:

1. Study carefully all available records on a pupil before the interview takes place.
2. Determine what gaps in the information need to be filled in.
3. Plan ways of filling in the gaps in the information.
4. Establish rapport with the student.
5. Give the student complete freedom to talk.
6. Tactfully elicit information from the student.
7. Help the student to think through his problem.
8. Help the student to formulate possible solutions to his problem.
9. Work out with the student a proposed course of action.
10. Set a time for the next conference at which the pupil's progress in solving his problem will be discussed.
11. Record the interview and file, preferably in the student's cumulative record folder. The summary of an interview may be recorded as follows:

Name of student:
Date, place, and time of interview:
Name of counselor:
Summary of interview:

Proposed Action:

Date, place, and time of next interview:

THE CASE STUDY

The case study is a convenient way of assembling all the materials and information about an individual who has a problem so that diagnosis may be made and treatment prescribed. The case study is a useful technique for studying a student in depth. Unfortunately, it is so time-consuming that the busy teacher will have to reserve this technique for study of special cases. A student who exhibits erratic behavior, unusual talent, or difficult behavior will make a valuable subject for case study.

Every bit of available evidence about a pupil should be included in the study. The teacher may put together in any logical fashion the various data he collects. The following outline for a case study may prove helpful:

Case Study

I. Introduction; general information
II. Identification of the problem
III. Data
    a. Physical data
    b. School data
    c. Family data
    d. Test data
    e. Activities and interests of the student
IV. Diagnosis and Treatment
V. Prognosis
VI. Follow-up

THE AUTOBIOGRAPHY

The autobiography is the student's life story told in his own words. As a counseling device, the autobiography is a technique that may throw light on a student's feelings and attitudes. As a guidance technique, it is one of the simplest to incorporate into the curriculum. With the help of a cooperative English teacher the autobiography could be a regular assignment for all students of English at a particular grade level. It is one of the few guidance techniques that double as an instructional device. While it supplies the counselor with essential information, the autobiography also gives the student needed practice in outlining, organizing his material, and using English effectively. By the selection of his experiences, by the emphases he gives to various episodes in his life, and by his choice of words, the student reveals to the counselor his ambitions and difficulties. The autobiography can provide clues in understanding the student.

Froelich gives a useful outline for the autobiography of a student:[5] This is one used at Hampstead High School, Hampstead, Maryland.

I. Childhood
    A. Years before school
        1. Description of your family

---

[5] From *Guidance Services In Schools* by Clifford P. Froelich, pp. 185–186. Copyright © 1958 by McGraw-Hill, Inc. Used by permission of McGraw-Hill Book Company.

2. Places where you have lived
3. Funny things you did and said as a youngster
4. Ways you amused yourself

B. Early school days
1. Friendships formed
2. Kinds of games, work, hobbies you liked
3. Incidents your family relates to you

C. Last years in elementary school
1. Chief desires and wishes
2. Favorite subjects

II. Adolescence
A. Social activities
1. What I do
   a. After school (favorite radio programs, etc.; movies, and magazines)
   b. During school
   c. In the evening
   d. On weekends
2. What I should like to do
3. Who my favorite pals are; kinds of people I like

B. School activities
1. My successes
2. My failures
3. My hopes
4. My plans for future work
   a. Several choices
   b. Why?
5. My suggestions for opportunities offered by our school
6. My favorite subjects; most disliked ones. What I would change about myself, my home, my school, etc., if I could.

The autobiography is recommended as a worthwhile guidance technique.

RECORDS AND FORMS

The work of the classroom teacher will be simplified by the use of various record and report forms which, with the possible exception of the cumulative record, can be duplicated locally. Among the more common records with which the classroom teacher should be familiar are the following:

THE CUMULATIVE RECORD

On the cumulative record the teacher records all significant data about an individual student. The most desirable form for the cumulative record is a folder printed on both sides. Information may be recorded on the inside and outside of the folder. Folders may then be filed in a central location for the use of teachers who are concerned about particular pupils. Additional materials about a pupil may be kept within the folding cumulative record. The National Committee on Cumulative Records recommends the following categories of information for inclusion on the record:[6]

Personal
    Name
    Date of birth
    Evidence of birth
    Place of birth
    Sex
    Color or race
    Residence of pupil and/or parents

Home and Community
    Names of parents or guardians
    Occupation of parents or guardians
    Are parents alive or deceased
    Ratings of home environment and/or economic status
    With whom does the pupil live
    Birthplace of parents
    Language spoken in the home
    Marital status
    Number of siblings, older and younger

Scholarship
    School marks by years and subject
    Special reports on failures
    Record of reading
    Rank in graduating class (with number in class)

Test scores and ratings
    General intelligence test scores
    Achievement test scores
    Other test scores
    Personality ratings

School attendance
    Days present or absent each year
    Record of schools attended, with dates

Health
    The following types of items are desirable if a school has a health program in which physicians and nurses are a part:
    Complete health record, to be filled in by physician or nurse

[6] *Handbook of Cumulative Records*, Bulletin 1944, No. 5, U.S. Office of Education (Washington: Superintendent of Documents, 1945), pp. 8–9.

Record of physical disabilities

Vaccination record

Disease census

If a physician or nurse is not available for examining school children a rating of the health of pupils may be made by the teachers, the type of rating depending upon the extent of the education of teachers in health matters. For suggestions regarding detailed items see the cumulative record forms given in the Appendix [of the National Committee's *Handbook*].

Anecdotal records

If an anecdotal records system is to be used, a special form should be developed. Anecdotal reports may be kept easily if filed in a folding type of cumulative record or where records are kept in envelopes.

Miscellaneous

Employment record during school years

Vocational plans

Counselor's notes

Extracurricular activities

Follow-up record after leaving school (Employment and further education)

Space for notations by teachers and others

The task of keeping the cumulative records current requires considerable time. Many schools have purchased excellent cumulative records but have failed to keep them up to date. The school administration has the responsibility of providing time and clerical assistance for the tedious but necessary job of recording data on the cumulative records.

Cumulative records are maintained in some schools by the homeroom teachers. In other schools the records are kept in the principal's or guidance director's office. Wherever the records are kept, they should be readily available for teachers to consult. Information in the student's file should be considered for professional use only.

THE QUESTIONNAIRE

A rapid way to obtain a large amount of significant data about a student is through the use of the questionnaire. The teacher may pass out a questionnaire to each pupil in his homeroom, class, or grade and let the students take the questionnaire home to fill out.

Following is the questionnaire used at Ribault High School, Jacksonville, Florida. This particular questionnaire is a simple form mimeographed on a single sheet. For a more lengthy and detailed questionnaire see the Basic Information Form of Hutchinson High School, Minnesota.[7]

7 Froelich, *op. cit.*, pp. 188–92.

GUIDANCE RECORD

Name .... Birth date ....
     Last   Middle   First
Address .... Phone ....
Father .... Age .... Occupation ....
Guardian
    or step-parent .... Age .... Occupation ....
(If father or mother is not living, simply draw a line across and put year
    of death. Divorced: D, Separated: S)
Circle highest level
Schooling of father: 1 2 3 4 5 6 7 8 9 10 11 12 College
              mother: 1 2 3 4 5 6 7 8 9 10 11 12 College
I am .... in a family of .... children. Own home ....
        1st, 2nd, etc.   How many?
Rent ....

                                             In the   In
                            Age Working Service School Married
Brothers, older ....
....
....

Sisters, older ....
....

Brothers, younger ....
....
....

Sisters, younger ....
....

Other people who live with us ....
....
....

HEALTH   Good   Fair   Poor   Describe ailments, if any
1. Father's ....
2. Mother's ....
3. Yours ....
Family Doctor's Name .... Address ....

Do you have a yearly health check? .... Date of last check .... Health Ins.? ......
Name of church you attend .... Denomination .... Member? .....
Father's church ....Member? .....
Mother's church ....Member? .....
Minister to whom you feel closest .... Address ....

What do you do for fun? (Out of school), hobbies, etc. ....

....

Jobs for which you have been paid ....

School activities: (Teams, class offices, special achievements, clubs, etc.)

....

Subjects best liked ....

Subjects least liked ....

General grade average ....

Attendance: Are you often absent? ....

Do you really like school? .... If not, can you name anything that might

make you like it better? ....

Life Work: What job would you most like to be doing 10 years from now,

regardless of expense, training, etc.? ....

....

Do you want more training after high school? ....

College .... Technical School .... Business School .... On the Job Train-

ing .... Nursing School .... Military .... Other ....

HIGH SCHOOL PROGRAM PLANS

The teacher-counselor will find useful a form on which he can plan with
the pupil a tentative schedule for the number of years of secondary school.
The teacher should have available a three-year or four-year or six-year
(depending on the grades in the school) program plan sheet on which to
record suggested courses the pupil will take.

Detailed information on the various curricula of the school and requirements of various colleges and occupations should be easily available. Information about the school's program is often included in a student handbook. The teacher, in planning a high school program with the pupil, will
use information on cumulative records, questionnaires, reports, and test
data. The objective in this academic counseling situation is to work out
the program most appropriate to the student's interests and capabilities.

Programs should be reviewed annually in consultation with the pupil.
Changes should be made as needed. No program should be considered
fixed and unchangeable. Movement between "college preparatory," "vocational," "commercial," and other tracks of the curriculum should be permitted. Some schools like to send the program plan sheets home for parents' signatures.

THE ANECDOTAL RECORD

The anecdotal record is a written account of an instance of the student's
behavior. The report is occasioned by an unusual incident in class or by
the teacher's desire to study carefully a particular pupil. By repeated obser-

vations of a student's behavior, the teacher may determine if there is a pattern of behavior. Since it would be difficult for a high school teacher to find time to keep anecdotal records on all his students, he can select students for special study. Among likely cases for study are the overaggressive, the docile, the emotionally disturbed, and the underachievers. Anecdotes should be recorded shortly after the behavior has been observed so that the teacher may have an accurate description of what took place. The student should not be aware that the teacher is recording instances of his behavior. The teacher may observe the student's behavior in the classroom, then record the behavior as soon as the class ends, during study hall or free period, or at the next available moment.

A definite distinction should be made in the anecdotal record between the objective recording of the student's behavior and the teacher's interpretation of the behavior. Any evaluation the teacher makes should be clearly labeled as such. Following is a simple form for an anecdotal record.

ANECDOTAL RECORD

Name of pupil .... Class ....

Date and time .... Place.............................

Behavior observed:

Evaluation:

Recorder ....

THE TEST PROFILE

The test profile is a graphic representation of the test scores made by an individual student on a series of tests. The profile may take the form of a bar graph or a line graph. A profile reveals clearly and quickly a student's strengths and weaknesses as shown by the test results.

Some of the test makers supply profile forms with their tests. These forms vary in size from a full sheet, as in the case of the Kuder Preference Record, to card-size, as in the case of the Iowa Tests of Educational Development.[8]

The profile sheet may be used by the test maker to report to the school or to parents ratings made by a student on the tests. The form may also be

[8] *Kuder Preference Record* and *Iowa Tests of Educational Development*, Science Research Associates, Chicago, Illinois.

filled out by the teacher and interpreted to the student. In some cases students may construct their own profiles. The profile sheet of the Kuder Preference Record is an illustration of the type of form which may be used directly by the students. With this form students participate in making bar graphs of their own scores. This exercise permits them to identify their own interests, to read their percentile ranks, and to interpret their own test scores.

The Individual Profile Chart used by the University Test Service, Department of Educational Research and Testing of The Florida State University to report scores and percentiles on the Florida State-Wide Ninth-Grade Testing Program furnishes us with an illustrative example. (See Figure 2.)

The Individual Profile Chart is an illustration of the type of profile that shows scores made in subtests of the same test or, in this case, on two tests. A profile may also be constructed of scores made on many tests. The teacher can create his own profile sheet for this purpose. Following is an illustration of a profile sheet which is simple to make (pp. 320–21). To use the form, determine from the table of norms the percentile rank of each score a student has made. Locate the percentile on the top or bottom of the graph. Plot the percentile rank for each score by placing a dot at the correct percentile on the line with each score. Join the dots to form a broken line. High scores are readily visible on the right side of the graph, low scores on the left.

THE REFERRAL

The classroom teacher cannot be expected to handle all types of student problems without assistance. Larger school systems provide specialized help in the form of nurses, psychologists, remedial reading teachers, and guidance counselors. The classroom teacher should make it a point early in his tenure at the school to learn the services available to him in the local school system. The classroom teacher has the responsibility of detecting students in his classes who need special help. He should advise students and parents on the availability of special help and should counsel them to take advantage of any opportunities provided. The teacher should keep in communication with the specialists so that he knows what action the specialists recommend.

Where the practice of referral is expected and customary, as between professional personnel in the school system, a referral form may be used. A simple referral form like that shown on page 319 may prove useful.

NAME OF STUDENT

FLORIDA STATE-WIDE NINTH-GRADE TESTING PROGRAM

SCHOOL & COLLEGE ABILITY TEST			METROPOLITAN ACHIEVEMENT TESTS ADVANCED BATTERY										
				LANGUAGE					ARITHMETIC			
VERBAL	QUANTITATIVE	TOTAL	READING	USAGE	PUNC. & CAP.	KINDS OF SENTENCES	PARTS OF SPEECH	TOTAL	COMPUTATION	PROB. SOLV. AND CONCEPTS	SOCIAL STUDIES INFORMATION	SCIENCE
40	25	65	34	15	22	5	13	55	27	24	35	41

RAW SCORES   RAW SCORES   RAW SCORES

PERCENTILE SCORES   PERCENTILE SCORES

| 61 | 40 | 53 | 56 | | | | | 53 | 23 | 16 | 46 | 69 |

PERCENTILE RANK

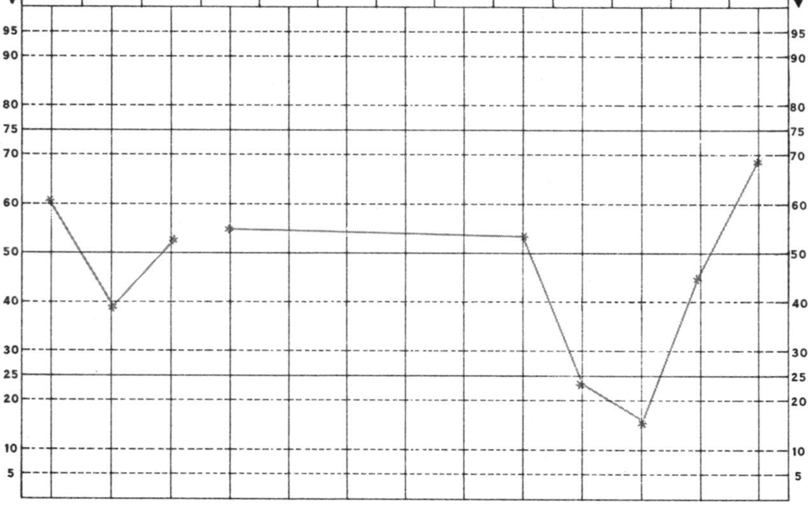

STUDENT NUMBER

NAME OF SCHOOL

SEX   YEAR

UNIVERSITY TEST SERVICE
DEPARTMENT OF EDUCATIONAL RESEARCH & TESTING
FLORIDA STATE UNIVERSITY, TALLAHASSEE

FIGURE 2

REFERRAL FORM

Name of student .... Date...................................

Referred to ....

Referred by ....

Purpose of referral:

A number of excellent resources available in the school and community are little used for purposes of referral. The teacher may often find assistance in dealing with specific problems from many of the following persons:

For assistance with educational counseling: teachers in special subject fields, teachers who are graduates of particular colleges, teachers who have traveled extensively, teachers who have had unusual experiences, teachers who have special hobbies, persons in the community who are graduates of particular colleges, persons in the community who have special interests and avocations, and persons who have traveled.

For assistance with vocational counseling: business and professional men and women in the community, workers in various jobs, and state employment service personnel.

For assistance with social and emotional counseling: psychologists, recreation workers, social workers, and clergymen.

For assistance with health counseling: school nurse, physicians, dentists, psychiatrists, physical education teachers, health education teachers, coaches, county and local health persons.

The classroom teacher need never feel alone in trying to help a student with his problems. Every school system and community has some resources which the teacher may use for referral.

NAME OF SCHOOL
TEST PROFILE SHEET

Name of student .... Grade .... Date ....

Percentile

SCORE 0 5 10 15 20 25 30 35 40 45 50 55 60 65 70 75 80 85 90 95 100

NAME OF TEST

Intelligence

Achievement

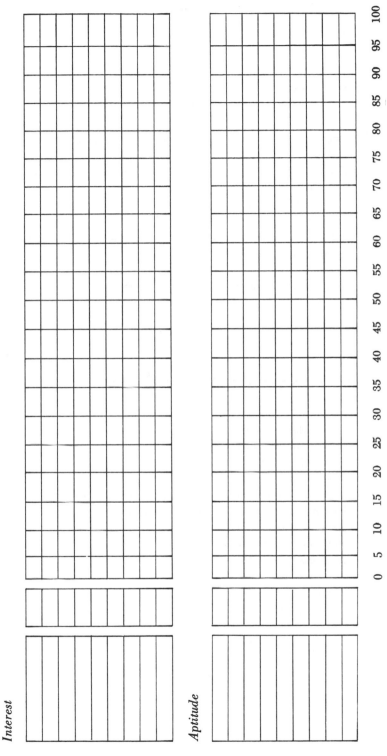

Interest

Aptitude

0 5 10 15 20 25 30 35 40 45 50 55 60 65 70 75 80 85 90 95 100

SUMMARY

Guidance is the advisement of students by a competent counselor on a wide range of personal problems. Every classroom teacher may expect to perform guidance duties. To render guidance services the counselor must be aware of the common needs and interests of adolescents in our culture, must gather detailed information about the individual pupil, must study the groups to which the student belongs, and must know how to use a number of guidance techniques. Among the essential techniques of the counselor are testing, interviewing, the case study, the autobiography, and the referral. The teacher will render more effective counseling if he makes use of suitable records, forms, and reference materials.

CLASS AND EVALUATION ACTIVITIES

1. Invite a guidance counselor from a local school to talk to the class on "The Meaning of Guidance."

2. Examine and report to class on the guidance programs in operation in several neighboring schools.

3. Discover and list some of the following guidance resources available in your college community or in your home town:
    a. occupational counseling
    b. social, emotional, and health counseling
    c. educational counseling

4. Find out and list some guidance materials available from:
    a. the federal government
    b. the state government
    c. the local government

5. Invite a religious counselor from the community to talk to the class on the topic, "Counseling Youth."

6. Write for catalogues and free materials from companies and organizations which have guidance materials.

7. Study and apply to an actual high school, if possible the Guidance Section, Section G, of the *Evaluative Criteria*, 1960 edition. Copies of the

Evaluative Criteria are obtained from the National Study of Secondary-School Evaluation, 1785 Massachusetts Ave., N.W., Washington, D.C. 20036.

8. Discuss the following questions:

    a. Can the principal render guidance services? If so, what services?

    b. Can the assistant principal render guidance services? If so, what services?

    c. Can the dean of boys (or girls) render guidance services? If so, what services?

9. List the needs and interests which you believe all American youth have in common. Record these on the blackboard.

10. List the kinds of information you believe it is necessary to know about an individual student. Record these on the blackboard.

11. Conduct a panel discussion on the topic, "Opportunities for Guidance in the Various Subject Fields." Form a panel in one of two ways:

    a. students majoring in different subjects.

    b. experienced teachers from different subject fields.

12. Debate the topic, "Resolved, that students in high school should be grouped homogeneously."

13. Map out a schedule of topics for a group guidance program for grades seven through twelve. If desired, work in small committees during this exercise.

14. Make a sociometric study of a student club or group from which you can obtain the necessary data.

15. Study copies of various types of standardized tests and their manuals. This may be done in one of two ways:

    a. The instructor will direct the students to purchase a kit of standardized tests, the titles of which he has chosen. Then the instructor may administer the tests in class or the students may administer the tests to themselves. Analyze the results.

    b. The students may examine specimen sets from files of the instructor, the college, or local school system.

Students should begin keeping a card file on standardized tests and guidance materials. They should prepare a separate card for each test, giving the name of the test, type, publisher, costs, and pertinent notes about the test.

16. Prepare a profile of your own test scores or of scores made by a student to whom you have administered a series of standardized tests. Write a summary of the test results.

17. From one of the class's nonstandardized examinations compute the median, the mean, and the mode of the scores on the test.

18. Select one intelligence test (group type), one achievement test, one interest test, and one aptitude test. Study the manuals of these tests. Compare claims made in the manuals with reviews of the same tests in Buros, *Mental Measurements Yearbook.*

19. Look up in Buros, *Mental Measurements Yearbook* tests in your own subject field. Record these tests in your card file.

20. Select a high school or college student and prepare a case study on him.

21. Role-play in class a number of typical interview situations. Among the situations may be:

    a. counseling a student who has no idea of his vocational ambitions.

    b. counseling a student who wants to know if he should go to college.

    c. counseling a student who is uncooperative in class.

    d. counseling a student who has a number of failing grades on his report card.

    e. counseling a boy who is too bashful to date.

22. Attend and report on a Career Day or College Night held at a school in the vicinity. If it is not possible to attend an actual Career Day or College Night, interview responsible officials in a school where a successful program has been held.

23. Write your own autobiography.

24. Examine a number of different forms of cumulative records from various localities and states.

25. Keep a time schedule of your activities for a week.

26. Visit a high school class, observe, and then write one or two anecdotal records. Do not identify the pupils in the records. Analyze the records in class.

27. Examine a number of student handbooks from various high schools. Judge their adequacy.

28. Familiarize yourself with the *Dictionary of Occupational Titles*. The *Dictionary of Occupational Titles* is available from the U. S. Department of Labor. The college library should have a copy. Copies may also be seen at the offices of the state employment service.

29. Visit the state employment service and find out what services are available from this agency.

30. Find out what the requirements are for graduation from high school in *(a)* your state and *(b)* your home town. Note the differences between minimum state requirements and requirements made by different communities.

31. Make a list of selected colleges and universities and record the number of high school units required in your subject field for admission to those colleges. Duplicate these lists and give to the students in class. In this way, students get an idea of college requirements in various subjects.

32. Prepare a philosophical statement on the aims of a high school guidance program.

33. Show the connection between guidance and

    a. the curriculum

    b. methods of instruction

    c. extra-class activities

    d. discipline

34. Evaluate the case study prepared as a class activity. Apply the following criteria to the case study:

    a. thoroughness and effort

    b. soundness of interpretation of the data

    c. logic of recommendations

    d. clarity of expression

35. Show in what way the needs of American youth differ from those of:

    a. Russian youth

    b. French youth

    c. Samoan youth

36. Given the following scores made on a series of standardized tests by an eleventh-grade boy in his first semester,

    a. Find the norms appropriate for his group on each of the tests.

    b. Construct the student's test profile.

    c. Write an analysis of the test results.

Standard scores on the Iowa Tests of Educational Development:

1. Understanding of Basic Social Concepts	18
2. General Background in the Natural Sciences	20
3. Correctness and Appropriateness of Expression	17
4. Ability to Do Quantitative Thinking	24
5. Ability to Interpret Reading Materials in the Social Studies	14
6. Ability to Interpret Reading Materials in the Natural Sciences	22
7. Ability to Interpret Literary Materials	16
8. General Vocabulary	19

Composite standard score for Tests 1–8	20
9. Uses of Sources of Information	21

Raw scores of the Differential Aptitude Tests (Form L):

Verbal Reasoning	35
Numerical Ability	36
Verbal Reasoning and Numerical Ability: Scholastic Aptitude	71
Abstract Reasoning	41
Clerical Speed and Accuracy	54
Mechanical Reasoning	56
Space Relations	84
Language Usage I: Spelling	57
II: Grammar	46

37. Prepare a well-thought-out, well-documented statement justifying your field of instruction in the high school program. Make your statement suitable for presentation to high school pupils.

38. Respond to the following questions:

a. What specific recommendations would you make to the administrator of a school who wants to start a guidance program?

b. What are the responsibilities and limitations implied in the statement, "Every teacher is a guidance person"?

c. Do current changes in the high school curriculum call for more or less guidance? Explain your answer.

d. What dangers do you see in maintaining and using cumulative records?

SELECTED BIBLIOGRAPHICAL REFERENCES

1. Black, Hillel. *They Shall Not Pass.* New York: William Morrow and Co., 1963. 342 pp.

   Highly readable presentation of the use and abuse of standardized tests. The author shows how "many young people in the U. S. are being penalized because of overemphasis by some test makers on the merchandising of tests and the ignorance of many school officials" (p. 255).

2. Foster, Charles R. *Guidance for Today's Schools.* New York: Ginn and Co., 1957. 362 pp.

   Comprehensive text on guidance with emphasis on guidance functions of the teacher.

3. Froelich, Clifford P. *Guidance Services in Schools.* 2nd ed. New York: McGraw-Hill, 1958. 383 pp.

   Comprehensive text on guidance which discusses ways of organizing guidance programs, techniques of guidance, and guidance services.

4. Gordon, Ira. *The Teacher As a Guidance Worker.* New York: Harper & Row, 1956. 350 pp.

   Book dealing with the meaning of guidance, human development concepts, and application of these concepts in the classroom.

5. Hatch, Raymond N., Dressel, Paul L., and Costar, James W. *Guidance Services in the Secondary School.* Dubuque, Iowa: William C. Brown Co., 1963. 206 pp.

   Simplified treatment of guidance services in the secondary school. It includes many practical suggestions.

6. Johnson, Walter F., Stefflre, Buford, and Edelfelt, Roy A. *Pupil Personnel and Guidance Services*. New York: McGraw-Hill, 1961. 407 pp.

   Textbook dealing with the nature and society of the pupil, roles of pupil personnel workers, and techniques of pupil personnel work. Contains samples of guidance forms for use in schools.

7. Lyman, Howard B. *Test Scores and What They Mean*. Englewood Cliffs, N. J.: Prentice-Hall, 1963. 223 pp.

   Paperback dealing with meaning of test scores. Helps teachers to understand and use test results. Especially useful for those who have not had specialized training in testing. Contains simplified treatment of statistics.

8. Miller, Carroll H. *Guidance Services: An Introduction*. New York: Harper and Row, 1965. 418 pp.

   Comprehensive treatment of the numerous guidance services that schools provide.

9. Ohlsen, Merle M. *Guidance Services in the Modern School*. New York: Harcourt, Brace & World, 1964. 515 pp.

   Revision of an earlier book by the author on guidance services. It is a comprehensive treatment of the many services provided by schools and includes a helpful appendix, on "Use of Statistics in Child Study."

INSTRUCTIONAL AIDS AND SOURCES

1. Charts, pamphlets, booklets, information sheets, etc. See catalogue of Science Research Associates, 259 East Erie Street, Chicago, Illinois, 60611.

2. Films

   a. *Learning to Understand Children*. New York: McGraw-Hill Book Co. The case study of Ada Adams.

   > Part 1: *A Diagnostic Approach*. 21 min. Sound. Black and white.
   > Part 2: *A Remedial Program*. 23 min. Sound. Black and white.

   b. *The Outsider*. New York: Young America Films. 10 min. Sound. Black and white.

   > The story of a girl who is rejected by her group.

   c. *Shy Guy*. Chicago: Coronet Films. 13 min. Sound. Black and white.

   > The story of a shy adolescent.

d. Teacher as Observer and Guide. New York: Teachers College, Columbia University. 20 min. Sound. Black and white.

This film shows classroom teachers guiding pupils.

3. Tests

See catalogues of test publishers, *The Mental Measurements Yearbook,* and *Tests in Print.* These latter two references are edited by Oscar K. Buros and are available from the Gryphon Press, Highland Park, New Jersey.

UNIT VI

DISCIPLINE AND CONTROL

OBJECTIVES OF UNIT VI

At the conclusion of his reading and correlated study-discussion activities, the reader should

A. understand that
1. discipline is an extremely complex question;
2. the aim of discipline is self-discipline;
3. matters of discipline are primary to instruction;
4. self-discipline is the desired goal of American education;
5. self-discipline is learned;
6. all behavior is caused;
7. a teacher should attempt to discover the causes of behavior problems;
8. symptoms and causes of behavior problems are not identical;
9. many corrective measures affect only surface conditions;
10. harsh, repressive measures are least effective in the achievement of the goal of self-discipline;
11. teachers vary greatly in their abilities to maintain order;
12. it is impossible to write a prescription for one method of discipline which would be applicable to all problem cases;
13. misbehavior is not necessarily directed personally against the teacher;
14. the most desirable forms of discipline are reformation and prevention.

B. show appreciation for
1. the classroom and school that stands out because of the absence of behavior problems,
2. the ability of the teacher who is master of the situation,
3. the self-disciplined citizen.

C. adopt attitudes of
1. reasonableness in regard to behavior problems and their treatment,
2. great care in the selection of corrective measures.

D. be able to demonstrate skill in
1. recognizing situations that produce disciplinary problems and in heading off difficulties,
2. perfecting the techniques of simple control,
3. selecting the best corrective measures,
4. providing situations that develop self-discipline,
5. maintaining a mentally healthful classroom climate.

CHAPTER 16

CAUSES OF BEHAVIOR PROBLEMS

Children now love luxury. They have bad manners, contempt for
authority. They show disrespect for elders and love chatter in
place of exercise. Children are now tyrants, not the servants of
their households.   —*Socrates*[1]

No single problem is such a challenge and causes teachers so much
heartache, frustration, and failure as the problem of discipline. Teachers,
administrators, students, and parents are all deeply concerned with discipline. The age-old question of discipline still occupies a large proportion
of the energies and time of teachers and administrators.

Problems of discipline are foremost in the thinking of beginning teachers,
because inexperienced teachers are often judged by students, administrators, and parents by their ability to maintain order and to control their
classes. The Purdue Opinion Panel of Purdue University, which surveys
attitudes and problems of school youth, found in its studies of some 15,000
teen-agers that students generally gave approval and support to their teachers.
The Panel reported that students complained of teachers who play favorites,
teachers who give no encouragement, and teachers who are too strict or too
impersonal.[2] Similar surveys of the attitudes of young people have dis-
closed general satisfaction with teachers and schools but some complaints
when the teacher was too strict or too lax in discipline.

No phase of secondary school life, with the possible exception of school
marking practices, is as apparent to outsiders as the management of pupil
behavior problems. Parents are easily aroused if the discipline of the school
is too strict, and they are generally dissatisfied if the discipline of the
school is too lax or confused.

[1] *The Education Digest* (January 1954), Ann Arbor, Mich., p. 20.
[2] H. H. Remmers and C. G. Hackett, *Let's Listen to Youth* (Chicago: Science
Research Associates, 1950), p. 25.

FREEDOM UNDER RESTRAINT

The central problem in the question of discipline is that of imposing restraint without destroying the individuality of the one restrained. Too much restraint can frustrate the creative and leadership abilities of the individual. Too little restraint can be responsible for the destruction of society. A middle ground must be found in which society's interests are protected and in which the individual's talents and abilities can be made to flourish.

The methods of restraint imposed by society depend upon the goals of that society. Totalitarian society imposes its restraints through force and complete subjugation of the individual to the state's desires. Democratic society relies upon self-discipline of the individual to maintain its dynamic status.

In democracy the limits of restraint are defined either by the mores of society or by the written and unwritten laws of the land. Within the law, a great variance in freedom of life, liberty, and the pursuit of happiness is possible. Law and its punishments protect society against the immature adult, the criminal, the extreme deviate, and the willful destroyer of group purposes and goals. Law at the same time protects the individual in the maximum freedom possible without grave harm to society and himself. Without some form of restraint or law anarchy would exist instead of democracy.

There is no question of the necessity for restraint. No brief is made for complete freedom of the adolescent. Punishment in the form of legal sanctions and social disapproval is ever present, even in democracy. The individual has to learn the effect of his conduct upon the groups with which he is associated and upon the welfare of society as a whole. Everywhere he turns the individual finds some form of restraint.

Deterrent effects of punishment alone, however, have not proven an answer to the problem of discipline for democracy. The simple observation of the number of criminals, petty and grand, attests the inefficiency of punishment itself. Only when self-control takes over is the cause of democracy served. The habit of obedience to law and control become fixed through either (1) subjection to enforced obedience, which results in citizens more suitable to totalitarian society than democracy, or (2) training in and through democratic processes, which results in citizens acceptable to democratic society.

The school's objective in democracy is clearly to turn out citizens for the preservation of our republic. The school must develop all the talents of every individual, teach him the importance of self-restraint, and impose restraint when necessary, for the education of the individual and for the welfare of the group.

To serve as guides to the teacher in understanding adolescent behavior problems, five categories of causes are discussed in the following pages. These categories are: (1) causes originating with the child, (2) causes originating with the child's group, (3) causes originating with the teacher and the school, (4) causes originating with the home and community, and (5) causes originating in the larger social order. Following each category are suggested remedial measures.

CAUSES ORIGINATING WITH THE CHILD

PHYSICAL FACTORS

Physical factors play an important part in the presence or absence of behavior disorders. The state of health of the child, his nutritional condition, the presence of physical handicaps and glandular deficiencies, and the phase of growth and development of the child directly affect his conduct. The effect of physical factors on conduct is illustrated in Case 1 following:

> *Case 1.* W., a sophomore boy, consistently came to class without his work done. He appeared dejected and lethargic most of the time. Investigation showed that his father was dead. He and an older brother, with their mother, managed the family farm. W. was up each morning at 5 A.M., doing chores. Arriving home in the afternoon, he was again occupied by farm work until supper time. At the end of the day, he was exhausted and unable to do his studies.

Physical deficiencies such as poor vision and hearing loss can create difficulties in the classroom. Pupils who cannot see the blackboard or hear the teacher are candidates for problem behavior.

It is not expected that a teacher or administrator be a physician. But it is vitally important that the teacher be able to sense when the pupil is exhibiting erratic behavior and refer that pupil for complete medical attention. Gross injustice may result if the teacher uses harsh measures to make a pupil conform when the pupil is actually physically unable to do so.

Physiologically, early adolescence is a period of rapid growth, sexual maturation, and muscular development. Too rapid spurts in growth result in the gangling awkwardness so typical of the adolescent stage. With maturation of the sexual organs, secondary sex characteristics create problems of adjustment for both boys and girls. This physical development accounts for increased interest in dating and establishment of satisfactory relationships between the sexes. Physical growth and development account for many psychological problems of the adolescent.

REMEDIAL MEASURES

The following remedial actions can be taken in the treatment of causes of behavior problems resulting from physical factors:

1. Thorough medical examination will provide data on the nature of physical difficulties.

2. Provision of minimum medical and dental attention in school—through the services of a school nurse and a dental hygienist—is a necessity.

3. Extra milk and opportunities for extra rest, when needed, can be provided by the school.

4. Reports to parents from the school physician and school nurse should be sent and followed up.

5. Enlisting the help of social agencies to assist poor children in obtaining needed medical and dental attention is a responsibility of school leadership.

6. A suitable physical education program and corrective therapy should be provided for the physically handicapped.

7. Seating and the scheduling of the child's program should be such as to conform to his physical condition.

MENTAL FACTORS

Mental factors must be considered as sources of behavior problems. The effect of mental factors on conduct is shown in Cases 2 and 3 following.

> Case 2. R., was a seventh-grade boy with a low IQ, reading ability of the fifth grade, and spelling ability of the second grade. He was required to use the same textbooks and attempt the same lesson assignments as students of greater ability in his class. Since he could not possibly succeed academically, he spent the day amusing himself with behavior annoying to his fellow pupils and to his teacher.

The slow learner, unable to do well in his school work, finds ways of satisfying his need for achievement through antisocial behavior.

> Case 3. B., a sophomore girl, was exceptionally proficient in mathematics. She completed a series of problems ahead of the rest of the class. Socially mature enough not to wish to disturb the others, who were concentrating on their problems, she took out a fiction book and began reading. The teacher, infuriated by this diversion, scolded her for not giving her complete and undivided attention to mathematics. The teacher had provided no additional work for the girl to do. In the teacher's opinion the girl should have spent her time uselessly rechecking work which later turned out to be accurate.

The gifted child can be a behavior problem, if provision is not made for him. Unlike the girl in Case 3 the pupil could be a disturbance to the class and teacher.

REMEDIAL MEASURES

Possible actions in dealing with mental factors as causes of behavior problems are:

1. The pupil's program should be adjusted to his abilities and interests. Groups sectioned by ability should be involved in work at their own levels.

2. Suitable instruction for varying levels of learners within each class should be provided. Expectations for slow students in heterogeneous classes should not be as high as expectations for bright students.

3. In severe cases the child should be referred to a psychological or psychiatric clinic.

SOCIAL AND EMOTIONAL FACTORS

Social and emotional needs are as strong in youth as in adults. Many of the disciplinary problems that arise are due to the pupil's seeking recognition in one form or another. An adolescent who cannot obtain approval from the teacher through scholastic achievement will often seek it from his classmates by becoming a behavior problem. An unsatisfied need for approval resulted in misbehavior in Case 4 below.

> *Case 4.* B., a sophomore boy, was a constant source of annoyance in his classes. He frequently dispensed with all homework. Intelligence tests revealed a high IQ. B. was given a leading part in a holiday dramatic show in the assembly. His conduct improved noticeably after a successful presentation of the play in assembly.

The need for affection is a driving force. In some cases the boy or girl does not find affection in the home. He may be rejected or an unwanted child, or he may be from a broken home. All human beings need affection. Many of the warped personalities of this age have become so by lack of affection. Such a lack led to the unhappiness of the boy in Case 5 below.

> *Case 5.* E., a bright boy in his junior year of high school, was confused, constantly worried, and spent a great deal of his time debating abstract questions with various faculty members. E. admitted that his home life was unhappy, that he was disliked by his stepfather.

The need for security creates many problem cases. Security may be lacking at home or school. Failure in school work as well as basic insecurity in the home can produce a mental case. The security of the boy in Case 6 following was shattered by the outburst of his teacher.

> *Case 6.* A seventh-grade boy was called upon to stand up and recite the

answer to a question posed to him by the teacher. The boy did not know the answer. The teacher, aggravated, shouted at him, "Sit down, you goddam dummy."

The need for success must be recognized by teachers. Success breeds success. Failure begets failure, disillusionment, and despair. Success is achieved in school mainly through academic channels. Failure in school work accounts for a large proportion of dropouts. Austin, French, and Hull state: "The worst behavior problems are found in those students who have few skills in which they can take pride and few wholesome interests in which they can lose themselves."[3]

Gregariousness and the sense of belonging are critical needs at the adolescent level. The desire to belong to one's peer group accounts for the fads and fashions that occasionally take the high school by storm. The overwhelming desire to be one of the crowd can cause maladjustment. An acute feeling of being an outsider on account of her manner of dress ended in scholastic tragedy for the girl in Case 7 below.

Case 7. V., a senior girl, left school in her final year. She felt her clothes were not fashionable enough and she was unable to purchase other clothes.

The need for movement creates many difficult situations. Unless they are suffering from some physical or mental handicap, adolescents exhibit a restlessness, a bountiful energy. It is a difficult task for an adolescent to sit through six or seven periods a day, giving complete attention to the intellectual tasks presented to him. Whispering, noisy disturbance of the class, shuffling around, teasing, and similar disorderly conduct can often be attributed to misdirected energies of the pupils.

The desire for new experiences and adventure is a prevalent phenomenon in adolescents. Curiosity abounds. Hero worship, preference by the boys for tales of violence and by the girls for romantic escapades, and formation of gangs to seek new thrills are common at the adolescent stage. A search for adventure led to truancy of the boy in Case 8 below.

Case 8. J., a freshman in a New York State high school, became bored with his school and home life, ran off without anyone's knowledge, and hitchhiked to Florida.

REMEDIAL MEASURES

Action that may be taken in dealing with social and emotional factors includes:

[3] David B. Austin, Will French, and J. Dan Hull, *American High School Administration* (New York: Holt, Rinehart & Winston, 3rd ed., 1962), p. 388.

1. Affection and sympathy from the teacher to help satisfy needs for affection, approval, and security.

2. Provision of guidance services to help the pupil solve some of his many problems.

3. The placing of responsibility on the pupil in keeping with his abilities in order to satisfy his need of approbation, independence, and new experiences.

4. Social functions and training in social manners to give the adolescent the necessary confidence and skills to establish good relationships with the opposite sex.

5. Group projects to develop group morale and to satisfy the desire for gregariousness.

6. Praise and publication of student achievements to satisfy the need for success.

7. Part-time work to give added opportunities to fulfill adolescent needs for security and independence. The school can assist in this training through diversified work-experience programs and through placement services.

8. Provision of outlets for excess energy and for talents not brought out in the academic phases of the curriculum. This can be done through extra-class activities, including athletics. Substitution of wholesome activities for unwholesome cuts down on behavior problems.

CAUSES ORIGINATING WITH THE CHILD'S GROUP

The groups of which the individual is a part have a pronounced effect upon his behavior. His family, his church group, his neighborhood associates, and his school classes each influence him to some extent.

The teacher will be especially concerned with the impact of the class group upon the individual. The class is not only a collection of individuals present for learning but also a social group living together for a period of time.

The teacher is always a group leader. Group leadership involves an understanding of the nature of groups and the ways in which they behave. As we have noted in our previous discussion, there are smaller subgroupings within each group. Some of the individual students are recognized by their classmates as leaders. Other students are not accepted by their classmates as full members of that group. The attitudes and conduct of pupils in the class are shaped in part by both the group as a whole and subgroupings within the class. The effective group leader learns how to utilize student leadership within a group. He can spot subgroups or cliques within the class and channel their energies into worthwhile tasks. The effective group leader seeks to develop unity, cohesiveness, and esprit de corps in the groups for which he has responsibility. He uses his authority, when necessary, to prevent deterioration of group unity through aggressive, antisocial behavior on the part of an individual or groupings of individuals within the total group.

The effective group leader is aware that student responses and participation are affected by students' views of themselves as members of the group. If they believe their classmates consider them as valuable, participating members of the group, they may make worthwhile contributions to group activity. If they see themselves as ineffective, worthless members of the group, they will contribute little to the group's activities.

Instruction in the school is a group endeavor. A teacher has not only one hundred and sixty students, let us say, but five groups of thirty-two students each. The teacher must think of the five group organizations as well as the many individuals. Teachers have the groups in mind when they state such things as "The fifth-period class is my best class." "Oh, that seventh-period class!" "Third-period class is the slowest." "My classes this year are even better than last year's." Obviously there are characteristics about the groups that permit us to consider them as entities. Group patterns of achievement, motivation, spirit, and conduct are identifiable.

A teacher can tell when a group is producing, when there is a spark of enthusiasm, where there is high rapport between the teacher and the class, when there is high-quality student leadership present, and when there are disrupting influences. A teacher must always be aware of atmosphere, or group climate, in the classroom. He should seek to foster a healthy, pleasant atmosphere which is conducive to learning. Every individual in the classroom is affected by the group climate. Fritz Redl, the psychologist, identifies four types of unhealthy group climates:

1. Punitive climate. The punitive climate is perhaps the most destructive of group morale and discipline of any classroom climate . . . some rebel, hate, and fight back and others identify themselves with the teacher out of fear and, therefore, have to become moral hypocrites in their attitude toward the other children. . . . The emotion of fear of reprisal and shame is in the air most of the time, the teacher as well as the onlookers receiving sadistic enjoyment of the chronic type. It is the kind of group climate that breeds sadists, bullies, and hypocrites. In this group it is a sign of character and courage to become a behavior problem.

2. Emotional blackmail climate. The teacher repeats that she "loves" all the pupils, will not punish them, enjoys self-induced guilt feelings. The children fear disapproval. The main casualties are those who want to grow up, be independent.

3. Hostile competition climate. This type of climate develops aggressiveness, defeatism, snobbishness, and hate.

4. Distorted group-pride climate. Vanity of the group is encouraged, as in the instance of an athletic team with distorted pride.[4]

[4] George Sheviakov and Fritz Redl, *Discipline for Today's Children and Youth*, revised by Sybil K. Richardson (Washington: Association for Supervision and Curriculum Development, N. E. A., 1956), pp. 49–51.

Redl estimates that at least ninety per cent of all discipline cases are in dire need of group psychological analysis.

In order to treat the causes of behavior problems that originate with the pupil's group:

1. Teachers should study techniques of group leadership. They should be skillful at handling group discussions. They should seek to involve all students in the work of the class.

2. The teacher needs to know the make-up of the group. He must know the backgrounds of the individuals, what kind of previous training the group has had, and what types of discipline the group has been subjected to in its school history. He needs to discover the students who are identified by their own classmates as their leaders. He should discover also the students who have been socially rejected by their classmates. Once the composition of the group is known, the teacher can deal with individual needs and can tackle the job of development of high group morale.

3. The teacher should seek to develop student leadership within his group. He should encourage students to accept leadership responsibilities. The group may study the qualities of an effective leader so that they have some idea of what qualities to look for in the persons they will choose to lead them.

4. Teachers must be aware of the type of group climate they are fostering. They must develop a happy, healthy, secure group climate with relationships of mutual respect between teacher and pupils.

5. The teacher needs to realize that his own personality both as an adult and personification of authority and his methods of instruction affect group development.

CAUSES ORIGINATING WITH THE TEACHER AND THE SCHOOL

The most important single factor in the problem of discipline is the teacher himself. Personality traits of the teacher can account for the presence of disciplinary problems or the absence of these problems. Analysis of personality differences in teachers sometimes reveals the source of behavior problems in pupils.

TEACHER ATTITUDES

Teachers' attitudes about the nature and seriousness of behavior disorders can cause considerable difficulty. Teachers frequently want strong discipline, meaning by this a high degree of order, authoritarian control, and quick punishment for infractions. Teachers need to examine their attitudes toward questions of morality. These attitudes determine ways in which a teacher reacts to pupil behavior. A third or more of the children in our culture belong to minority groups. Teachers must harbor no prejudices against individuals or groups. The teacher has the obligation to instruct and guide the pupils of minority groups in his classes as well as those of the majority group. Slurs against racial and religious backgrounds can create behavior disorders and arouse a segment of the public.

Masculine and feminine roles must be strictly adhered to. Adolescents are quick to spot deviations from culturally established roles. The masculine woman or the effeminate man will find control a big problem and may be condemned by pupils and parents alike.

Too much erudition can provoke problems. Young teachers, particularly those fresh out of college, may forget that they are dealing with immature boys and girls. Though standards of scholarship on the part of the teacher should be of the highest, the teacher must take care that he speaks and presents his material at the level of the learner.

PHYSICAL ATTRIBUTES

The voice plays a great role in control. A high-pitched, squeaky, shrill-toned or booming voice will not control a group of adolescents as easily as a pleasant, well-modulated tone of confidence and self-expression. A resonant, quiet, unemotional tone commands respect.

Grooming is more important in teaching than in many other vocations. Teachers are subjected to the public scrutiny seven days a week. Teachers are cast into a certain role by the public and are expected to dress well, neatly, and conservatively. Ostentatious dress may provoke laughter and ridicule.

Posture and walk contribute to the presence or absence of respect that a teacher will receive. A slouching posture does not command the attention of pupils.

Mannerisms and gestures have significance in the problem of control. Use of the hands and facial expressions may be effective for teaching or may be sources of merriment to the pupils. Startlingly unusual mannerisms and gestures may cast the teacher in an unfortunate role in which it will be difficult to maintain respect.

POPULARITY

Most teachers want to be liked by their students. But teachers who vie for popularity in the eyes of students will find to their dismay that they are not as well respected as are those who couple genuine liking and mutual respect with a professional attitude. To be "one of the boys" is a regrettable mistake. Contempt arises not only from students with whom the teacher has bartered respect for cheap popularity but also from fellow colleagues who resent this type of unprofessional competition.

PERSONAL LIFE

Personal life should, as a general rule, be kept out of the classroom, unless it can serve to illustrate some instructional purpose. When a teacher is disturbed, worried, or ill, he needs to be doubly cautious that he does not project his own troubles on the boys and girls in his classes. The moody teacher presents the adolescent with conflicts, since the student does not know from one day to the next what the mood of the teacher will be. A consistently pleasant mood is conducive to good mental health and to the absence of disciplinary problems.

The maladjustment of the teacher is in some cases a source of disciplinary difficulties. There is no doubt that our schools house teachers who have nervous disorders, worries, and anxieties which actually interfere with their teaching.

A teacher must analyze his own values and standards of conduct. Overly strict teachers may find that bitter dissatisfactions in their own personal lives have contributed to stern treatment of the pupils in their charge. They may be using pupils to satisfy their own needs for someone to love, their desire to dominate others, or their craving for approval and recognition.

Teachers need to be conscious of their own state of adjustment and willing to accept lacks as elements calling for improvement. The maladjusted teacher who is inwardly aware of his disturbance should seek professional counseling for himself. The maladjusted teacher who is not aware of his state of adjustment, as is often the case, may have to be required by his school administrator to obtain professional help. If the teacher refuses to obtain help and if his degree of maladjustment is sufficiently great, he may be discharged.

PERSONAL TRAITS

Sarcasm is unacceptable and ineffective in achieving the goal of self-discipline. The use of sarcasm is unjust in that the teacher is taking advantage of his authority, employing a technique denied to the pupil. It leads to further disciplinary problems by arousing the group to the defense of the unfortunate victim. Humiliation of the pupil by the teacher is universally condemned.

Hypocrisy is a trait detected by adolescents. The teacher must be the example of good conduct. Pupils will pattern their own behavior after adult models. Hypocritical behavior on the part of teachers provides justification for misbehavior on the part of boys and girls. The maintenance of a double standard of conduct, one for pupils and one for teachers, is a dangerous practice.

Confidence is of primary importance. Lack of confidence accounts for many of the failures among teachers. Expression of confidence and poise should be exhibited from the first day in the classroom.

A sense of humor is indispensable in human relations. The ability to laugh with the pupils and at one's self can go a long way in the establishment of a healthy group climate and in the elimination of behavior problems. A sense of humor will not only make the class experiences more pleasant, but also will ease the teacher's strain. Some teachers feel that, if they exhibit the very natural tendency toward humor, they will undermine their prestige and bring disrespect to themselves. A well-balanced sense of humor will, in fact, raise group morale. Redl states: "A sense of humor is obviously the most essential characteristic of skillful handlers of discipline problems or tough group situations and its possession must be among the prime requisites of the teacher. . . . The fear of exposure to ridicule has caused more intangible discipline problems than anything else."[5]

Temper outbursts either frighten the pupil or beget temper outbursts from him. They destroy group morale. They are a means of relieving teacher's feelings, an abuse of authority, and damaging to immature personalities.

Numerous other personality traits are the obvious ones required of any one who seeks success in a profession where the ability to get along with people is the principal task.

SCHOOL-CREATED PROBLEMS

The curriculum offered by the school causes a large percentage of behavior problems. Programs and courses of study that are not in keeping with the needs and interests of the young people cause much trouble for teachers. For a full treatment of the topic of curriculum see Unit II of this book.

Lack of articulation between the elementary school and the secondary school can create problems. The elementary school pupil leaves the class where he has been accustomed to spend the whole school day with one teacher and is thrust into a junior high school program with a complicated schedule and many teachers. The pupil can become lost during his early days of secondary school, confused by its complex arrangement and many requirements, and discouraged if he cannot keep up with the numerous assignments.

Methods of instruction are primary sources of behavior difficulties. Methods inappropriate for specific classes or groups may be found to provoke disciplinary problems and frustrate teaching entirely.

Feminization of the school staff presents a problem. Boys and girls need

---

[5] *Ibid.*, pp. 59–60, 63.

association with both men and women. Ideally, a fifty-fifty percentage would be desirable. Male and female points of view need equal representation among adolescents.

Lack of guidance may be blamed for a pupil's failure to be placed properly in the school program, thus contributing to misbehavior. All too frequently there is no one to whom the pupil can turn for individual help. For a full treatment of the topic of guidance see Unit V of this book.

Lack of cooperation among faculty members is an unhealthy condition contributing to pupil misbehavior. Enmities among faculty members may cause a pupil to develop loyalties to one side or another or to be split with conflict. Inconsistency by various faculty members in applying school policies can result in pupil insecurity. Youth learn to use to advantage divisions among teachers and to play one teacher off against the other.

REMEDIAL MEASURES

Guidelines for the teacher to keep in mind in attempting to handle causes of behavior problems originating with the teacher and the school are:

1. The teacher should know himself. He should take inventory of personal strengths and weaknesses. He should seek help on weaknesses. If he has a thick enough skin, he can let the pupils rate him anonymously on various personality and scholastic traits. If his speech stands in need of improvement, he can enroll in a college course or adult education course in speech or dramatics.

2. Provision of a clean, attractive, well-equipped school plant and physical environment dispels many problem cases.

3. Change of course, teacher, or school is sometimes warranted.

4. Orientation should be provided for elementary school pupils entering the secondary school. Orientation for college and vocations is further required at the senior high school level.

5. Methods of instruction must provide opportunities for success, recognition, and a sense of security.

6. Extra help is necessitated in counseling, conferences, and academic work.

7. Courses in psychology, hygiene, and adolescent problems have been offered for pupils with success in many secondary schools.

CAUSES ORIGINATING WITH THE HOME AND COMMUNITY

Family background accounts for a large percentage of behavior problems. Factors in the family setting which must be considered are the attitudes of the parents, the socioeconomic level of the family, the status of the home (whether it is broken by separation, divorce, or death in the family), the handling of discipline in the home, and the extent of training given the children in manners and morals. The tragic effect of unpleasant family background was felt by the girl in Case 9 following:

> *Case 9.* E., a freshman girl, was considered "lazy" by her teachers. An examination of the home situation showed that E's mother had left home with another man. E. carried the burden of taking care of the home, making meals for her father, and assuming at an early age her mother's house-keeping tasks. Besides, she bore the stigma attached to her mother's delinquent behavior.

The home environment of the pupil is frequently depressing and sordid. The discrepancy between home and school life sets up conflicts that are sources of real concern to the pupil.

Imitation of elders is a cause of behavior problems. Adolescents have been taught unconsciously many attitudes and ways of undesirable behavior by adults in their home, community, and nation. Immature, pliant, and impressionable adolescents, aware that their parents and other adults indulge in misconduct and unethical behavior, adopt similar modes of conduct themselves in the mistaken belief that these ways of behaving are accepted and approved by society. The use of profanity, the "fixing" of a traffic ticket, the sale of shoddy goods, the swindling of partners, unsavory business practices, and the double sex standard demonstrate ways of conduct to the young which they may assume are acceptable.

Cliques are important in the development of adolescent behavior. The development of cliques, gangs, and clubs can be related to the adolescent need for gregariousness. The attitudes of the clique are often more influential than the attitudes taught by the home and the school. Davis says:

> The example of the adolescent's play group and of his own kin, however, is the crucial determinant of behavior. Even where the efforts of the parent to instill middle-class mores in the child are more than half-hearted, the power of the street culture in which the child and adolescent are trained overwhelms the verbal instruction. The rewards of gang prestige, freedom of movement, and property gain all seem to be on the side of the street culture.[6]

A simple behavior problem caused by a boy's association with his gang is cited in Case 10 below.

> *Case 10.* S., a sophomore boy with above-average IQ, did extremely poor school work and was a frequent disciplinary problem. It was learned that S.

---

[6] Allison Davis, "Socialization and Adolescent Personality," in *Adolescence*, 43rd Yearbook of the National Society for the Study of Education, Part I (Chicago: The National Society for the Study of Education, 1944), p. 210.

was running around town with a gang of boys older than himself. S. found their behavior patterns more exciting than his own life.

REMEDIAL MEASURES

Approaches to the treatment of causes of behavior problems originating in the home and community may be outlined:

1. Visits to the home may establish rapport and furnish necessary information about the pupil's background.

2. Part-time work for the student may solve some of the family's economic difficulties.

3. Adult education can provide parents with help in the problems of growth and development of their boys and girls. A course such as "Understanding the Teen-ager," taught by a competent specialist, would be found popular in many communities.

4. Retraining the young people from disadvantaged environments must be handled tactfully and patiently.

5. Adequate and available physical recreation facilities in the school can do much to counteract neighborhood conditions and provide a healthful environment under adult supervision.

6. Cooperation with outside agencies, such as Boy Scouts, Girl Scouts, community centers, churches, etc., attacks the problem of unfavorable home and neighborhood environment.

7. Teachers have discovered that in many cases little can be done by the school about home environment. They have the responsibility of seeking any measures which may be helpful and, at the same time, not augmenting the pupil's conflict by mentally unhygienic treatment in school.

Patience is necessary with parents who interfere either by opposing the methods of discipline used by the school or by actively encouraging the pupil to be uncooperative and disrespectful to the authorities of the school. Some parents are continuing maladjusted patterns of behavior they have learned. Others are projecting their disgruntled frustration at their own lack of success in school by encouraging defiant behavior in their children. Some parents are jealous of the position the teacher holds in the estimation of the pupil. Adult education may reach some of these problem parents.

CAUSES ORIGINATING IN THE LARGER SOCIAL ORDER

Circumstances beyond the control of the individual and conditions found in the intricacy of the social order in which the individual is imbedded give rise to adjustment difficulties experienced by many of the young people. The coming of the machine age with the Industrial Revolution has produced tremendous changes in society. The forces of technology have liberated men in a material sense and have bound them closely together in a social sense. In the course of some one hundred fifty years the machine has produced a giant of industrial power on the American continent. The modern age of science, improving and at the same time endangering mankind's existence on this small planet, has rocked the stability of the old agrarian society and created problems of conflict between the two opposing patterns of life, nineteenth-century agrarianism and the twentieth-century space era. It has become an ever-increasing battle for human society to adapt itself to the new cultural patterns evolved by the scientific age. Lag in the social institutions of society may be traced to the failure of these institutions to keep pace with the rapid technological advances and the concomitant results of these advances. The impact of the changes in the culture, brought about through technological changes and the resulting effect on behavior, bear examination.

CHANGES IN FAMILY ROLE AND STATUS

The Age of Technology has changed the American family considerably. The family, like all institutions in our technological society, has undergone the process of specialization of function. The family of the agrarian society was self-sufficient. Several generations lived at the family homestead and prided themselves on their productive power. As the Industrial Revolution made its inroads, more and more goods were produced outside the family. Services once performed by the family have now been taken over by outside agencies. The members of the home began to slip away from the hearth into the newly created industrial jobs. Women found employment outside the home, radically changing the style of living of the family.

The commercialized entertainment world has taken over much of the recreation function of the family. Schools have been assigned much of the education function of the family. Churches perform most of the religious function. The protective function is now largely in the hands of public agencies. The status of the family, formerly dependent on lineage, is now established in the industrial society by competencies of the members of the family. The family tree is now frequently a subject of comedy rather than a serious support for status.

These changes lessened the authoritarian function of the father. Whereas the father of the agrarian society was present twenty-four hours a day, the father of this age is absent from the home eight to ten hours a day and often sees his children only a few short hours a day, if at all. In many cases both parents are away from the home during the working day, leaving the children in care of relatives, friends, or day-nurseries. Attitudes and values of both parents, then, have little opportunity to be inculcated. The industrial age has called for an entirely new attitude on child-rearing and has resulted in the absolute necessity for self-disciplined citizens, since the citizens of this age are no longer subjected to family controls throughout their lifetime. The modern family, thus, has different functions from those held by the family of agrarian society.

Industrial society has resulted in the weakening of the primary group, the small circle of friends and relatives in which formerly one lived and developed one's values and attitudes. The element of mobility and the very complexity of modern society result in the individual's disassociation from his primary group and consequent association with larger, special-interest groups. The mobile individual is exposed to conflicts in the values held by different groups. This requires an adjustive personality. It requires experience and training in socializing with any and all types of personalities.

The impersonal relationships cause the individual to lose the identity he would have in his own small primary group. The democracy of technological society is an interdependent association of many specialized functions. Since the family and the primary group are not so effective in controlling the conduct of the individual, self-discipline assumes a role of leading importance.

CONFLICT IN MORES

The mores or customs of society regulate the individual's behavior in his social group. The mores of one group differ from the mores of other groups. Teachers, as a group, are products of the middle class and thus hold middle-class standards and values. The pupil from a lower socioeconomic class experiences conflicts when confronted in school with different standards and different values for which he has not learned the expected responses.

Middle-class adolescents are taught to disguise their aggression in forms of competitive striving for middle-class goals of success and material rewards. They are taught to conform to conventions that have been established so that the middle-class goals may be obtained.

The adolescent is caught in the vise of the culture in which he is reared. Teachers and administrators must be conscious of the discrepancy that arises between the way adolescents have been taught from birth to react and the way in which teachers would like them to respond. Ericson notes the problem of frustration in middle-class training: "Middle-class children are probably subjected to more frustration in the process of achieving these learnings and are probably more anxious as a result of these pressures than are the lower-class children. Lower-class families tend to be more permissive than the middle-class families in the training of their children in all areas."[7]

[7] Martha C. Ericson, "Social Status and Child-Rearing Practices," in *Readings in Social Psychology*, Theodore M. Newcomb, and Eugene L. Hartley, editors (New York: Holt, Rinehart & Winston, 1947), p. 501.

The very differences from community to community in mores and accepted practices require that a teacher or administrator move slowly in instituting radical changes, whether they be changes in discipline or any other change. A more desirable form of discipline cannot be established overnight in a community where, for generations, the traditions of discipline have been repressive measures and corporal punishment. Under these circumstances the educator must proceed gradually to allow new traditions of discipline to grow and develop.

ANXIETY OF THE TIMES

The strains of the current period, the antagonisms between East and West, limited wars, and the threat of falling off the "brink" into World War III have done much to increase adolescent difficulties. The continued existence of totalitarian systems throughout the world is a menace to the very security of the nation. The threat from aggressive communism has appeared close to home in our own hemisphere. The fact that young men of today will most certainly face military service for a good many years to come has heightened the problem of discipline for these times. Adolescents find themselves in a world they did not create. They are being asked to accept the burden of military service and to risk their lives for causes that we have not always helped them to understand. Young women find it difficult to adjust to the fact that eligible males may be forced to leave their homes and careers and to postpone marriage because of military service. Insecurity is prevalent in today's adolescents. They have never known a period without war or threat of war. In their seeking for security and meaning in their lives, they may at times show erratic behavior.

The problems of unemployment and economic stress strike the average family hard. Some of the young people are forced to find jobs to help support the family. Consequently, attitudes of indifference to book learning and neglect of studies may exist with adolescents, who do not know where the world is headed or why. They may seek the thrills of the moment instead of postponing them for some obscure and uncertain future.

PREVALENCE OF UNETHICAL CONDUCT

As young people read the newspapers they are periodically treated to a sordid display of undemocratic lack of ethics and moral values. Crime still flourishes. The use of influence to obtain special benefits has been frequently reported in the press in recent years. Unethical and illegal practices have been unearthed in government circles, the sports world, the ranks of labor, the highest levels of management and the entertainment world.

How much of the widespread lack of ethics on the part of young people may be due to unconscious imitation of adult behavior patterns cannot be known. Yet, the world outside the schools is education unparalleled. The child learns daily through scandalous reports in the mass means of communication, the radio, the newspaper, and television, that unethical behavior is everywhere engaged in and may, therefore, be the thing to do.

IMPACT OF URBAN CULTURE

The forces of technology have produced the rapidly growing modern city. While there were but twenty-four cities of twenty-five hundred or more population in 1790, there are now over four thousand cities in the United States. More than half of the country's population now lives in urban areas. With the mass means of communication the culture of the metropolitan area has been thrust on the rural area.

City culture is dominant since the influential means of shaping thought are city-controlled, the difficulties of transportation that formerly separated the city and country life are nonexistent today, and cities are still growing in population. In many locations the city has spread out and engulfed the surrounding suburban area to make one giant urban complex. The differences in urban and rural mores result in conflict, especially pronounced among rural adolescents upon whom this alien culture is thrust. To many rural adolescents the city culture looks superior to their more prosaic way of life and intensifies their desire for adventure, glamor, and urban vocational pursuits. Urban organizations, urban social pursuits, and urban tastes in reading, art, and fashion are imitated and adopted by the country.

REMEDIAL MEASURES

No one can, of course, blame all the ills of society on the public schools, though some critics of modern education often appear to do so. Home and community environments are extremely potent factors in the development of such evils as delinquency and crime. Yet, schools have the responsibility to work for improvement of our society. Possible approaches to the treatment of behavior problems resulting from causes originating in the larger social order can be outlined:

1. Orientation to youth problems will help adolescents understand the reasons for military service, the problems of democracy, and the reasons for the necessity of participation in the processes of democracy.

2. Vocational education and guidance are essential to provide the youth with salable skills.

3. Instruction in school must encompass some of the pressing controversial issues of democracy in search for solutions. Typical of the unresolved problems which distress youth and the nation and which must be faced are the issues of segregation, unemployment, slums, and medical care.

4. Discussion of the individual's role in an industrial society must be

emphasized in secondary education. In this way the adolescent is made to consider his place in society, to recognize his obligations, and to sense his responsibilities.

5. Prejudices and special-interest narrowness can be counteracted by providing opportunities for heterogeneous groups to live and work together. Objective teaching of information to dispel irrational discrimination is a function of schools in a free society. The school can combat social class divisions by providing a truly democratic atmosphere of social cooperation.

6. Adapting the curriculum for the locality will serve to resist alien urban influences on the small localities.

7. The school can provide opportunities for the development of social skills of manners, cooperation, and teamwork.

8. Attention should be given in every course to citizenship from the local level to world responsibilities.

9. As much attention should be given to the imperative needs of our society as is given to the imperative needs of youth.

CHAPTER 17

DISCIPLINARY ASPECTS OF THE SECONDARY SCHOOL PROGRAM

Ideally, a well-disciplined school is recognized by the absence of disciplinary problems. The ideal is, of course, extremely difficult to obtain. Even in those schools where disciplinary problems are trivial, there is no guarantee that self-discipline is being learned. A repressive atmosphere can check the majority of disciplinary offenses. Self-discipline must be consciously sought and opportunities for training in self-control must be provided.

The problem of discipline runs through all aspects of the school program. A concerted attack on all deficient aspects of the program is required to cope with the problem of discipline on a school-wide basis.

We will at this point examine briefly some of the aspects of the high school program, giving emphasis to the opportunities available for developing self-discipline. As self-discipline develops, disciplinary problems decrease.

CURRICULAR OFFERINGS

The functions of the curriculum are the transmission of the cultural heritage to the pupils in proportion to their abilities to learn, the development of the mind, body, and character of the individual, and the development of self-disciplined citizens. Knowledge, citizenship, vocational preparation, and self-discipline are all fundamental aims of the curriculum.

Disciplinary problems arise whenever the curriculum is out of step with the needs of learners. Is not the curriculum out of step when we:

1. neglect the average learner, catering to either the slow or the fast student?

2. deny pupils opportunities for participation in formulating school policies?

3. gear instruction to a middle level, making no allowances for extremes in scholastic aptitude?

4. diminish vocational programs in order to augment the academic?

5. assist pupils in finding college placement and not job placement?

6. stress interscholastic athletics and starve intramural programs?

7. provide no time in the schedule for clubs and other worthwhile student activities?

8. pride ourselves on how many students go on to college but ignore students who go directly to work on graduation from high school?

9. feel no responsibility to students who have dropped out of school before graduating?

Disciplinary problems are fewer and the attainment of self-discipline is greater in a school that gears its curricular offerings to the needs of its students.

PROVISION FOR THE EXCEPTIONAL CHILD

Provision for the bright pupil, the average pupil, the slow pupil, and the handicapped pupil must be made in the entire curricular program and within each class. To diminish behavior problems and to permit maximum educational development, provision for the exceptional student is frequently made through (1) individualized instruction, (2) flexible programming of courses, (3) ability grouping, and (4) special classes.

For the gifted special opportunities need to be created in the form of extra work, thought-provoking problems, leadership responsibilities, special privileges, independent study, admission to night school for special courses, use of correspondence courses, cooperation with other educational agencies and institutions in the community, and acceleration in certain subjects.

Special classes are of particular necessity for the seriously retarded pupils who cannot hope to achieve much academic success in the regular classes.

Remedial classes and after-school instruction should be given to all those who need additional work. Special concessions in time and "standards" must be given to the physically and emotionally handicapped. By providing for the exceptional pupils the school can decrease the number of disciplinary problems.

PUPIL PARTICIPATION IN GOVERNMENT

Pupil participation in control and in government is one of the best ways for providing training in the democratic processes, for teaching group cooperation, for instruction in governmental operations, for training in citizenship, for raising the morale of the student body, for reducing teacher burdens, for facilitating administration, and for fostering self-discipline. Let us compare the practices of three high schools regarding pupil participation in government:

COMPARISON 1

School A. The senior high has a student council. The junior high school in the same building is not represented and has no council of its own. No student participation .on policy committees exists. The council is merely a rubber stamp of the principal. Discussion of school rules and regulations is not permitted anywhere in the school. Criticism of school policies is not allowed in the school newspaper. There is a corridor traffic squad.

School B. There is a student council with representation by junior and senior high schools. The council initiates many activities, subjected to the principal's veto. Discussion of policies is encouraged in the school paper and group guidance programs. No channels are provided for student participation on policy committees.

School C. There is a representative student council in this six-year high school. A student committee has regular representation on an advisory council which considers policy matters. Participation in control exists in the advisory councils, class activities, traffic squad, and classroom procedures.

Students in School A are subjects of the school, not citizens. They have been taught under a system of enforced obedience. This type of training is decidedly not the type required by a dynamic democratic society in which the welfare of all is conditioned by the competence of the individuals.

Even in the competitive world of work it has been found that democratic worker-manager cooperation in control is superior to exclusive management control. Golden and Ruttenberg conducted a well-known study of labor and management cooperation. They discovered that under those conditions in which labor and management both participated in research and planning, with workers sharing equitably in the profits, production soared. They conclude that when the workers have creative participation in the productive process, the prerogatives of management become more secure, though less exclusive.[1]

School B goes further in pupil participation in government than School A, but has not set channels of participation as effectively as has School C. Experiences in pupil participation must be started early in the school life of a class, in the primary grades. Beginning early is safer than attempting to thrust suddenly upon unprepared pupils in the secondary school a program of student participation in control. A plan of pupil participation can only be

[1] Clinton S. Golden, and H. J. Ruttenberg, *The Dynamics of Industrial Democracy* (New York: Harper & Row, 1942), p. 262.

started by the fullest cooperation between staff and students, by starting on a small scale, and by gradually increasing responsibilities as the students develop competencies in participation in government.

Staff attitudes are extremely important to the success or failure of pupil participation. Teachers must first be convinced of the merit of the program and be willing to give their complete support or the program is doomed to failure. If student participation in government is established with the idea of setting up a model form of democracy without the experience in democracy, it is better not to have any form of pupil participation in government at all.

Teachers and pupils alike may feel insecure at the first experimentation in pupil participation in government. Yet, it is to be emphasized that pupil participation does not mean that the pupils rule themselves.

Participation gives the students a psychological lift, makes them feel important, raises their morale, and provides training in self-discipline.

SUPPLEMENTARY ACTIVITIES

As we have seen in our commentary on the supplementary curriculum in Unit II, student activities have developed in response to the social needs of growing adolescents and to the diversified interests of the large numbers of children now being educated in our schools. Through student activities excess energies are absorbed in creative and educational pursuits. The supplementary program can provide training in group cooperation, can develop school spirit, can awaken interest, and can be used in solving adjustment problems of pupils. Since these activities are more informal than classroom situations, satisfactory teacher-pupil relationships have additional opportunities to develop.

The Association for Supervision and Curriculum Development reveals:

> . . . In most schools where participation was studied, it was found that rarely more than twenty percent of all students are actively involved in clubs, student government, and similar activities . . . those who do not participate tend to come from the sub-groups in the community which are already out of touch with each other and with the active groups.[2]

Teachers have an obligation, whether they sponsor an activity or not, to make the supplementary program a success. Among their duties are the encouragement of pupils to join activities, advice on the selection of activities, limitation of homework assignments on the eve of important school-wide functions, and provision for members of activities to make up instruction they have missed because of school-sponsored activities.

[2] *Fostering Mental Health in Our Schools* (Washington: Association for Supervision and Curriculum Development, N. E. A., 1950), p. 30.

Student activities are excellent substitutes for otherwise undesirable behavior. Through participation in control of supplementary programs—especially through the Student Council—pupils achieve additional training in self-discipline. They select activities they need, help to formulate policies concerning the program, charter activities through the Student Council, set dates for activities, make arrangements for their functioning, plan their programs, formulate goals, devise ways of reaching these goals, and determine qualifications for membership in their activities. There is a positive correlation between a well-balanced supplementary program and an absence of disciplinary problems.

TEACHER LOAD

To fulfill his job the classroom teacher has to have few enough pupils, classes, and assignments to give effective instruction and guidance.

COMPARISON 2

School A. Each teacher is assigned to six class periods per day. Classes average 35–40 pupils. In addition teachers have activities to sponsor. Physical education men receive supplementary pay for extra duties.

School B. Teachers average five class periods per day, 30–35 pupils per class, one study hall, one activity to sponsor plus added duties, faculty meetings, committee meetings after school. No extra pay for extra duties except for coaching.

School C. Teachers average five class periods per day, one study hall per day, one activity to sponsor. They have 2–3 free periods per week. School is dismissed last period once a month for in-service program. Other meetings outside of school hours. Extra pay is granted for extra duties. School time permitted at beginning of the year for home visits or conferences with parents.

School D. Teachers have four class periods per day. Classes are 25–35 pupils. One free period per day. There are no study halls.

School E. This school has gone into a number of team teaching programs. Teachers in the teams are assisted by teacher-aides and other clerical workers. Each team has one planning period per day. Responsibilities of teachers who are members of the team include instruction in large groups, direction of small group work, and assisting students in individual study.

Teaching loads vary with the community, depending on size of enrollments, number of staff available, and types of curricular offerings. Loads in typical school patterns run from an ideal of four class periods per day with 25–35 in a class as in School *D* to large groups six periods a day as in School *A*. In many communities swelling enrollments have caused schools to start double and even triple shift programs.

In classes too large the children are being short-changed in their education and the teachers are overworked. Teachers who must handle heavy assignments often become disillusioned and may either give up teaching entirely or simply attempt to keep order as best they can and let instruction suffer.

Schools *C* and *D* attempt to release their teachers through free periods during the week for preparation of classes, study, extra help to pupils, record-keeping, and conferences. School *E* seeks maximum effectiveness with large enrollments by a team approach. Provision of school time for planning, in-service training and conferences with parents contributes to high teacher morale, which in turn is reflected in student morale. Where teacher morale is low, student misbehavior is immediately detected.

If schools and communities are to expect teachers to accept tasks required by a modern program of education, provision for equitable loads and for school time for some of the assigned duties must be made. No teacher can adequately guide 150 to 200 young people each day. With smaller teaching loads teachers can get to know their pupils well and disciplinary problems may be expected to decrease.

GROUNDS AND PLANT

An attractive, well-planned, well-equipped, well-kept building and grounds will foster school spirit and pride, whereas dirty, run-down physical facilities will beget behavior problems. A casual visitor can surmise that disciplinary problems are many when he walks into a school and finds broken panes of glass, profane writings on the walls, streaks of paint on the doors and walls, holes in the plaster, and gum spattered on the floors.

Ways for developing pride in dull and poor plants have been found in soliciting help from students in the school and from adults in the community for cooperative projects of beautifying the grounds and plant and for construction of needed facilities.

It is important to develop within the students the attitude that school property is their property. One school, for example, with an excellent plant displays many reproductions of famous paintings throughout the school. All paintings are selected by the principal. In another school many paintings which have been done by the pupils themselves are displayed. In the school where the principal selects all paintings, though they add to the beauty of the school, an excellent opportunity for art appreciation by students and faculty is lost. If the paintings were selected by a student-faculty-principal committee, the paintings themselves would be more highly appreciated and studied. The selection process would provide an added opportunity for pupil participation in the affairs of the school.

As long as many students have the idea that the school, its buildings and grounds belong to the authorities who rule them, carelessness with public property will exist. If pupils are consciously taught through participation that the school, its plant and equipment belong to them all equally, pride in the school will develop.

When the foregoing aspects of the high school program are functioning well, behavior problems will be fewer and self-discipline will be encouraged.

Chapter 18

CORRECTIVE MEASURES AND PUNISHMENT

Discipline and punishment have been considered synonymous by many teachers. Punishments of varied sorts can be found in use in most high schools. In this section of the discussion we will consider a number of corrective measures and judge whether or not they are desirable, undesirable, or questionable techniques to use.

The employment of any corrective measure must be evaluated in terms of the philosophy of discipline a teacher has, the nature of the behavior, the nature of the pupil, and the objectives of the school. In the commentary that follows we will appraise fifteen disciplinary measures.

SIMPLE CONTROL

By simple control is meant a look at the offender, signifying disapproval, waiting for attention before continuing the instruction, a mild reproof, posing a question to a pupil whose attention has wandered, switching seats of offenders, movement of the teacher about the room to trouble centers, and laughing off trivial infractions.

ADVANTAGES

a. It is a fairly easy means of control.
b. It allows instruction to proceed.
c. It avoids unpleasant scenes.
d. There are few harmful effects on the personality.

DISADVANTAGES

a. This measure attacks surface behavior only.
b. It may be ineffective.
c. Success in using this technique depends largely on the personality of the teacher.

Much of the success in using simple control measures rests upon the tacitly implied dissatisfaction of the teacher. Most adolescents quickly comply with methods of simple control, since they are unaware of the exact nature of what the teacher is thinking. This system rests upon the authority of the teacher but may be found expedient in maintaining order in the classroom for instructional purposes and for the general welfare of the group. (In difficult, unruly classes, however, simple measures of control may be ineffective.)

INDIVIDUAL CONFERENCES WITH PUPILS

The individual conference between the pupil and the teacher is, by far, the most desirable single corrective measure that can be employed by the teacher. A serious and frank talk would appear to be the logical first step in the understanding of behavior problems.

ADVANTAGES

a. The individual conference provides an opportunity for a private talk between the teacher as a guidance person and the pupil who has exhibited a behavior problem.

b. It affords the teacher a chance to obtain further information.

c. It provides the pupil with a chance to express himself and to air his problems.

DISADVANTAGES

a. Many teachers are incapable of carrying on an interview or a conference with an offender because of (1) lack of knowledge, (2) lack of time, (3) lack of interest, (4) lack of understanding of adolescent problems, (5) feeling of moral indignation at the offender's actions, and (6) inability to achieve rapport between teacher and pupil.

All teachers should have some familiarity with the use of interview techniques. Conferences can be helpful if they are designed to understand the causes of misbehavior, to find out more about the problems the pupil has, and to interpret school regulations as desirable for individual and group welfare.

HOME-SCHOOL COOPERATION

This measure of control recognizes the fact that the behavior problems a child evidences may be rooted in his home environment. Genuine cooperation between home and school through conferences, home visits, and social contacts can achieve remarkable results, provided both the home and the school are sincere in wanting to help the child.

a. This affords an opportunity for establishing rapport between the home and the school.

b. Parent and teacher may supply each other with valuable information.

c. It provides opportunities for joint attack upon causes of misbehavior.

d. Visits provide opportunity to see the child in his home environment.

DISADVANTAGES

a. Teachers are not trained in many cases to deal with parents or to conduct home visits.

b. Teachers do not always understand causes of behavior themselves. They are unable, therefore, to interpret pupil behavior to parents.

c. It is sometimes difficult to get the parents into the school and for the teacher to find time to visit the home.

d. Too many reports annoy parents, who may feel that their child is being abused or that the teacher is shifting a problem to them.

Home-school cooperation can produce fruitful information and lead to correction of misbehavior. The method of handling the conferences or visits is important. Teachers must avoid "summoning" a parent. Parents readily resent this display of authority on the part of the teacher. The teacher-parent conference is certainly not an opportunity for the teacher to "tell off" the parent. This antagonizes the parents against the school, creates ill will, destroys good public relations, and defeats the purpose of solving the youth's problems. Tact and persuasion are called for in soliciting parental cooperation in treatment of behavior disorders.

RESTITUTION AND REPARATION

Restitution of things taken and reparation for things damaged or destroyed willfully are generally conceded to be effective and fair forms of punishment.

ADVANTAGES

a. Restitution and reparation associate the punishment in a natural way with the offense.

b. These measures teach the child that damage done through willful action on his part must be rectified.

c. These measures can be administered justly, fairly, impartially, and unemotionally.

DISADVANTAGES

a. Children may not have the money to pay for damages.

b. Children may obtain the money too readily from parents, thus destroying the educative values of the punishment.

To be effective this form of punishment must educate the child to realize that what he destroys affects the welfare of the entire group. It teaches him that he must make amends. The teacher's responsibility lies in explaining the reasons for the punishment to him and following through to see that restoration is made. If the child is financially unable to pay expenses of reparation, the school should find a way by which he may work out the damages and pay off his debt. Where parents are too free with money, the school should solicit their cooperation to make the punishment educative, permitting the child to work out his own debt to society.

LOSS OF PRIVILEGES

Loss of privileges, particularly those of a social nature, is generally accepted in the interests of training the child.

ADVANTAGES

a. This form of punishment enables the child to feel that, if his behavior destroys the group's effectiveness, people will disapprove of that action by not associating with him.

b. This measure corresponds to the type used to a large extent in the home. The child is accustomed to this form of punishment.

DISADVANTAGES

a. This means of control may, if wrongly used, deny the child the very thing that he may need most—social participation.

The child's behavior must be understood before loss of privileges is applied. Care must be exercised not to apply this sanction too long. Ways must be made available so that, after the pupil has had time to examine his conduct with the help of the teacher, he can restore himself to full privileges. This corrective measure is one method of teaching the child that privileges in a democracy have corresponding duties.

REWARDS AND PRIZES

Schools use various types of rewards and prizes to obtain specific kinds of student behavior.

ADVANTAGES

a. These are positive measures instead of negative.
b. They appeal to desires for recognition and approval.

DISADVANTAGES

a. Rewards may become ends in themselves instead of means to good conduct.

b. Rewards may not be made available to all students on an equal basis.

c. Tangible money and material prizes appeal to greed.

The use of rewards is justified if rewards are available to all and if they appeal to higher motives such as group welfare, citizenship, and service. Praise from the group, recognition of useful service by the school and local newspapers, certain exemptions, use of the student in assisting others, certificates of achievement, use of the honor rolls, and honor study halls under student leaders may be suitable rewards.

DETENTION

Detention, or keeping a student after school, is an ancient disciplinary device.

ADVANTAGES

a. Detention substitutes for harsher forms of punishment.

b. Detention serves as a deterrent for those who have something to do after school.

c. It is easily administered.

DISADVANTAGES

a. It does not consider causes of behavior.

b. The child can readily sense that he is keeping the teacher in at the same time and that the teacher is not anxious to remain.

c. It prevents the child from getting outside recreation and exercise after school.

d. It prevents the teacher from getting outside recreation and exercise after school.

e. It makes an unnecessary demand on the teacher's time.

f. Parents may need the child at home. Detention may alienate the parents.

g. The child may have a job after school. The home may need money from his work. Keeping the child from his work increases parental antagonism toward the school.

h. After-school appointments with the dentist or doctor, music lessons, and tutoring cause conflicts.

i. Conflicts arise with other school activities, particularly with sports and other extra-class activities. Frequently, this measure may cause friction with other faculty members who want the child for some purpose after school.

j. What to have the child do during detention becomes a problem. If he does nothing but sit, there is no worthwhile learning taking place. He may sit nursing his resentment. If he does homework, he is learning further to detest school, since his homework becomes punishment, or he may, in some cases, take the attitude that this is an opportunity to get his homework done so he will not have to do it later. This destroys the punishment effect of detention. If he does tasks other than homework, the punishment is no longer associated with the behavior for which he was detained.

k. This type of control is often used for all types of offenders, making little or no distinction in fitting the corrective measure to the offense and to the offender.

Teachers sometimes act rashly without understanding the behavior of the child and rapidly "sentence" the pupil to detention. This solves the problem of the teacher's indignation at the pupil's behavior but it does not help the pupil with his adjustment problem.

It is a frequent practice to send pupils to a detention room, where violators from all classes are kept under supervision of a teacher. The detention hall procedure is doubly unsound. Each behavior problem is the teacher's responsibility. The detention hall teacher is a policeman giving no help in solving the youth's behavior difficulty. Weak teachers make it difficult for their own colleagues by sending large numbers of pupils to detention, passing their problems on to someone else. The presence of fellow sufferers among the pupils serves to ease their burdens and lessens the corrective value of the measure. That this system is ineffective is seen by the large numbers of repeat offenders visiting the detention room during the year.

Detention after school can be justified on three grounds:

1. For extra help the teacher gives to the pupil.
2. To enable the pupil to make up work.
3. To hold individual conferences with the pupil.

If the practice of detention must be used, it should be understood by the pupils, teachers, and parents alike. Parents will then know what to expect and will not be angered by the child's remaining in school. This is but another phase of good public relations.

Detention at recess or noon is condemned by most educators, since it denies healthful opportunities to relieve excess energies during the day and recreation for the pupil and teacher alike.

DISMISSAL FROM CLASS AND ISOLATION

Some teachers send misbehaving pupils out of their classrooms or isolate disorderly pupils from the rest of the class.

ADVANTAGES

a. The teacher gets rid of the troublemaker or silences him.

b. This procedure may be effective, since it bars a child from association with his group.

DISADVANTAGES

a. Dismissal from class

1. This measure bars a pupil from necessary instruction.

2. It creates a scene and can be humiliating to the offender.

3. The pupil may become a hero, getting considerable attention.

4. This may be exactly what the pupil wants—relief from the boredom of the classroom situation.

b. Isolation: This means of control may not be harmful in the same classroom, but supervision is required if the pupil is isolated elsewhere.

c. Sending a pupil elsewhere in the building

1. A teacher in sending a pupil elsewhere in the building is shifting his burdens to another faculty member, who naturally resents the extra burdens. If a classroom teacher sends his problem cases to a study hall, then logically a study hall teacher should be able to send his behavior problems to the classroom teacher.

d. Sending pupils to the principal's office

1. The child is barred from instruction.

2. The teacher is transferring his problem to other authority.

3. The principal's time is consumed.

The practice of sending pupils to the principal's office may be justified in severe cases. But principals frown upon a large number of petty cases being sent to the office. The teacher who sends many pupils to the office is not fulfilling his responsibilities and is creating a "bogey-man" out of the principal.

In extreme circumstances sending a pupil to the office may be justified. But the following precautions must be taken:

1. The teacher must tell the child where to report. The teacher must make sure that the pupil gets to his destination and does not loiter about the building. The pupil should be instructed what to do if the principal is not in.

2. The teacher must report the incident either by going to the office with the offender, which means that the class is left to its own devices, or by a note sent to the principal, or by use of the intercommunication system. The teacher must be aware that the pupil can misrepresent the case if he goes to the principal alone.

3. The teacher should be aware of the principal's attitude concerning this practice. The teacher needs to know the principal's schedule. Since the principal's duties may be pressing, he may dismiss the offender with a simple warning. This will disturb the teacher who expects the principal to do something drastic, even though the offenders may be merely mischievous. Principals tend to deal gently with routine cases of misbehavior sent to their offices.

PUNISHING THE GROUP FOR THE OFFENSES OF ONE PERSON

Occasionally a teacher or administrator will punish a whole group when he is not able to discover which student in the group has committed some wrongdoing.

ADVANTAGES

a. It may be an expedient way of arousing group disapproval toward the offender.

DISADVANTAGES

a. It may align the group against the teacher.
b. It creates a hostile group climate.
c. It is patently unjust to punish the innocent for the offense of one guilty person.

This corrective measure is condemned by all educational authorities.

EXTRA TASKS

This punishment technique includes the assigning of additional homework, an extra project, janitorial work, and the writing of a sentence, for example, 500 times.

ADVANTAGES

There are no worthwhile advantages to this measure.

DISADVANTAGES

a. Punishment bears no connection to the behavior.
b. It creates added distaste for school work and destroys incentive to learn.

This corrective measure should be avoided.

ENFORCED APOLOGIES

Some teachers force students to apologize for wrongdoings.

ADVANTAGES

a. The teacher may be satisfied that social conventions have been observed.

DISADVANTAGES

a. It stirs up the pupil's resentment.
b. It embarrasses the pupil.

c. It teaches the pupil to be hypocritical if he gives an apology without meaning it.

If the pupil can be shown how his actions are undesirable, and if he can be induced to apologize with sincerity, the method may be useful. Otherwise, it is a poor practice.

LOWERING THE MARKS

It is relatively common to find teachers who lower the marks of students who misbehave.

ADVANTAGES

a. This procedure satisfies the teacher's need for surface order.

DISADVANTAGES

a. It does not treat causes of misbehavior.
b. It is a misuse of marks, which are supposed to be indications of achievement.

The teacher should not find it necessary to curb misbehavior by lowering a pupil's achievement grades.

OTHER UNDESIRABLE PUNISHMENTS

Further undesirable practices which most educators do not sanction are (1) personal indignities and tortures, (2) threats and warnings, (3) humiliation before others and ridicule, (4) satiation, or saturation-repetition of the offense ad nauseam, (5) money fines, and (6) nagging, scolding, tongue lashing, diatribes.

Questionable is the practice of demerits used in some schools. Though they may be effective in maintaining order, they do not attack causes of misbehavior. They entail unnecessary bookkeeping for already burdened teachers. Such time could be better given over to counseling and in-service study.

CORPORAL PUNISHMENT

Corporal punishment is rejected by most educational authorities, particularly its use on adolescents. Even those who recommend its use specify it as a last resort.

ADVANTAGES

a. It is drastic and dramatic.
b. It associates punishment with pain.
c. It relieves the teacher's needs.

DISADVANTAGES

a. It may humiliate an older pupil.

b. It may be ineffective with older pupils, who may not mind it at all.

c. It may create a personal battle between the pupil and teacher. The pupil may act in self-defense, further complicating the punishment.

d. It deepens resentment, creates a further hatred for school, arouses hostility toward all authority, and creates a feeling of injustice.

e. It may alienate parents.

Corporal punishment is based on the psychology of fear. The administration of corporal punishment presents a dilemma. For those pupils who do not fear it corporal punishment is no punishment at all. Some youngsters are willing to take their "licks." Some prefer corporal punishment to other types of punishment, such as suspension or loss of privileges or involvement of parents.

Corporal punishment is often administered in a state of anger. Punishment based on sound principles of mental hygiene must be unemotional. Corporal punishment may arouse the sentiment of the entire group against the teacher, thus augmenting the teacher's troubles.

This measure of control is prohibited by law in some states and by some school boards, though we do see some recent efforts of school systems to reinstate corporal punishment. Any teacher contemplating the use of corporal punishment should ascertain local and state laws on the measures to avoid possible legal action.

If acceptable ever, corporal punishment should be employed only with boys who are classified as "unruly," "defiant," and "completely unmanageable"; it should not be employed with girls. Harsh methods should be abandoned as soon as the individuals have developed the ability to manage themselves.

Corporal punishment should be used only after every other means is attempted. In applying this measure the following precautions need to be taken:

1. The pupil must be guilty of some major offense beyond all doubt.

2. The teacher must find out what the laws are regarding corporal punishment.

3. The school should obtain the parents' consent first.

4. The punishment should be administered in private with one adult witness present.

5. The person administering the punishment should not be brutal. He should not leave any marks, bruises, or scars on the body.

6. The face, ears, or head should not be struck.

7. Corporal punishment should not be administered in a rage.

8. The offense and the punishment should be recorded. A report should be filed in the principal's office.

Teachers may find it expedient to inform the parents of the child's misbehavior and may discover that the parents themselves in some cases will administer corporal punishment. This, too, must be done with caution, since some parents can be brutal.

Generally speaking, corporal punishment is an unsatisfactory corrective measure to use with adolescents.

SUSPENSION

The act of suspending a pupil from attendance in school for a stipulated period of time can be used with the reservation that it is a serious form of punishment.

ADVANTAGES

a. It removes the offender from the situation.
b. It allows the pupil time to consider the seriousness of his actions.

DISADVANTAGES

a. It bars the pupil from instruction, causing him to fall behind in his work.
b. It does not treat the causes of misbehavior.
c. It may be exactly what the pupil wants, reprieve from the scholastic setting.
d. It involves the parents, who may resent this extreme action.

Suspension may be justified only in very unusual circumstances and not for trivial misbehavior. Although action may start with the teacher, the principal and the board of education should be the only authorities to suspend a pupil. Pupils who are suspended must be permitted to make up the work they have missed. Suspension should be revoked as soon as the pupil is aware of the seriousness of his actions.

EXPULSION

Expulsion is considered desirable only as the very last measure that a school can take. It is reserved for those cases of erratic behavior for which there is no hope for improvement under school conditions. The welfare of the group has to be seriously endangered to justify expulsion.

ADVANTAGES

a. It empowers the school to get rid of extreme deviates, such as mentally deranged youth, severe delinquents, homosexuals, etc.

DISADVANTAGES

a. It removes the pupil from a normal setting.

b. It alienates the parents.

Expulsion is usually regulated by state law. The principal or superintendent and the board of education must be the final authorities for expulsion. In expelling a student within the compulsory age limits of education, provision must be made for other instruction, such as committal to an institution. Expulsion arouses public interest, but if it is justifiable, public sympathy will support the administration.

GUIDELINES ON CORRECTIVE MEASURES

1. Corrective measures must be based upon the understanding of the student and sound guidance procedures.

2. The purpose of any correctional device is to improve the adjustment of the individual and of the group.

3. Measures must be taken for the welfare of the individual and for the welfare of the group. A measure applied to an individual must not be destructive either of the individual's personality or of the group climate. In case a choice has to be made between the welfare of the individual and the welfare of the group, the group's welfare must take precedence.

4. In using punishment the simple measures should be used before resorting to the more severe kinds.

5. Punishment should be administered impersonally, objectively, unemotionally, and privately.

6. The corrective measure should fit the offense and the offender. Intent of the offender should affect the choice of corrective measures.

7. All sources of idleness and lack of interest must be eliminated and all preventive measures taken prior to using corrective measures.

8. Punishment has to be certain.

9. Fixed penalties should not be established. They cannot anticipate all forms of misconduct. They may encourage pupils to "pay the price." They erroneously assume that all offenses of the same type are actually identical and that the same corrective measures should be applied.

10. Punishment should be exercised swiftly, though at times, a short delay may be effective to enable the pupil to consider his actions.

11. Teachers must remember that most offenses are not personally directed at them, though it may seem so on the surface.

12. Desirable corrective measures are simple control, individual conferences, cooperation with parents, restitution and reparation, loss of privileges, and the use of rewards.

13. Undesirable or questionable measures are detention after school, dismissal from class, sending to the office, punishing the group, extra tasks, enforced apologies, lowering the marks, personal indignities and tortures, threats and warnings, humiliation, sarcasm and ridicule, satiation, money fines, nagging and scolding, and demerits.

14. Corporal punishment, suspension, and expulsion are to be used in extreme situations only and then with appropriate precautions.

A word might be added about our "tough" schools, the "Blackboard Jungles" sometimes found in large cities. It should be pointed out that the blackboard jungles are explosive culminations of all categories of causes of behavior problems brought together into one volatile institution. Perhaps the best thing we could do with our blackboard jungles is to close them and start over. It might be desirable to split up their student bodies among well-disciplined schools or create special schools for difficult and delinquent cases, as has been done in the "600" and "700" schools of New York City. It might even be desirable to reverse the trend in bus routes and take the urban children of our blackboard jungles into the country environment. Surely, the cost of transportation for purposes of re-education of these victims of educational anarchy would be cheaper to the state and nation than the price of crime that is bred in this unwholesome atmosphere. We would be just as mistaken, however, to believe that the blackboard jungle with every conceivable problem is the typical American high school as we would be to paint a utopian picture of a school without the blemish of a problem.

The strength of America lies not in the atypical blackboard jungles nor in idealistic utopias but in the backbone of our strong, wholesome American high schools.

BASIC CONSIDERATIONS ABOUT DISCIPLINE

DISCIPLINE IS AN EXTREMELY COMPLEX QUESTION

The roots of behavior problems reach deep into the character of the disturbed individual, into the composition of the group, into the home and community environment, and into the larger social order. Teachers who believe they experience no disciplinary problems because they constantly suppress the forces at work may be contributing to more serious maladjustments either in the present school life of the pupil or at a later stage in the child's growth. It is difficult to take time to discover the causes of problem behavior, to counsel the student, and to feel genuine concern for the student's difficulties. Yet it is only through complete, well-rounded growth in every aspect of the pupil's social and emotional as well as intellectual development that the child is able to take his place in present-day complex society with a minimum of maladjustment.

THE AIM OF DISCIPLINE IS SELF-DISCIPLINE

The aim of discipline in this society is the development of self-disciplined citizens for democracy. High schools must be as fervid about the creation of democratic citizens as the totalitarian societies are in the creation of citizens for their cultures. This nation has produced a unique civilization. It has sought through one of the noblest experiments in history to extend to every child a free public school education.

IT IS IMPOSSIBLE TO WRITE A PRESCRIPTION FOR ONE METHOD OF DISCIPLINE WHICH WOULD BE APPLICABLE TO ALL PROBLEM CASES

Methods of discipline used by a teacher will vary with the individual, with the school, with the home, with the community, with the teacher, and with the group. Methods will differ with the behavior shown, even with the weather, the day of the week, the physical condition of the child on the day that misbehavior is apparent, the teacher's condition on that day, and the condition of the school and classroom on that day. This explains why it is impossible to write an advance prescription for any specific type of behavior disorder. In fact, one cannot anticipate in advance the ingenious and varied types of misconduct that may arise.

SUMMARY

The type of discipline sought by American high schools is self-discipline. Discipline should be conceived of as a problem permeating the entire school program and organization. This unit attempts to convey basic understandings needed for coping with the universal problem of discipline. It suggests possible courses of remedial and punitive action for correction of misbehavior. It places misbehavior in its psychological, sociological, and philosophical setting.

CLASS AND EVALUATION ACTIVITIES

1. Write your definition of discipline and read to the class. Compare and discuss the various definitions.

2. List common behavior problems that teachers encounter.

3. Define *(a)* retributive, *(b)* punitive, *(c)* reformative, and *(d)* preventive discipline. Decide which of these types of discipline is best.

4. Observe and record ten instances of misbehavior and the methods the teachers used in handling the situations. Analyze and criticize.

5. Observe and record ten simple techniques teachers use for keeping their classes, pupils, and learning situations under control.

6. Find out the policy of a high school or high schools on corporal punishment and detention. Interview the principals and several teachers regarding the effectiveness of these two corrective measures.

7. Debate the topic, "Resolved: That corporal punishment should be banned by law in the schools of this state."

8. Conduct a panel discussion or buzz groups on "How Do We Achieve Self-Discipline?"

9. Observe and record or recall from personal experience peculiar mannerisms or traits of teachers which could provoke disciplinary problems.

10. *a.* Rank in order of seriousness the twenty behavior problems below. Number one will be the behavior problem you consider most serious, number twenty, least serious. Keep your ranking exercise in your notebook until the conclusion of your study of discipline.

Ranking Exercise

Rank these behavior problems in order of seriousness. Rank from 1 to 20, 1 being the most serious behavior problem in your estimation.

____ Laziness	____ Stealing
____ Disorderliness in class	____ Untruthfulness
____ Depression	____ Overcriticalness of others
____ Unsocialness	____ Cheating
____ Fearfulness	____ Truancy
____ Suspiciousness	____ Destroying school property
____ Cruelty	____ Impertinence
____ Sensitiveness	____ Obscene notes
____ Shyness	____ Disobedience
____ Resentfulness	____ Selfishness

b. Have several counselors or psychologists or psychiatrists or mental hygienists rank the same behavior problems. Compare their rankings with rankings made by students in the class. See if there is any appreciable difference in the rankings. Account for noticeable differences.

11. Take the *Minnesota Teacher Attitude Inventory*. Compare your scores against the norms furnished in the test manual. (See p. 377 for source of this inventory.)

12. Search the newspapers and magazines for court cases arising from the use of harsh corrective measures in schools.

13. Poll a faculty for their views on selected corrective measures, such as expulsion, suspension, corporal punishment, loss of privileges, extra homework, janitorial tasks, lowering the student's marks, etc.

14. Conduct a class discussion on which works better—reward or punishment, the carrot or the goad.

15. Make a case study of a student who is a serious disciplinary problem.

16. Hold a class discussion on "Why Is Self-Discipline Necessary in a Democracy?" Contrast this type of discipline with types found in Nazi Germany or Soviet Russia.

17. Invite a psychiatrist or psychologist to talk to the class on his views on behavior problems and discipline.

18. Invite a police officer or state trooper or a jurist or a penologist to talk to the class on his views on discipline.

19. Arrange a panel discussion on "How Much Truth Is There to the Saying, 'Spare the Rod and Spoil the Child'?" Members of the panel could be a mother, a father, a teacher, a clergyman, a policeman, a psychologist, and a sociologist.

20. Prepare individual oral reports to the class showing the relation-

ship between discipline and *(a)* health, *(b)* socioeconomic background of the pupil, *(c)* group pressures, *(d)* methods of instruction, *(e)* curriculum of the school, and *(f)* personality of the teacher.

21. Study the following disciplinary measures and decide if they are desirable, undesirable, or questionable for use in the school. Place a check for each measure in the appropriate column. Keep this exercise in your notebook with the conclusion of your study of discipline.

Disciplinary Measures

Do you believe the following widely used disciplinary measures are desirable or undesirable? Place a check in the *D* column if you believe the measure is *desirable,* in the *U* column if you believe the measure is *undesirable,* and in the *Q* column if you believe the measure is *questionable.*

Disciplinary Measures	D	U	Q
1. Simple control (waiting for class attention, looking at a student, etc.)			
2. Individual conferences with students			
3. Home-school cooperation			
4. Threats			
5. Sarcasm and ridicule			
6. Money fines			
7. Personal indignities			
8. Satiation (repetition of the offense ad nauseam)			
9. Restitution and reparation			
10. Loss of privileges			
11. Use of rewards and prizes			
12. Dismissal from class			
13. Isolation			
14. Detention after school			
15. Extra tasks			
16. Punishing the group			
17. Enforced apologies			
18. Lowering the marks			
19. Corporal punishment			
20. Suspension			
21. Expulsion			

22. Consult recent manuals of the U. S. Army for the Army's current views on discipline.

23. Prepare small group reports to the class on the topics, Juvenile Delinquency, Crime in the United States, Prisons, Juvenile Offenders and the Law, Slums, Minority Groups, and Sociological Changes in American Life.

24. Answer in writing or discuss the following:

a. Give five categories of causes of behavior problems.

b. List one of the specific causes of behavior problems under each category and give a possible remedial measure for that cause.

c. Show the relationship between the following aspects of the high school and discipline:

    1. Pupil participation in government

    2. Scheduling

    3. Teacher load

    4. Marking practices

d. List five desirable corrective measures which a teacher or school can use.

e. List five undesirable corrective measures in use in schools. State why these measures are undesirable.

f. Contrast the advantages and disadvantages of the following corrective measures:

    1. Detention after school

    2. Corporal punishment

    3. Suspension

    4. Expulsion

State your own position on each of these corrective measures.

SELECTED BIBLIOGRAPHICAL REFERENCES

1. Larson, Knute G. and Karpas, Melvin R. *Effective Secondary School Discipline.* Englewood Cliffs, N. J.: Prentice-Hall, 1963. 206 pp.

    Generalized treatment of the topic of discipline. Easy reading. Review of teaching techniques and administrative policies and practices that have a bearing on discipline.

2. Sheviakov, George V. and Redl, Fritz. *Discipline for Today's Children and Youth.* Revised by Sybil K. Richardson. Washington: Association for Supervision and Curriculum Development, N.E.A., 1956. 64 pp.

Highly readable booklet on the meaning of discipline, democratic principles of discipline, and discipline in classroom practice. Emphasizes the application of psychological theory to problems in the classroom. First issued in 1944.

INSTRUCTIONAL AIDS AND SOURCES

1. Film: *Maintaining Classroom Discipline.* 14 min. Sound. Black and white. New York: McGraw-Hill Book Co.

   This instructional film contrasts two approaches to classroom discipline. It demonstrates rigid, authoritarian methods of control and contrasts these with methods based upon sound psychological principles.

2. Test: Walter W. Cook, Carroll H. Leeds, and Robert Callis. *Minnesota Teacher Attitude Inventory.* New York: The Psychological Corporation, 1951.

   Interesting standardized inventory consisting of one hundred and fifty statements about children and teaching. The person taking the test expresses agreement, disagreement, or indecision on each of the statements.

UNIT VII

EVALUATION

OBJECTIVES OF UNIT VII

At the conclusion of his reading and correlated study-discussion activities the reader should

A. understand that
1. evaluation is a part of the instructional process;
2. evaluation is a continuing process;
3. there are numerous means of evaluating pupil progress and achievement;
4. evaluation means more than testing and measurement;
5. the effects of evaluation on the pupil are serious and long-lasting;
6. tests and marks are a source of great concern and anxiety to students and parents;
7. evaluative techniques appraise the teacher's effectiveness as well as the pupils' progress and achievement.

B. show appreciation for
1. a well-planned evaluation program,
2. the relative difficulty of determining reliable and valid evaluative techniques,
3. well-constructed teacher-made tests,
4. a well-balanced testing program,
5. a marking system which has been carefully worked out and explained to all affected by it,
6. a reporting system which truly and accurately reports.

C. adopt attitudes of
1. willingness to seek reliable and valid means of evaluation,
2. care in test construction,
3. caution in assigning marks,
4. readiness to explain to students and parents marks assigned,
5. desire to make marks reliable indicators of progress and achievement,
6. awareness of the difficulty of reporting progress and achievement in symbols,
7. willingness to use varied means of evaluation.

D. be able to demonstrate skill in
1. identifying good test items,
2. constructing essay tests,
3. constructing objective tests,

4. scoring tests,
5. using means of evaluation other than tests,
6. determining marks,
7. reporting pupil progress and achievement.

E. know the following:
  1. the meaning of the terms
    a. evaluation
    b. measurement
    c. essay tests
    d. objective tests
      1) recall
      2) completion
      3) true-false (alternate-response)
      4) multiple choice
      5) rearrangement
      6) matching
  2. procedures for determining marks,
  3. various systems of reporting and varied types of report cards.

CHAPTER 19

THE MEANING OF EVALUATION

Evaluation is a part of our daily life. We decide one commodity is better than another. We choose one way of solving a problem over another. We try out a new technique and make conclusions about its efficacy. We not only evaluate other persons, products, and techniques but we also evaluate ourselves. We are constantly evaluating our own achievements. Sometimes we are pleased with our own performance, sometimes we are our own worst critics. Some of us underrate our accomplishments, some overrate them.

WHAT IS EVALUATION?

Evaluation is the process of making judgments about the worth or value of an item or a person. Evaluation is the process of appraising a person or thing. Translated into a school situation, evaluation is the process of appraising pupil progress and achievement. Generally, evaluation as applied to the school is the process a teacher follows in judging pupil progress and achievement. The pupil frequently enters into the process of evaluation by judging his own progress and achievement and by evaluating with others the success of his learning group on some project or portion of a course. The skilled teacher helps the student and the group to develop these skills of self-evaluation.

Another kind of evaluation continuously in operation in the classroom is the pupils' evaluation of the teacher's progress and achievement. This third kind of evaluative process is rarely recognized formally. Pupils do make judgments on the skill, scholarship, and personality of their teachers but they do not normally voice their judgments to the teacher himself, unless, of course, their judgments are positive and favorable. Never do the pupils top off their evaluations with a symbol or grade for the teacher.

Since we are primarily concerned with the classroom teacher, we will but note that in a school situation principals and supervisors evaluate teacher performance and pupil progress. The school board and the lay public make judgments on the achievement of pupils, teachers, and administrators.

EVALUATION AS PROCESS

Since evaluation is present continuously and in so many different situations, we have used the term "process," instead of "act." We speak of evaluation as a process of making appraisals rather than as an act of making appraisals. The distinction is more than a semantic difference. An act implies a single, completed effort. When we make global assertions such as "That boy is stupid" or "That girl is lazy" or "He should not be in my class," we are often following the conception of evaluation as an act rather than as a process. When we base our judgments of pupil performance on limited data, we are using evaluation as a momentary, finite, terminal activity. Accurate evaluation can never be momentary, finite, or terminal. Rarely is a learner "stupid" in all areas of human endeavor or even in all aspects of one area of human endeavor. Rarely is a learner "lazy" in respect to all subjects or activities or even in all aspects of one subject or activity. The process of evaluation seeks out strengths and weaknesses, likes and dislikes. Evaluation is a never-ending process. Students develop and change as they mature. The progress made by individual students in one school year can be astounding. The process of evaluation considers pupil progress and achievement in depth over a period of time. Evaluative judgments must be based on ample evidence. The teacher must be aware that even the best judgments are subject to error.

Through the process of evaluation we decide whether or not we have accomplished our objectives. We have then carried through a program of learning experiences. We appraise pupil's achievement and our success in presenting a topic. We ask ourselves if we are moving toward our predetermined goals. As we move through the study of a particular topic, we revise our goals and activities wherever evaluative procedures indicate revision is necessary. When we have completed the study of a topic, we attempt through evaluative means to determine how successful we have been in reaching our objectives.

MEASUREMENT AND TESTING

We should distinguish "evaluation" from two of its phases, "measurement" and "testing." Measurement and testing are both parts of the total process of evaluation. Testing is the act of employing instruments which seek to measure progress and achievement. Measurement is the act of calculating the amount or degree of progress and achievement. Most tests used in the classroom are written exercises created by the teacher or standardized tests from test publishers. Tests are the instruments used in measurement. Tests yield numerical scores which teachers can inspect, average, calculate, and convert to symbols for reporting purposes. We use test scores to measure the amount or degree of pupil progress and achievement. Measurement is the system of devising, administering, and scoring tests. It is a system of counting, figuring, and interpreting scores. Measurement can involve scaling scores, establishing curves, and using norms. Tests are the means of measurement.

Teachers who are overly preoccupied with test scores and letter grades limit their concept of evaluation to testing and measurement. They utilize almost exclusively formal written tests as their tools of evaluation They attempt to reduce the evaluation of learning outcomes to a set of scores and symbols. The usual classroom test lends itself best to the measurement of subject-matter achievement. The teacher whose objectives are limited to subject-matter achievement may very well be satisfied with testing as his only means of evaluation. But what of the learning objectives such as attitudes and appreciations? They do not lend themselves so readily to precise measurement. It is difficult, if not impossible, for the teacher to create a valid and reliable instrument for the measurement of attitudes and appreciations. Must we then ignore these vital learning objectives? If we agree that attitudes and appreciations are worthy objectives, then we should seek ways to evaluate the attainment of these objectives. We must use evaluative techniques in addition to tests. We will use means which will not necessarily follow the principles of precise measurement. We may have to find new means for reporting symbols of pupil progress. Evaluation is a much broader process than either testing or measurement. Testing and measurement are significant parts of the process of evaluation but should not be accepted as the entire process. We limit our evaluative process to testing and measurement for varying reasons.

1. *We are not clear on our educational purposes.* We seek the development of facts and skills but ignore or play down other outcomes of learning.

2. *We are deceived by the apparent objectivity of measurement techniques.* We deal with numbers. We can set an arbitrary passing point. We can set up scales for converting numerical scores to letter grades. We are often unaware of the lack of validity and reliability in the testing instruments used.

3. *We are accustomed to measurement techniques as the principal evaluative system in high school and college, and to a lesser extent, perhaps, in some elementary schools.* We have carried our report cards home with their quota of *A*'s, *B*'s, *C*'s, *D*'s, and *F*'s. As students we have experienced the system of measurement in action. As teachers we perpetuate the system with which we have had experience.

4. *Tests are dramatic.* They serve to arouse student interest in the course. Since they are weighted so heavily and since they hold such a prominent place in the academic scheme of things, students study for the tests.

5. *Tests are widely used outside the classroom as well as in school.* The public is test-conscious. We are in an era of great stress on testing of all kinds. This general receptivity to testing makes it relatively simple for the classroom teacher to limit his evaluative techniques to testing.

Testing will and should continue to hold a prominent place in the process of evaluation. The classroom teacher can perfect his skills of testing so that tests will represent reasonably accurate appraisals of subject matter achievement. He will bring into his repertoire of evaluative techniques means of evaluation in addition to the usual classroom tests.

The following discussion is concerned with the various phases of evaluation, including testing and test construction, forms of evaluation other than tests, determining and assigning marks, reporting marks, and promotion of pupils. As we move into more specific areas of evaluation we should keep in mind the following general principles:

PRINCIPLES OF EVALUATION

1. *Evaluation is a continuous process.* The teacher evaluates pupil progress and achievement daily. Pupils constantly evaluate their own performance.

2. *Evaluative techniques should be related to the objectives of learning.* They should be designed to determine whether the learning objectives have been met. Some effort should be made to appraise success in each of the planned objectives of instruction.

3. *Evaluation should be conducted in a variety of ways.* The teacher should not limit himself to the use of one specific technique such as, for example, objective tests. The teacher can use formal means of evaluation such as essay and objective tests as well as informal means such as observation and oral questioning.

4. *The major function of evaluation is assistance to the pupil.* Evaluation should reveal pupil strengths and weaknesses. Evaluative techniques should provide diagnoses of pupil achievement so that pupils may work to overcome their weaknesses. The major function of evaluation is not the accumulation of test scores nor the calculation of marks nor the provision of a basis for report cards. These latter are, of course, tasks of the teacher but they are by-products of evaluation, not the central purpose.

5. *Evaluation provides the teacher with necessary information for improving his instructional program.* Evaluative techniques will reveal areas

where pupils need further help as well as areas that pupils have mastered. The results of evaluation should continuously affect the teacher's planning.

THE PURPOSES OF TESTING

Testing occupies a time-honored position in our schools. Indeed, it would be difficult for us to imagine an instructional program without testing. Pupils are conditioned from the earliest grades to undergo tests of various types. They approach tests in varying frames of mind. Many pupils take tests in stride as an inevitable, though often unpleasant, part of the educational process. For some students tests represent a challenge. For others each test is a traumatic experience. The extent of the trauma depends upon the stress that teachers and parents have placed on the tests. It depends also on the weight assigned to the tests by the teacher for purposes of marking.

Stress is an appropriate word to use when we refer to testing, for it has a two-fold meaning. On one hand, it means "emphasis" and on the other hand, it implies "anxiety." We are placing considerable emphasis today on academic achievement and college preparation. Our college-conscious students and their parents are greatly worried over the often reported lack of room for students in colleges. Consequently, scholastic competition is keen. Tests are the instruments of scholastic competition. Pupils not only take the teachers' quotas of tests but also enter into a variety of merit and scholarship examinations. The parents of college-bound students are most anxious that their children obtain high test scores and marks, scholarships to ease the financial burden, and admission to the college of their choice.

Tests are used to fulfill a number of purposes:

EVALUATION OF INSTRUCTION

Tests provide an indication of the effectiveness of instruction. When a class performs at a high level on a well-constructed teacher-made test, the teacher may feel that he has been successful in reaching the objectives evaluated in the particular test. When a class as a whole performs poorly on a test, there is a strong possibility that the instruction has not been effective. As a general rule, when more than half of a class receive failing or close to failing grades on a test, the teacher should analyze the preceding instruction, determine the difficulties of the students, and give remedial instruction where needed. When a class as a group achieves poor results on a test, the scores made by the students should not be counted. After a period of review and further instruction a second test can be administered. If it then appears that the class as a group has achieved satisfactory results, test scores can be recorded.

Principals often gauge the effectiveness of a teacher's instruction by analyzing scores made by pupils on both teacher-made and standardized tests. They are often more concerned with test results on standardized tests, in order to make comparisons between performance of pupils in their schools with performance of pupils elsewhere throughout the nation. They like, with some justification, to be able to tell parents that instruction in their school compares favorably with the best instruction to be found in the nation.

If the standardized tests are carefully selected and if they represent a fair approximation of what is being taught in the courses that use the tests, it is helpful to examine the results made by pupils on standardized tests. The test results should be considered informational only. They may or may not reveal needed directions in instruction in an individual school. The individual teacher must decide whether the test results have meaning for him with his particular classes. If the teacher has had no control over the selection of a test, as in a state-wide testing program, the test may not be valid for his classes. For example, in the field of foreign languages, a standardized test may measure achievement in reading and writing skills. The pupils of a teacher who has emphasized speaking and understanding the language may not perform as well on the standardized test of reading and writing at the beginning stages of their instruction. A principal inspecting the test results might conclude erroneously that instruction in foreign languages in his school was ineffective. He might even wrongly ask his teacher to revise his program so that students achieve higher scores on the standardized tests. What the principal should do is to find out if the particular test is appropriate for the instruction in his school. If the test is not appropriate, then it should not be used.

If a test is clearly not appropriate, it is a much more sound practice to change or eliminate the test than to change the instructional program. A test should never dictate the instructional program. When undue emphasis is given to standardized tests, particularly if they are used by principals to judge effectiveness of instruction, teachers tend to teach so as to have their pupils do well on the tests. When this happens in a school, the teacher's individual creativity is stifled. He finds it more difficult to plan unique programs for his particular classes. One of the most critical problems in the field of evaluation today is how to utilize standardized tests in the school without harming both teacher and pupil creativity.

DIAGNOSTIC FUNCTION

Tests reveal difficulties pupils are experiencing. They show points that pupils have mastered and places where pupils need help. They provide the teacher with information he can use in planning his next lessons. Studying the results of a test he has administered, the teacher can decide whether he must go back and review points covered or whether he can proceed with new material.

REVIEW AND SUMMARY

Tests serve as a review and summary of the important features of instruction during the preceding period. In preparing a test the teacher selects for inclusion the most important points. Attention of the pupils is in this way called to the more significant aspects. Appearance of selected items on a test serves to emphasize and reinforce in the pupils' minds the essential features of the previous instruction.

SOURCE OF MOTIVATION

Tests act as extrinsic forms of motivation. Students who wish to do well on the tests will be motivated to study. Teachers are prone to overdo this function of testing. You will often hear teachers say, "This will be on the test." "You'd better study this; it will be on next Thursday's test." "Tomorrow we'll begin our review for the test." "You'd better listen so you'll do well on the test." Pupils get caught up in the spirit of testing by asking such questions as, "Will we have this on the test?" "What will the test cover?" "How much will the test count?" Realizing the powerful effect that tests may have on a group, teachers sometimes use tests as disciplinary measures to keep a group under control. It is not uncommon to hear a teacher exclaim, "If you're not quiet, I'll give you a test." This practice cannot be defended. The test becomes a punitive device, rather than the instructional device it should be. The use of tests as disciplinary measures reveals a weakness in the teacher. The motivational aspects of testing should be kept on a positive plane and should not be permitted to degenerate into negative and punitive measures.

INDICATORS OF PUPIL PROGRESS

By administering a series of tests during the course of the school year the teacher is able to see some of the progress made by his pupils. After each test the teacher can determine whether his pupils have continued to make satisfactory progress. The teacher will find it helpful to have the pupils maintain files of their tests, either in their notebooks or in folders kept in the classroom. In this way they have a continuing record of their performance. Samples of the pupils' tests are often of great benefit when parents come to see the teacher about their children's work.

INFORMATION FOR PLACEMENT

Tests are widely used to make decisions about a pupil's placement in the school. They supply part of the information needed in sectioning or grouping pupils. Teachers of advanced courses can decide with the help of test data whether pupils are ready for the advanced levels of a subject. For example, a standardized or teacher-prepared test of first-year algebra can be used in helping to decide if a pupil is ready for second-year algebra. Decisions of this type are common in the case of students transferring into a school. Decisions on placement in the individual courses are most difficult when the school to which a pupil is transferring has received no records of the pupil's academic work. Placement tests assist school officials in overcoming this difficulty.

DATA FOR MARKING

Tests provide statistical data which the teacher can use, in part, as bases for marking. Since teachers are charged with the responsibility of determining and reporting marks for pupils in their courses, they must find means of gathering data about the pupils' achievement. Tests offer some tangible evidence of achievement. Since tests play such a large part in school marking practices, they should be as reliable and valid measures of achievement as possible. The more reliable and valid the tests, the more reliable and valid are the marks that are placed on the students' report cards.

Tests provide, then, an indication of the effectiveness of instruction, diagnosis of learning difficulties, review and summary of important points, a source of motivation, indications of pupil progress, information for placement in courses, and data for marking purposes.

CHAPTER 20

TYPES OF TESTS

In Unit V we considered the nature and types of standardized tests, including intelligence tests, achievement tests, interest inventories, aptitude tests, and personality tests. At this point we will confine our attention to achievement tests created by the classroom teacher. If the teacher becomes involved in intelligence, interest, aptitude, or personality testing, he must rely on commercially prepared standardized instruments. Consequently, the classroom teacher is not customarily occupied in the production of instruments other than tests of achievement. The teacher has a primary interest in learning how his pupils are progressing in his course. He must continuously design achievement tests to measure his pupils' progress and achievement. He is not vitally concerned with nationwide or statewide or even local norms. He is interested in knowing how well his pupils have achieved the goals that together they have set out to achieve. The background information secured by the administration of tests of intelligence, interest, or aptitude may prove helpful to him, but this information is tangential to his major concern: appraising the accomplishments of his pupils in their immediate studies. He must create his own tests in the light of the experiences of his own classes.

Standardized tests cannot replace the teacher-prepared tests; they may only supplement them. However appealing the use of standardized tests might seem, as long as the teacher holds a teaching position he will continue to prepare tests for his own special classes. On the basis of his own tests and whatever additional data he may have the teacher will determine and assign marks. From his knowledge of the material his pupils have studied and from his knowledge of the pupils themselves, the teacher can create test items that he knows his pupils can handle. The preparation, administration, scoring, and use of teacher-made tests deserve more than cursory study in the education of the teacher. Testing requires on the part of the teacher specialized knowledge and skill which can be developed with some experience.

DECISIONS ON TESTING

As the teacher plans his tests, he is confronted with a number of decisions. Each time he wishes to give a test he must make several choices:

WRITTEN VERSUS ORAL

Should the pupils respond in written form to written questions, in written form to oral questions, in oral form to oral questions, or in oral form to written questions? By and large tests in most classrooms of the secondary school require written responses to written test questions. The decision to use written tests is a practical consideration in most cases. Large enrollments make it difficult and often impossible to use oral tests to any great extent.

The preparation, conduct, and scoring of oral examinations are more time-consuming than is true of written examinations. There are some few teachers who write out their tests and then administer them orally to their students. Generally speaking, this is an inefficient use of class time. The oral reading of test items keeps all pupils at the same pace. Some pupils will require a longer period of time on some items. Others might quickly finish the whole test if it were presented in written form and turn to other constructive activities. Errors creep into orally administered tests when pupils misunderstand the teacher or fail to hear cor.ectly what he has said. Only in cases where the objectives demonstrate a need for this type of test should it be used. A dictation exercise in English or a foreign language or in shorthand can obviously be conducted properly only through oral means. But it is a sheer waste of time for a social studies or mathematics teacher to stand in front of his class and read aloud test questions. As a practical or frequent testing procedure the oral examination can be ruled out.

The teacher may wish to administer an individual oral examination on occasion to a pupil who cannot for one reason or another express himself in written form. If the teacher wishes to know specifically if the pupil has understood the work covered and not necessarily whether the pupil can write well or express his thoughts clearly in writing, he may schedule an oral examination for a student. He may wish to do the same for a pupil who cannot read as well as he should for his grade level. In some cases the teacher may wish to follow up a written test with an oral test.

The written test which is duplicated and distributed to the pupils for their written answers continues to be the most feasible type of test for the majority of classes. The foreign language and the shorthand teacher, and to a lesser extent a few others such as the music teacher, English teacher, and speech and dramatics teacher, will utilize oral questions and oral tests. Even they, however, will seek to economize in the use of their valuable time. They will keep oral examinations to the minimum number essential and limit the length of responses. A Spanish teacher readily discovers, for example, that he can save himself five hours in scoring taped oral talks of one hundred and fifty students if he restricts the length of the talks to three minutes instead of five. The French teacher can check quickly the students' abilities to comprehend orally by having them respond to oral questions with a simple written symbol, a T for True or an F for False, or a plus sign for True and a minus sign for False. The decision to use either written or oral test questions depends not only upon the objectives being evaluated but also upon the time available to students for answering and to the teacher for administering and correcting.

GROUP VERSUS INDIVIDUAL

Should the test be administered to the class as a whole or individually to each student? Group tests conserve the teacher's time. Individual tests would not represent a realistic choice in most circumstances. The constant demands on the teacher's time would not permit him to schedule individual tests for large numbers of students. True, there are some limited uses of the individual test that are lost in group testing. When the teacher administers a test individually to a pupil, he can observe how the pupil goes about responding to the questions. He can study the facial expressions of the pupil at greater length than he could when the pupil is a part of a group being tested. If the teacher administers the individual test orally, he can hear how the pupil expresses himself. He can detect difficulties in the pupil's oral expression as well as difficulties pertaining to content. He can sense where the pupil is confident of his answers and where he is hesitant. Yet, such advantages would not be sufficient to justify individual testing as a standard procedure. At times the teacher will find it necessary to administer an individual test, either written or oral, to a student who has been absent from class on the day a test was given. If the student has a legitimate excuse for his absence from class, the teacher is bound to give him the opportunity to make up the test he has missed. As a general procedure, however, the teacher will gather his test data from group tests rather than individual tests.

PAPER-AND-PENCIL VERSUS PERFORMANCE

Should the test be a paper-and-pencil type or an actual demonstration of some proficiency in a skill? Should the agricultural student, for example, write a description of how to raise watermelons or should he actually grow some watermelons? Should the student of auto mechanics take a written test on automobile tune-up or should he go through an actual tune-up with the teacher? Should the science student describe on a written test a classic experiment or should he perform the experiment in the laboratory? The physical demonstration of some competency leaves no doubt whether the student has achieved a skill or not. Tests of typing and physical fitness, for example, require the pupil to demonstrate his proficiency. The teacher of typing, though, is in a more favorable position to conduct proficiency examinations than is the teacher of auto mechanics. Each of the typing teacher's pupils has a typewriter, and the teacher can administer a test to his whole class simultaneously. The teacher of auto mechanics may have but one automobile in the shop. In that case each pupil must proceed through a test in turn, a process which requires an undue amount of the teacher's time. In order to administer demonstration-type tests adequate facilities and time must be available. The science student obviously cannot conduct an experiment if there is no laboratory or if the school does not have the requisite materials for the experiment. The agricultural student cannot grow watermelons unless he has the land available for planting.

In a sense, of course, all tests are tests of proficiency. We are all aware, however, of persons who have the ability to verbalize without the ability to carry through the verbalization into action. They can explain all the fine points of bowling, for example, but they cannot themselves bowl. They can explain the duties of citizens in our society but they do not demonstrate civic competence in their daily behavior. Tests must be constructed so carefully that they measure the kinds of proficiency the teacher is seeking to evaluate. The test items must be designed so that they yield the specific responses that the teacher is looking for rather than answers that avoid or talk around the questions asked. If data can be secured in no other way than by physical demonstration of proficiency, then tests of actual performance must be used. No paper-and-pencil test can under any circumstances replace a performance test in the typing classroom.

Economy of space and economy of time must be considerations in the choice of tests to be employed. It would be an uneconomical use of both the pupils' and teacher's time to have each student in the science classroom perform as part of a testing situation a science experiment in the laboratory. Presumably, they would be repeating an experiment which they had already performed in previous laboratory work. They would find it necessary to set up the equipment, obtain the appropriate materials, disassemble equipment, clean up and put away materials. Carefully prepared items on a written test can quickly reveal whether pupils have understood the purposes, procedures, and conclusions to be drawn from previous experiments they have undertaken.

We can at this point draw two inferences in respect to the choice of test. We should select the type of test that most nearly measures the objectives of instruction and is most economical in respect to space, facilities, and time. Further, we should prepare tests that evaluate achievement in respect to previous instruction.

TRIALS VERSUS MEASUREMENT

It may be well at this point, since we have introduced the illustration of the science test, to distinguish between a test which is in reality a try or an attempt at discovery and a test or examination which is given to measure achievement and to obtain scores which can be utilized in marking. Tests that are simply tries or trials can be an important aspect of instruction. It is highly desirable for students to work through science experiments, drawing their own conclusions. Students who wish to try out new and advanced experimentation should be permitted to do so under the supervision of the teacher. Creativity is fostered when students are allowed to try out new ideas, whether in science or English or mathematics. The teacher's observation and judgment of their efforts and ingenuity form a part of the total process of evaluation. Students who are learning through trying out new ideas, that is, testing their ideas, should be freed of the burden implied in test scores and marks. Test items for scoring and marking purposes should be based on the preceding work which students have been doing in the course.

PREPARATION VERSUS SURPRISE

Should the test be announced in advance or should it come as a surprise to the students? All major tests should be announced well in advance of the test date in order to give students ample time for study and review. Prior announcement of the test date will soften the psychological impact of the test. It will give students time to prepare and thereby gain confidence in their ability to do well. Announced tests carry with them the implication that the teacher and students are working together for mutual success. Unannounced tests underscore the teacher's authority to control a group. Unannounced tests may show whether pupils are keeping up with their work; on the other hand, they may also arouse considerable antagonism on the part of the students who have been surprised by the test. Feelings of antagonism and hostility toward the teacher may affect the test results in such a way as to give an inaccurate appraisal of pupil achievement.

The teacher who wishes to use unannounced tests should let his pupils know at the beginning of the year that he uses that technique. By laying the groundwork he may use this type of test without creating a great deal of hostility. Unannounced or "pop" tests, as they are often called, should be kept very brief. They may serve to point out to the students the necessity for keeping up with their work. The teacher may give several of these "pop" tests during the year. The credit assigned to the unannounced tests should be minor. In this way if a pupil comes to class one time or even a few times unprepared for a "pop" test he will not be unduly penalized. We must remember that the major purpose of testing is to appraise pupil progress and achievement. We should be primarily concerned, not with punishing a student who does not do his homework, but with knowing whether a pupil can with proper instruction and study achieve a measure of success in a course. The announced test accomplishes this purpose better than does the unannounced test. A combination of announced tests and unannounced tests may be effective if, as we have suggested, the students are made ready for the use of unannounced tests, but the surprise test should not be used as a disciplinary device. Such usage defeats the purposes of testing and turns testing into a form of punishment.

QUIZ VERSUS LONG EXAMINATION

Should the test be a quiz, i.e., a short test, or a thorough examination requiring considerable time? Experienced teachers generally give tests of varying lengths. Some tests require only five minutes or less, others take a full period. Length of the test depends upon the number and relative importance of the topics previously studied, as well as upon the individual teacher's decision on time allotments and his beliefs about the values of testing. It is fairly standard practice for teachers to administer short tests of varying lengths during the marking period with a full-period test scheduled at the end of the marking period. It is also common to find full-period tests administered at intervals during the marking period. Tests at frequent intervals over a period of time yield a broader and truer picture of students' achievement than do tests at infrequent intervals. When a number of tests are given during a marking period, the relative value of each test is not as great. The use of frequent tests of varying lengths in effect decreases emphasis on tests, since pupils become accustomed to tests as a part of instruction and do not feel that each test is a harrowing, threatening experience.

SHORT-TERM VERSUS COMPREHENSIVE

Should the test cover only the work of the immediately preceding period or should it be comprehensive in nature, covering everything that has taken place in the classroom from the first day of the year? In current practice many, perhaps a majority, of teachers limit the content of their tests to questions about the work just completed. Tests that come at the end of a marking period of six weeks, for example, measure achievement on the work of that period. Following this practice, if we divide the school year into six marking periods, each major test at the end of each period would deal only or mainly with the instructional experiences of that marking period. This is frequently true even for the last test given at the end of the year. The final examination may be a full-period test which simply evaluates achievement of pupils during the last six-week marking period rather than a test of one to three periods which evaluates achievement of pupils during the whole year.

Over the years the long, comprehensive final examination has lost ground as an evaluative instrument. In the past schools have administered long, rigorous final examinations upon the bases of which students were promoted or failed. Teachers came to realize that it was unwise psychologically to place students under the severe strains of all-or-nothing examinations. It was unfair to the students to make success or failure rest upon one examination. This practice encourages cramming—superficial review at the last minute—and allows neglect of systematic progress during the year. Students who have the ability to retain what they have learned during the year or who have the knack of cramming would show up well on the final comprehensive examination. Few schools, if any, today allow success or failure in a course to ride on one examination. Where final comprehensive examinations are given, the test results are added to the results made by pupils on previous tests. The stress has been removed from the final examination by making it a part of the teacher's testing program along with other tests and means of evaluation.

Some teachers use a full-period test to check on the achievement of pupils during the last marking period and follow this with a longer final examination, often scheduled for a block of time during an examination period. In New York State, where the Regents examination program has been in effect for many years, teachers must administer final comprehensive examinations to those pupils who are working for a Regents, i.e., state, diploma. State-prepared examinations in the various subjects are sent to the local schools for administration by teachers at specific times scheduled by the state.

We would probably be unwise in abandoning entirely the final comprehensive type of examination. We can use it along with the test at the end of the marking period. We may play down the role of the final, comprehensive examination by arbitrarily weighting it as equivalent to two, or at most, three regular full-period tests. College-bound students especially should be given practice in taking the comprehensive type of examination because they will be confronted with tests of this nature during their college careers. Further, the comprehensive examination does require review of the essentials of the course. It summarizes and brings into focus important aspects of the subject. The teacher may wish to use a comprehensive examination at the end of a semester and then another at the end of the year. A complete testing program would consist of short tests, full-period tests at the end of each marking period, a comprehensive test at the end of a semester, and a final, comprehensive test at the end of the year.

SINGLE VERSUS DIFFERENTIATED FORMS

Should one form of the test be prepared or more than one form? Like lesson plans, tests must be created for particular classes. The teacher should ask his classes questions only on work that they have studied. Ideally, tests should be tailor-made for each class. Practically, however, a test may be used with more than one group of students provided (a) the groups are at approximately the same ability level and (b) the teacher is certain that they have all had the previous work involved. As is the case with lesson plans, sometimes the same test may be used unchanged with more than one class. At other times minor modifications are necessary. At still other times completely different tests are in order. Where high schools group students homogeneously, the teachers must make separate tests for the varying ability levels which they teach. The purpose of grouping is to permit differentiation of instruction. A test designed for an average group of students would be too simple for an accelerated group and too difficult for a slow group.

If teachers had unlimited time, which they do not, it would be ideal for them to have comparable forms of the same test for administering to groups of the same relative abilities. The teacher with five average groups might create two or more forms of the same test in much the same way commercial publishers produce multiple forms of the same test. The teacher could then give different forms of the same test to different classes. This practice would cut down on the information which is passed along from class to class concerning the test items. However ideal and statistically sound the use of multiple forms might be, it does not represent a realistic solution to test design. Most teachers have all they can do to construct one good test for each ability level.

OPEN-BOOK VERSUS CLOSED-BOOK

Should the test be given in the classroom or should it be taken home for answering? Similarly should the teacher forbid the use of books and notes during the test period or permit their use in responding to test questions? When teachers and students think of tests, they normally think of closed-book tests taken in the classroom. Few are the high school students who have the experiences of a take-home test and an open-book test. Most teachers seem to feel that students demonstrate learning only when they are able to respond to test items without any aids. Actually, a knowledge of the appropriate sources and aids and skill in using the right aids is a part of the learning process. There is the mistaken notion that take-home and open-book tests are easy. That such is not the case can be attested by students who have had the opportunity to take these types of tests. Many students would prefer, if given the choice, to elect closed-book tests rather than open-book tests.

The take-home test does present students with a temptation for cheating. Yet, trust and self-discipline are taught by providing students with opportunities to demonstrate these qualities. Take-home tests give students the opportunity to demonstrate power and utilize resources. They permit students to work at their own speeds. Open-book tests allow students to use tools which they may need in the solution of test items. A well-constructed open-book test will be difficult enough so that students will not have time to look up all the answers to questions which they should know. They may look up a key idea or a key formula for use in their answers, but they would have to know where to locate the idea or formula quickly, and the test item should lead them into application and elaboration. The closed-book test in the classroom can remain the primary type of test given by the teacher. It is worthwhile, however, to give an occasional take-home and open-book test if only as an added means of putting variety into the testing program. College-preparatory students in particular would profit from the exposure to take-home and open-book examination since these types of tests are used to some extent on the university level.

OBJECTIVE VERSUS ESSAY

Should the test items be essay questions or objective questions? Should students be made to compose their own answers in narrative style or should they respond by means of underlining the correct answer, checking the right response, encircling the number of the correct response, or blackening in a number or letter which corresponds to a correct answer? Sharp controversy has raged in academic circles in respect to the use of essay or objective tests. There are those persons who see no value at all in essay tests. Others would eliminate objective tests. In the following sections we will consider the purposes and values as well as the limitations of essay and objective tests. Suffice it at this point to state that both essay and objective tests have their place in the classroom. They should be used for the purposes which they accomplish best. Neither the essay test nor the objective test has a clear superiority for all testing purposes. In choosing the types of tests they will use, teachers must keep in mind the purposes of the tests and the time, space, and facilities at their own and the students' disposal.

ESSAY TESTS

We have all in our academic life pondered over such questions as "Discuss the Korean War" or "Compare the ancient empires of Darius the

Great and Alexander the Great" or "Describe Hemingway's style." Each of these is an essay question, though not necessarily in its best form. The illustrations, though, are typical of thousands of brain-teasers presented to young people in high school classrooms daily. An essay test is an examination which requires pupils to respond to one or more essay questions. The nature of the test items, the essay questions, is such that pupils must respond at length in expository form. They cannot answer an essay test item with a check mark, a single word, a line, or a symbol. They must write a longer answer. They cannot use a standard form of an answer sheet on which to indicate their answers by blackening in little spaces. They must use blank paper on which they will compose their own original answers. Each answer is formulated in the student's own words, not in the words of the test maker.

Essay questions may take slightly different forms but they all have in common the requirement that pupils think through their responses, organize their thoughts, and write out their answers. Following are useful types of essay questions:

DISCUSSION

Pupils are asked to write in narrative form on the topic presented by the teacher in the test item. The discussion question is one of the most frequently used, and often abused, types of essay items. The discussion question appears deceptively simple to prepare. It requires but little thought on the teacher's part to jot down such blockbusters as "Discuss the Korean War," as cited above, or "Discuss *Don Quixote*" or "Discuss the Age of the Dinosaurs." As a general rule, any test question which requires little thought is probably a poor question. Questions like "Discuss the Korean War" lack sharp focus. They permit students to ramble around in answering. They are difficult to score. The teacher may have some preconception of a complete answer to the question but the pupils may come up with variations on the answer. Many pupils wonder "When is enough, enough?" As a result they write lengthy answers, throwing in much extraneous material. The length of an answer often impresses the teacher and results in a higher score. Thus, there is the tendency for discussion questions to encourage verbosity.

Essay tests are often referred to as subjective tests. That is, the student composes his own answers and the teacher must judge each answer and place a score on it. Scoring of essay questions can be notoriously unreliable. Different teachers who score a question like "Discuss the Korean War" are likely to assign differing scores to the answers because they look for different things in the answer. The same teacher may score the same question answered by the same pupil differently on different dates and at different times. When he is tired or hungry or irritable, he may score an essay question lower than he would if he were in a happy mood. Though subjectivity cannot and perhaps should not be completely ruled out of testing, it should be carefully controlled and minimized. Since test scores do mean a great deal to pupils and do affect the marks they receive, effort should be made to make the tests as reliable as possible. Ideally, two or more scorers should obtain the same or close to the same scores when grading the same test item. The teacher should assign the same or close to the same score to an answer regardless of the time at which he reads the answer. Discussion questions can be made more reliable if they are written in such a way as to give pupils some clues as to the direction the answers should take, the length of reply required, and the points which must be included in order to receive full credit for the answer. Let us take our illustration, "Discuss the Korean War." A slight improvement can be achieved by narrowing the question to one aspect of the Korean War, as, "Discuss the causes of the Korean War." Students would receive further help so that they could know what might constitute a full answer if the question read: "Discuss four reasons for the entry of the United States into the Korean War." We might give the student a real workout with a detailed question such as "Discuss the Korean War, including in your answer the major causes; the military forces opposing each other; losses suffered on both sides; the roles of MacArthur, Truman, and Eisenhower; terms of settlement; and current situation in Korea." Admittedly, the discussion question with the requisite information as illustrated in the longer item requires much more time and thought than does the oversimplified, "Discuss the Korean War."

COMPARISON OR CONTRAST

Questions of this type ask the student to show the likenesses and differences between two things. Though there is a slight semantic difference between "compare" and "contrast," the two terms are generally used interchangeably. "Compare" is a broader term, for it implies a discussion of both likenesses and differences. "Contrast" suggests an emphasis on differences. A question asking students to compare or contrast two items can cover considerable ground, requiring the students to demonstrate knowledge of both items included in the question.

We encounter the same necessity for providing specific direction to the question of comparison or contrast as is the case with discussion-type questions. The question "Compare the ancient empires of Darius the Great and Alexander the Great" leaves too much latitude for response. Knowledgeable students can go on in great detail about any phase or phases of life in the empires of these two greats of history. The question would be sharpened if it were to read: "Compare the ancient empires of Darius the Great and Alexander the Great in respect to size, boundaries, administration, and contributions to civilization." The students responding to this longer version would know what points were expected for a complete answer. "Compare the Protestant King James version of *The Holy Bible* with the Catholic Douay-Rheims version" could be improved by specifying several points desired in the comparison. It might well state: "Compare the Protestant King James version of *The Holy Bible* with the Catholic Douay-Rheims version, including in your answer differences in style of writing, differences in content, and clarity of translation." If the direction the answer is to take is clear, no further elaboration of the question is necessary. Assuming prior study, students should be able to handle the question: "Contrast the meaning of the word 'democracy' as it is used in the United States with the meaning of the word as it is used in the Soviet Union."

Questions of comparison and contrast may be limited to a single item to compare or contrast or they may be expanded to include a number of items. Length of the essay question should depend on the previous study, importance of the items included in the question, and time allotted for answering the question. "Compare the objectives of the French Revolution with the objectives of the American Revolution" limits the comparison to a single feature of the two revolutions. A more complex and considerably longer answer is called for in the question: "Compare the French Revolution with the American Revolution in respect to objectives, justification for revolution, duration, conduct of the revolution, and final outcomes." The teacher controls the length and direction of the answer by the features he incorporates in his question.

EXPLANATION

Students are expected on questions of this type to make clear explanations of the problems presented to them. They may be asked to respond to the question: "Explain the steps by which a federal bill becomes a law." The science teacher may ask them: "Explain what is meant by the 'nitrogen cycle.'" Or, more directly, "What is meant by the 'nitrogen cycle'?" An English teacher may ask: "Explain the origin and meaning of the expression, 'Never send to know for whom the bell tolls.'" There are times when essay questions of explanation resemble discussion questions. In fact, some teachers use the words "explain" and "discuss" interchangeably. There are, to be sure, small differences in these terms. If we changed the question: "Explain the steps by which a federal bill becomes a law" to read: "Discuss the steps by which a federal bill becomes a law," we should get essentially the same answer. On the other hand, "Discuss the nitrogen cycle" might produce a much different answer from "Explain what is meant by the 'nitrogen cycle.'" As we have seen before, the term "discuss" without further clues lacks precision and makes it difficult for the student to know the direction his answer should take. A discussion of this question might lead a student well beyond a simple explanation of the nitrogen cycle into a treatise on the element nitrogen, the commercial use of nitrates, and agricultural methods. Nor is the interchange of the words, "discuss," and "explain," always possible. It would be poor English usage to substitute "Explain the ancient empires . . ." for "Discuss the ancient empires . . ." The nature of the question and of the expected responses will determine whether "explain" may be substituted for "discuss."

DESCRIPTION

Essay questions may ask a student to describe a situation or thing. Descriptive questions often require elements of shape and color in the answers. "Describe Fishermen's Wharf in San Francisco" would provide students with the opportunity to paint in prose the color and excitement of that famous landmark. An art teacher or social studies teacher might use a question of description such as: "Describe a flying buttress and explain its purpose." The teacher is calling for both description and explanation in this question. In health class or physical education a student might be given the question: "Describe the method of artificial respiration currently recommended by the National Red Cross." A social studies teacher would permit sketches in an answer to the question: "Describe, using diagrams, the battle plans of the Union and Confederate forces at Gettysburg."

"Describe," "explain," and "discuss" are often used in similar ways. When the teacher is constructing essay questions, he may find a number of alternatives possible. For example, the following question could be phrased in the following ways:

> What were the political and economic reasons for the United States' entry into World War II? (direct question)
>
> Discuss the political and economic reasons for the United States' entry into World War II. (discussion)
>
> Explain the political and economic reasons for the United States' entry into World War II. (explanation)
>
> Describe the political and economic reasons for the United States' entry into World War II. (description)

Each of these means of stating the question should yield essentially the same results.

SUMMARY

It is apparent that essay questions test not only the student's mastery of content but other knowledge and skills as well. In the previous illustrations we can see that essay tests can provide the teacher with information about the pupil's ability to discuss, compare, explain, and describe. The summary type of question tests not only for content but also for the ability to summarize. The pupil must decide what the significant points, conclusions, principles, or findings have been. He must state these briefly. The teacher can place a limitation on the length of the answer by including the length desired in the question; for example, "Summarize in about 200 words the plot of *Great Expectations*." Or, on another occasion the pupil might be asked, "Summarize in about 100 words the advantages of the heat pump." The teacher can combine a summary question with a question of contrast by asking to summarize and to contrast in the same answer, as, for example, "Summarize the principal differences between the French system of education and the American system of education."

OUTLINE

A student may be asked to give his answer in outline form rather than in narrative form. An outline question would show whether the student could pick out the salient features of the work studied. He might be asked: "Outline in not more than one page the chief events of the War of 1812." A question of this type presupposes that students have been taught how to prepare an outline. If students do not know the correct procedures in outlining, the teacher should give them ample instruction and practice before using this type of question as a test item.

CRITICISM

A question of criticism asks students to make judgments. When giving this type of question, we should remind the students that criticism implies both positive and negative judgments. In popular usage the word "criticize" has negative connotations. A student should not be permitted to submit an answer which bears only negative criticism. He should be developing the skill of judging strengths and weaknesses. We most often use questions of criticism in reference to the fields of art, philosophy, music, and literature. We might ask the student: "Criticize the performance of Sir Laurence Olivier in the filmed production of Shakespeare's *Henry V*." We can give a more specific direction to the answer; for example, "Criticize James A. Michener's *Hawaii* in respect to historical accuracy." A much lengthier reply would be required by the question: "Criticize the writing of William Faulkner in respect to descriptive passages, syntax, vocabulary, and ability to sustain interest."

ANALYSIS

When students analyze a problem, they break it into its component parts. An illustration of this type is the question: "Analyze the situation in Germany between 1919 and 1932 which created opportunities for the rise of Hitler."

A student can be asked to take some trait and analyze it. This is done in the question: "Analyze the qualities of democratic leadership." An analysis question expects not only a statement of the answer but some interpretation. "Analyze the motives for the departure of the early American colonists from the Old World" would produce a different answer from the more simple: "State the reasons why the early American colonists left the Old World" or "List the reasons why the early American colonists left the Old World." Both "state" and "list" do not imply that interpretation or elaboration is necessary.

DECISION OR OPINION

A decision question seeks an expressed judgment or opinion on the part of the student. The pupil takes a position and then supports that position. The supporting reasons for his position are the essential features of this type of question. Following are examples of essay questions which force the student to take a position and defend that position:

> Do you believe that works of literature should be read in condensed versions? Why?

> A number of influential persons have stated that we should never have dropped the atomic bomb on Japan. Do you agree with them? Give your reasons.

> In your opinion who has contributed more to our civilization—Albert Einstein or Henry Ford? Support your position.

Since there is the element of opinion involved in questions of this nature, more than one answer can be "right." In questions involving a choice between two items or a position for or against an item, both items or both situations may be "correct." The teacher must exercise care that he does not give an opinion-type question and then expect the answer which he has in mind. If the teacher wishes the student to make only the choice or hold the opinion he, the teacher, has in mind, he should not use opinion-type questions. He should structure his questions in such a way that he obtains the kinds of responses he is seeking. The most significant portion of the answer to a decision or opinion-type question lies in the supporting reasons a student gives for his position. Students should be able to receive full credit for their answers if their supporting reasons are logical and if the facts they use are correct.

SHOWING RELATIONSHIPS

Essay questions can be formed which ask students to give the relationships between two or more factors. An illustration of this type is: "Show, giving appropriate examples, the relationship between poverty and communism."

More intricate is the question: "Show the interrelationships between federal spending, federal taxation, and the national economy."

ILLUSTRATION OR APPLICATION

Questions of this type ask for examples of a principle or application of knowledge. A student would have to demonstrate knowledge of a principle and creative application of the principle in answering the question: "Give four original sentences in Latin using the ablative absolute." Application of knowledge is again required in the question: "In what countries outside of the United States would you expect to find oranges being grown? Why would you expect to find them there?"

RAISING QUESTIONS

The ability to raise intelligent questions is a sign of knowledge. Essay questions can be designed in such a way that they show whether students have sufficient knowledge of a topic to raise thoughtful questions. We may provide the student with a situation to which he may react, as in the following instance. "At a public forum Congressman X has just completed a severe condemnation of our national foreign aid program. As a citizen and taxpayer raise several questions which you might address to him in order to help you understand the issue better." The ability to raise judicious questions would help a learner to understand the following situation: "Several prominent critics of American education have suggested that we adopt in our schools patterns of European education. Pose several questions which you would want answered before you could decide whether or not to agree with them." A question of this nature provides a student with an opportunity for creative thinking.

RECOMMENDING SOLUTIONS

A highly creative exercise is the type of question that asks students to propose solutions, make recommendations, suggest alternatives, and offer original ideas. In this vein are questions such as the following:

> What suggestions could you make to the local board of education to help alleviate the dropout problem?
>
> What recommendations would you make to your local representative for state legislation on civil rights?
>
> What can we do to combat juvenile delinquency in our city?
>
> Southeastern United States has a plentiful supply of Spanish moss. Can you suggest any ways to turn this into a commercial product?

From the foregoing illustrations of essay questions we can see that the teacher has available a number of types of questions which can make for variety in form of response. We have not in our summary of types of essay questions exhausted all possibilities. We can ask students to evaluate or interpret or clarify. There are enough variants of the essay question so that teachers need not overuse any one form, such as "Discuss. . . ." Pupils will find greater stimulation in the questions if they encounter a variety of situations.

ADVANTAGES OF ESSAY TESTS

It is apparent that essay questions test more than content. True, a student must be knowledgeable in order to perform well on essay tests. Essay questions do, however, test pupils in other aspects of learning as well as the acquisition of content. They test the student's ability to write coherently and to express himself in an organized way. Each answer is an exercise in language usage, giving the teacher an opportunity to check on spelling, punctuation, and sentence structure.

Essay questions are somewhat easier to prepare than are objective test items. Since essay tests require pupils to give longer answers, there are fewer test items than would appear on objective tests. Although wording is important in any test item, it is, perhaps, not as crucial in an essay question as in an objective test item. The choice of a poor, inexact, or inappropriate word can completely invalidate an objective item, whereas the meaning of the essay question might come through in spite of the wording.

To sample content plus writing skills essay questions are unexcelled. Pupils can and should have the experience of writing intelligible answers. Most educational authorities are in agreement that pupils do not get enough practice in writing during their school years. English teachers cannot alone accomplish the task of teaching students to write well. Every teacher who utilizes essay questions is helping pupils to learn to write. To sample content alone, however, the objective test excels the essay test. Each time the teacher prepares a test he must decide on his purposes for giving the test.

DISADVANTAGES OF ESSAY TESTS

Essay tests are much less reliable than are objective tests. That is, they are not consistent in the results they yield. We have mentioned the fact that different teachers assign different scores to the same essay question. We have also mentioned that it is possible for the same teacher to assign different scores to the same answers to essay questions. If a test is reliable, it should yield essentially the same score whether it is graded by several teachers or graded by the same teacher at different times.

Essay tests have low validity as well as low reliability. Both the questions and the scoring often permit the student to avoid coming to the point, to pad his answer with extraneous material, and to bluff. Students who can say nothing well are often rewarded with higher scores than are received by students who say a great deal poorly. The scorer often allows his knowledge of the student to affect the grade he assigns to a question. It is very difficult to abstract one's attitude toward the student when grading tests. We have a tendency to make excuses for those students whom we favor. We say to ourselves, "He can't mean this." His score does not suffer because we know that he knows better. The boy who is a constant disciplinary problem had better make sure that his answer is full and correct. We can be very subjective in our scoring. We read into answers things which are not there. Since we are usually pressed for time, we read the answers hurriedly and overlook essential points.

The essay test provides a relatively small sampling of content and skills. Since essay questions require considerable time to answer, the teacher can ask but few of them on any one test. The teacher will ask those questions he has deemed to be most important. He must omit whole areas of knowledge. A pupil might be better prepared to answer questions on topics other than those chosen by the teacher. The essay test may be more a demonstration of what he doesn't know than a demonstration of what he does know. Every essay test is a gamble. Will the teacher ask a question on the topic the pupil knows best? The lucky students are those who have spent time studying and reviewing those areas that appear on the test. The unlucky ones are those who have spent their time studying and reviewing areas that do not appear on the test. Students are often discouraged when they have studied for a test and discover there are no questions on it on topics which they can handle best.

Scoring of essay tests is difficult. How much weight should the teacher give to content and how much to other aspects? How much should spelling and punctuation count? What values should be assigned to each .question and to parts of each question? How do we score quantitatively the ability to express one's thoughts? Should handwriting affect the score assigned? How do we judge original answers? How close must the student be to the answer the teacher has in mind to get full credit? Should we penalize the student for poor grammar? Should neatness influence our assigned score? Should the science teacher even consider English usage when grading his papers? Should the ability of the student be considered when scoring a paper? When scoring essay questions the teacher has many judgments to make.

IMPROVING ESSAY TESTS

Essay tests can be made more effective instruments with care in preparation, administration, and scoring. When preparing the test the teacher should:

1. Clearly formulate in mind the purposes of each essay question.

2. Carefully relate the questions to the work which the class has studied.

3. Make sure the questions evaluate objectives of instruction.

4. Improve the sampling by increasing the number of questions and shortening the length of the responses. Four or five short essay questions sample the work of the course better than do one or two long essay questions.

5. Word the questions in such a way that students understand the specific areas to be discussed.

6. Decide what factors he intends to consider when scoring the papers. He should decide at the beginning whether he will count spelling, handwriting, style of writing, and other skills as well as content.

7. Vary the form of the essay questions included on the test.

When administering the essay test the teacher should:

1. Inform the students what factors will be counted. Even though the teacher customarily considers such factors as grammar and spelling on all his tests, it is well to remind pupils of this fact at each testing session.

2. Allow sufficient time for the slowest pupils to complete their answers.

3. Present the questions to students in duplicated form rather than orally or on the blackboard. In this way students have the questions directly at hand for close study and analysis.

When scoring the essay test the teacher should:

1. Prepare a key for each question. This key will contain the specific points to be looked for in each answer. The key should contain in outline form the minimum number of points that must be covered in order to receive full credit.

2. Assign values to each of the factors he is considering. He must set values for the content, writing abilities, and other skills he wishes to evaluate. We should stress the point that if the teacher does not wish to evaluate writing skills he should not be using essay questions. He should use objective questions instead.

3. Score one question at a time on all the papers. That is, he should read the first question on all the papers, then go back and read the second question on all the papers, and so on. By doing this he can keep in mind the points he is looking for in the answer. This will be fairer to the students since he will be looking for essentially the same points.

4. Write the value given beside each question. He may wish to note this value in the amount of credit he has assigned to the answer or in the number of points he has deducted from the answer. At the end he should total the

number of points which the student has obtained and place this score in a prominent position at the top of the first page of the student's answer sheets.

5. Watch out for wordy answers which do not come to grips with the question. Attractive writing style can be deceptive. The teacher must make sure that the pupil has really answered the question. He must not be misled by fine but empty phrases and sentences.

6. Guard against rewarding or penalizing a student because of his personality.

Two other recommendations for scoring often made by test experts may prove helpful under some circumstances. It is considered good practice in scoring essay questions to read each question twice, once to appraise the over-all organization of the answer and the second time to make a detailed evaluation. Certainly, this procedure would be a desirable one if the teacher has sufficient time. Since teachers do not always have enough time for two readings, one careful reading should prove sufficient.

A second often-made recommendation on scoring urges the tester to grade each paper without knowing who wrote the paper. Students may omit their names and write on their papers instead a code word, number, or letters. Although the recommendation to conceal the names of the test writers may be statistically sound, it is not always a practical procedure for high school teachers. The teacher who knows his pupils well can usually tell the handwriting of each of his pupils. If he does not readily identify the handwriting, he can often recognize a pupil's paper from the quality of the work or from the phraseology the pupil uses.

OBJECTIVE TESTS

Harry Golden, noted author and editor of *The Carolina Israelite*, has observed:

> In the old days, the teacher asked, "Who discovered America and in what year?" When a kid rose to answer, either he knew or he didn't know. No one asks that question today. Instead the question is worded, "Who discovered America? Choose one. (1) Bernard Baruch, (2) Christopher Columbus, (3) Nathan Hale, (4) Mickey Mantle."
>
> These are called multiple choice questions. I believe they discourage genuine education. The multiple choice question has banished facts. It has made the fact unimportant. You can guess at the fact. You have a 25 per cent chance of hitting it.[1]

[1] "Now Kids Guess Who Discovered America," *Chicago Sunday Tribune Magazine* (June 26, 1960), 22.

Golden's comments are aimed directly at objective tests. These tests are in wide use in the classrooms. They constitute the major forms of commercially made standardized tests. Objective tests consist of a series of objective items of varied types. Regardless of type of item, the objective test has as its major purposes an increase over essay tests in reliability, an increase in validity, and a reduction in subjectivity of scoring. Objective tests seek to eliminate personal judgments and opinions of the scorer. They can be scored fairly and simply by an aide or even by a machine. Most teachers have not had facilities for machine-scoring their own objective tests, but such procedure is well within the realm of possibility.

There has been considerable controversy over the use of objective tests. Some teachers feel that we have overdone their use. Certainly we do overdo the use of objective tests if we permit them to force out essay tests and to become our only means of measurement. Both essay testing and objective testing have their places in the classroom. They should both be used for the purposes that suit them best. We have indicated that essay tests are superior in measuring the combination of content plus writing skills. One of the unfortunate products of the elimination of essay tests is the decrease in writing practice that students get.

ADVANTAGES OF OBJECTIVE TESTS

For measuring content, however, the objective test is clearly superior. It samples content widely. The teacher can prepare many small objective test items covering a much wider scope than he can by using essay items. An essay test may reveal depth of knowledge on one or more selected topics, but the objective test reveals breadth of knowledge. The content of an entire course can best be examined by means of objective items.

If the test items are well constructed, objective tests yield answers that are clearly right or clearly wrong. Well-prepared objective tests are consistent in the results they yield and accurate in measurement. The student must react to the questions presented to him by the test maker. He does not have an opportunity on objective tests to avoid coming to grips with the question, as he often does on essay tests.

Objective tests can be scored very rapidly with the use of a key. A full-period objective test requires but a few minutes for scoring each paper. A set of essay tests may require hours or days to score. This time factor is one of the reasons that objective tests have grown in popularity with teachers.

Many students prefer objective tests to essay tests. It is undoubtedly true that part of this preference stems from a distaste for writing and lack of ability in writing coherently. We should not abandon essay tests because students do not perform well on them. They need the practice that essay writing gives. But part of the preference also comes from the legitimate feeling that objective tests are fairer than essay tests. For one thing, students need not worry about the teacher's subjectivity in scoring. The scores cannot be affected by the teacher's attitude toward students. For a second reason, if they go blank on one item, they will not necessarily suffer severely. They can miss some items and still achieve satisfactory scores on an objective test. The objective test calls for knowledge of many points and gives the student the chance to demonstrate his knowledge on a wider scale than can be done on essay tests.

Objective tests have advantages in wider sampling of content, increase in reliability and validity, and, as their name implies, an increase in objectivity.

DISADVANTAGES OF OBJECTIVE TESTS

The most frequent criticism of objective tests is that voiced by Harry Golden. They may permit guessing. There are certain types of objective items, specifically recall and completion items, which eliminate guessing. Items such as true and false and multiple choice do introduce the element of guessing. We must ask ourselves whether the error introduced by guessing on objective tests is more serious than the error introduced by subjectivity on the essay tests. In spite of the factor of guessing objective tests can measure achievement with more precision than can essay tests.

We can minimize guessing in a number of ways. We can employ questions that ask the student to fill in a response. He must recall the appropriate response without the assistance of a number of choices. We can increase the number of choices we give with a question. When we present a student with two choices, as in a true-false question, he has a fifty-fifty chance of guessing the correct answer. When we give him three choices, he has a one-out-of-three chance to guess correctly. By increasing the number of choices to four or five we cut his chances for outright guessing. We can further reduce the effects of guessing by applying a scoring formula, as is done in many standardized tests. The scoring formula penalizes the pupil who guesses wrong. A student who does not know the answer to a question finds when a scoring formula is applied that if he omits the test item he suffers less in loss of credit than if he guesses incorrectly. The standard formula which is applied is:

$$S = \frac{R - W}{n - 1}$$

in which S is score; R, number of correct responses; W, number of wrong responses; n, number of choices in each question. Thus, the formula applied to a true-false test would be:

$$S = \frac{R - W}{2 - 1} = R - W$$

Here n is 2, because each true-false item provides two responses. The scoring formula for a multiple-choice test consisting of items that provide four choices would be:

$$S = \frac{R - W}{4 - 1} = \frac{R - W}{3}$$

As a general rule, teachers do not resort to the use of a scoring formula for their own class tests. The calculation involved requires more time than is justifiable. They are also reluctant to kill one of the minor academic pleasures, the thrill of guessing an answer correctly. The only time when it is better practice to use a scoring formula in ordinary high school tests made by the teacher is in the case of long true-false examinations. Pupils should be advised before they take the test that a scoring formula will be used. In that way they can decide for themselves whether they wish to guess. When they know a formula is to be used, they may be more cautious in their guesses. They may omit items which they realize they do not know and guess at items which they are not completely sure of but which they feel might be right.

Objective tests are difficult to construct. It requires a good deal of time and thought to create a good test item. One vague or inexact word can throw the student off the track, or the injudicious use of a word in the item may reveal the answer to the student. The teacher must carefully review the work studied by the class and make detailed selection of the content to be included in the test items. Since pupils can respond very quickly to objective items, the teacher must prepare a sizable quantity of questions for each test. Depending on the difficulty of the material students can run through one hundred or more items in a single class period without too much strain. The use of teacher time in essay tests and objective tests is almost reversed. Essay questions are easier to construct, but scoring is time-consuming. Objective questions are more difficult to write, but scoring is easy.

Teachers tend to limit their use of objective tests to the measurement of facts. They examine the retention of specific data more frequently than application of knowledge. They deal with details more often than with generalizations and understandings. Objective questions often test students on minute data that they will quickly forget after taking the test. Objective tests can encourage memorization rather than reasoning. The teacher has the obligation to be sure that test items have importance to the learners. He should not ferret out esoteric data for questioning. There are so many important learnings which young people must attain that they should not be burdened with trivial data. Why, for example, should every pupil have to learn the names of all the Vice-Presidents in our country's history? They will do reasonably well if they learn the names of all our Presidents.

The teacher can create objective test items that measure more than retention. He can devise questions to test application of facts. He can write items that test for generalizations and understandings. These kinds of items are difficult to create, but not impossible.

TYPES OF OBJECTIVE TESTS

The most common types of objective tests are (1) recall, (2) completion, (3) alternate response, (4) multiple choice, (5) rearrangement, and (6) matching. We will consider the advantages and disadvantages of each of these types of objective questions and illustrate each.

RECALL

A recall item is a statement or question that asks for a direct answer. The student must supply the answer. He is given no choices. There is, therefore, no opportunity for selecting one of the teacher's prepared responses. The student may guess, but the teacher supplies no clues to guide his answer. The recall item calls for a brief answer or answers. A recall item may be phrased as a question as in the examples: "Who is the Chief Justice of the U.S. Supreme Court?" "How much are 5 and 7?" "What color will blue litmus paper turn when dipped into an acid solution?" Each of these questions requires one definite answer. There is no elaboration or explanation necessary.

Recall items may be cast in the form of statements, such as:

Give a synonym for "beautiful."
Translate the word *le cheval*.
Mention four contributions of the ancient Greeks.
Name the Secretary General of the United Nations.
List five species of trees which are native to Colorado.

Each of these questions asks for specific information which the student must possess. As we can see from the illustrations, we may ask for more than one answer. The test scorer must be aware of all the correct possibilities for answers. Occasionally, pupils will come up with original answers which are correct but which the teacher had not anticipated. There is an element of subjectivity in scoring questions of this type. When pupils supply answers which are technically correct, they must be given credit for the answers even though they may be different from the ones the teacher expected. A further element of subjectivity enters when the teacher makes the decision as to whether he will count spelling of the answer. If he decides to count spelling, how much weight should he give to this factor? Must the answer be spelled absolutely correctly or will he allow partial credit for the correct information but incorrect spelling?

We must take great care in constructing items so that we get the answers we want. When we ask the student to "mention four contributions . . . ," we will surely be aware that there are more than four contributions. In fact, we are making it simpler for the student by limiting his answer to a certain number of responses. Where we encounter difficulties is in preparing a question without being aware that multiple answers are possible. Harry Golden's question, "Who discovered America?" affords us an excellent illustration of this problem. The test-maker would apparently expect the answer, "Christopher Columbus." A poorly informed student would have little difficulty with this question. He would reply "Christopher Columbus" and move on to the next question. But the bright student who is well informed could easily give the "wrong" answer. Who did discover America? Was it Columbus, who landed in the West Indies in 1492? Or, was it the Vikings, who discovered the North American continent in the 10th century A.D.? Or, was it Amerigo Vespucci, whom some people credit with the discovery of South America, and for whom America is named? When the student replies to the test question, is "Christopher Columbus" the only answer acceptable?

If the teacher is reasonably careful in constructing recall items, he will discover that they are relatively easy to prepare in comparison with multiple-choice items, for example. They require little space on the examination paper. The teacher can sample a wide range of subject matter using recall items.

COMPLETION

A completion test item is a variation of the recall item. Instead of a question or complete statement the student is given a statement with a blank or blanks to be filled in. We can recast our Columbus example in the form of a completion item, as follows: "The name of the famous explorer who landed in Hispaniola in 1492 was —————." Since they are essentially recall questions, completion items reduce guessing to a minimum. The student may supply a wild guess. If the test items are well made, however, they will have precise answers which the students must give to receive credit. Lack of precision in writing the item can invalidate it. There should be but one correct answer for each blank to be filled in. The answer might consist of more than one word, but there should be only one right response. What should the student reply when he is asked to fill in the following: "Abraham Lincoln was born in ——————." The teacher may be expecting the answer, "1809." But "Kentucky" would be a reasonable answer. So would "a log cabin." The teacher may not have been expecting the latter two answers when he composed the test item. There are some few teachers who will give the students credit only for the responses which they, the teachers, have had in mind when they prepared the test item. We should follow the same general rule suggested with recall items. If the teacher gives a test question which has more than one plausible answer, he is bound to give full credit for each plausible answer. The fault is not the students' in not

being mind-readers but the teacher's for not devising test items which yield only one response. Our "Abraham Lincoln" illustration is an extremely poor item. It is not unusual, though, to find items such as this on teacher-made tests. We can improve our item in two ways. We can restate the item: "The year in which Abraham Lincoln was born was _____." Or, we can start with our original form and supply a clue to the information wanted, as, "Abraham Lincoln was born in _____."

(year)

The teacher should avoid providing helps which give away the answer. Blanks should be of consistent length for all completion items, so that students cannot judge the answer by the length of the blank. Words like "a" and "an" in the answer should be avoided if possible. The student is aided considerably in this vocabulary item: "A word which means a collection of literary works is an _____." Obviously, the answer starts with a vowel. In this illustration we can leave the statement as it is and simply omit the "an" or we can turn the statement around: "_____ is a word which means a collection of literary works." In either case we should still obtain "anthology" as the response.

Completion items can be used in many subject fields. In some cases the teacher needs to supply some preparatory information so the students will know how to proceed. If the French teacher, for example, wishes the students to change nouns used as objectives to objective pronouns, he might prepare the following illustration: "Voici le livre. _____voici. Voici les livres. _____voici." He provides the form which the students must change. He must, of course, have given the general directions for answering the questions at the beginning of the test items. Occasionally, we may wish to include more than one word in our response, as the same French teacher might when he asks pupils to change both a noun used as a direct object and a noun used as an indirect object to pronoun objects. To illustrate, "Je donne le livre à Jean. Je _____ donne." If the teacher wishes, he could divide the blank into two parts, as "Je——————— donne." The teacher has the option of giving part credit for one correct portion of the answer or of giving credit only if both portions are correct. The teacher aids in clarity by underlining the words which are to be converted.

It is helpful though not absolutely essential to have the students place their answers in column form at the right of the statements, as in the following:

1. The unit of electrical resistance is . . . . .   1. _____
2. The unit of intensity of electric current is . . . . .   2. _____
3. The unit of electromotive force is . . . .   3. _____

Scoring is simplified and speeded up when the answers are placed in column form. When well-constructed, completion items are effective test questions.

ALTERNATE-RESPONSE

An alternate-response item gives the student two choices of answer and asks him to select the correct one. The most common form of this test is the true-false item. Since students have a fifty-fifty chance to guess the right answer, alternate-response items are the poorest of objective types. Following are some examples.

He (don't, doesn't) know about it yet.

The student may strike out the incorrect response or he may write the correct response in a column at the right. The form of the item may be altered slightly:

don't
He   know about it yet.
doesn't

The student can be asked to check the correct response, as in the following cases:

For each statement that forms a complete sentence place a checkmark in the YES column; for each statement that does not form a complete sentence place a checkmark in the NO column.

	YES	NO
1. The fundamentals of bridge are not hard to master.	———	———
2. Since you brought up that matter.	———	———

Each of the following sentences contains an underlined word which is either an adjective or an adverb. Decide whether the underlined word is an adjective or adverb and place a checkmark in the appropriate column.

	ADJECTIVE	ADVERB
1. He is a healthy individual.	———	———
2. Tommy works hard.	———	———

True-false items have been very popular with some teachers. Perhaps one reason for this popularity is the deceptive simplicity of such questions. They appear to be easy to compose. The teacher feels he can dash off a statement and the pupil can reply by indicating whether the statement is true or false. True-false items are far from easy to write. They must be written with such precision that pupils cannot possibly misunderstand or misinterpret the meaning. It is very easy to introduce into a statement qualifying words which either give away the answer or are subject to misinterpretation. How would you answer the following true-false questions if you were taking a test on which they appeared?

True ☐ False ☐   A straight line is always the shortest distance between two points.

The chances are good that the word "always" will lead you to false, which is the correct answer. If we did not know of great circle routes, we could still guess the answer correctly.

True ☐ False ☐   The red light on a set of traffic signals is never placed below the green light.

Even if we had never seen a topsy-turvy set of signals which some communities use, the word "never" points the way to the correct answer, which is false.

Words like "no," "little," "always," "never," and "sometimes" often give away the desired response. Qualitative words can cause pupils to go astray in their answers. How would you reply to the following questions?

True ☐ False ☐   The largest city in the United States is New York.

Would you say "True" or would you say "False?" Either answer might be correct. The answer depends upon what you mean by *largest*. *Largest* is a qualitative word. Does the test-maker mean largest in the sense of total number of inhabitants within the city limits? Or, does largest refer in this case to the geographic size of the city as measured, for example, in square miles? Would Los Angeles not be as reasonable an answer as New York City?

What would you do with the item: "True ☐ False ☐ Pineapples are the most important industry of Hawaii"? "Most important" opens the door to interpretation. Perhaps some people know Hawaii best for its pineapples. Some people might consider orchid production "most important." In total production sugar cane is actually the largest agricultural crop. Tourism occupies a "most important" position in Hawaiian industry. To answer this question we would have to know the meaning of "most important." Do we mean most important in respect to total number of persons employed in the industry? Do we mean in respect to total income produced? We have to ask ourselves, "Most important to whom?" To the teacher who has asked the question? To the majority of residents of Hawaii? To the United States as a whole? To the world? "Most important" in what way?

True-false items are improved if they are kept as brief as possible. Long involved statements throw the students off the track before they reach the end of the statements. The intent of the statement is generally clearer if the use of double negatives is avoided. "Castles are commonly seen in Spain" is clearer to the reader than "It is not uncommon to see castles in Spain."

The teacher may direct the students to respond to true-false questions in a number of ways. They may encircle the word True or the word False.

They may place a checkmark in the True column or in the False column. They may write the word True or the word False in a column at the right of each statement. They may use the letter T instead of the entire word True, and F for False. Many teachers prefer to use the symbols, $+$ for True and $-$ for False.

Alternate-response items can survey a good deal of the subject matter. Students can answer more alternate-response items in the same time it would take to respond to fewer completion or multiple-choice items, for example. Alternate-response items are useful in testing specific facts. They are easy to score. The teacher should guard against setting a consistent pattern of responses. Bright students can quickly spot the pattern, which will give them the answers. It might be easier for the teacher to score a paper if the answers were organized to form a pattern, as three true followed by three false or one true followed by two false, but the test is rendered useless when students detect the pattern.

Alternate-response items used in moderation lend some variety to objective tests. An objective test may consist of several types of objective items, including alternate-response items. It is best practice to avoid extensive use of alternate-response questions, primarily because of the guessing factor. Though some teachers do give long tests consisting completely of alternate-response items, we cannot recommend this practice. Should the teacher resort to long alternate-response tests, however, he should apply the scoring formula, $S = R - W$, in order to discourage guessing.

MULTIPLE CHOICE

A multiple-choice item offers a number of responses from which the student must select one. Usually four or five responses appear with each question. Multiple-choice questions are widely used on both teacher-made and standardized tests. Testing experts prefer the multiple-choice item over other types of objective items. A multiple-choice test is a flexible instrument. It can examine pupils on both simple factual data and on complex ideas. Clever multiple-choice items can test the pupils' ability to reason, to interpret data, and to apply facts. In a number of ways, they are superior to recall and completion items. The teacher need not interpret multiple-choice answers. He can score tests very quickly by following his scoring key. Recall and completion items slow down scoring because the teacher must read each answer. Reliability of recall and completion tests is lower than for multiple-choice, since the teacher must often decide whether unexpected answers to recall and completion items are correct. He must also make some decision on whether to give partial credit for an answer. No decisions of this kind enter into multiple-choice tests.

Multiple-choice items are preferred to alternate-response questions because they cut down on the guessing factor. Although wording is extremely important in all types of questions, it is, perhaps, not quite as crucial in the multiple-choice as an alternate-response items. One word can throw off a whole alternate-response question, causing students to supply the wrong answer. With multiple-choice items we give the student a series of carefully controlled answers, so he may be able to select the right answer even though the teacher has inadvertently included an inept word or two in the stimulus.

A typical multiple-choice question calling for knowledge of specific facts is the following:

> The common seaway used by France, Switzerland, and Germany for shipping goods to distant markets is:
> a. the Elbe
> b. the Rhine
> c. the Oder
> d. the Danube

We can save space with the following form:

> The common seaway used by France, Switzerland, and Germany for shipping goods to distant markets is (a) the Elbe, (b) the Rhine, (c) the Oder, (d) the Danube.

Students can respond to multiple-choice items by underlining the correct answer, writing the correct answer in a column at the right, writing the letter or number of the correct answer in a column at the right, or using a standardized answer sheet on which they may blacken in the letter or number of the correct response.

Multiple-choice items are difficult to construct. The teacher must design a carefully controlled item and then devise a set of plausible answers. The teacher must use his imagination in inventing or providing logical responses. Items that test reasoning, interpretation, and application are particularly challenging to make. Reasoning is involved in the following test item, which requires the pupil to think through the method for solving a problem:

> Mr. Myers drove 480 miles in 8 hours. To find out how many miles per hour he went we should
> a. multiply 480 by 8
> b. divide 480 by 8
> c. add 8 to 480
> d. subtract 8 from 480

The student must make an interpretation when he is asked to reply to the following item:

> When you hear someone say, "Scratch a Russian and you find a Tartar," he means
> a. Russians are descended from Tartars.
> b. Russians are good-natured.

c. Russians can be rough at times.
d. Russians have calm personalities.

We are asking students to apply their knowledge when we prepare test items as follows:

If a pot of water is taken to the top of a mountain and heated:
1. The water will boil at a higher temperature than at sea level.
2. The water will boil but not as vigorously as it boils at sea level.
3. The water will boil at a lower temperature than at sea level.
4. The water will not boil under any circumstances.

Select the sentence that you believe is the best example of English usage:
1. My cousin, John, strives to do good in all his classes.
2. My cousin, who's name is John, strives to do well in all his classes.
3. My cousin John strives to do well in all his classes.
4. My cousin, John, strives to do well in all his classes.

We can design a more complex item, such as the following, which requires a knowledge of two points rather than just one:

Newcastle is to Great Britain as _____ is to Germany. (*a*) the Black Forest, (*b*) the Ruhr Valley, (*c*) the Elbe Valley, (*d*) Heidelberg.

The student must decide first the significance of Newcastle to Great Britain. He must then choose the place that has the same relevance to Germany, in this case, the Ruhr Valley with its coal.

The multiple-choice item takes on greater complexity when students must decide whether none or all of the responses are correct. For example,

Which of the following cities are ports on the Mississippi River?
a. St. Louis.
b. Cairo
c. Memphis
d. New Orleans
e. All of the above

To pick out the correct answer, "all of the above," the student would have to know that each city in the list was a port on the Mississippi River. A more complicated version of the same type of information is the multiple-choice item that supplies a number of stimuli followed by a number of responses. As an illustration:

Which of the following cities are ports on the Mississippi River?
a. St. Louis
b. Cairo
c. Memphis
d. Peoria
e. New Orleans

1. all of the above
2. none of the above
3. *a, b, c,* and *e* but not *d*
4. *a, b, c,* and *d* but not *e*
5. *b, c, d,* and *e* but not *a*

The multiple-choice test question shows its flexibility again when we construct an item asking for the wrong or incorrect response. We could cast our Mississippi ports question in the following form:

Which of the following cities is *not* a port on the Mississippi River?
a. St. Louis
b. Cairo
c. Memphis
d. Peoria
e. New Orleans

It is always helpful to the students taking the test to underline or capitalize key words like "not," "best," "least," and "wrong." This is especially necessary if on the same test the teacher mixes types of multiple-choice items.

Multiple-choice items require more time to construct than recall, completion, or alternate-response items. They also require more space, which means additional school supplies. Nevertheless, the reliability, validity, and flexibility of multiple-choice tests make them excellent instruments for measuring achievement. Multiple-choice items can be improved if the teacher will follow a few simple rules. The responses provided for each question should be consistent in form. If the correct response is a single word, all responses should be single words. If the correct response is an adjective, all responses should be adjectives. If the correct response starts with a capital letter, all responses should start with capital letters. Responses should be approximately the same length. The correct response should not be significantly shorter or longer than the other responses. If it is shorter or longer than the other responses, students who do not know the answer will tend to guess the item that is different in length. The knowledge that pupils will do this may be used in constructing a test item so that one of the *incorrect* responses is somewhat longer or shorter than the correct response. An item of this nature is the following:

Sir Walter Scott is the author of all the following novels *except:*
a. Ivanhoe
b. Kenilworth
c. The Heart of Midlothian
d. Trilby
e. Waverly

The student who cannot recognize the titles of Scott's works may guess at *The Heart of Midlothian* because it is different. This guess would not be correct. *Trilby* is the only one of the novels mentioned that was not written by Sir Walter Scott.

The series of answers should form no consistent pattern. A wise student can quickly guess if all the correct responses are *b*, for example. The position of the correct responses should be varied. It is desirable to avoid placing the correct response in the position of first choice. To keep guessing to a minimum, at least four choices should be given with each item. Consistency in number of choices is generally good practice. If the teacher wishes to use items with four choices and five choices both, he should group the two types so that all items with four choices are together and all items with five choices are together. Rarely is it necessary to provide more than five choices. The more choices that appear on the examination, the longer it takes pupils to read and to reply. This cuts down the number of questions which can be asked and answered in the testing time. For practical purposes the use of a scoring formula on teacher-made, multiple-choice tests is unnecessary, particularly if the teacher has provided at least four choices for each item.

REARRANGEMENT

The rearrangement item is useful in discovering whether pupils know a particular sequence of events, can rank responses in a particular order, or have an understanding of the chronology of a situation. A ranking item might appear as in the following illustration:

> Rank the following countries in order of number of barrels of oil produced annually, using 1 for the country producing the largest number of barrels, 2 for the second, etc.
> ( ) Saudi Arabia
> ( ) U.S.S.R.
> ( ) Iraq
> ( ) Venezuela
> ( ) U.S.A.
> ( ) Iran

A knowledge of the chronology of events is tested in the following item:

> Place the number 1 at the left of the event that occurred first, 2 beside the event that occurred second, etc.
> ( ) The Japanese attack Pearl Harbor.
> ( ) The Germans march into Poland.
> ( ) The United States declares war.
> ( ) Great Britain declares war.
> ( ) Hitler seizes Czechoslovakia.
> ( ) Hitler invades the Rhineland.
> ( ) Hitler becomes Chancellor.
> ( ) The Munich Agreement is signed.

Rearrangement questions are helpful for the limited purposes they serve. If the teacher wishes to determine whether pupils know a particular sequence, rearrangement items provide him with the means. They do require considerable space on an examination. They require time for pupils to read and figure out the sequences. They are more difficult to score than alternate-response or multiple-choice items. The teacher must check to see that each number is in the right position. When scoring rearrangement questions the teacher must have made a prior decision whether he will allow credit only if the entire sequence is correct or whether he will allow credit for each correct response.

Rearrangement items are easiest for the students to handle if the spaces for the answers are placed to the left of each item. If the teacher wishes to use a separate answer sheet, the students can work out the sequence first on the examination paper and then transfer the answers to the answer sheet.

Since we are dealing with fixed sequences, all responses in a rearrangement question must be applicable.

MATCHING

A matching question asks students to relate a given set of stimuli with a given set of responses. In the following illustration students would match the names of the cities given as the stimuli with the names of rivers provided as the responses.

Match the cities with the rivers on which they are located by placing the number of the appropriate city in the blank space at the left of each river.

	———— The Moscow
1. Paris	———— The Neva
2. London	———— The Tiber
3. Vienna	———— The Rhone
4. Rome	———— The Thames
5. Geneva	———— The Rhine
6. Leningrad	———— The Danube
	———— The Amazon

You will note that we provide more responses than there are stimuli. We do this to make the question a little more difficult. If we provided an equal number of stimuli and responses, the student who knew all but one of the pairs would have the last one given to him. If there are additional responses, he does not have the last item presented to him gratis. He must still know the final pair.

If we wish, we can repeat the numbers of our stimuli in several responses. We might set up our matching question as follows:

Match the rivers with the cities that are located on the rivers by placing the appropriate number of the river in the blank space at the left of each city. Numbers may be repeated if more than one city is located on the same river.

	_____ Basel
	_____ London
1. The Moscow	_____ Geneva
2. The Danube	_____ Rome
3. The Thames	_____ Cologne
4. The Seine	_____ Vienna
5. The Rhine	_____ Leningrad
6. The Rhone	_____ Budapest
7. The Tiber	_____ Paris
8. The Neva	_____ Lyon
	_____ Rotterdam

Variation in number of responses is at the discretion of the teacher. As a general rule, six to a dozen responses would be sufficient for an average matching question.

Matching questions permit the teacher to ask many questions in a short space. They measure the student's ability to identify and associate items that have a relationship. They can survey a considerable amount of subject matter.

When writing a matching question the teacher should guard against providing clues to the correct relationships. For example, if we provided Moscow as one of the cities in the list of responses in the matching question above, it is most likely that students would guess that Moscow is on the Moscow River. They would, of course, be correct. It is preferable to avoid placing the correct response on the same line as the correct stimulus. Responses should be placed in such a way that there is no pattern possible. We would not want, for example, responses positioned in such a way that the answers would read 8, 7, 6, 5, 4, 3, 2, 1. After he has filled in the first few answers, the student could quickly discern the pattern.

Matching questions require skill in construction. The teacher must be careful when intending to use a stimulus only once that he does not inadvertently provide more than one response which calls for the stimulus. He must tell the students if he wishes the numbers or letters repeated in the set of answers. So as not to be confusing and time-consuming, an entire matching question should be placed on one page. Portions of the question should not carry over onto a following page.

SEMI-OBJECTIVE TEST ITEMS

A few varieties of test items are difficult to classify as either objective or essay type. They have elements of both but are not truly either fully objective or fully essay. They require answers that are not short enough to be objective or long enough to test writing skills to any extent. Two of these semi-objective types are (1) questions asking students to identify or define and (2) true-false items that ask students to explain why false items are false. Both types require some narration, which will vary in length depending upon the nature of the test item.

We might dispose of the question "Identify: Rembrandt" in three words, "a Dutch painter." On the other hand, a question like "Define: capitalism" may take more than a few words. It would not be difficult to explain why the following true-false item is false: "True ☐ False ☐ Robert E. Lee founded the University of Virginia." We can simply correct the statement to read, "Thomas Jefferson founded the University of Virginia." But it takes more than the mere change of a name to explain why the following item is false: "True ☐ False ☐ The Republican Party, headed by Herbert Hoover, caused the great depression of the 1930's."

With questions of this type the teacher must decide what answers he will allow. Suppose he asks the students to identify Eisenhower. Will he accept "five-star general," "former President of the United States," "former President of Columbia University," or "author of *Crusade in Europe*"? Each of these answers is correct. Perhaps the teacher did not have all of the answers in mind. He should allow full credit, however, for any correct response. If he is not willing to allow credit for all reasonable and correct answers, he should use a different type of test item. Subjectivity of scoring is involved in these semi-objective items. Identify and define items are easy to write but hard to score unless the question limits the answer to a word or two. With identify and define items the teacher has a problem similar to that in recall and completion items. Should he allow credit if the answer is right but spelled wrong? With true-false and explanation items should he allow credit if the answer is right but the explanation wrong? In both cases it is preferable to allow part credit for the right answer and take off credit for improper spelling and incorrect explanation. Spelling should be penalized more lightly than should an incorrect explanation. Semi-objective items can be used to add variety to a test. They can be made to approach objective items if the teacher constructs the items so that answers are kept brief and to the point.

POST-TEST DISCUSSION

In making use of any type of test the teacher should inform the students of their scores and errors as soon as possible after they have taken the test. Tests should be considered a part of the total process of instruction. They should be used for instructional purposes. Whenever possible the teacher should hand back the tests and go over the questions so that students may see where they have made mistakes. This rule should apply to final examinations as well as other tests. Unfortunately, many schools allow final examinations only at the last meeting of a class. There is little to justify this practice. It is of little instructional value to the students. It protects the teacher from criticism for a poor examination or poor test questions. If a teacher makes an error in scoring an examination, the student has no knowledge of this and, therefore, no recourse for correcting the error. There are some teachers who are so defensive about their scoring of final examinations that they refuse adamantly to show students their final examination papers after they have been scored even if they have the opportunity to do so. Far better practice would be to administer the final examination in advance of the last meeting of the class, using the last class meeting to go over the examination.

The industrious teacher will strive to make his tests truly effective instruments for measuring pupil progress and achievement.

CHAPTER 21

TECHNIQUES OF EVALUATION
OTHER THAN TESTING

We have devoted a large portion of this unit to the subject of testing because of its highly technical nature. We return now to the point made early in the discussion of evaluation that testing is but one means of evaluation. Differing objectives of learning call for different means of evaluation. Written teacher-made tests do not readily measure some of the desired outcomes of learning. They do not measure appreciations effectively. The student can indicate on a test a knowledge of good literature; he may even know which pieces of literature have the stamp of approval of the public or the critics or the teacher; but whether he goes of his own free will to the library and selects a work of literature is a matter a test cannot measure.

Tests do not measure attitudes well. They can measure whether a student can verbalize an attitude. The student may state on a test that we should be law-abiding citizens, but does the student translate this attitude into behavior? Is he a good citizen at school? What happens when he takes his place at the wheel of a car? What kinds of attitudes does he show then?

Although we do have standardized tests of values, it is difficult to measure actual moral and spiritual values; for a student may recognize democratic values, but not follow them in practice. A student may know that he should subscribe to honesty, integrity, and love of his fellow man; and on a test, he may say that he believes in human values—but are these values a part of his character?

Tests are silent on most character traits. They do not show persistence or initiative or resourcefulness, all of which are traits the school should seek to develop. Tests are limited in their ability to reveal student creativeness. Occasionally, test items do allow for creative solutions. Standardized tests to determine creativity in students are in the process of development.

As a general rule, however, creativity in the arts or in academic pursuits or in thinking does not show up on tests.

Tests do not customarily measure students' abilities to express themselves orally. Let us distinguish clearly oral practice from oral testing. When we speak of an oral test, we mean a structured examination which we score. Even language teachers use oral tests to a more limited extent than they use written tests. Other teachers may on a rare occasion conduct an oral test. We do not appraise oral expression and discussion skills by most classroom tests.

We would agree, no doubt, that positive attitudes, appreciations, values, character traits, creativity, and oral skills are worthy goals of education. We can see that test instruments do not effectively measure attainment of these goals. In fact, we cannot measure attainment of these goals in the same sense as we measure subject matter achievement. It is difficult to place a precise score on an attitude, for example. How much is an attitude worth? How many points should we allow for the student who chooses a good book from the library? How do you score initiative? If we believe these goals to be significant, then we must find ways of evaluating their attainment even though we are bound to make subjective judgments in the process of evaluation.

Experienced teachers make use of a number of techniques of evaluation other than testing. Among these techniques are the following:

OBSERVATION

IN-CLASS BEHAVIOR

Observation of a student's work in class is one of the most common techniques of evaluation. In the case of a discerning teacher it is also one of the most effective. Some teachers are blissfully unaware of what is going on in their classrooms. Others can tell the significance of a student's facial expression. Some teachers seem to be insensitive to occurrences and interpersonal relationships in the classroom. Others can, to borrow the cliché, read their class like a book. Skill in observation can be developed through experience.

A skilled teacher can analyze student participation in class. He knows whether all students are taking part. He knows which pupils hesitate to respond. He can tell from the contributions to class discussion whether students have studied the subject. He can detect difficulties from the questions students ask. He knows who is not paying attention. He can tell which students have respect for others' views. He can watch how students go about tackling a problem he has given them. He knows if some students tend to dominate the class discussion. He spots individuals who try to throw him and the class off the track. He can study facial expressions and detect when a student has difficulty understanding a point, when he has suddenly understood, and when he is bluffing on a point. He can evaluate students' abilities to express themselves orally. He can, if he carefully plans, place a value or letter grade on some aspects of pupil achievements which he observes, such as class participation. He should be clear on what he means by class participation.

The pupils must also be clear as to what class participation means and should know the teacher is assigning a grade to this factor. The teacher should spell out each factor he is grading. In this case it may mean attentiveness and interest, frequency of participation, quality of questions, extent of volunteering, and contribution of significant illustrations pertinent to the class discussion. The teacher may find the use of a rating scale or check list helpful in evaluating some objectives. We can set up our elements of class participation in a simple rating scale form.

Evaluation of Class Participation

Name of student ....

CHARACTERISTIC	A Excellent	B Good	C Fair	D Poor	F Failing
Attentiveness and interest shown					
Frequency of participation					
Merit (quality) of questions and answers raised					
Extent of volunteering					
Contributions of significant anecdotes, illustrations, and facts to assist in topics under discussion					

Total Letter Grade———

We are combining our evaluation of class participation with grading. The teacher is making subjective judgments on the pupils' performance. We cannot rule out subjectivity completely, but we can control it by spelling out the bases by which we grade. We have in the rating scale spelled out the bases for grading class participation. Other teachers may decide to grade upon different bases or not to grade class participation at all. The important thing is that the teacher has carefully spelled out what he means by class participation and this information has been related to the students.

We must admit that some of the objectives of instruction do not lend themselves to grading. We must not feel compelled to assign marks for every goal. We may evaluate, but this does not mean we must assign a numerical or letter value for every objective we evaluate. We are on shaky ground, for example, when we start to mark attitudes. We may agree that tolerance is a positive value that all individuals should develop. How would we grade the students' achievement in tolerance? Can we even be sure that we are developing the "right" attitude or value? To many individuals tolerance implies a condescension and does not have the positive connotation that other individuals give the word. Again, what of honesty? How do we grade this? Is a white lie as dishonest as a whopper?

Attitudes are normative. We decide we "should" do something or we "ought" to do something. Sometimes our norms or standards of behavior are endorsed by society. Society agrees that we should love our neighbor at least to the extent that we do not rush over without cause and poke him in the nose. But what about the unresolved issues? How would we grade a student's attitude on the issue of whether the federal government should or should not provide financial aid to education? Honest men differ on this issue. In order to attain a score must the student agree with the writer of the textbook, the teacher, the school board, the Democratic party, or the Republican party? The teacher should find out whether the student has examined both sides of an unresolved issue and then allow the student to decide the issue for himself.

The teacher can observe and evaluate student class work without resorting to grading daily recitations. There is no need for the teacher to stand over a group of pupils with his grade book open, recording a symbol every time a pupil recites. This practice destroys a class discussion. It overstresses marks and adds an atmosphere of tension to the classroom. The practice stems from a misinterpretation of the function of the teacher. If the teacher is guiding learning, he does not have the time to grade pupils on their daily recitations. He is aware also that the extra bookkeeping involved is scarcely worth the bother. Very often the teacher who resorts to the extreme of marking pupils on their daily recitations is employing this technique as a means of controlling the behavior of the group.

OUT-OF-CLASS BEHAVIOR

Some of the goals of learning are more readily appraised in out-of-class situations. We can spot leadership talent in the supplementary or extra-class program. Creativity shows up in many activities out of class. We can discover if the school is having any impact on the development of civic and social skills by observing student behavior in the corridors, in assemblies, at athletic contests, and at school social events. It is helpful to know if the student is pursuing some hobby or interest outside of school. We can evaluate student progress toward some of the educational objectives if we are aware, for example, that a pupil takes lessons in vocal or instrumental music after school, participates in a community base-ball league, has a paper route, caddies at the golf course, or repairs radio and television sets. We can observe some aspects of a pupil's behavior our-selves in situations in which we have contact with the pupil. Some of the information on pupil interests and activities may come to us second-hand through other students, other teachers, the principal, or guidance direc-tor. Questionnaires administered as part of a guidance program often provide information about pupil activities outside of class. Certainly, we should have some concern over whether pupils are carrying over into their daily lives outside of class and the school some of the learnings that the school seeks to teach. This knowledge helps us to evaluate not only pupil performance but also the program of the school. We are, of course, evalu-ating in this case, not measuring. We are making observations and judgments and we are gathering information, but we are not marking students on their out-of-class successes and failures.

ASSIGNED WRITTEN WORK

The teacher evaluates pupil progress by means of written assignments. Typical assignments include daily written homework (often based on text-book exercises), compositions, essays, and research papers. Some teachers check the class notebooks of students or require them to prepare a scrap-book devoted to a particular topic. Written reports of books, movies, tele-vision shows, and trips are common assignments.

The teacher can and should grade written assignments. We should, perhaps, modify our concept of grading, if we mean assigning a numeri-cal or letter grade in the case of daily homework. Today's teacher rarely has the time to grade all the daily homework of all his students. Most of the time the daily homework is checked in class, in itself a form of eval-uation. It is satisfactory procedure for the teacher simply to make sure the pupils have turned in their homework papers after checking them in class. He may record a simple checkmark in his grade book for each home-work paper that is turned in. If he has a bit more time, the teacher should spot-check the homework to see if the students seem to understand the work they have done. He should not attempt to mark these. It would be unfair to mark some of the papers and not all of them. Further, the teacher can never be sure that homework papers represent the individual work of the pupil. Nor is it entirely necessary that the routine daily assignments always be the individual work of the student. Homework often consists of practice exercises. A student who does not understand a point or a process may legitimately enlist aid from other pupils or from his parents. This does not mean that anyone should do the work for the student. It means simply that he can seek help with his work.

When a teacher gives a written assignment which he will grade, he should make clear the instructions for performing the assignment and the criteria on which the assignment will be graded. Let us say that an English teacher wishes to make as an assignment the preparation of a research paper. He should precede his assignment with instruction on the nature of a research paper. He should provide samples of research papers. When the students are ready for the assignment, the teacher should give them specific instructions on how to proceed. He should let them know when the paper is due, how long it should be, in what form he would like it, and where they can expect to find resources. He should let them know what factors will be considered when he grades the papers and how they will be weighted. He might elect to evaluate content, documentation, i.e., footnotes and bibliography, and English usage. When he grades a student's assignment, such as a research paper, he should place comments either on the paper or on a separate sheet showing where he took off credit, how much he took off, and why he deducted the credit. He should also place comments on the paper showing agreement and approval as well as disagreement and disapproval. He should show how he has graded each of the criteria which he supplied when he made the assignment. Nothing is so annoying to a student as receiving back from the teacher a paper with the letter *B* or *C* or other grade without comment. Even an *A* paper should bear suitable comments and suggestions for improving future papers.

It is doubtful that the teacher should grade students' individual notebooks. He should preserve the prerogative of examining the students' notebooks to see if they know how to take notes and if they show an understanding of the subject, but students can argue with some justice that the notebooks are their own, kept for their own purposes, and written in their own inimitable ways. A notebook which must be turned in for grading becomes a production for the teacher rather than an aid to the student.

ORAL REPORTS

Students may demonstrate their knowledge of a topic and their abilities to express themselves orally through various types of oral assignments. Students may make individual reports to the class. The teacher may provide for group reports in the form of panels and symposia. A group may prepare a dramatic enactment of a topic. A debate can be an effective means of presenting a problem to the class. A variety of oral assignments not only help the teacher to evaluate the attainment of learning objectives but also lend variety to the class program.

To evaluate oral assignments the teacher may draw up a simple rating scale which bears the criteria he deems essential, as in the accompanying Individual Oral Report.

Individual Oral Report

	1	2	3	4	5
Was there evidence of preparation on the speaker's part?					
Was the speaker's presentation clear to the listeners?					
Was his voice audible?					
Was his voice free of monotony?					
Was there correct language usage?					

A similar rating scale, such as the one following, may be used for a group's oral report.

Group Oral Report

	1	2	3	4	5
Was there evidence of preparation in respect to content?					
Was there evidence of preparation in respect to organization and presentation of the report?					
Did all the students in the reporting group have the opportunity to participate in the report?					
Did all the students speak audibly?					
Did all the students use language correctly?					

The teacher should devise his own criteria for each of these types of reports and he should describe them clearly to the pupils when he makes the assignments, especially if he wishes to grade the students on their oral reports. Grading will be simpler for individual students than for groups. An individual who goes to some trouble to prepare a report for the class will expect a grade for his report. He will want his work to count. In the case of groups it is difficult to determine accurately whether all students in a reporting group have performed equally well. It is common practice in almost all functioning human groups for some individuals to carry more responsibility than others and for some to ride along on the work of others. Since much of a group's report is planned and prepared outside of class time, it is not always simple to detect with any degree of precision the quality of work of the individual members of a group. The teacher can evaluate more accurately the actual performance of the group in class at the time of reporting. Since it is so difficult to grade individuals in a group report separately, many teachers assign one grade to the total report and record this grade for each of the members of the group. Though this has an element of unfairness to the pupils in the group who have worked hardest, it is fairer than attempting to grade pupils without sufficient evidence. Should this system not appeal to the teacher, he has the alternative of not grading group reports at all. In the long run it may be a wiser technique to grade individual reports and omit grading of group reports.

If the classes are mature, the teacher can have the class members apply the rating scale to individual and group reports. The teacher using this technique encourages the students to develop skills of evaluation. Class members check copies of the rating scale which the teacher distributes to them. The rating scales are then turned in to the teacher or used as a basis for a follow-up discussion. By evaluating class reports, students become more conscious of the criteria. They listen to the reports more attentively. The teacher must watch, however, that in follow-up discussions pupils do not become overly critical and vindictive. When starting pupils on the task of evaluating the reports of their fellow members, the teacher should lay firm ground rules. Pupils should be told that criticism must be accurate and constructive, pertinent but not petty. The teacher who wishes to introduce class evaluation of reports may begin by permitting the students to react to reports given by some of the more capable students and by students whose confident nature makes them less sensitive to criticism by their fellows. It should not be necessary to point out that class participation in evaluation is an exercise in evaluating, not in marking. The teacher will assign any marks which are to be given. He cannot turn over to the class the responsibility for assigning marks.

EVALUATION CONFERENCES

A friendly private chat with a student can be informative. Even a brief conference affords the teacher an opportunity to discuss a student's progress with him. The student should be given an opportunity to explain some of the difficulties he is having and to raise questions about his work. An evaluation conference gives the teacher and the pupil a chance to compare their ratings of the pupil's work. The teacher may find out whether the pupil has made a realistic appraisal of his own work. The teacher can help the student to see his achievement in relation to his ability and to see why he has received certain marks. If the teacher has graded a student low in class participation, for example, he can suggest to a student ways to improve his work. It would be ideal if the teacher could schedule an evaluation conference with each of his pupils at the end of a marking period, preferably just before assigning grades for that marking period. The teacher could then inform the student of his evaluations and at the same time verify some of his evaluations. Should he discover that he has made any errors as determined by further evidence supplied in a conference with a pupil, the teacher can still make a change of grade. Unfortunately, time and space are often unavailable for secondary school teachers to conduct evaluation conferences with each of their many pupils. As a result, conferences are often scheduled during the lunch hour or after school with those pupils who seem most in need of the teacher's help and those from whom he needs additional information. The teacher should make time available for any pupil who requests a conference with him.

OPINIONNAIRES

An opinionnaire is an inventory on which students register their views and attitudes. Many opinionnaires offer students a series of statements with which they may agree or disagree. We may think of these instruments as attitude inventories. There are some standardized attitude inventories on the market, for example, the *Minnesota Teacher Attitude Inventory*.[1] College students and teachers who take this attitude inventory react to one hundred and fifty statements that reflect attitudes toward children and school work, indicating whether they strongly agree, agree, are undecided, disagree, or strongly disagree with each of the statements.

The Minnesota Teacher Attitude Inventory is a type of opinionnaire. The teacher will find the opinionnaire a useful technique in surveying student attitudes and values. We should say, perhaps, with more precision that an opinionnaire surveys what students report to be their attitudes and values. The attitudes and values surveyed may or may not be translated into behavior. We can at least discover what students say their attitudes and values are. Other techniques, such as observation and conference, may reveal to us whether students follow their expressed attitudes and values in everyday behavior.

A teacher uses the opinionnaire when he and his classes are dealing with normative material. Administration of an opinionnaire is an effective means of initiating a class discussion on controversial subjects and unresolved issues. The teacher can draft a number of statements and ask the students to express agreement or disagreement with each statement. If we were studying the Bill of Rights, we might include the following items in an opinionnaire:

Encircle *A* if you agree with the statement and *D* if you disagree.

A   D   1. The President of the United States should have the power to suppress newspapers which report his actions unfavorably.

___

[1] Walter W. Cook, Carroll H. Leeds, and Robert Callis, *Minnesota Teacher Attitude Inventory* (New York: The Psychological Corporation, 1951).

A   D   2. A court should not accept evidence in a trial from anonymous witnesses.

A   D   3. The State should require daily reading of *The Holy Bible* in the public schools.

Answers to these statements will show some understanding or lack of understanding of the Bill of Rights.

We should help the student distinguish between attitudes sanctioned by law and attitudes that stem from unresolved issues upon which men honestly differ. The illustrations above reflect attitudes that strike at the heart of our democratic society. There must be central values to which our nation as a whole can subscribe. The school must seek to develop these values. The rule of law illustrates a central value to which all American citizens should subscribe. The rule of law as opposed to the rule of men is part of the fabric of our society. The student does not have the option of rejecting the rule of law. He cannot choose to be a law unto himself. He cannot expect to be exempted from his duty to obey the laws of our nation, state, or locality. He cannot decide to enter into a life of crime without society's efforts to deter him and to punish him if necessary. A student should learn the differences between attitudes that have the sanctions of law and custom and attitudes that represent free choices. A student should learn the reasons why some attitudes and values have the support of law and custom. For this reason opinionnaires may be used with two purposes in mind: (1) to find out if pupils do recognize the attitudes and values that are central to our society and (2) to open discussion and analysis of unresolved issues. An example of the latter type of opinion item is the following:

A   D   The federal government should provide financial aid to parochial schools.

This issue has not been conclusively resolved. Some claim that federal financial aid to parochial schools is unconstitutional and is in opposition to the first amendment to the Constitution. Others claim that federal financial aid to parochial schools is legally permissible. They cite previous precedents of federal and state aid to parochial school children and to institutions of higher education. The opinionnaire item itself can introduce an intriguing subject of study. Perhaps eventually the federal government through Congressional legislation will provide financial aid to parochial elementary and secondary schools. Perhaps the United States Supreme Court will support this action, if challenged, or declare legislation of this nature unconstitutional. The student should further understand that in a democracy he may continue to object to a law and he may labor through legal channels to change the law. He does not, however, have the choice of breaking the law. Americans have not had this choice since 1789.

SELF-EVALUATION

Youth should develop skills in appraising their own progress and achievement. They should develop the ability to judge whether they are making satisfactory progress or not. The teacher can help students to become more skillful in evaluating their own work by continuously providing opportunities for their self-evaluation. He may find rating scales helpful in training pupils to judge their own work. For example, the teacher can very simply change the "Evaluation of Class Participation" rating scale which we saw earlier in our discussion to a "Self-Evaluation of Class Participation" rating scale. Instead of the teacher's rating of the pupil, the pupil rates himself on each of the characteristics of the scale. When a committee of students prepares a report and presents it to the class, a self-evaluation form such as the one illustrated is helpful in providing a technique for individual members of the committee to rate their own work.

Evaluation Form for Committee Member

Please rate yourself on each of the following phases of your committee's work by encircling the appropriate letter.

Planning   (Extent of your participation in planning sessions)
            A   B   C   D   F

Preparation   (Library research, search for materials, committee work outside of planning and class sessions)
            A   B   C   D   F

Teaching   (Performance during class periods devoted to your topic)
            A   B   C   D   F

Composite grade: ————————————————
                        Write A, B, C, D, or F
Name: ....

Use of a self-evaluation rating scale reinforces the criteria in the student's mind. It gives the student a chance to say to the teacher how he feels he has done. The teacher should consider the information supplied advisory in nature. He is not bound to accept the rating as an accurate appraisal of the student's work. One effective way of utilizing self-evaluation instruments is through follow-up conferences after the instrument has been filled out. Particularly are conferences beneficial when the teacher's rating and the student's rating are far apart. The teacher and the student should sit down together and talk over the reasons for the discrepancies in rating. Perhaps as a result of a conference each of the two parties would want to modify the ratings. A joint evaluation form on which both the student and the teacher record marks which they would give for specified criteria provides an excellent basis for an evaluation conference. Such a form may appear as follows.

Name of student ....

Place an A, B, C, D, or F in each blank.

Student's Appraisal   *Teacher's Appraisal*

	Weight		
Achievement (Tests)	———	⅖	Achievement (Tests)	———
Written assignments (Homework, class work, research papers, term reports, book reports)	———	⅛	Written assignments (Homework, class work, research papers, term reports, book reports)	———
Reports to class (Preparation, delivery)	———	⅛	Reports to class (Preparation, delivery)	———
Assigned readings (Completed, understood)	———	⅛	Assigned readings (Completed, understood)	———
Participation in class discussions (Value of contributions, frequency, attentiveness)	———	⅛	Participation in class discussions (Value of contributions, frequency, attentiveness)	———
Total Grade	———		*Total Grade*	———

The teacher will discover that students do not always relish the idea of evaluating themselves. Many prefer to leave this task to the teacher, since they do not have a clear understanding of their own attainments. This is all the more reason why students should be helped to evaluate themselves realistically. The teacher may be surprised to discover how many students underrate as well as overrate themselves. The author has found that even teachers who are graduate students at the university level are often reluctant to rate themselves and when they do, many underrate their performance. Students do not possess this skill because schools have traditionally provided few opportunities for them to rate themselves.

GROUP EVALUATION

At the end of a particular unit or topic of study it is often advisable to sound out the group on its accomplishments. A general class discussion directed by the teacher brings out student conceptions of what they got out of a topic. The group takes a look back at what has taken place and attempts to evaluate its successes and failures. Not only is a group evaluation session helpful to the immediate group which is concerned with the task of evaluating its work, but a session of this nature aids the teacher in improving instruction for future groups.

A group may be asked by a teacher to evaluate a course that they have just completed. The teacher might wish to supply a brief questionnaire, to be filled out anonymously, which has the students rate aspects of the course. He may ask students to register their reactions about the helpfulness of specific elements of the course. He might design, for example, a five-point scale and have students rate the effectiveness of outside readings, field trips, use of resource units, tests, lectures, committee reports, laboratory work, use of audio-visual aids, and any other aspects of instruction. If the teacher has a tough skin, he should ask the students to rate the effectiveness of the teacher. Student reactions to this item are often illuminating. A questionnaire can provide additional information if the teacher includes an open-ended question or two, such as "What ways would you suggest for improving this course?"

To preserve the anonymity of students a small committee from the class may be selected to receive the completed questionnaires, tabulate the results, and report the results to the class as a whole. The questionnaires may then be destroyed. This is the fairest means of handling an evaluation exercise of this nature. Anonymity is maintained. There is no danger that the teacher will recognize the handwriting of students who have answered the questions on the instrument. The class as a whole is apprised of the results of the questionnaire. A group has a greater sense of identity with the work in which it is engaged if it is afforded the opportunity periodically to evaluate its accomplishments.

Evaluation is improved when the teacher utilizes a variety of techniques besides testing. We have considered eight of these techniques: observation of a student's work in class, observation of the student's out-of-class behavior, evaluation of written work, oral reports, evaluation conferences, opinionnaires, self-evaluation, and group evaluation. Surely no teacher need be so limited in evaluative skills that he must confine himself to written tests as his only means of appraising pupil progress and achievement.

Chapter 22

MARKING PUPIL PROGRESS

A mark is a symbol which the teacher assigns to a student's work. It is the expressed value that in the teacher's judgment reflects the quality of work the student has done. The words *mark* and *grade* are used synonymously, as are the terms *marking* and *grading*. This is, perhaps, an unfortunate language usage, since we speak of grades and grading in reference also to the vertical organization of the school.

The teacher assigns a mark to each major piece of work the student does. Each test begets a mark. The teacher records in his grade book all the separate symbols the student has earned during a particular period. At the end of each marking period, which may come twice, four times, or six times a year, the teacher "averages" all the marks he has in his grade book for each student and assigns a composite mark for the marking period. At the end of each semester or at the end of the year or both times he determines a grand composite mark which signifies the quality of work the student has done for that entire period. Nothing appears simpler. Nothing is, in fact, more difficult. Teachers do more soul-searching over marking than over any other single phase of teaching. Marks have a way of becoming permanent. They remain in a pupil's record ad infinitum. The teacher must be concerned that the mark he assigns is an accurate approximation of the student's work.

The many studies of the reliability or rather, we should say, of the unreliability of teachers' marks should make us seriously consider our marking practices. We have mentioned previously that unreliable test instruments will yield unreliable grades. We know that it is not only possible, but highly probable, that teachers within the same subject field will grade essay tests, compositions, and reports differently, assigning different marks to the same paper. Parents must always wonder when their children bring home a grade of *C*, for example, in Social Studies exactly what that *C* means and how it has been derived. The student knows that a *B* from a teacher who has earned the reputation of being a "hard marker" is not the same as a *B* from a teacher who is an "easy marker." It is common knowledge that grades vary from school to school, as well as from teacher to teacher within a school. Discrepancies in grading show up when students transfer from one school to another. The truly amazing thing about marking is that in spite of all its pitfalls it is still a serviceable practice.

THE PURPOSES OF MARKING

Before we analyze some of the problems of marking practices we should ask why we mark at all. Teachers customarily cite the following as purposes of marking:

1. *We report the mark to the student so that he may be aware of his progress.* If his progress is not as high as it should be, he can take steps to improve his work.

2. *We report the mark to parents so that they may be aware of their children's progress.* If they believe their children's progress is unsatisfactory, they may seek measures for improvement.

3. *We report marks to colleges to assist colleges in deciding whether students will be admitted.* We might emphasize the point here that we are assisting the colleges, not the students. We assist the bright student who has high grades when we report his grades to colleges. We are not helping the student with low grades, however.

4. *We use marks in determining promotions from one class to the next or from one grade level to the next.*

5. *We use marks in determining honors, such as awards at graduation, scholarships, admission to honor societies, and inclusion on the honor roll.*

6. *We use marks as extrinsic forms of motivation.* Many students are motivated to study in order to attain high marks.

With many students marks are more important than the actual learning. By pressuring students constantly to achieve high grades teachers and parents have overstressed the motivational aspects of marking. "Grade-conscious" students are creations of our school systems. Our overemphasis on marks may stem from a fear that students will not work without extrinsic motivators, but there is limited evidence on the current scene that students will pursue academic work for pleasure and self-improvement. A number of schools have offered after-school and Saturday courses without credit for students who were interested in taking the work. Such courses have met with enthusiastic response from students. Students enrolled in these non-credit courses have been, by and large, more scholastically inclined students who had the particular interest in pursuing the additional work.

Though the six purposes of marking stated above are sufficient grounds for justifying a marking system, we must admit that each of the purposes could be achieved by means other than assigning symbols. We could report our interpretation of the student's progress to him in narrative form or in an evaluation conference. We could write a few sentences summarizing his achievement for a marking period and suggesting ways to improve his work. We could report to parents through narrative reports or in a conference with them what the student has accomplished. Elementary schools follow these practices. They prepare narrative reports of achievement, some of which are very detailed. They cite strengths and weaknesses of the pupils and make suggestions for improvement. Some elementary schools do this in conjunction with letter grades, which are often different from letter grades used in the secondary school.

We could find alternate means of reporting to colleges. We might send a simple statement to the effect the student has passed a course or to the effect that the student has been graduated from high school. We could conceivably send a narrative statement to the college. The best solution would be to let the college determine for itself the suitability of an applicant. This would mean that the college would have to conduct or require a standardized test for admission. Hundreds of colleges already do this, though most require a high school transcript as well.

Teachers could judge without marks whether students should be promoted. Discerning teachers would know what students have accomplished in their courses. Honors could be awarded on the basis of competitive tests. The motivational purpose of marking is the one most difficult to replace. True, if we could engender the interest of all students in all courses we would reach a happy stage in education. We might then dispense with marks. True also, we have never really attempted on any scale to get along without marks. If we could find sure-fire ways of developing intrinsic motivation in pupils, we could do without extrinsic motivation.

Conceivably we could accomplish the purposes ascribed to marking by means other than marking. We might even accomplish these purposes more effectively. But time and tradition are on the side of marking. The busy secondary school teacher would not have the time to write lengthy narrative reports and to conduct conferences with all students and parents even if he so desired. Nor can we completely upset tradition, which has for generations demanded a marking system of one type or another. Ideally, we might do without a marking system, abandoning both marks and report cards. Practically, we cannot do this. Our task as teachers is to make a marking system work. We can live comfortably with a marking system if (1) marks are based on reliable data, (2) marks are used as positive motivation, not negative, and (3) no student is penalized by a marking system.

TYPES OF MARKING SYSTEMS

We could use *W, X, Y, Z* or Roman numerals or Greek characters as the symbols of a marking system. There would be no objection to doing this if all persons "to whom these came greeting" understood the meaning of the symbols. Any symbols used as marks should be understood and accepted in the school community where they are used. Since we have no national ministry of education dictating what marking symbols we must use, localities are free to devise whatever systems seem most suitable to them. For this reason, we find a variety of symbols in use. With a few exceptions and a few minor modifications, we find in use three basic types of marking systems, namely: (1) the one-hundred-point or percentage system, (2) the five-point or letter grade system, and (3) the fewer than five-point system, often two-point, which also uses letters.

THE PERCENTAGE SYSTEM

The percentage system is the oldest of the three systems. Marks are reported in numbers from 0 to 100. All tests and assignments are graded on a percentage system. Students receive grades to the most precise percentage point. A student may carry home a 77 in English on his report card and an 82 in algebra. Marks have meaning in relation to an arbitrary passing grade. Schools vary widely on the points which they have set as passing grades. There are schools with a passing grade as low as 55 and others as high as 75. Seventy appears to be the most commonly agreed-on point of passing. The percentage system per se has been superseded in most schools by a letter grade system. This has happened for a number of reasons.

First, teachers have come to realize that the percentage system is not as objective as it appears on the surface. Nothing looks sounder mathematically than the percentage system. We might say that the percentage system is deceptively objective. It implies a greater precision than is possible. When we give a student a grade of 77 in English, we are saying that the student has not achieved either 78 or 76. We are saying that we know for a fact that the student's achievement is 77, or more exactly, 77 per cent. Does this mean 77 per cent of perfection? The percentage system with its one hundred gradations does not have enough of a range in any one grade. A system with fewer symbols and broader range for each symbol would permit a margin of error.

Second, not all accomplishments can be rated to the nearest percentage point. Should Abraham Lincoln have received a 97 or a 98 for the Gettysburg Address? Can the industrial arts teacher evaluate the worth of a student's newly made table as 88 instead of 89? Can an original painting be appraised at 74 rather than 75? Human achievements do not lend themselves to such precise rating.

Third, in the percentage system all ratings must be related to 100 per cent. A test score of 66 must indicate 66 points out of 100, not 66 points out of 66 or out of any other total. If we should give a test which yields a score of 66 out of 66 we must convert all the scores to our percentage scale before we can average them. Thus 66 equals 100 per cent, 33 equals 50 per cent, and so on. Teachers avoid this awkward calculation by constructing tests using factors of 100. They create tests with 10, 20, 25, 50, or 100 items. Each item then counts 10 points, 5 points, 4 points, 2 points, or 1 point, respectively. No converting of scores is necessary. The construction of tests to contain a number of test items which is a factor of 100 unnecessarily restricts the teacher. He has to omit some items he might like to ask or he has to invent superfluous items.

THE FIVE-POINT MARKING SYSTEM

The five-point marking system is an attempt to correct some of the ills of the percentage system. The five-point system with but few modifications is in universal use in our secondary schools. The most common symbols used in this system are *A, B, C, D,* and *F*. Most schools also employ the symbol *I* for Incomplete. We find a few minor variations. Hamilton, Ohio, for example, uses *A, B, C, D,* and *U*. The P. K. Yonge Laboratory School at the University of Florida uses *A, B, C, D,* and *E*. The *E* in this case means Unsatisfactory. The use of the symbol *E* presents some confusion. Some teachers use *E* on papers to mean Excellent. A few school systems designate *E* as conditional pass, which gives them a six-point scale, *A, B, C, D, E,* and *F*. The Muskegon County, Michigan, junior high school teachers are advised in their handbook that marks to be used on junior high school cards are *A, B, C, D,* and *E*. The handbook states very clearly that *E* means "Very Low Achievement" and is not to be considered failure. This *E* is neither a passing grade nor a failing grade. The handbook explains:

A pupil is promoted if he receives all D, or above, marks.

A mark of E means very low achievement and *not failure*. A pupil could receive a mark of E in every subject and still be allowed to progress with his group. He would be "assigned" in such cases. In general, a pupil is "assigned," even though there is low achievement in some subjects, whenever it is felt that he can no longer profit from repeating that grade.[1]

[1] Muskegon County Board of Education, *Reporting Pupil Progress, Junior High School* (Muskegon, Michigan, 1958), p. 9.

The five-point scale alleviates some of the objections to the percentage system and introduces some of its own. Each letter grade represents a range of achievement. Pupil performance does not have to be rated down to the nearest percentage point. Teachers do not have to limit their tests to a number of items which is a factor of 100. The five-point scale clearly says to students and parents that we are not so omniscient that we can pin-point achievement with the accuracy implied by the percentage scale. On the other hand, each of the letter grades covers a wide range of achievement. A *B* may include a multitude of sins. It stands for a low *B*, a middle *B*, and a high *B*. Some teachers and parents have not been content with the blanket nature of a five-point scale, so they have resorted to *A+*, *A*, *A−*, etc. This practice, of course, destroys the value of the five-point scale, for it converts the five-point system into a fifteen-point system.

COMBINED PERCENTAGE AND LETTER SYSTEMS

Most secondary school marking systems combine elements of the percentage system and the five-point letter-grade system. Although final marks are reported in letter grades, the percentage system is used to help calculate the marks. Letter grades are equated to percentage points. It is of interest to note the cut-off points for each letter grade. Five school systems within the state of Florida have arrived independently at different percentage values for their letter grades. These values are given on their report cards as:

	Brevard County	Dade County	Fort Myers Jr. H. S.	Hillsborough County	Pinellas County
A	95–100	93–100	94–100	95–100	94–100
B	89–94	85–92	87–93	88–94	85–93
C	77–88	77–84	77–86	76–87	75–84
D	70–76	70–76	70–76	70–75	70–74
F	Below 70	69–Below	Below 70	0–69	Below 70

The differences in scales, though small, can be significant. For example, in the *B* range Brevard County has the narrowest range with six points. Pinellas County offers the widest range, nine points. Two of the remaining three school systems have a *B* range of seven points, one, eight points. Perhaps, we might conclude that it is more difficult for a student to get a *B* in Brevard County than in Pinellas County. This hypothesis would, however, bear testing.

A letter system can be effectively combined with a percentage system. When both systems are in use, the teacher can record test scores in percentages for those evidences of student behavior which can be evaluated in percentage points, for example, objective tests. He can record letter grades in evidences of student behavior which are not best rated by percentage points—for example, an original short story. The teacher can average his percentage points separately from his letter grades. He can convert his percentage points to a letter grade. He can study this letter grade and the pattern of other letter grades to determine the final mark he will give the student. A letter system should not, however, become a percentage system in disguise. The teacher must not feel that he must evaluate all student behavior in percentage points, which he simply totals up, averages, and converts to a final letter grade. If this is done, we are back where we started, with a percentage system based on one hundred gradations. We are then using the letter grade to obscure the fact that we are following a percentage system.

OTHER MARKING SYSTEMS

A two-, three-, or four-point scale increases the range at each point. When we use a two-point system, such as *S* for Satisfactory and *U* for Unsatisfactory, we include a great range of achievement, particularly within the Satisfactory range. An *S* mark would include achievement equivalent to *A*, *B*, *C*, and *D* categories on a five-point scale. A two-point scale tells students and parents even less than a five-point scale. For this reason, it has not been a popular system on the secondary school level. Whether we agree with their views or not, parents want to know where their children stand in comparison to other children. They not only wish to know where their children stand in comparison to other children in their class but also where they stand in comparison to other children in the state and nation.

The *S-U* system has gained a great deal of popularity on the elementary school level. Some elementary schools have created a three-point system with *S*, *U*, and *N* or *I*. The *N* or *I* usually signifies Needs Improvement. Some have set up a four-point system with *H*, *S*, *U*, and *N* or *I*. *H* is used to designate High Achievement. When *S* and *U* appear on secondary school report cards, they normally refer to growth in personal and social traits. They are frequently used as symbols for reporting attitude, conduct, citizenship, work-study habits, and social attitudes. Scholastic achievement in the secondary school is regularly reported with the symbols *A*, *B*, *C*, *D*, and *F*.

We can assume on the basis of general practice in the secondary schools that the *A-F* marking system will continue to be the standard system. Of the three systems mentioned the *A-F* system represents the most functional system. It is easily understood. It is with slight modifications in universal use throughout the United States. Try as we may we will not discover a marking system without defects. Every marking system contains some elements which are rather hard to defend. Our job as teachers is to maximize the defensible elements of a marking system and minimize the indefensible elements.

DETERMINING MARKS

It is the end of the marking period. It is time once again for the soul-searching job of grading the pupils. The biology teacher reviews Elizabeth's work for the past six weeks. The school requires the teacher to record a single grade on the report card beside the name of the subject. He reads the report card, finds "Biology," and pens an *A* in the square that designates the appropriate marking period. How has he arrived at this *A*? We may form several hypotheses. Elizabeth may have received all *A*'s on the tests she took during the period. She may have turned in all her homework. She may have participated well in class discussions. Perhaps she always had the right answer to each of the teacher's questions. Perhaps she volunteered readily, not only information but her assistance in cleaning the room. She may have been more cooperative. She was certainly more cooperative than most of the boys. The boys as a group were making lower grades. The teacher may know Elizabeth's parents well. He may recognize that Elizabeth comes from an influential family in the community. Perhaps Elizabeth is the daughter of the president of the school board. She may have made great effort this marking period, for which the teacher feels she should be rewarded. She may be a cheerful girl, who always greets the teacher when she comes into the room. She may show considerable interest in the course. She may ask for additional work to do outside of class. Teachers have been known to consider many of the foregoing elements when deciding upon a grade. It is not at all unusual for teachers to be influenced by conduct, personality, and socioeconomic background of pupils.

This teacher's problem is complicated by the fact that he must decide upon a single grade, which will encompass a number of factors. A marking systems that calls for a single grade in each subject is a time-honored practice still in vogue in many school systems. More modern marking systems provide for two or even three grades to be assigned in each course for various types of growth. In some newer systems the teacher assigns a grade in the subject and another grade in "conduct" or "citizenship." In other more modern systems the student is assigned three grades: one for achievement in relation to other members of his class, one for achievement in relation to his own ability, and one for progress in other kinds of growth.

A marking system must be based upon the purposes of the school. Schools of today recognize their responsibilities for developing many types of growth, not only intellectual. A marking system which permits but a single symbol for reporting all types of growth in a course is not adequate for the modern school.

CONCERN FOR SEVERAL KINDS OF GROWTH

Since we have a commitment in this country to provide an education for all youth who can profit from it, our modern schools must be concerned with several kinds of growth. A marking system in a modern school should appraise a student's scholastic achievement in relation to other members of the class, which some refer to as comparative achievement; scholastic achievement in relation to the student's own ability, which is referred to as personal achievement; and growth in certain personal and social traits. In light of our heterogeneous student population a marking system that limits marks to a single grade representing comparative achievement in each course is feasible, but unjust. Comparative achievement grades are based upon a set of absolute standards of achievement, usually determined by the teacher. All students are rated against these standards. In practice standards are set at mid-level of difficulty. They are, thus, too easy for bright pupils and too difficult for slow pupils. All students compete with each other to meet the teacher's standards. Students of low ability may compete in vain.

A marking system which limits marks to a single grade representing comparative achievement, personal achievement, and other traits is an awkward system. Better practice would allow separate marks for each of the three areas of growth in each course. Most reporting systems in use, however, provide report forms which call for either a single grade which may or may not represent all three areas of growth in each subject or two grades, one of which usually represents comparative or a combination of comparative and personal achievement, the other, progress in personal and social traits. Few marking and reporting systems provide separate grades for personal achievement. Although we give a great deal of lip service to the importance of differences in ability of boys and girls, our marking practices do not always reflect a concern for these differences. Achievement is usually reported with the symbols *A-F*. Personal and social traits are commonly reported with a different set of symbols, for example, *S* and *U*. Occasionally, schools use *A-F* for reporting personal and social traits and habits as well as for achievement.

NEED FOR DEFINITION OF SYMBOLS

Regardless of whether a marking system provides a single symbol for each course or more than one symbol for varying types of growth, it becomes fair and feasible as the meaning of the symbols used is defined. Marks used by a school system should be clearly defined. It is desirable for a school system to set some basic policies on marking which will provide guidelines to all teachers in the system. Though some will argue to the contrary, it is not good practice for each teacher to be a law unto himself. Marks lose their meaning when they vary radically from teacher to teacher within a school system. Certainly there should be some latitude for the teacher in any marking system. A system-wide policy on marking does not mean that all freedom is denied the teacher. Such a policy protects the teacher as well as the student. A school policy would define letter grades in broad terms and explain what is meant by "citizenship," "health habits," and "work-study habits." It would advise teachers whether they should consider a student's ability when assigning a mark. Any policies to which teachers must subscribe should be developed cooperatively by all parties concerned.

We encounter definition of grades at its lowest level when we substitute a word or words for the symbol. A parent is told, for example, that *A* is Excellent; *B*, Good; *C*, Average; *D*, Passing; and *F*, Failure. Or, *A* is Superior; *B*, Good; *C*, Average; *D*, Poor; and *F*, Failure. Or, *A* is Superior Development; *B*, High Development; *C*, Average Development; *D*, Low Development; *E*, Unsatisfactory. Or, *A* is Outstanding Achievement; *B*, Above Average; *C*, Average; *D*, Below Average; and *E*, Very Low Achievement. If we think of words as symbols, we are merely substituting one symbol for another. We have still not defined the meaning of an *A* or *B* or *C* or *D* or *E* or *F*. We define the meaning of a grade when we decide upon the competencies which a student receiving the grade should demonstrate or possess. Some schools interpret their grades by describing the *A* Pupil, the *B* Pupil, the *C* Pupil, the *D* Pupil, and the *F* Pupil; an example of such an effort follows.

A Pupil

is superior in scholastic ability
has a thorough knowledge of the subject matter
consistently does more than assigned work
consistently takes part in class activities and discussion
demonstrates a high degree of ability to organize his work
consistently shows initiative and resourcefulness
regularly has creative ideas which contribute to class' work
consistently turns in work of superior quality, including tests
is always cooperative
has superior study habits
has an excellent attitude

B Pupil

is above average in scholastic ability
has an above-average knowledge of the subject matter
occasionally does more than assigned work
frequently takes part in class activities and discussion
demonstrates moderate degree of ability to organize his work
frequently shows initiative and resourcefulness
frequently has creative ideas which contribute to class' work
usually turns in work of above average quality, including tests
is usually cooperative
has good study habits
has a good attitude

C Pupil

is average in scholastic ability
has an average knowledge of the subject matter

does only the minimum assigned work
occasionally takes part in class activities and discussion
demonstrates average degree of ability to organize his work
occasionally shows initiative and resourcefulness
occasionally has creative ideas which contribute to class' work
usually turns in work of average quality, including tests
is usually cooperative
has fair study habits
has a fair attitude

D Pupil

is below average in scholastic ability
has below-average knowledge of the subject matter
starts but does not complete assigned work
rarely takes part in class activities and discussion
demonstrates low degree of ability to organize his work
rarely shows initiative and resourcefulness
rarely has creative ideas which contribute to class' work
regularly turns in work of below-average quality, including tests
is frequently uncooperative
has poor study habits
has a poor attitude

F Pupil

lacks scholastic ability
has little or no comprehension of the subject matter
does little or none of the assigned work
takes no part in class activities and discussion
is not able to organize his work
shows no initiative or resourcefulness
never has creative ideas which contribute to class' work
consistently turns in work of failing quality, including tests
is usually uncooperative
has very poor study habits
has a very poor attitude

We note that elements of comparative achievement, personal achievement, and personal and social development have been incorporated into the foregoing description of letter grades. Although the description leaves much to be desired, it does show the effort of a school to explain its bases for marking; and it does provide a guideline, however erroneous the guideline may be. For example, personal and social traits such as "attitude" and "cooperation" should not be mingled with academic achievement; but since many schools do this very thing, they should describe to students and parents just what they are doing. For that reason a further refinement of the descriptive statement would call for a definition of vague terms such as "attitude." Such a descriptive statement of grades, as the foregoing with careful subsequent refinements, can be used in a marking system that requires a single grade in each subject.

If we were working with a marking system that permitted three grades, we could define the symbols for each of the types of growth. We could convert the above description of grades to a description of grades for comparative achievement by eliminating references to personal achievement, such as "is superior in scholastic ability" and references to personal and social development, such as "has an excellent attitude" and "is always cooperative." We would have then a description of the grades of comparative achievement. We would proceed to define the grades of personal achievement and the symbols of personal-social development. An interpretation of grades for personal achievement might appear as follows:

A Pupil

Works up to the peak of his ability. Shows unusual interest and effort.

B Pupil

Works well in relation to his ability. Shows considerable interest and effort.

C Pupil

Work is average for his ability. Shows interest and effort.

D Pupil

Works below average for his ability. Shows little interest or effort.

F Pupil

Works well below his ability. Shows no interest or effort.

A personal achievement grade would be determined in reference to the student's intelligence or mental ability as revealed by standardized tests. In deciding a grade of this nature the teacher must make a judgment as to how well the student lives up to his own ability.

A comparative achievement grade would be determined as the result of tests, assigned written work, and teacher's observation of student performance. The comparative achievement grade would show the student's progress toward a set of standards set by the teacher. It would reflect the student's position in the class relative to other members of the class.

MARKING PERSONAL AND COMPARATIVE ACHIEVEMENT

A personal achievement grade is based on relative or personal standards for the individual student rather than a set of absolute standards. When a student receives a personal achievement grade he is, in effect, competing with himself. If we can separate the grades, i.e., for comparative achievement and personal achievement, we can resolve a few problems of marking. We can inform students and parents how well students do both competitively and personally. We can report the comparative grades to college.

We can demonstrate to the public that the school does have a concern for individual differences and that we have taken into consideration differences in ability. We can make the student aware of whether he is living up to his own capacity.

What usually happens, however, is that we must report a single grade for achievement, not two grades. In this situation we find teachers who mark students only on a comparative basis. We find other teachers who combine a comparative achievement grade and a personal achievement grade into one mark. Their letter grades in achievement reflect the student's mastery of the subject in relation to the effort he expends and the ability he possesses. The stickiest problem in marking is the question of how to handle the factor of the student's ability to achieve. Specifically, each school must answer the following questions:

Do you consider ability in grading students who are grouped heterogeneously?

Do you consider ability in grading students who are grouped homogeneously?

Do you consider ability in grading students in courses that are required of all students, i.e., general education?

Do you consider ability in grading students in courses that are chosen by the student, i.e., electives or specialized education?

We find extremes in practice as proffered solutions to this problem. In some schools all classes are grouped heterogeneously and pupils are marked competitively without concern for the factor of ability. Other schools which utilize heterogeneous grouping mark pupils with some consideration of student ability to achieve.

MARKING IN HOMOGENEOUS GROUPS

Schools that group pupils homogeneously have adopted varying solutions to the problem. Some schools permit the entire range of grades, as A-F, to be assigned in each of the homogeneously grouped sections. That is, students in the slow groups may earn top grades in their sections just as bright pupils may earn top grades in their sections. Slower groups use simpler materials and have lower standards of achievement than the average or fast sections have. Students in these slower sections are marked on their achievement at their own levels. They are, in a sense, competing with other members of their class, but at their own level of ability.

Although this is a fair solution to the problem of handling the ability factor, many schools are dissatisfied with this practice. They claim it is not fair to assign the same letter grades to slow and fast pupils. They argue that it is not just that a slow student receives an *A* which appears the same as the bright pupil's *A*, because persons outside the school, as well as colleges, will not understand the differences in achievement involved in the two letter grades. For this reason some schools have resorted to classifying the grades with some sign which identifies the level of the student. Thus, we find A_1 used to identify the *A* given to a pupil in a fast group and C_3 as a grade given to a pupil in a slow group. The use of subscripts and exponents has not proved a popular solution to the problem. It involves extra bookkeeping, and the possibility still remains that persons outside the system may not understand the meaning of the grades. Further, if an explanation is to be given with a reporting form, it would be just as simple to leave the symbols alone and explain the nature of the section to which the student has been assigned. All grades could then be interpreted in the light of the section in which the student was a member. The school which is unduly concerned with what college admissions officers will think when they receive the transcripts of students has a very simple solution. The principal may write boldly across the transcript, "This student was in a slow group. I do not recommend him for college."

Some schools which practice homogeneous groupings have decreed that students in their slow sections must not receive grades higher than *C*. Students in the slow sections know that regardless of how hard they work they can never make higher than a *C* grade. It is difficult to defend this practice. Certainly, it kills the morale and motivation of many of the students in the slow sections. The marking system has been rigged against them. Many of them elect to drop out of school rather than bear the frustration and discouragement wrought by this system. What schools do when they follow this practice is to group students homogeneously for instruction, then mark students with reference to the entire range of abilities. A *C* is the top grade in the slow group so that it will not detract from the *A*'s made in the average and fast groups. A *C* is the top grade in the slow group because an *A* must be interpreted to be that grade made by a student of high mental ability and achievement. If we are going to follow this marking practice, we might just as well keep the students in heterogeneous sections instead of sectioning them by ability.

Conant, an advocate of ability group, subject by subject, has suggested an intelligent answer to this thorny problem. He states:

> In order to assist the counselors in their work of guiding the students into programs which the students can handle effectively, the teachers of the advanced academic elective courses—foreign languages, mathematics, and science—should be urged to maintain high standards. They should be told not to hesitate to fail a student who does not meet the minimum level of performance they judge necessary for a mastery of the subject in question. In other words, the work in the academic elective courses should be judged on a standard of performance so high that students who do not have the

ability to handle the subjects are discouraged from electing these courses and prevented from continuing in the sequence. On the other hand, for the required courses another standard should be applied. Since these courses are required of all, irrespective of ability, a student may be given a passing grade if he has worked to full capacity whether or not a certain level of achievement has been reached.[2]

Conant's recommendation is a compromise solution. It does not go as far as the directive on reporting pupil progress in the School Code of Hawaii, which says:

Grades in academic subjects should be given on the basis of a student's ability to achieve as determined by a national percentile rating on standardized mental maturity tests and other available data.[3]

Conant's proposal should meet with rather widespread approval as a practical solution to the problem of how to treat the factor of ability. If we follow his proposal, we would consider ability when marking in the required courses but not in the elective courses.

MARKING ATTITUDES AND HABITS

Effort and ability are interrelated elements. When we speak of a student working up to his full capacity, we imply not only that he is living up to his potential but he is also working hard, exerting great effort. Aside from effort and ability we should screen out of our marks all other extraneous factors, such as attitude, work habits, personal habits, citizenship, and conduct. These factors have no place in an achievement score. Aspects of learning such as attitude, work habits, health habits, citizenship, and the like are important. But they should be evaluated, marked, and reported separately or not at all. Many schools do report separate marks for development in personal and social traits. They have not always defined these marks carefully. The word "citizenship" appears on many report cards without definition. Most frequently, teachers equate citizenship with conduct or deportment. Conduct is often equated with docility. Therefore, a docile student is a good citizen. Of course, we are exaggerating slightly to make our point that all objectives which are to be rated must be defined. If we are attempting to define "effort," for example, we might rate it on a five-point scale, as follows:

1. Fails to complete assignments
2. Completes assignments minimally

2 James B. Conant, *The American High School Today* (New York: McGraw-Hill, 1959), p. 48. By permission of A Study of American Education, Princeton, N. J.

3 State of Hawaii, "Reporting Pupil Progress," *School Code of Hawaii*, No. 5124, Sec. 3 (July 1960).

3. Completes assignments faithfully and well
4. Completes assignments faithfully and well; occasionally does extra work on own
5. Completes assignments faithfully and well; frequently does extra work on own; asks teacher for extra work

The "extra work" mentioned in the rating scale could be of a remedial nature for slow pupils or an enrichment nature for fast pupils.

DEFINITIONS OF PERSONAL AND SOCIAL DEVELOPMENT

Some schools have worked out thoughtful definitions of traits of personal and social development. Clark County, Ohio, teachers evaluate Character Development, using a plus sign to signify outstanding, no mark for satisfactory, and *U* for unsatisfactory. Character Development is broken into two parts, Social and Work Habits. Social Development is described as:

Respects rights and opinions of others
Accepts responsibility
Is careful with property
Practices self-control

Development in Work Habits is detailed as:

Is attentive
Thinks and works independently
Uses time to advantage ,
Follows directions accurately
Daily assignments prepared
Regular in attendance

Hana High School at Hana on the Island of Maui, Hawaii, rates Personal Development in five categories, as follows:

Participation: growth and interest in discussions, meetings, committee work, school activities, school government affairs, etc.

Work Habits: growth in planning work, working independently, using time wisely, attending to work, carrying out instructions, using resource materials, etc.

Social Attitudes: growth in cooperation, maintaining group discipline, accepting responsibility, consideration of opinions, rights, feelings, and property of others, etc.

Personal Habits: growth in good manners, self-control, honesty, carrying out health and safety rules, good grooming, neatness, cleanliness, etc.

Speech Development: growth in quality of speech in formal, recitation activities; informal, conversational activities.

Personal Development is rated at Hana High School with 1 as Good, 2 as Average, and 3 as Poor.

We find less standardization of symbols when it comes to rating personal and social traits. University High School, University of Hawaii, rates social, emotional, and physical development with the symbols *E* for Excellent, *S* for Satisfactory, and *U* for Unsatisfactory. Kawananakoa Intermediate (Junior High) School on Oahu, Hawaii, rates personal development with a plus sign for commendable, a check mark for normal, and a minus sign to show need for improvement. Muskegon, Michigan, junior high schools rate growth in attitudes and behavior with *C* for commendable, no mark for satisfactory, and *N* for needing improvement.

These schools recognize the necessity for marking objectives of learning in addition to subject matter achievement. Some schools have moved further than others in spelling out the meaning of the grades they assign. Whatever marks are reported, whether they are marks of comparative achievement, personal achievement, personal-social development, or any combination of these areas of growth, they should be clearly defined.

Chapter 23

REPORTING PUPIL PROGRESS

As we have developed our discussion of marking practices we have inevitably been drawn into a discussion of reporting practices. Marking and reporting go hand in hand. Reporting is a natural consequence of marking. If we were to abolish report cards, we could also do away with marking, but it is not likely that we will abandon either of these cherished practices.

Our purposes in reporting are similar to those for marking. We wish to inform the student of his progress. A report card or reporting form simplifies the procedure for letting the student know how well he is doing. An alternate procedure would be an evaluation conference, which normally consumes too much time at the secondary school level. Secondary teachers have responsibility for too many pupils to deliver a report on progress to each student individually in a conference. Report cards inform the parents of their child's progress. With the information goes the hope that the school and home can work closely together to help a child who needs help. Report cards act as extrinsic motivators in the same way that marks do. Students prefer to take home report cards with high grades. The desire to show up well at reporting time motivates many students to achieve. Some students who are severely pressured by their parents to attain high grades are, in fact, fearful of taking home an unsatisfactory report card.

A reporting system provides means of recording information for administrative purposes and for counseling. The marks a student makes become a part of the permanent records of the school, referred to over the years when requests come from colleges, employers, and the students themselves. The record of marks reported by teachers is used in determining promotion, honors, and scholarships. Marks have the unfortunate characteristic of longevity. There are times when we might wish that the marks had not been so carefully preserved. There are many cases of students who have turned in a mediocre performance in high school and who have gone on to make outstanding records in college. Many of the World War II veterans who returned to college after the war provided evidence of this fact. Factors of maturity and motivation can work to effect changes in the performance of students.

Reporting practices reflect the philosophy of the school. If the school honors comparative scholastic achievement only, the report cards will provide for this goal only. If the school accepts responsibility for the personal development of pupils in areas besides scholastic achievement, report cards will allow space for ratings in personal development.

The years have brought many changes to reporting systems. A couple of decades ago report cards like the one below from a New York State high school were in common use.

_____ High School					
Monthly Report Of					
1st Half School Year 19__ 19__					
			Month		
Subjects	I	II	III	IV	V
Sessions Absent					
Times Tardy					

On the reverse side of the card were five lines for the parent's signature and date at each reporting period. Teachers placed on the card, which measured 3 by 5 inches, percentage marks for achievement in each subject. At the end of each month the card was filled out by the teachers, slipped into a simple brown envelope, and handed to the students to take home.

Instead of this rather austere type of report card we find in use today numerous varieties. As we examine report cards of various schools we find differences in several respects:

1. *Size and shape.* The small 3-by-5-inch card can still be found in a few high schools but much less commonly than in previous years. There is no standardized shape or form. Some report forms are printed sheets, some of which are as large as 8½ by 11 inches. Size varies with the amount of information given on the card. Machine-processed forms appear as elongated slips of paper with limited information. A common type of card now in existence is the 8½-by-11-inch card which folds in the middle to make four pages, each 5½ by 8½ inches. Cards of this kind provide a great deal of information. They show a school's concern for progress in several areas of growth in addition to scholastic achievement.

2. *Information provided.* The larger, more extensive cards report progress in scholastic achievement, in personal-social traits, including citizenship, and occasionally in extra-class activities. They provide some explanation of the symbols used, allot space for teachers to comment, and also provide room for parents to write comments.

3. *Frequency of issue.* The older-type, small report card illustrated above was issued once a month. In that school one card was issued each semester. The number of marking periods varies from school system to school system. Many high schools issue report cards six times a year. Others issue them four times a year. Almost without exception schools issue all report cards on the same date. There is no reason why schools could not issue report cards on a staggered schedule, for example, cards for grades seven and eight on one date, for nine and ten on another date, and for eleven and twelve on still another date. This could simplify the problem of processing the report forms and not put so great a burden on teachers all at one time.

4. *Number of report cards issued.* Many school systems issue a separate report card for each subject rather than a single report card for all subjects. Some schools feel that they gain in efficiency when they issue separate cards for each subject. Students in schools which have separate cards take home a small packet with them at the end of each marking period. Separate cards can provide additional information, but unless they do so there is little to recommend them over the single report form.

5. *Number of copies of each card.* In order to make reports more readily available to all parties concerned many schools now make carbon copies of each report form. Forms of this type are usually printed on paper rather than on cardboard. Some schools prepare as many as five or six copies of each report. In some cases these are copies of single forms which report all grades. In other cases schools make carbon copies of cards for separate subjects.

When multiple copies are made, they are ordinarily distributed to the student, the parents, the guidance counselor, the principal, and the homeroom teacher.

TRENDS AND COUNTERTRENDS IN REPORTING

MACHINE-PROCESSING

Until very recently many schools were using report cards which provided information on several types of growth, provided space for teachers' and parents' comments, and explained the meaning of the marks. With increasing enrollments large school systems have turned to machine-processing. Cities as far apart as Honolulu and Miami now process report cards by machine. The student's report card in Honolulu schools which are using machine-processing is a slip of paper with the subject and a single grade. *A* through *F* are the symbols used. The card also reports total days absent. The Miami Progress Report lists courses with scholarship grades, rated with *A-F;* effort grades, rated 1 for Satisfactory, 2 for Improvement Shown, and 3 for Unsatisfactory; and Conduct, rated *A-F.* The processed card also reports days absent and times tardy and contains a blank line for parent's signature.

Machine-processing permits administrators to handle a great many marks expeditiously. Machine-processing is not to be preferred to a personal, individual type of reporting which gives generous information to parents and pupils. Certainly, school systems that can avoid it should not jump into machine-processing. Although J. Lloyd Trump was speaking of scheduling when he wrote the following remarks, his observations appear to this author to have relevance also to machine-processed report cards:

> Modern electronic data-processing equipment can be a boon to the further development of quality in education. It can also be used to do faster what should not be done anyway and thus delay or forestall changes that could improve dramatically the service of schools to individual students. . . .[1]

Those schools that go into machine-processing for one reason or another should find ways of supplementing the meager information given on the machine-processed slips.

SUPPLEMENTARY REPORTS

When reports are sent home, parents usually want to know how the student who has made poor grades can improve his work. Unfortunately, a whole marking period has gone by before a parent realizes the student is doing

[1] "Developing and Evaluating a Class Schedule To Help Each Pupil Learn Better," *Journal of Secondary Education,* 36 (October 1961), 338–45. See also, "Flexible Scheduling—Fad or Fundamental," *Phi Delta Kappan* (May 1963), 368.

poor work. A preliminary warning notice of unsatisfactory work mailed to the parents during the marking period is commendable practice. If the notice is sent early enough, there is still time for the student to improve his work before marks come out. Parents appreciate the advance warning so they can check more closely on their boys and girls, aid them, if possible, or see that they obtain aid. Roosevelt High School in Honolulu uses the form shown on p. 463 to notify parents that their children are not doing satisfactory work.

A supplementary report such as Roosevelt High's can be most helpful. It does mean some extra clerical work on the teacher's part, but the extra work may produce enough beneficial results to make it worthwhile. A report such as this which explains why the student is having difficulty is an improvement over the simple notice some schools send home announcing only that the student is doing failing work in a subject without offering any suggestions for improvement.

A modern reporting system will be clear and informative. It will not limit itself to a single grade in scholastic achievement but will include evaluations of other areas of growth as well. Report forms should be kept simple enough so all persons can understand them.

PROMOTIONS

One of the major purposes of marking and reporting is to establish a basis for deciding upon promotions. Ultimate promotion, i.e., graduation, rests upon completing a specified number of units. The increased stress on scholarship has tended to push up the total number of credits schools are requiring for graduation.

In the secondary school promotion is based upon the number of credits earned. Promotion in each course is determined by the marks a student makes and the judgment of the teachers as to whether he will profit more from continuing on in the next course or from repeating the course. If we follow the Conant proposal on marking, i.e., according to ability of the student in the required courses, and according to comparative achievement in elective courses, we have an answer to promotion. A student passes a required course when he completes work that is satisfactory in terms of his own ability. If he refuses or fails to do what he is capable of doing, he is not passed. Negligence and disinterest can cause the student to fail the course. Promotion in the elective courses will be based upon completion of high standards of achievement. There is no reason why a teacher should pass a student from a beginning course in a sequence, say from Algebra I, to an advanced course, as Algebra II, if the student has not mastered the fundamentals of the beginning course. We are now assuming that Algebra I is an elective course. Now and then we find a small school whose offerings are so

ROOSEVELT HIGH SCHOOL
Special Report to Parents

Date ....

Student ....Homeroom ....

Subject ....Period ....

Dear Parent:

This student is doing unsatisfactory work. Unless corrective measures are taken immediately, a failing mark will be given at the end of the next grading period. My evaluation of the difficulty is given below:

........1. Is content with minimum results.

........2. Does not do homework. Comes to class unprepared.

........3. Needs to establish more effective study habits.

........4. Fails to turn in written work.

........5. Is careless and inaccurate in his written work.

........6. Does not make up work missed because of absence.

........7. Does not participate in class discussions.

........8. Requires constant supervision and prodding.

........9. Wastes time in class.

......10. Seems to study hard but makes little progress.

......11. Lacks sufficient background for the subject.

......12. Does not bring necessary equipment to class (notebook, book, pencil, etc.)

......13. Shows a general lack of interest in school.

......14. Is inattentive in class.

......15. Lacks self-control and distracts others in class.

......16. Is rude and disrespectful in class.

......17. Does not cooperate with others.

......18. Resents constructive criticism.

......19. Fails to follow directions.

......20. Is irregular in attendance.

......21. Is immature for grade and age.

......22. Seems to have too many outside interests.

......23. Accepts the privilege of coming to school without assuming the obligations and responsibilities.

....
Teacher's signature

Parent's comment: (Use other side if necessary.)

....
Parent's signature

Please acknowledge receipt of this report by signing and returning it to Roosevelt High School. If a conference with the teacher is desired, please call 575391 and ask for the grade counselor.

PARENTS	ROUTE TO:	INITIAL	ACTION TAKEN
DO NOT	1. Teacher		
USE THIS	2. Counselor		
SECTION	3. File		

463

limited that some courses such as algebra, which should be elective, are required of all pupils. In this case we apply the standard of marking based on the student's ability. We ought not penalize a student for the lack of a suitable curriculum.

As students are guided to elect courses in which they can succeed, promotion is a regular, expected event for all students who make the effort to achieve. The student who does not have the aptitude for algebra should probably not be in algebra in the first place. The student who has demonstrated a low (D) level of achievement in first-year foreign language should not go on to second-year foreign language. If C represents an average grade, however, students should be permitted to continue in the next level. A teacher should not expect to teach only A and B students, however pleasant that might be. Nor should teachers resort to the practice of failing just as many students as possible at the beginning of the course to "weed out the dead wood." The teacher should start with the positive attitude to help all students succeed who can possibly do so.

As students accumulate the requisite number of credits they approach graduation. When they have earned enough or more than enough credits, the high school will place its seal of approval on them by handing them a diploma at an impressive commencement ceremony. A storm rages over this piece of paper, which in former days was parchment. Should all students receive a diploma regardless of the courses they have taken? Should all students receive the same diploma? Don't we "water down" the diploma when the masses of students receive it? The answers to these questions lie in the school's philosophy. If the school believes that all students who can profit from a high school education should continue in programs that best suit their abilities, all of these receive a diploma. The value of the diploma itself is not "watered down." The meaning of the diploma has changed since the "good old days" when a minority of adolescents completed a high school education. A diploma today means that a normally intelligent student has completed a high school program satisfactory for him. This meaning should be sufficient for a piece of paper which is often stored away in a forgotten trunk in the attic. All students other than special or retarded students may receive the same diploma, which simply certifies completion of a high school program, not necessarily the same high school program.

Some schools have experimented with issuing more than one type of diploma. If the school organizes its program of studies into separate curricula, such as vocational, commercial, college-preparatory, it could with little benefit or little harm type on the diploma the name of the curriculum in which the student was enrolled. In general, the diploma should be basically the same. For this reason it is not advisable to give diplomas of different colors for the various curricula. Nine times out of ten the college-preparatory diploma would be accorded the most prestige. Since the college-preparatory

sequence traditionally bears the stamp of prestige, there is no need to reinforce the prestige factor at commencement with an obviously different
diploma.

The problem is most keenly felt in connection with students in special
classes or retarded students. Many schools prefer not to give special students
a regular high school diploma, since they do not complete a typical high
school program. They are awarded instead a certificate of attendance. A
special student who sticks out a twelve-year program deserves some recognition. His achievement is in some respects greater than is the achievement of
a pupil for whom learning comes easily. At a commencement ceremony the
certificate, similar in size and shape to the high school diploma, should be
presented to the special student without any unnecessary qualifying remarks.
The certificate could state that the student has been in attendance at the
school for a specified number of years.

A high school should take pride in the number of bona fide graduates it
turns out, not in the number of students it loses along the paths toward
graduation.

SUMMARY

Evaluation is the process of appraising pupil progress and achievement. Evaluation involves the use of tests and other techniques. We aim to create reliable and valid test instruments. Two basic types of tests are widely used in the classroom, the essay test and objective tests. Each type has its merits and disadvantages. Both types are useful for specific purposes.

Teachers' marks are often low in reliability because they are based on insufficient and unreliable data. A marking system should provide sufficient data on each student's achievement. Marks should be defined carefully.

Reporting systems inform parents and others of student progress. Report cards vary from school to school. A satisfactory report card tells clearly how a student is progressing in several aspects of growth.

Failure in a required course is indicative of the student's lack of use of his own ability. Failure in an elective course is indicative of lack of attainment of the standards of the course. Promotion should be a natural outcome of progress, particularly if adequate counseling is provided by the school. All students with a normal range of intelligence should be expected to complete a high school program and graduate. A diploma will mean that a normal student has completed a high school course appropriate for him.

CLASS AND EVALUATION ACTIVITIES

1. Define "evaluation," "testing," and "measurement."

2. Discuss the relative merits, uses, and limitations of teacher-made tests and standardized tests.

3. Observe one or two teachers during a class period and analyze the evaluative means being used.

4. Visit a school and find out if there are any school-wide policies on evaluation, testing, grading, reporting, and promotions. The principal or guidance person should be able to help you on this.

5. Find out if there are any state-wide policies, set forth by the State Department of Education, on evaluation, testing, grading, reporting, and promotions.

6. Take a short essay written by a high school student. Duplicate the essay and let all members of the class score it. Note the range of scores. Determine reasons for the range.

7. Repeat activity 6 with another essay. This time, however, determine with the class some criteria for scoring the essay, then score it. Note the range of scores this time. Compare the range of scores in activity 6 with the range of scores in activity 7.

8. Collect specimens of tests and/or test items from teachers or student teachers. Examine the test items carefully and decide if they are good items or poor items. Show how each poor item might be improved.

9. Obtain a major test and the set of scores made by pupils in a high school class. Analyze the scores. Decide (a) whether you believe the pupils performed well on the test and (b) whether you feel the previous instruction on points covered in the test had been adequate.

10. Obtain a set of scores pupils made on a major test in a high school course. Find the median (middle) score. Convert the test scores to letter grades. Explain how you did this.

11. Consult some cooperative teacher and ask him to explain how he determined the grade that he assigned to a specific student at the end of a marking period.

12. Suggest as many means as you can think of for evaluating pupil progress and achievement other than by means of written tests. List these on the board.

13. Discuss:

   a. What factors should be taken into consideration in assigning a grade for the marking period, for example, at the end of six weeks?

   b. What part should the pupil's ability play in assigning grades?

   c. What part should the pupil's effort play in assigning grades?

   d. How should ability grouping affect grading?

14. Respond to the 70-item opinionnaire, "Points of View on Marking and Reporting," to be found in William L. Wrinkle's book, *Improving Marking and Reporting Practices in Elementary and Secondary Schools*, pp. 10–15.

15. React to the six cases presented by William L. Wrinkle in *Improving Marking and Reporting Practices in Elementary and Secondary Schools*, pp. 36–37. Assign a mark to each case and compare your marks with those given by the P.T.A. officers mentioned in the book.

16. Find out the numerical values that several schools assign to their letter grades, e.g., *A* is 94–100. Find out what numerical grade is considered "passing" in each school. Compare the numerical values of the various schools.

17. Construct sample test items in your subject—both essay and objective test items. Let the entire class analyze and comment on these items.

18. Role-play the following situation: An irate mother (or father) whose

daughter received a *C* in your class storms in to see you, the teacher, and questions the accuracy of your grade.

19. Suggest means for encouraging self-evaluation on the part of the student.

20. Collect samples of report cards from different schools. Compare the information given on the cards. Develop criteria for good report cards.

21. Debate the question: Resolved: Report cards should be abolished.

22. Take a report card that has on it some actual marks and interpret to the class the symbols you find in each subject.

23. Define "citizenship" in such a way that you can evaluate it.

24. Discuss:

   a. Should all pupils be promoted? If not, who should be retained? For how long should they be retained?

   b. What does high school graduation mean?

   c. Should all high school graduates receive the same type of diploma?

25. Find out and report on several schools' policies regarding the awarding of high school diplomas.

26. Apply to the school you know best the following criteria for an evaluation program:

   a. Evaluation is an integral part of instruction.

   b. There is a direct relationship between the techniques of evaluation used and the objectives of the course.

   c. Varied means of evaluation are used.

   d. Many areas of growth are evaluated.

27. Apply the following criteria for a testing program in some subject field of the school you know best:

   a. Test items are significant.

   b. Tests are both reliable and valid.

   c. Diverse types of tests are used.

   d. Tests measure more than specific facts.

   e. Test questions are carefully worded.

   f. Tests are objectively scored.

28. Apply the following criteria to several essay tests from the subject field that you chose in question 27 above:

   a. Questions are related to important phases of the course.

   b. Questions are worded in such a way that the student knows exactly what is wanted in the answer and what he must do to receive full credit for his answer.

   c. Purposes of the essay questions are understood by the teachers.

   d. Scoring is fair.

29. Apply the following criteria to several objective tests from the subject field that you chose in question 27 above:

   a. Test items are carefully phrased.

b. Varying types of objective items are used on tests.

c. Test items seek to evaluate more than memorized bits of information.

30. Apply the following criteria to the marking system of the school that you know best:

a. Marks are based on ample data.

b. Marks are based on reliable data.

c. Marks are understood by all persons affected by the marking system.

d. Marks are explicitly defined.

e. Marks are assigned in various aspects of growth, not only in scholastic achievement.

f. Marks in required courses reflect the ability of the student.

g. The school has in force a policy on marking.

31. Apply the following criteria to the reporting system of the school you know best:

a. Reports are understood by all persons affected.

b. Report cards provide sufficient information.

c. Report cards are issued at fairly frequent intervals.

d. Supplementary reports are issued during the marking period to notify parents if a student's work is not satisfactory.

32. Define "conduct" in such a way that you can evaluate it.

33. Tell the class how you would go about discovering whether a pupil is working up to his capacity. Be specific.

34. Obtain access to the scholastic records of a school and see if you can determine whether it is true that boys in that school generally make lower grades than girls in that school.

35. If you consider a pupil's ability to achieve: Should a slow student who works up to his capacity receive a top grade? Should a fast student who makes all *A*'s on assigned minimum work be required to do more work for his *A* because he is capable of more?

36. Each of the following test items has some deficiency in construction. Identify that deficiency and change the item so that it will be a useable item.

a. T ☐ F ☐ Shakespeare is the greatest dramatist that the world has so far produced.

b. The population of the United States is —————.

c. The longest suspension bridge in the world is
   1. Golden Gate
   2. Verrazano-Narrows
   3. George Washington

d. Match the capital city with its state.
   1. Albany   ————— California
   2. Sacramento   ————— Maryland

3. Annapolis   _____ Florida
4. Tallahassee   _____ New York
    e. Discuss the philosophy of Plato.

37. Create a report card that you feel would be functional. This can be a group project, if desired.

38. Decide whether you would prefer to use a single report card that gives grades in all subjects or separate report cards for each subject.

39. Prepare evaluation forms for:
    a. oral reports in class
    b. group projects

40. Write statements that you feel would be suitable as school system policies on (a) marking, (b) reporting, and (c) promotions.

41. What are some of the erroneous beliefs or assumptions teachers hold about marking? In what way are they erroneous?

SELECTED BIBLIOGRAPHICAL REFERENCES

1. Ahmann, J. Stanley and Glock, Marvin D. *Evaluating Pupil Growth*, 2nd ed. Boston: Allyn and Bacon, 1963. 640 pp.

    A comprehensive work on evaluation, covering the role of evaluation in education, teacher-built tests, statistics, and standardized tests.

2. Grambs, Jean D., Iverson, William J., and Patterson, Franklin K. *Modern Methods in Secondary Education*, rev. ed. New York: Holt, Rinehart & Winston, 1958, Chapters 17 and 18.

    These two chapters illustrate testing instruments and discuss problems of grading and reporting student progress.

3. Green, John A. *Teacher-Made Tests*. New York: Harper & Row, 1963. 141 pp.

    This small book deals with construction and use of various test forms, scoring, grading, and assigning marks. It includes elementary statistics.

4. Ross, C. C. *Measurement in Today's Schools*. Revised by Julian C. Stanley. Englewood Cliffs, N. J.: Prentice-Hall, 1954. 485 pp.

    Standard text on fundamentals of measurement, including test construction and statistics.

5. Wrinkle, William L. *Improving Marking and Reporting Practices in Elementary and Secondary Schools*. New York: Holt, Rinehart & Winston, 1947. 120 pp.

A simplified, interesting presentation of marking and reporting practices with a view to improvement. Old, but still useful. Includes self-tests and exercises that help the reader to clarify his thoughts on marking and reporting.

INSTRUCTIONAL AIDS AND SOURCES

1. Specimens of tests and test items from teachers or student teachers.
2. Sample report cards from different schools.

INDEX

INDEX